URBAN WORKERS IN THE EARLY
INDUSTRIAL REVOLUTION

CROOM HELM STUDIES IN SOCIETY AND HISTORY
Edited by Richard Price

Social Conflict and the Political Order in Modern Britian
James E. Cronin and Jonathan Schneer

The Transformation of Intellectual Life in Victorian England
T.W. Heyck

Ben Tillett
Jonathan Schneer

South Wales and the Rising of 1839
Ivor Wilks

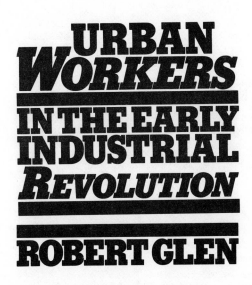

URBAN WORKERS IN THE EARLY INDUSTRIAL REVOLUTION

ROBERT GLEN

CROOM HELM
London, Canberra

ST. MARTIN'S PRESS
New York

©1984 Robert Glen
Croom Helm Ltd, Provident House, Burrell Row, Beckenham, Kent BR3 1AT

Croom Helm Australia, PO Box 391, Manuka, ACT 2603, Australia

British Library Cataloguing in Publication Data

Glen, Robert
  Urban workers in the early industrial revolution. – (Croom Helm studies in society
  and industry)
  1. Industry – Social aspects – Stockport (Greater Manchester: District)
  2. Stockport (Greater Manchester: District) – Industries – History
  I. Title
  303.4'83'0942734   HD60.5.G7

  ISBN 0-7099-1103-3

All rights reserved. For information, write:
St. Martin's Press, Inc., 175 Fifth Avenue, New York, NY 10010
Printed in Great Britain
First published in the United States of America in 1983

Library of Congress Cataloging in Publication Data

Glen, Robert.
    Urban workers in the Industrial Revolution.

       1. Labor and laboring classes - England - Stockport
(Greater Manchester) I. Title.
HD8400.S72G53 1983   305.5'62'0942734   83-43002
ISBN 0-312-83472-1   (St. Martin's Press)

CONTENTS

For Elsie Glen and Agnes Grieme,
My Grandmothers

PREFACE

The Industrial Revolution in England seems to have a perennial fascination for historians, and rightly so. As the first instance of successful industrialisation, it can still provide many social and economic lessons and also furnish essential evidence for continuing debates over ideology and theory. This study focuses primarily on the early Industrial Revolution (c. 1780-1820), a period which has received less attention than the later Industrial Revolution – probably because of the smaller number of sources available for the earlier period. Parliamentary inquiries were not so numerous before the 1820s as after, and the same could be said for workers' periodicals, independent social investigations, and so forth.

The Stockport district poses special problems. It did not have its own newspaper until 1822. Its legal and administrative records are scattered, in part because it lies on the boundary between two counties. Thus, many relevant items are to be found either in Lancashire or Cheshire repositories, while the Assize documents relating to Stockport are in the Public Record Office in London. Compounding the problem was the fact that down to the 1970s, the major local manuscript collections were split inconveniently between the Stockport Public Library and the Stockport Municipal Museum. This helped to assure that Stockport would be the subject of few detailed studies. A large Victorian compilation by Henry Heginbotham (2 vols., 1882-92) was followed nearly a half-century later by George Unwin's justly famous work on Samuel Oldknow and his role in the industrialisation of the Stockport district (1924). Only a few things of consequence appeared during the ensuing 50 years.

Yet a revival is currently underway. The first Cheshire volumes of the Victoria County History (1979-) contain much material on Stockport and north-east Cheshire. The same can be said of the new periodical, *Cheshire History* (1979-), and the publications of the Stockport Historical Society, Poynton Local History Society, Marple Antiquarian Society and other history groups in the area. In one sense, the present work comprises merely the latest addition to this renaissance of local and regional history.

I owe a debt of gratitude to many people for helping me in this endeavour, which was first produced as a 1978 Berkeley doctoral dissertation. My adviser, Lewis P. Curtis, Jr, helped me immensely in that undertaking. To Sidney Pollard I give credit for kindling my first serious interest in the social and economic changes brought about by the Industrial Revolution. I offer thanks to the numerous archivists and librarians who helped me at the Cheshire Record Office, the Public Record Office, the Manchester Central Library and elsewhere. I want to express my sincere appreciation to David and Naomi Reid of Stockport who have been a constant source of information and encouragement. Finally, my thanks to Pauline Barker for producing the map which is found in Chapter 2.

R.G.
New Haven

1 DEBATE OVER THE 'WORKING CLASS'

In England, modern society is indisputably most highly and classically developed in economic structure. Nevertheless, even here the stratification of classes does not appear in its pure form. Middle and intermediate strata even here obliterate lines of demarcation everywhere (although incomparably less in rural districts than in the cities) . . . Physicians and officials, e.g., would . . . constitute two classes, for they belong to two distinct social groups, the members of each of these groups receiving their revenue from one and the same source. The same would also be true of the infinite fragmentation of interest and rank into which the division of social labour splits labourers as well as capitalists and landlords – the latter, e.g., into owners of vineyards, farm owners, owners of forests, mine owners and owners of fisheries. [Here the manuscript breaks off.] – Marx, *Capital*, vol. III (1894), last chapter

The old Cheshire saying that 'when the world was made, the rubbish was sent to Stockport' had particular relevance to the period of the Industrial Revolution. By the second quarter of the nineteenth century, Stockport and its district contained scores of factories, cramped brick houses no longer red but sooty black, innumerable beer shops and pawn shops and, as a final mark of advanced industrialisation, a heavily polluted river system. Having passed through the town on many occasions, Friedrich Engels could write with some authority in 1845 that Stockport was 'notoriously one of the darkest and smokiest holes in the whole industrial area, and particularly when seen from the [railway] viaduct, presents a truly revolting picture'.[1]

Stockport thus comprised precisely the sort of industrial setting in which a mature 'working class' might be expected to emerge. Indeed, Engels referred specifically to Stockport as one of a group of medium-sized industrial towns in which occupational stratification was highly visible. When discussing such towns, Engels divided their populations into only three groups: a mass of factory workers, a small number of shopkeepers and a mere handful of factory

1

owners. He further claimed that workers in such towns 'form an even larger proportion of the total population than in Manchester'. According to Engels, rapid urbanisation of the kind Stockport experienced contributed to the class formation which inevitably accompanied industrialisation.

> Urban life tends to divide the proletariat from the middle classes. It helps to weld the proletariat into a compact group with its own ways of life and its own outlook on society. . . . In this way the great cities are the birthplace of the working-class movement.[2]

Whether or not the workers of Stockport and its district comprised this sort of 'working class' will be the subject of detailed investigation in this work.

As a necessary preliminary, the tangle of historiographical, ideological and semantic difficulties inherent in any usage of the term *working class* must be examined. The literature on these topics is enormous, of course, and only a brief sketch can be presented here.[3] For the purposes of analysis it is possible to discuss the emergence of a working class with regard to at least three parameters: (1) the chronology of its appearance; (2) its composition; and (3) what might be called its 'ideological' characteristics, focusing especially on the interrelated topics of consciousness and collective behaviour. A Marxist-Leninist conception of the working class has long pervaded discussions of English labour history. Marx and Engels held that an individual's class was determined by the role he or she played in the productive process, with the fundamental distinction existing between those who owned the means of production and those who did not.[4] When a new mode of production appeared in the last third of the eighteenth century, Marx believed that there began to emerge new class relationships featuring a wage-earning working class at fundamental odds with those who controlled the means of capitalist industrial production. A characteristic feature of the new system was that workers were subordinated to the monotonous pace of power-driven machines in increasingly large factories which were typically involved (during the earliest years of industrialisation) in the production of cotton yarns and textiles.[5] This factory proletariat produced ever larger amounts of goods but received minimal and often decreasing amounts of wages in return. The result was expanding profits for the capitalist factory owners and a profound feeling of alienation for the proletariat. 'The object that labour produces, its product, confronts it as an alien being, as a power independent of the producer,' Marx believed.

> Therefore, [the worker] does not confirm himself in his work, he denies himself, feels miserable instead of happy, deploys no free physical and intellectual energy, but mortifies his body and ruins his mind . . .He is at home when he is not working and when he works he is not at home.

The factory proletariat, in other words, becomes alienated from the goods it produces, from nature, and from itself.[6]

This working-class nucleus continued to grow in size after the onset of industrialisation, Marx argued, due in part to the successive proletarianisation and alienation of shopkeepers, artisans and peasants. Marx's analysis simultaneously *described* what had happened since the advent of industrialisation and *predicted* what would continue to occur until the inevitable demise of the capitalist system. In terms of chronology and composition of the working class, therefore, Marx played both the Sociologist and the Prophet and held two related but somewhat incompatible views: one was that the working class appeared suddenly with the onset of the factory mode of production in the 1760s; the other was that the working class evolved slowly towards maturity as it came to incorporate those who were, over time, caught up in capitalist modes of production.

As to ideological patterns, Marx believed that concomitants of class formation included class consciousness and class conflict. 'With its [the proletariat's] birth,' Marx wrote, 'begins its struggle with the bourgeoisie.'[7] But again, Marx linked this remark to an evolutionary viewpoint. Consciousness and conflict take time to mature. Reinhard Bendix and Seymour Martin Lipset have discussed a few of the facets of capitalist industry which Marx believed would promote the maturation process. These include: (1) 'easy communication between individuals in the same class-position so that ideas and action programs are readily disseminated' – this specifically occurring in large factories situated in populous urban centres; (2) 'profound dissatisfaction of the lower class over its inability to control the economic structure of which it feels itself to be the exploited victim'; and (3) 'conflicts over the distribution of rewards between the classes'.[8] From initial attempts merely to destroy machines, factories and wares which 'compete with their labour', workers become interested in maintaining and advancing wage levels. National trade unions ultimately appear on the scene and objectives become explicitly political. By these criteria, the English working class had not reached maturity by the middle of the nineteenth century: 'as yet in its infancy,' Marx stated, '[it] offers . . . the spectacle of a class without any historical initiative or any independent political movement.' Or again: ' . . . the proletariat is still in a very undeveloped state and has but a fantastic conception of its own position . . .' English workers, in other words, comprised a rather passive 'class in itself' which occupied a specific socio-economic position but which possessed little consciousness of an identity of interests and had only rudimentary organisations and theories with which to oppose the bourgeoisie. They had not yet become a true 'class for itself.'[9] Marx's perplexity and frustration with the lack of solidarity among workers from the late 1840s to the 1880s is well known[10] and suggests that he believed that English working-class formation was still in progress – that is, still incomplete – during those decades.

Lenin closely followed Marx's descriptions of class formation, class consciousness and alienation, and agreed that workers might fall prey to 'false consciousness' of the kind which appeared in the mid-Victorian years and which blinded workers to the true interests they shared with other workers in opposition to their capitalist oppressors.[11] Lenin also added to Marx's analysis in a number of ways, one of which has received extended treatment in certain recent commentaries on the English Industrial Revolution. It concerns Lenin's stages of conflict in industrial societies. The initial stage involved only trade union consciousness and did not lead to the dominance of the proletariat. The latter could only be achieved when political or 'mature' working-class consciousness emerged in a succeeding stage under the leadership of a small, disciplined working-class 'vanguard', and a struggle ensued for power in the state. Lenin found true working-class consciousness appearing for the first time in history in the English Chartist movement of the late 1830s and the 1840s.[12]

British labour historians writing during the first half of the twentieth century sometimes used both Marxist and Leninist chronologies without attempting to reconcile possible discrepancies.[13] On the one hand, it was held that the 1880s marked the onset of sustained political or socialist consciousness. The preceding period included two subdivisions. From 1760 to 1848, sporadic revolts against the industrial system occurred, but during the mid-Victorian years (1848-80) a process of 'acclimatisation' took place in which workers accepted industrialism but were not yet strong enough to make a bid for political and economic control. This view closely follows Marx's chronology, which encompassed his view that the English proletariat was in its infancy in 1848 and was not highly developed during the remaining 35 years of his life. G.D.H. Cole led the twentieth-century exponents of this position, which also gained the tacit endorsement of E.J. Hobsbawm at the outset of his professional career.[14]

On the other hand, Cole also sometimes followed Lenin's chronology and argued that full working-class consciousness appeared between 1832 and 1848, a time of heightened urban and rural trade union activity, of anti-Poor Law agitations and of political radicalism under the banner of the People's Charter. Cole agreed that working-class consciousness before the Chartist age had been merely latent.[15] The young Hobsbawm also came to embrace this view. He pointed especially to fundamental divisions between the highly skilled 'aristocracy' of labour and the less skilled workers, and also to the different status levels *within* these two categories during most of the Industrial Revolution. He concluded that before the 1840s, 'it is . . . doubtful whether we can speak of a proletariat in the developed sense at all, for this class was still in the process of emerging from the mass of petty producers, small masters, countrymen, etc., of pre-industrial society, though in certain regions and industries it had already taken fairly definite shape'.[16]

Yet even as Hobsbawm was writing these words during the 1950s new scholarly impulses were fostering changes in the Marxist-Leninist formulations and their derivatives. Economic historians, for example, were accumulating increasing evidence which demonstrated that industrial mechanisation and the factory mode of production directly affected only a small percentage of workers before the mid-nineteenth century. Factory workers, moreover, were not continuously in distress but were in fact among the more highly paid workers of the day. The factory proletariat thus came to appear neither so important numerically nor so systematically impoverished as previous commentators had believed.[17]

Urban studies provided a second impetus for reappraisals of 'working-class' formation. Asa Briggs, in particular, came to emphasise two distinctive types of urban socioeconomic development. Many cities and towns, including the Midlands industrial giant, Birmingham, continued to produce goods in small artisanal workshops in which masters and men worked side by side. Occupational and social mobility were relatively easy, and there was little control or interference by capitalist merchants, at least during the early decades of the nineteenth century. In urban centres such as this, Briggs found little evidence of class formation and even came to believe that co-operation among different social strata was more typical than class conflict. Factory towns like Manchester and Leeds, on the other hand, did witness class formation and class conflict in the first part of the nineteenth century, much as Marxists and others had long maintained.[18] Briggs' implicit conclusion was that in only a relatively few urban settings of the northern Midlands, Lancashire and the West Riding was there evidence of a working class. Like the work of economic historians on the factory proletariat, Briggs' research in a sense narrowed the boundaries in which discussions of the working class could be carried on. No longer did it appear possible to speak of a national working class in the Industrial Revolution, except of course for polemical effect.

A third impetus came from the oscillation theory of 'working-class' development which became especially popular during the 1950s and 1960s. Hobsbawm dealt with the issue in a brief, early essay and concluded that trade unions advanced in times of prosperity while political agitations (and, to a lesser extent, 'social movements' like Luddism) flourished in times of economic distress.[19] The idea that 'working-class' movements oscillated between industrial and political objectives was reiterated by Briggs and George Rudé,[20] but received little systematic investigation. By the early 1960s, the precise geographical and chronological extent of these oscillations and the mechanisms by which they promoted 'working-class' formation remained to be determined.

Among those who have addressed themselves to issues such as these over the past 20 years, E.P. Thompson, Harold Perkin and John Foster deserve special attention. In his *Making of the English Working Class* (1963) and subsequent writings, Thompson has produced a vigorous reinterpretation of Marxist-Leninist approaches to working-class formation. Like Marx, Thompson perceives the onset of class formation at the start of English industrialisation. But Thompson follows the convention of economic historians – writing since about 1950 – to the effect that the Industrial Revolution began in the 1780s, not in the 1760s as Marx, Arnold Toynbee, the

Hammonds and others had maintained. If the onset of class formation began in the last two decades of the eighteenth century, according to Thompson, it ended in the early 1830s. For Thompson, class formation was 'the outstanding fact of the period'. He does not, in other words, follow Marx and Engels in believing that the formation process was a long-term, cumulative phenomenon which was not near an end by the time Marx died in 1883. Thompson believes quite simply that 'to step over the threshold, from 1832 to 1833, is to step into a world in which the working-class presence can be felt in every county in England, and in most fields of life'.[21] By including skilled artisans, domestic workers, miners and agricultural labourers in his analysis of working-class formation, Thompson moves his discussion significantly beyond Marx's working-class nucleus (the factory workers) and often beyond those urban centres in which factory workers predominated. He is thus able to surmount certain of the objections which were being raised about Marxist-Leninist formulations during the 1950s and early 1960s. Indeed, he attacks such critics on their own territory. 'The Birmingham of 1833 was not the Birmingham of 1831,' he writes, perhaps with Asa Briggs in mind. By the later date, 'the characteristic ideology of Birmingham Radicalism, which united employers and journeymen in opposition to the aristocracy . . . was beginning to fall apart.'[22]

Thompson does not 'see class as a "structure", nor even as a "category", but something which in fact happens (and can be shown to have happened) in human relationships'. Class is a relationship which occurs over time. It 'happens when some men, as a result of common experiences (inherited or shared), feel *and articulate* the identity of their interests as between themselves, and as against other men whose interests are different from (and usually opposed to) theirs'. Class thus involves the existence of conflict relationships. But there are important aspects of class beyond 'feelings' of conflict and their articulation. The conflict relationship must be acted out by people in their day-to-day lives. So a class is also a group of people acting in discernably 'class' ways, and this necessitates at least two such groups found on opposing sides of a conflict situation. Furthermore, 'the class experience is largely determined by the productive relations into which men are born – or enter voluntarily'.[23] This assumes that the categories of people in conflict must, by definition, be workers who possess only their labour power and the capitalists and their allies who control the means of production.

While Thompson embraces the oscillation theory of working-class development, he does not make it a crucial feature of his analysis and seems to hold that such oscillations ended once the class was formed in 1832.[24] Thompson also includes religious revivalism as part of his oscillating cycles of workers' experience, but this approach has been effectively criticised.[25] It will be the task of the present work to analyse possible political-industrial oscillations to determine what role, if any, they played in the formation of class.[26] Probably in response to the work of John Foster, Thompson has also taken into account the stages of consciousness postulated by Lenin. But Thompson's formulations are only superficially Leninist. Whereas Lenin saw 'trade union consciousness' as a horizontal relationship emerging in industrialising societies, Thompson's stage of 'trade consciousness' involves vertical relationships occurring within the paternalistic moral economy of pre-industrial societies. Thompson argues that the succeeding stage, that of horizontal working-class consciousness, appeared as soon as industrialisation began to break down the framework and assumptions of the old moral economy towards the end of the eighteenth century.[27]

Critics of Thompson characteristically express reservations as to the size and composition of his 'working class' and the continuity of its conflict orientation. Thompson is forthright in his claim that by 1832 'most' English workers exhibited class consciousness. Yet such statements as to the feelings and opinions of the majority of workers are not susceptible to careful testing.[28] Thompson bolsters his claims by focusing on such conflict situations as strikes and political agitations, and then by showing that they included geographically widespread, occupationally diverse and numerically large groups of workers. Since Thompson frequently cites the Stockport district in his narrative, a more intensive examination of that district can perhaps furnish further evidence to support or contradict his conclusions.

Hobsbawm's judgements on this matter have tended to converge with Thompson's, and no doubt the two men greatly influenced each other's thinking and writing during the early 1960s, as before and afterwards. By 1962, Hobsbawm had come to believe, for example, that working-class consciousness appeared 'between 1815 and 1848, more specifically about 1830'. He had also come to see the importance of a greatly expanded view of the composition of the working class or 'labour movement', which he admitted was therefore not 'a strictly "proletarian" movement' in the Marxist sense.[29] At the end of the 1960s, in the wake of Thompson's work, he felt able to reassert the oscillation theory with a considerable degree of confidence.

> Phases of the movement stressing political reform and trade-unionist agitation tended to alternate, the former being normally by far the most massive: politics predominated in 1815-19, 1829-32, and above all in the Chartist era (1838-48), industrial organization in the early 1820s and 1833-8. However, from about 1830 all these movements became more self-consciously and characteristically proletarian.[30]

His last remark would seem to indicate that his chronology of class formation remains similar to that of Thompson.

If Hobsbawm can be discussed in conjunction with Thompson, Harold Perkin requires individual treatment. In his *Origins of Modern English Society* (1969) he perceives working-class formation in the context of a wider 'social revolution' which resulted in the emergence of a Victorian class society characterised 'by the existence of vertical antagonism between a small number of horizontal groups, each based on a common source of income'.[31] He counters Thompson's analysis in at least three important respects. First, Perkin does not follow Thompson's chronology. Perkin doubts, for instance, whether the Jacobins of the 1790s, or any group before Waterloo, really gained the allegiance of workers *en masse*.[32] Instead, he sees a working class based on workers from numerous trades emerging between 1815 and 1820, that is, during the explosive parliamentary reform agitations of the immediate post-war years.

Second, he stresses that class formation occurred primarily because of social rather than economic changes. Instead of focusing on changing modes of production, Perkin sketches the rise of three classes (working, entrepreneurial and professional), the revival of a fourth (the aristocracy), and the complex interrelationships among all four. Whereas Thompson, by dealing primarily with workers, sees the working class heroically forming itself in new industrial surroundings, Perkin points to influences not exclusively or substantially the product of workers' collective activities. Sectarian religion, for example, reflected and fostered decreasing deference and dependence on the part of workers and thus receives extended treatment. The 'abdication on the part of the governors', which involved the rejection of paternal protection and responsibility by the nascent middle class, is likewise accorded much greater weight by Perkin than by Thompson.[33]

While Thompson tries to describe and explain the emergence of a working class possessing a unique cultural heritage, Perkin attempts to show the development of all the major groups in society simultaneously. With this broader perspective, Perkin concludes that between 1780 and 1880, a major theme was the triumph of the entrepreneurial ideal and its emphasis on thrift, hard work, sobriety, charity, minimal activity on the part of government, and so forth. A necessary corollary of this was the relative lack of success of the working-class ideal. Perkin consequently diverges from Thompson in a third respect by conveying none of the latter's confidence as to the degree of workers' solidarity or the depth of their commitment to social conflict in the early Victorian years. Workers sought a wide array of objectives in the spheres of parliamentary reform, trade unionism and co-operative ventures. And they employed disparate means in their attempts to achieve such objectives, means ranging from peaceful petitioning to quasi-revolutionary outbursts. Although a working class definitely existed according to Perkin, 'the divisions of the working class, between urban and rural, skilled and unskilled, "aristocracy of labour" and common or garden workers, were proverbial right down the nineteenth century'.[34]

This being said, it is also true that some areas of similarity exist between Perkin's and Thompson's conceptions of the early working class. Both believe that a working class was formed at some point during the early industrialisation process, that it was perhaps most visible in urban areas, that it was not primarily composed of factory workers,[35] and that it exhibited class consciousness and a conflict orientation – aspects of the 'working class ideal', to use Perkin's terminology. As a result, the major criticisms of this aspect of Perkin's work have resembled the criticisms of Thompson already cited. Specifically, critics wonder to what extent the 'working-class ideal' described by Perkin was really shared by all or most English workers before or during the Victorian Age. And they attack the label 'social cranks' Perkins applies to those who did not accept the ideals of their class.[36] Whether such social cranks were rare or not in the Stockport district will comprise part of the investigation into the pervasiveness of the 'working-class consciousness' Perkin claims to have detected in England after Waterloo.

Unlike either Thompson or Perkin, John Foster has closely

followed Lenin's chronological framework in examining Oldham in his *Class Struggle and the Industrial Revolution* (1974). Thompson quickly came to regard this as 'a major area of dissent' between himself and Foster. He labelled Foster a 'platonist Marxist' who was guilty of 'idealist reductionism'. Specifically, Thompson criticised the 'structure' of Foster's argument and his 'notion of a "correct" historical model of class maturation to which Oldham working people largely conformed until the mid-1840s . . .'[37]

Foster's model encompasses distinct stages of social change. The first, lasting from the 1790s through the 1820s, was characterised by trade union or labour consciousness of the kind Lenin postulated. This form of consciousness elicited 'the involvement of a large part of the labour force in economic struggle'; an occupational solidarity which was 'radically new, specifically illegal and in its practical application a direct challenge to state power'; and the cementing of 'the relationship between the radicals and industrial action'.[38] In other words, Foster broadly agrees with Thompson that before the early 1830s, trade unions were common, solidarity among different trades was manifest, and radical political ideas deeply influenced this labour bloc and helped to ignite numerous collective outbursts during these years. But the two writers disagree as to the significance of these findings. Thompson argues that inter-trade links and oscillations between trade union and political activity (two types of agitation sometimes involving the same personnel) were so pervasive geographically and chronologically that they indicate the existence of full class consciousness by 1832. Foster, on the contrary, emphasises that collective activities before the 1830s were highly sporadic – he uses Lenin's term 'festivals of the oppressed' to help convey their infrequent and special nature. Such outbursts relied too heavily on the leadership and support of a weakly organised body of handloom weavers, and this in turn meant that outbursts were typically dependent on the existence of adverse economic conditions, that is, on 'desperation', for widespread support. Such movements, moreover, lacked the permanence that intellectual convictions could have furnished. According to Foster, radicalism before the 1830s usually included no concept of an alternative economic order but only offered notions of an 'ill-defined Jacobin republic'.[39] Whereas Foster regards the latter as an insufficient foundation for mature class consciousness, both Thompson and Perkin include it as an important part of an emergent, distinctive 'working-class' ideology.

Foster's second stage, lasting from the 1830s to about 1848, was characterised by full class consciousness of a form 'sufficiently convincing for Marx and Engels to use it as a basis for their own political analysis' – that is, of a revolutionary political form. This 'fundamental *intellectual* reorientation' helped to replace merely sporadic outbursts by a '*permanent* subordination of all sections of the working population to radical control' and, ultimately, by a '*sustained* rejection of bourgeois forms'. Foster emphasises the increasingly popular ideal of a co-operative commonwealth which supplanted earlier dreams of a Jacobin republic of small and independent producers. He focuses especially on the Short Time Movement as a continuous and specifically anti-capitalist agitation which contributed significantly to the formation of Oldham's mass revolutionary consciousness.[40]

The works of Thompson and Perkin contain a number of passages which are in disagreement with Foster's discussion of the early-nineteenth century. Both Thompson and Perkin, of course, believe that a working class was formed by the beginning of Foster's second stage, not during the course of the 1830s and 1840s. And while Foster focuses on alternatives to capitalism, Thompson and Perkin merely incorporate such alternatives, along with reformist objects of various kinds, into their analyses of these two decades. More specific criticisms of Foster's presentation have come from other quarters. D.S. Gadian argues that the tradition of co-operation (or collaboration) among different social groups in Oldham remained strong during the Industrial Revolution. This resulted in part from the fact that the scale of industrial units was not so large, and the concentration of ownership not so prominent, as in other cotton towns. He concludes that in terms of the broad contours of economic and social development, Oldham resembled Birmingham more than Manchester.[41] Gareth Stedman Jones attacks Foster from another direction. He points out that Foster's argument as to the continuity of revolutionary consciousness rests chiefly on episodes occurring in 1834 and 1842, that is, on the same kind of sporadic outbursts which occurred in the first stage. While Jones agrees that the Short Time Movement was anti-capitalist in its objectives, he can not accept that it was therefore socialist or revolutionary.[42] Since the present study will not deal with this stage in great detail, it should be noted that such reservations seem to apply with particular force to the Stockport district. The sporadic and often weak nature of collective outbursts in the 1830s and 1840s,[43] the timidity of the Stockport Short Time Movement, at least in the 1830s, and the belated influence of Owenism and co-operative ideals would all seem to support this conclusion.

While Foster warns that probably not many other towns exhibited 'exactly' the same social development he claims to have occurred in Oldham, he does speak of 'parallel consciousness' and of the idea that this general pattern probably existed elsewhere. He refers specifically to Bolton, Bury, Rochdale, Ashton and Stockport as places which duplicated Oldham's economic (and, implicitly, its social) experiences in significant ways.[44] Derek Fraser, one of Foster's critics, has advocated the study of other cotton towns for different reasons.

> There was less political violence in Oldham than elsewhere, less independent working-class activity, more middle-class radical leadership and in the town's response to the new Poor Law, class collaboration was maintained longer than elsewhere. ... Stockport, for instance, [was] far more socially divided.[45]

Thus, if a study of Stockport can provide local evidence relating to Thompson's and Perkin's national conclusions, it can provide an ideal point of comparison or contrast to Foster's work on Oldham.

Additional local evidence also seems necessary because those who have disagreed with the hypotheses that working-class formation occurred or began during the early industrialisation process have seldom done so in a detailed or systematic manner. Briggs confined his objections to Thompson's work to a brief review. Henry Pelling has offered his reservations in the form of crisp assertions. 'It would be a mistake ...,' he writes in one place, 'to speak of a homogenous "working class" in Britain at any time before the later nineteenth century. Contemporaries did not use the expression, at any rate in its singular form.' A.E. Musson has revealed his views by agreeing with Pelling's position and deftly attacking Foster.[46] Furthermore, semantic difficulties have crept into many of these brief comments. Briggs has shown that the singular term 'working class' appeared soon after Waterloo, and he claims that the appearance of the term reflected the emergence of the class.[47] Yet for most of the nineteenth century the plural term 'working classes' was employed at least as often as the singular form. This would seem to vitiate Briggs' argument, however interesting his findings. Problems of usage should also be noted. When referring to the food, clothing, shelter and leisure pursuits characteristic of workers, writers often lapse into expressions such as 'working-class diets', 'working-class clothing', 'working-class housing' and 'working-class pastimes'. *Class* here simply becomes a synonym for *group* or *category*, but the impression left in readers' minds is that a single, unified, self-conscious class exists. To give but one example of this usage, Derek Beales argues that divisions within the ranks of workers were so pronounced from 1815 to 1885 that he chooses to employ 'the more realistic terminology of contemporaries, "the working classes" '. Yet on the same page on which he announces that decision, he refers to 'working-class activity' and 'working-class violence'.[48] Thompson does not eliminate the ambiguity of this issue by referring to workers as 'the working class' during the period (c. 1780-1832) when the class was in the process of being 'made'.

Debates over the 'working class', like those over the middle class and the lower-middle class, have tended to be inconclusive. A case study, by its very nature, can not resolve the deadlock. It can, however, provide fresh evidence on the daily experiences of workers in the past, precisely the kind of material which can be used to help test the hypotheses of Thompson, Perkin and Foster.[49] These hypotheses suggest a series of specific questions about workers in the Stockport district from the 1770s to the 1820s. What kinds of workers managed to organise, and to what extent were labour organisations widespread? What were the aims of such organisations? Did such organisations exhibit inter-trade solidarity? Whether united or not, did such organisations endorse and act upon radical political ideologies? Or to put it another way, to what extent were the radical circles or radical 'vanguards' which existed in most towns of the period able to secure mass support? And if there existed this conjunction between radicalism and trades' support, were the resulting actions sporadic or more or less continuous? These, then, will comprise the major lines of inquiry into workers' behaviour in the Stockport district. The time period examined includes not only the early Industrial Revolution proper (c. 1780-1820) but also an additional decade before and after in order better to determine origins and consequences of significant social and economic developments.

The increase in the population and extent of Stockport were almost incredible; instead of the obscure and miserable place which formerly appeared on the Cheshire side of the river Mersey, a new town was erected as if by inchantment; streets and houses annually increased on the hills and in the vallies; manufactories were erected, and thousands of busy hands employed in a new and productive staple of national wealth; artizans attracted by the hope of gain flocked hither, and the scene became equally gratifying, interesting, and important, to the merchant, the philosopher, and the statesman. – Corry's *Macclesfield* (1817)

The Stockport district occupies a position of considerable geographic interest, lying as it does on the boundary between hill-country and plain. To the east rise the foothills of the Pennines which, according to the radical-poet Samuel Bamford, resembled 'a region of congealed waves'. To the west lie the wooded and grassy plains of Cheshire and south Lancashire parted by the gently flowing waters of the Mersey river and its tributaries. One eighteenth-century traveller was impressed by the latter vista, 'a boundless flat country sloping down as far as the eye can reach towards Liverpool and the Irish Sea'.[1] For the sake of precise investigation, this topographically variegated 'Stockport district' can be defined to include an area within a radius of three or four miles from the Stockport Market Place encompassing 26 townships in four parishes:

County	Parish	Townships
Cheshire	Stockport	Bramhall, Bredbury, Brinnington, Disley, Hyde, Marple, Norbury, Offerton, Romiley, Stockport, Stockport Etchells, Torkington, Werneth
	Cheadle	Cheadle Bulkeley, Cheadle Moseley, Handforth cum Bosden

	Prestbury	Poynton, Woodford, Worth
Lancashire	Manchester	Burnage, Denton, Didsbury,
		Haughton, Heaton Norris,
		Levenshulme, Reddish

Of the four parishes, only Cheadle was contained wholly within the boundaries of the Stockport district. Most of Stockport parish was included, however, with only the single detached township of Dukinfield being omitted (see Map).[2]

The town and its district possessed some economic importance before the eighteenth century because Stockport lies at the point where the meandering Tame and Goit rivers join to form the Mersey. The earliest settlements on the site probably resulted from the fact that the Mersey is fordable just 60 yards west of the Tame-Goit confluence. A bridge supplemented the ford at least as early as the fourteenth century and thereby further enhanced Stockport's position. It became, and remained for centuries, the only bridge-crossing between the West Pennines and the town of Warrington at the head of the Mersey estuary. The bridge also helped to confirm Stockport's position as the major gateway from the rich Cheshire farm lands to Manchester and other towns of eastern Lancashire. An account of 1634 referred to Stockport as 'an ancient Markett Towne, to which there doth weekly resort a great concourse of people in respect of the Markett as upon other occasions . . .' During the eighteenth century the importance of Stockport's market is indicated by the fact that prices of provisions there were said to exert a strong influence over prices in Manchester.[3]

I

Yet it was the construction of silk factories in the town of Stockport from the 1730s to the 1770s which began the process of transforming Stockport into a smoky industrial 'hole' of national renown. Demographic changes began throughout the district in the middle decades of the century. Stockport township soon took the lead, however, and attained its most rapid rate of growth in the 1780s (Table 2.1). This general pattern of population growth shows that early industrialisation was primarily an urban phenomenon in this instance. To be sure, there were early industrial villages in outlying parts of the district and two famous ones (Styal and Mellor) just outside the district. Cottage industries also flourished. But most of the early industrial activity – and a disproportionate share of the population growth – was occurring within Stockport township. John Byng, an unusually perceptive traveller, wrote with some amazement in 1790 that 'Stockport . . . increases hourly'.[4] By 1801 the town contained 38 per cent of the population of the entire district (Table 2.2), a higher percentage than it was to attain at any other point in the eighteenth or nineteenth centuries.

The notion that popular disorders inevitably go hand-in-hand with rapid population growth does not gain support from the Stockport district. By that reckoning disturbances should have wracked Stockport township in the 1780s, its suburbs in the years from 1790 to 1841, and the Hyde-Denton area from 1801 to 1841. That pattern simply did not occur. Disturbances were typically confined to Stockport township. They began in a small way in the 1790s and picked up momentum after the turn of the century (especially from 1811 to 1821) as population growth rates in Stockport *decreased*. The Hyde-Denton area rarely played a leading

Table 2.1: Patterns of Population Growth in the Stockport District, 1664–1871

Period	Stockport Township	Suburbs [a]	Hyde-Denton Area [b]	Remaining Out-townships [c]
1664–1754	Slow	Slow	Slow	Slow
1754–65	Moderate	Moderate	Moderate	Moderate
1765–79	Rapid	Moderate	Moderate	Moderate
1779–90	Very rapid	Rapid	Rapid	Moderate
1790–1801	Rapid	Very rapid	Rapid	Moderate
1801–41	Moderate	Very rapid	Very rapid	Moderate
1841–71	Slow	Slow	Slow	Slow

Key:

Slow	=	0.0–1.00% annual average increase
Moderate	=	1.01–2.50% '' '' ''
Rapid	=	2.51–3.50% '' '' ''
Very rapid	=	3.51% + '' '' ''

Notes: (a) Brinnington, Cheadle Bulkeley and Heaton Norris townships. This term *suburb* is used merely as a convenient shorthand description for these townships. They were technically semi-urban in that they included both built-up areas which were extensions of the urban core and rural, agricultural areas.

(b) Hyde, Denton, Haughton and Werneth townships.

(c) That is, 18 townships.

Sources: See sources for Table 2.2.

role in workers' movements, at least down to the 1820s. Even Stockport's suburbs remained relatively backward in such matters. While some workers' leaders lived in Edgeley, Heaton Lane and Portwood, that is, just outside the borders of Stockport township, hardly any of them resided further afield in the suburban townships.

There were two demographic features which might help to explain this phenomenon – absolute population size and population density. By each measure Stockport township was in an entirely different category from any of the other 25 townships in the district. During the early Industrial Revolution no other district township attained even as much as half the population or density of Stockport. It was the urban locus *par excellence* with all that that meant in terms of the availability of newspapers, pamphlets and printed matter of all kinds and the ease of communications with other urban areas. Stockport's appreciably greater density probably helped activists to organise clubs, meetings and demonstrations, since propinquity would have made recruitment much easier than in townships where

Table 2.2: Stockport District Population, 1754–1831

Date	Stockport Township	Suburbs	Hyde-Denton Area	Remaining Out-Townships	Total
1754 [a]	3,144	1,321	1,679	6,689	12,833
	(2.3)[b]	(1.6)	(1.8)	(1.1)	(1.6)
1779	5,572	1,969	2,612	8,812	18,965
	(4.6)	(5.4)	(2.7)	(1.8)	(3.3)
1801	14,830	6,235	4,716	13,112	38,893
	(1.7)	(4.2)	(2.8)	(1.8)	(2.3)
1811	17,545	9,446	6,230	15,685	48,906
	(2.2)	(2.7)	(4.0)	(1.5)	(2.3)
1821	21,726	12,311	9,255	18,248	61,540
	(1.6)	(4.7)	(5.8)	(1.4)	(2.9)
1831	25,469	19,453	16,312	20,953	82,187

Notes: (a) The figures for 1754 are based on population enumerations for 13 townships and estimates for the remaining townships derived primarily from interpolations from the 1664 hearth tax data and local censuses of the 1770s.

(b) Figures in parentheses indicate rates of growth per annum (in percentages) during the intervening periods.

Sources: The nineteenth-century data are from the official census reports. The 1754 and 1779 figures for Stockport parish townships are from Bodleian Library, MS Topography Cheshire b.1., Watson MSS, 129. Figures for Cheadle parish townships in 1778 can be found in CRO, EDV 7/1/85. A 1774 census of the Manchester parish townships is located in Chetham's Library, 'An Enumeration of the Houses and Inhabitants in the Town and Parish of Manchester', III (1774). Estimates have been used for Poynton, Woodford and Worth in 1779. A convenient listing of local 1,664 hearth totals can be found in MCL, Burton MSS, V, 260. (For the abbreviations used in this and all subsequent tables, see the 'Prefatory Remarks' to the Notes.)

workers were spread out in a series of industrial villages or isolated hamlets.

The exact role migration played in total population growth will probably never be determined because deficiencies in the parish registers preclude accurate calculation of the district's 'natural' increase or decrease per annum.[5] Despite this, all evidence points to the conclusion that a large part of the population growth during the early Industrial Revolution was due to migration into the district. In 1792 the Stranger's Friend Society was established specifically to aid those who were moving into Stockport. In 1816 a magistrate's clerk thought that over half of the 1,117 unemployed weavers in Stockport were migrants who did not have a legal settlement in the township.[6] Some of these people, of course, had settlements in nearby townships within the district. Scrutiny of Quarter Sessions removal orders for 1811-13, a period of considerable population movement, also reveals a number of cases in which families and individuals had moved from villages and hamlets fairly close to the Stockport district, a pattern not unknown in other years.[7] The rector of Wilmslow (a parish bordering on the southern edge of the Stockport district) stated that during the boom of 1824-5, 'the influx to the towns was very considerable; to the villages by no means so; in fact the tide flowed from the villages to the towns'.[8] Other industrial towns in the cotton districts also provided many of the migrants to Stockport. Some came from Manchester, of course, but there seems to have been a greater influx of people from places more nearly resembling Stockport in size – places like Bolton, Oldham and Ashton. The Stockport district also attracted migrants from urban areas at a somewhat greater distance. These came from Lancashire and Cheshire towns located outside the cotton manufacturing areas and from counties bordering on Cheshire (the West Riding, Derbyshire, Staffordshire and Shropshire). Migrants from towns in north Wales must also be included in this category.

There were, finally, groups of migrants from distant areas. From the 1770s to the 1810s there were large numbers of children sent from London orphanages and workhouses to work in Stockport district silk and cotton factories. Many more migrants came from Scotland and Ireland. One commentator, in comparing the situation in 1800 to that 15 years previously, expressed astonishment at the results of such long-distance movements:

> What were Stockport and Bolton? What are they now? Has not the cotton business stretched out into larger and larger circles? Has it not drawn into its vortex an immense population from other counties, from Scotland and from Ireland?[9]

The Scottish migration is difficult to trace because migrants from North Britain seemed to become assimilated quite easily after their arrival in the Stockport district. It appears that influxes from southern Scotland to northern England during harvest time had already become an annual event by the late-eighteenth century – not unlike certain elements of the Welsh migration. Permanent industrial migrants thus could have followed the routes earlier established by seasonal agricultural workers. Yet no separate

Scottish neighbourhoods in the Stockport district can be identified. Unlike the Welsh or Irish, they had no need to establish new religious denominations but could join any of a number of long-established Presbyterian congregations. Some, like Coulton Hampson, a Dumfries hatter who arrived around 1830, easily entered skilled trades.[10] Despite the dearth of evidence on the subject, it seems reasonable to suggest that the Scottish migration into the Stockport district was relatively modest, certainly only a small fraction of what the Irish migration was to become.

For most of the eighteenth century few Irish settled in the Stockport district. Diocesan visitation returns for 1778 and 1789 indicate that there were not more than ten Catholic families in the district.[11] Even if all of them were Irish (which is doubtful) there are clearly no grounds for arguing that there existed a large Irish influx in the earliest years of the Industrial Revolution. In the 1790s, however, Irish began arriving in increasing numbers in all the urban centres of the Manchester district.[12] Stockport's Stranger's Friend Society was soon established in part to aid Roman Catholics, which was almost certainly an allusion to Irish migrants. The growing Irish Catholic population of Stockport merited a visiting Catholic priest in 1798 and a resident priest in 1799. Four years later a Catholic congregation of 300 helped to consecrate the Church of SS Philip and James in Edgeley.[13]

Before 1821 the Irish in the Stockport district probably never exceeded two per cent of the total population, that is, about 1,200 people. They were involved in some low-paying occupations like road and canal construction, but that was not inevitably the case. They moved with relative ease into calico printing, which was highly-paid, and handloom weaving, which still had occasional years of prosperity (1802 and 1814, for instance).[14] Moreover, the Irish were largely integrated into the neighbourhoods of English calico printers and handloom weavers. Edgeley provides the only significant example of a separate Irish enclave before the 1820s. Thus, Irish workers comprised a tiny minority which was not rigidly segregated, either occupationally or residentially, from the English majority. It is consequently not surprising that the Irish were well-represented in workers' movements of the early Industrial Revolution.

From the 1820s to the mid-Victorian period the character of the Irish influx changed in various ways. With the advent of regular steamship service across the Irish Sea, there were many more transient Irish arriving each year to help with the harvest in the

Stockport district or elsewhere. The Denton curate referred to such Irish families, who, he thought, 'are always migrating backwards and forwards'.[15] At the same time the number of permanent Irish residents grew both in absolute and percentage terms. Already by the early 1830s they numbered 5,000 or about six per cent of the total population. Few from this rather substantial minority could hope to obtain permanent, high-paying employment in calico printing in the out-townships or in handloom weaving since neither type of employment retained its former importance after 1820. These changes affected many townships, including Disley, whose curate could write in 1821 that 'there are no regular Catholic families; but the calico printers from Ireland are often going and coming'.[16]

Irish males found themselves overwhelmingly consigned to one low-paying occupation, construction. Many took part in the building boom of the 1820s as bricklayers' helpers, an occupation they quickly came to dominate.[17] Others would help to build roads and canals, as some of their predecessors had done in the 1790s. Their successors in the 1830s and 1840s helped to build Stockport district railways. Many Irish women and children were able to find employment in the cotton factories. But their husbands' low-paying occupations seemed to determine family status and to assure that the Irish would live apart from English workers. Many Irish enclaves began to appear, notably in the Hillgate (especially around Edward Street) and the Adlington Square-Carr Green area. According to an account from the 1830s, the Irish 'retain, in a great measure, their former habits; in their manner of living they do not assimilate themselves much to the English'; and for their part, 'the English do not assimilate themselves to the Irish, and rather feel a pride in keeping a superior state of the house . . .'[18] The Irish also seemed to be less prominent in major workers' movements. They did not, by and large, embrace the infidelism which became fashionable in some radical circles during the 1820s. They likewise played less visible roles in trade unionism and in organised political radicalism in general.

This coincided with increasingly frequent perceptions at all levels of society that the Irish were not merely distinctive but actually degraded in character and reprehensible in conduct. As more and more Irish drinking establishments opened (the Harp of Ireland, the Harp and Crown, and so forth) few could ignore the propensity of the Irish to drink to excess. On one occasion, when some barrels of gin fell off a wagon and broke open on the pavement, one Irishman drank himself into unconsciousness from the gutter. Pitched battles between English and Irish occurred in and around certain public houses. In 1826 the *Stockport Advertiser* reported on another phenomenon, a gang of robbers who stole goods for later sale at an Edward Street lodging house inhabited chiefly by Irish. By 1836 fully one-third of the persons brought before the magistrates were Irish, and Irishmen committed over half of the highway robberies.[19] An *Annual Report* of the Stockport Sunday School alluded to such problems without mentioning the Irish by name.

> The demand for additional labour has brought an influx of population that forms a striking contrast to the native inhabitants; the uncivilized manners and squalid appearance of their persons and of their children are only exceeded by the filth and disorder of their habitations. They are evidently from the darker regions of moral degradation where society is only a remove from the level of brutish ignorance.

About the same time, however, the Stockport Sunday School Tract Society issued a moralising pamphlet directed explicitly at the Irish.[20] In short, one consequence of altered migratory habits after 1820 was the creation of a significant ethnic division in the Stockport district.

Overall, Stockport district migration patterns conform to general observations made in other areas. It appears, for example, that workers who possessed special skills could move more easily than those who did not. In trades with tramping systems, like hatting, shoemaking and tailoring, workers could be fairly mobile over long distances. Spinners were more restricted geographically, but their work experience could easily be transferred from one factory to another within the cotton districts. Mobility of the unskilled was closely related to the demand for their labour, a demand which was intermittent but which might be quite strong during boom periods or during the duration of large construction projects. Handloom weavers moved around quite a bit. But if they were successful enough to own their own looms, they might find themselves caught in a discouraging paradox. As a Bolton weaver put it: 'it is an extremely hard matter, when a man is poor, to shift his looms and his family, it would take more than he is worth . . .'[21]

Migrants into the Stockport district added greatly to the diversity of the early industrial working classes. It seems likely that most were less educated than the average person in the Stockport district if only because the facilities for education were becoming more highly developed within the district than in most areas of Ireland or the North of England. In referring to the large number of migrants who had arrived during the preceding three decades, the *Annual Report* of the Stockport Sunday School for 1822 stated that 'it is known to every observer, that these are generally more ignorant and more vicious than our native inhabitants'. By bringing new types of religion they added to the complexity of the district's denominational make-up. Migrant families probably had been fairly regular in their attendance at divine services in the small towns and rural parishes of England, Wales and Ireland from whence they came. If so, they may also have contributed to the general religious vitality of the district. Still, one should not conceal the degree of conjecture involved here, especially since the migrants themselves were so heterogeneous. While Scottish migrants probably had high levels of literacy, Irish migrants were probably mostly illiterate. Migrants likewise varied widely in their abilities to become assimilated.[22] Whereas some quickly joined the ranks of the 'respectable', others became highly visible examples of the 'rough' and the disorderly.

II

The various newcomers had to vie with Stockport district residents to obtain intermittently scarce housing. In preceding centuries, many houses had been built of oak, but by the eighteenth century timber was in short supply and expensive enough to be sold in small lots at special auctions. The switch to bricks was easily made, however, since surface clay deposits existed throughout the district and could sometimes be found in adequate quantity and quality on the building sites themselves.[23] In the town of Stockport, topographical irregularities necessitated the construction of houses in tiers.[24] A description of a walk through a group of houses popularly called 'Newton's Whim' gives some sense of the resulting jumble of buildings.

The entrance to this whim from Bridgefield was through a

narrow entry. On each side of this entry were doors admitting
to small dwellings. When we had got through this passage we
entered a kind of court yard, with dwellings all around. From
this court yard ascended a flight of steps, which led on to a
landing. Here were dwellings again. From this landing we
entered another entry, which led into Stewart-street.

Owners or occupiers of such houses had one advantage in that
they were able to excavate parts of the slope adjoining their premises
in order to make new rooms, a custom noted in Stockport by the
start of the nineteenth century.[25]
  The seemingly insatiable demand for housing required increasing
amounts of land and capital. Both were forthcoming. In 1773 the
Rector of Stockport obtained a parliamentary act enabling him to
lease large sections of the glebe to 'any Person or Persons who
shall be willing to take, build upon, and improve the same...'
People in all walks of life, from gentlemen to workers, leased
parcels of land and contributed the capital needed to construct
new houses – entirely new streets lined with houses in some cases.
John Byng immediately noticed the phenomenon on one of his
visits: 'Astonishing is the increase of buildings about this town, and
they go on most rapidly; ...in every field adjoining, is land to be
let for building.'[26] Artisans, both within the building trades and
without, took advantage of the myriad opportunities involved in
Stockport's growth. Some artisans built houses on their own account,
whether on glebe lands or elsewhere, and others speculated in the
housing market. During the 1780s and 1790s, a stonemason built
nine houses in Chestergate; a carpenter and a weaver jointly built
houses in Edward Street; a joiner-turned-machine maker owned
six houses in various locations; a shoemaker owned 15.[27] Along
with new construction, some older buildings were being converted
into multiple dwellings. In the 1790s there appeared an advertisement for a building which had been subdivided into 21 flats, and
there were additional references to cellar and garret dwellings. All
of this meant that in the town of Stockport (if not in its suburbs)
the persons-per-house ratio did not change appreciably by 1811
(Table 2.3).[28]
  From 1811 to 1821 the persons-per-house ratios increased noticeably in most parts of the district. That decade, in fact, ranks as the
most notable in terms of housing shortages of any decade in the
Industrial Revolution. This shortage resulted from continued

population growth in conjunction with mounting building costs and severe economic dislocations affecting a variety of industries. Many people were forced to become lodgers, while, in turn, many families were forced to take in lodgers in order to supplement family incomes. It seems likely that an unusually high persons-per-house ratio achieved in a relatively short period of time would have been a contributory factor to popular discontent.[29] The rate of increase in Stockport township's ratio seems especially remarkable in this respect, as do the workers' disorders which occurred there during the Regency period. By contrast, the comparatively quiescent workers in the 18 out-townships were much less affected by the housing shortage.

Table 2.3: Persons per House in the Stockport District, 1774–1831

Date	Stockport Township	Suburbs	Hyde-Denton Area	Remaining Out-townships	District Total
1774	(5.6)[a]	5.9[b]	5.3[c]	5.6[d]	5.6[e]
1801	5.8	5.5	5.8	5.6	5.7
1811	5.6	6.2	6.0	5.6	5.7
1821	6.4	6.3	6.5	5.9	6.2
1831	5.1	5.3	6.2	5.8	5.5

Notes: (a) An estimate.
(b) This figure is for Heaton Norris township only.
(c) This figure is for Denton and Haughton townships only.
(d) This fugure is for Burnage, Didsbury, Levenshulme and Reddish townships only.
(e) This figure is only for the seven townships mentioned in notes (b), (c), and (d) above.

Sources: See sources for Table 2.2.

The period between the censuses of 1821 and 1831 brought further important changes. Stockport township again stands out because its persons-per-house ratio dropped to a lower level at a faster rate than the other three areas, although its suburbs made rapid strides in the same direction. Thirty per cent of the district's net gain in housing stock for the decade occurred in Stockport, which meant that on the average, one new house was being built every 2.5 days. The 1820s marked the beginning of a new era in housing for Stockport township, since the persons-per-house ratio was to remain low (around 5:1) for the rest of the century. Stockport's suburbs and the rest of the district soon followed the same pattern.

This precipitous and prophetic change in Stockport township during the 1820s came about largely by means of lowering the quality of housing. Demand pent up during the previous decade of war and successive economic difficulties was simply too great to be restrained during a period of relative prosperity. Some of the demand, of course, came from the increasing numbers of Irish whose low-paying occupations allowed for only minimal outlays on rent. The *Stockport Advertiser* recorded a case in 1825 of 18 Irish crowded into one house. At the same time, the amount of land available for house-building was becoming increasingly scarce. Conversion of older premises naturally continued in such circumstances. The once-stately Heavily Hall was converted into eleven flats, for instance.[30] The new houses of the 1820s were often smaller in size than those built in the early Industrial Revolution. Whereas before, workers' houses often had four rooms ('two-up, two-down') whether in row configurations or not, in the 1820s they increasingly had just two rooms ('one-up, one-down') in back-to-back rows. The latter type is well known in the annals of execrable housing, its chief defect being the lack of cross- or through-ventilation.[31] But they could be built quickly and cheaply, especially because some were of a smaller size (four by five yards) than that often found in earlier decades (that is, five by five yards). This new housing of the later Industrial Revolution unfortunately lasted for generations. Three hundred courts consisting of quadrangles of back-to-backs still existed in early-twentieth-century Stockport and provided a curious vestige of past building practices to parliamentary investigators of the time.[32]

The decline in the quality of housing during the prosperous 1820s seems a rather ironic turn of events. Still, one must keep in mind the limits of this change. Before the 1830s the deterioration was chiefly confined to Stockport township. Workers in other townships with much lower population densities did not have to crowd into back-to-backs or cellar dwellings (although this would change later on). Within Stockport township, as the overall quality of new housing declined, the persons-per-house ratio also declined, which amounted to an improvement of sorts. This makes general conclusions difficult, especially in the absence of statistics which would reveal whether the average *per capita* amount of space within houses was increasing or decreasing during the 1820s and 1830s. Nor does one know in how many individual cases the new housing betokened a decline in standards. For former lodgers and newly-arrived Irish, occupying a new back-to-back may in fact have comprised an improvement in housing conditions. In short, one can not add Stockport's housing situation to the body of pessimistic evidence in the standard of living debate without numerous qualifications.[33]

The variations in housing were quite pronounced during the 1820s, which is what one would expect in a context in which workers' wages and styles of life likewise varied enormously. Ample data on housing from the early 1830s give a sense of the continuing trends and suggest certain of the major variations which existed. Some workers owned their own houses. Many of the cottages in Brinnington, for instance, were described as being owned by 'the labouring class'. Most workers, of course, rented, and rent payments for some of the larger houses could approach or exceed £10 per annum, especially if they had cellars or adjoining workshops. The two-up, two-down cottages owned by Thomas Ashton at Hyde did not have such extra space but did have private privies and small yards. They rented for £8 per annum. Somewhat less desirable two-up, two-down cottages with privies shared by three, four or five cottages rented for £6-7 per annum. A Stockport agent who collected rent for 150 of these cottages stated that they were tenanted by factory workers and skilled artisans (hatters, joiners, bricklayers).[34] One-up, one-down cottages rented for £5-6 per annum. Cellar dwellings, which comprised 11.3 per cent of the dwellings in Stockport township in 1831, generally went for £2-4 per annum. A bed in a lodging house would often cost a penny per night, or the equivalent of about £1 10s. per year.[35] At the upper end of the scale, in other words, workers' housing would qualify their residents to vote under the Great Reform Act and thereby help to incorporate them into the political life of the nation. At the lower end, housing conditions provided an overt sign of the presence of the recently-arrived, the unemployed, the poor.

Most of the housing in Stockport township, whatever the type, was built by individuals for their own habitation or by entrepreneurs of various sorts outside the cotton industry. 'Factory housing' built in conjunction with specific factories and owned by the factory master was not much in evidence.[36] In other district townships, by contrast, this phenomenon was much more pronounced from the onset of the Industrial Revolution through the 1820s and 1830s. Before 1795, for example, there were workers' cottages associated with Hope Hill Mill, Brinksway Mill, Grove Mill and the Heaton Mersey bleach and printworks in Heaton Norris; William and Cephas Howard's mill in Brinnington; John Howard's mill in Hyde; and the Reddish Vale Printworks. A questionnaire answered by owners of 46 Stockport district factories in the early 1830s revealed that 21 owned the houses of at least some of their employees. Complaints about the quality of this type of housing, whether from tenants or disinterested observers, were rare. Indeed, Thomas Ashton's two-up, two-down cottages in Hyde were often mentioned as models of the genre.[37]

The number of factory cottages owned by a specific firm might be quite large. Both the Ashtons of Hyde and the Andrews of Werneth owned scores of workers' cottages, and Brinksway Mill had 40 cottages associated with it. It is not unreasonable to assume that each cottage contained an average of two people employed by the cottage-cum-factory owner. If that were the case, then over half of the employees at Brinksway Mill would have lived in the owner's cottages. There would have been many more cases in which a substantial minority of workers would have been in a similar situation and thus especially susceptible to masters' pressures. One would consequently expect that the formation of trade unions in the cotton industry outside of Stockport township would have been inhibited and would certainly have been less pronounced than in the town itself. That was precisely the pattern which emerged.

Some owners' vigilance extended beyond workers' combinations, as three examples from factories established before 1810 illustrate. H. Sidebotham of Haughton stated with reference to his tenants: 'we give them tickets of admission to Sunday schools in the neighbourhood, and request them to attend.' James and Robert Gee of Cheadle Bulkeley stated: 'we frequently visit their houses, and can bear testimony to their domestic cleanliness and to their moral conduct.' Rooth and Mayer of Heaton Norris stated: 'if they are not moderately clean both in their persons and in their house, we should discharge them.'[38] In other words, the control of some workers' housing at as many as two-fifths of the cotton factories in the district provided owners with a direct and significant means to inform, exhort or threaten some of their workers on social, religious and political topics. The masters generally hoped that their employees would conform to the views and habits of the middle classes and would, in so doing, furnish examples to others unsusceptible to this type of paternal coercion. It is thus not surprising that Thomas Ashton and others like him in the district were compared to 'feudal lords'.[39]

A sense of 'industrial paternalism' was strengthened by the locations of the houses of the factory masters. Many lived within sight of their mills and therefore close to, if not in the midst of, the workers they employed. This pattern had occurred earlier, as when Joseph Dale chose to build his silk mills next to his Adlington Square home around 1770. Later examples abound. Peter Marsland's Woodbank House, the Gee's Hollywood House, Thomas Marsland's Holly Vale House, Thomas Ferneley, Sr's Avenue House, and the Sykeses' Edgeley house were all within sight of their owners' respective factories, printworks or bleachworks in Stockport or its suburbs. The custom of owners living at some distance from their mills does not appear to become common before the 1820s when, for instance, the Stockport industrialist John Bentley was occupying distant Haughton Hall and Joseph Horsefield moved from his mill site to the more gentrified setting of Arden Hall.[40] The phenomenon of a poor urban core and a more affluent periphery was a product of the late, rather than the early, Industrial Revolution at Stockport.[41]

Soot from the increased use of steam engines during the 1820s and thereafter probably played a major role in this shift. The improved forces of order may also have contributed. Before, masters themselves often had to keep order in the vicinities of their factories, whether by exhortation and cajolery or by joining the special constables, Volunteers or similar groups. When many masters still lived with their families close to their factories, it was clearly in their direct personal interest to suppress or prevent riots and strikes. When they began moving away from their mills, strict supervision would have been less possible and also less necessary to the security of their homes and families. Furthermore, by the 1820s there had emerged a host of institutions (from the Stockport Police Commission to the Sunday schools to the religious tract societies) nurtured by the industrialists themselves and designed to maintain order and instil respectable conduct in local workers. By the 1820s, in short, it was becoming less essential for industrial lords to live on their fiefs.

III

The long-term growth of Stockport district population and housing
during the early Industrial Revolution conceals numerous short-
term economic fluctuations which can be traced in the vicissitudes
of certain leading industries. Already by the early 1770s the various
branches of the cotton industry had become fairly well established
in the district and were benefiting from the general prosperity in
the trade which had been apparent to Arthur Young on his famous
northern tour.[42] Spinning and weaving of cottons and fustians were
being carried on in the Stockport district, but the most distinctive
local advances occurred in the finishing branches. A considerable
amount of bleaching and some dyeing was being done in Heaton
Norris, Reddish and Levenshulme, for example. Calico printing
had been established around 1760 in Romiley (Chadkirk) and was
in evidence in the town of Stockport by 1770.[43]

It was not, however, through the systematic growth of these
early enterprises that the cotton industry rose to a position of local
prominence. Rather, it was through the collapse of the silk industry
in the early 1770s that the revolutionary change occurred. Two
large silk firms went bankrupt at that time, and in 1773 only 350
Stopfordians were still employed in throwing silk. Just a few years
before there had been 1,600.[44] With large numbers of experienced
factory workers unemployed and certain mills and workshops intermittently standing idle, the 'cotton revolution' could proceed quite
swiftly in the Stockport district.

The major local stimulus for the switch to cotton probably came
from the Lord of the Manor, Sir George Warren. In the mid-1770s
he began clearing the ruins of Stockport's medieval castle in order
to erect the spectacular Castle Mill. Run by water fed through
tunnels from the Goyt river, it was filled with the latest spinning
machines – probably pirated Arkwright water frames. From about
1778 to 1782 it was supervised by John Milne, a former machine
maker who had previously patented machinery for milling grain
and flour and who proceeded to develop improved roving machines.
For some reason, though, the pioneering Castle Mill never functioned properly, and it was finally converted into a 'Muslin Hall' in
the late 1790s. Henry Marsland had better luck. A former shopkeeper, he carried on cotton spinning to the south of Stockport at
Bullocksmithy in the 1770s and even patented a new machine for
the purpose, one so close to Arkwright's that it allegedly infringed

on the latter's patents. Undeterred by legal niceties, Marsland purchased the 50-year-old Park Silk Mills in 1783, converted them to cotton spinning by installing his new machines, and thereby laid secure foundations for what was soon to become one of the largest manufacturing enterprises in the district.[45]

Both Warren and Marsland typified the successful early cotton magnates in their ability to perceive how to exploit technological advances by rapidly marshalling the requisite capital. Neither was typical, however, in terms of his background. The ranks of gentlemen and general shopkeepers provided few of the early cotton entrepreneurs in the Stockport district. Most fell into three categories. As at Oldham, many of the early factory masters had been prominent locally in some phase of textile marketing or manufacturing before the 1780s. William Lavender and Charles Turner, for example, had been drapers. Charles Davies, a silk throwster, purchased the Lower Carrs Mill in 1781 to begin cotton manufacturing. In the Higher Carrs Mill, Wells and Co. were throwing silk in the 1770s but spinning cotton in the 1780s.[46]

A second category of early industrialists had been involved in textiles outside the Stockport district. Included in this group were William Sykes, the Edgeley bleacher who had started as a West Riding mercer and draper and, most notably, Samuel Oldknow, the son of a Nottingham draper who settled in Stockport's Hillgate area in 1784.[47] His activities provide an interesting case of an early but ultimately unsuccessful attempt to achieve vertical integration in the cotton industry. By the early 1790s he was spinning and weaving in Stockport with the help of an 8 hp Boulton and Watt engine (the first steam engine to be used in the district's cotton industry), and he was bleaching and printing calicoes at Heaton Mersey. The slump of 1792-3 forced him to contract his business, however. He gave up the Heaton Mersey works in 1793 and his weaving operations by 1795. Thereafter, his spinning concern at Mellor was to become the major focus of his attention.[48]

Skilled craftsmen comprised a third category of early leaders in the Stockport cotton industry. This was especially so if they possessed skills in some way related to textile manufacturing. Joel Needham was a machine maker in the 1780s, a cotton manufacturer in the 1790s. John Bell, a joiner, owned a small spinning concern in 1791. William Platt was described as a clockmaker, cotton machine maker and cotton spinner, perhaps indicating the successive accretion of his occupations. William Radcliffe worked for 18 years as a skilled spinner and weaver before becoming a master manufacturer.[49]

For most of those entering the cotton industry from the late 1770s to the early 1790s it seemed easiest to locate in and around the town of Stockport. The availability of labour, housing, transportation facilities and mills which could be quickly converted to cotton no doubt played a major role in siting decisions. Few early cotton mills were built outside of Stockport and its suburbs. For many of the same reasons, early printworks and bleachworks were also established fairly close to Stockport – especially at Cheadle, Heaton Norris, Brinnington and Reddish. This early geographic concentration naturally put a great deal of strain on power supplies. Mention has already been made of the elaborate network of water tunnels under the town to provide power to mills not situated on river banks. Small brooks were dammed mercilessly. When the dam on one such rivulet burst in 1785, it was stated that the mill pond had reached two acres in extent.[50] Windmills in Edward Street and Heaton Norris were being used to manufacture cotton in the 1780s and 1790s. It is not surprising, therefore, that the larger industrialists folowed Oldknow's lead into steam. As Peter Ewart wrote, to the Boulton and Watt Factory, just at the point he got Oldknow's engine working in August 1791: 'there will soon be plenty of orders from this neighbourhood, but you will never get them executed half soon enough.' By 1793 there were 67 steam engines at work in Stockport cotton mills.[51]

The decade after the War of American Independence was clearly a time of high hopes, with the downturns of 1784-5 and 1788 having only an insignificant impact on the burgeoning economy of the district. Looming above it all were cotton princes like Oldknow, who reputedly made £17,000 in profits in both 1789 and 1790. He, the Marslands, Robert Gee and other major Stockport industrialists were beginning to achieve prominence not only within the Stockport district but also in Manchester public affairs. Even a blind man, when he heard that such men were 'getting loads of money', purchased six jennies from a Stockport machine maker and set about trying to make a fortune of his own from cotton.[52]

Then the tide turned. The 13 years after 1792, coinciding as they did with a series of wars with revolutionary and Napoleonic France, constituted a rather unsettled period for the Stockport district economy. The slump of 1792-3 was remembered by one contemporary as 'the most distressing period ever known by the oldest living'. The slump of 1797-8 affected many master spinners, weavers and calico printers. Disaster struck firms of all sizes. The smaller ones – some of which were capitalised at £100 or less – had virtually no means to assure steady supplies of cotton and probably had little cash to help tide them over difficult times or hold back goods from the market when prices were low. At the other end of the scale, three of the four largest Stockport district firms went bankrupt during this period: Abraham Illingworth in 1793, Alexander Hunt in 1796 and John Whitaker in 1797. Illingworth's collapse in turn helped to bring down the Stockport Bank, a two-year-old note-issuing institution which had become too deeply involved with making industrial loans.[53] Even the great Oldknow was affected by these slumps. When his sales sagged during the first quarter of 1793, he found it increasingly difficult to pay his 1,500 employees. Despite extraordinary exertions involving highly unorthodox marketing techniques, he was able to pay only partial wages during the first three weeks of April. Then he sent Peter Ewart, his 25-year-old partner, to Liverpool, where he met with Dr James Currie and explained that his mission was to

> raise a few hundred guineas, to get over another week and keep his people alive. He told me [Currie] that he and his partner had been constantly amongst them, and by entering into all their distresses, had prevailed on them to be extremely patient and reasonable... As I looked at this young man, I perceived that his countenance seemed actually withered with care and sorrow.

In 1798 Oldknow had to beg for a delay in paying Boulton and Watt the premium due on his Hillgate steam engine, complaining, *inter alia*, about his 'world of fixed capital'.[54]

These slumps were not so severe as they might have been for the working population of the district because they did not coincide with significant increases in the prices of foodstuffs. During the slumps of 1792-3 and 1797-8, food prices were moderate. When food prices were high in 1795 and 1800-1, the cotton trade was fairly prosperous. This pattern was not invariable, however. From late 1801 to early 1803, the cotton industry was buoyant and food prices were low. One person later recalled, 'The best time that I ever knew in the spinning [branch] was about 1802...'[55] In other words, despite the wars and the economic difficulties they engendered, seasons of prosperity were not unheard of. As another observer of the British cotton industry later stated, from about 1793 to 1800 'the trade was rapidly increasing, and every fluctuation and depression only seemed to give it renovated elasticity.'[56]

In such a situation some economic expansion occurred, and some innovations were introduced. By 1805 there were at least 26 steam engines at work in the district averaging 13-14 hp each (for a total of about 350 hp).[57] Since 10 hp consumed about one ton of coal per day, the need for coal grew enormously. Old pits in the district were worked more intensively, and new ones were opened. Many gentry families benefited (as did the Warrens from their seams at Poynton and Worth, the Ardens at Bredbury and the Leghs at Norbury), but so, too, did far-sighted industrialists. Oldknow had pits in Marple, for example, and the Ashtons acquired pits in Hyde. Conveyance of coal in turn provided the major stimulus for construction of Stockport district's first canals during this period and helped convince leading citizens of the need to improve roads. Better transportation facilities were also needed because of the diffusion of the cotton industry outward into the farthest corners of the district. It was during this period that Horsefield, Turner, the Ashtons and the Howards became industrialists in Hyde. There were also at least three printworks established in Disley and one bleachwork established on the southern boundary of the district in Handforth township.

At the same time, notable technological improvements were being made. Jennies were constructed in increasingly large sizes, which meant that they were becoming unsuitable for use in domestic manufactures. The change was barely underway in 1794 when Ann Radcliffe visited a Stockport 'crowded with buildings and people, as much so as some of the busiest quarters of London, with large blazing fires in every house, by the light of which women were frequently spinning...'[58] That jenny spinning continued to thrive in Stockport down to about 1820 while it rapidly declined in other cotton towns is not easily explained. It is clear, however, that by the turn of the century it was becoming a male occupation undertaken in jenny spinning workshops. Women who thereby lost one type of domestic employment could still easily shift to handloom weaving.

Powerloom weaving was not yet highly developed, but it received stimulation of a most crucial sort from at least three Stockport industrialist-inventors. From 1803 to 1807 William Radcliffe took out four patents relevant to weaving, William Horrocks took out two, and Henry Marsland's son, Peter, took out three.[59] As a result of their efforts, Stockport would soon be regarded as a major centre of powerloom weaving in all of Britain. Advances likewise occurred in the finishing branches. By 1805 steam engines had been installed at Cheadle Grove printworks and the Sykeses' Edgeley bleachworks, making them two of the earliest enterprises in which steam power was being applied to textile finishing processes.[60]

The succeeding years contained the most severe economic dislocations in the Stockport district of any period in the early Industrial Revolution. The same could be said for many other districts. The 26 commissions of bankruptcy in the cotton trade in 1806, for instance, constituted the largest number that had ever been recorded. It would not be exceeded until 1826.[61] Major slumps in 1807-8 and 1811-12 were separated by an upturn which can only be described as moderate and brief. Disruptions in foreign trade after promulgation of the Berlin and Milan Decrees, the Orders in Council and the United States' Embargo Act (1806-7) were major causes of the difficulties. As a consequence, many in the Stockport district joined the 'mad burst of speculation' to South America in 1808-10.[62] When few stable, lucrative markets were found there, Stockport entrepreneurs joined those of Manchester and Liverpool in pressing the government to end the East India Company's monopoly. A separate Stockport petition in 1813 requesting that greater attention be paid to the moral and religious condition of the inhabitants of India was undoubtedly related to Stopfordians' desires to penetrate the Indian market.[63]

In addition to trade problems, local entrepreneurial miscalculations from 1806 to 1812 made the situation in the Stockport district especially precarious. It was a time when industrialists should have been husbanding their resources, postponing new construction and deferring the installation of expensive new machinery. Some could not resist the temptation to expand or innovate, however, especially when it came to powerloom weaving. Among other things, the seductive new technology might help to keep twist out of the hands of Britain's enemies, to calm or at least circumvent factious handloom weavers, and to allow for tighter control over production schedules and embezzlement of materials.[64] Older accounts scarcely do justice to this early surge when they claim that there were only 14 powerloom factories in the greater Manchester district in 1818. Even if those figures referred to factories devoted exclusively to powerloom weaving, they seem too low.

William Radcliffe had personal knowledge of the existence of powerlooms in about 30 factories in 1808.[65] Steady growth in powerloom weaving in the Stockport district, whether in separate new factories or converted sections of pre-existing mills, suggests that Radcliffe's higher figure was accurate. By 1812 powerlooms were being used by at least six Stockport firms. To speed up the diffusion of the new technology, Radcliffe formed a powerloom manufacturers' club in 1811. Workers' discontent over powerlooms in 1812 thus occurred not when the new technology was in its infancy, strictly speaking, but rather when it was well on its way to becoming an established industrial process.

Radcliffe was one of those who did not follow the counsel of prudence and who consequently found themselves involved in rather spectacular failures. At his Hillgate Mill Radcliffe carried on spinning operations, put out cotton yarns to as many as a thousand handloom weavers, worked on new machinery and devoted increasing amounts of time and energy to the operation of his new powerloom weaving concern. These exertions took their toll, and Radcliffe declared bankruptcy in 1807. The Hillgate Mill was taken over by J.B. Spencer, a Manchester industrialist who soon set about building a costly addition to a Chestergate mill in Stockport which he also owned. In 1812 Spencer, too, declared bankruptcy.[66] Millgate Factory provides a similar case study. Built around 1806 by relatives of the inventor Thomas Horrocks, it contained 19,000 square feet of floor space, nearly 8,000 spindles, 100 of the new powerlooms, a steam engine and a steam heating system – the first such system installed in any factory in Stockport. The Horrockses were bankrupt by 1808, and the firm passed into the hands of John Goodair, a London merchant. As an outsider (like Spencer) he apparently believed that bold measures would secure great profits in this distant provincial town. He thus set about building Edgeley Great Mill which had 22,000 square feet of floor space, 8,000 spindles, and a steam engine of 36 hp. He also built a small adjoining weaving factory in which he installed 200 of the new powerlooms. Goodair had to declare bankruptcy in 1810, although he continued to oversee the affairs of his Stockport interests until all the relevant legal issues were settled.[67]

The major failures in the finishing branches during these years probably also occurred as a result of over-investment in fixed capital. Isachar Thorp had operated the calico printworks at Reddish Vale since about 1784. In 1805 he and his partner were trying to sell or lease one of their mills, which they described as 'newly erected'. Among other things, the elaborate millwork for the new edifice included a weir on the Tame and a canal from the river to the printworks which was 1,000 yards long. Thorp and his partner found no one interested in taking over these premises and consequently still had possession at the time of their bankruptcy in 1807.[68] Thorp thus shared with Radcliffe, Goodair and others a propensity to expand their firms and install new machinery in inauspicious circumstances and thereby to cause the failure of their respective enterprises. This trio also had another dubious distinction in common: in 1812 their hapless enterprises became targets of 'Luddite' attacks (see Chapter 8).

Some economic problems continued in the seven years after 1812, a period which included a major slump in 1816-17 and a minor downturn in 1819. Demobilisation contributed to these difficulties and meant that hundreds of men were returning to the Stockport district to search for employment. There were numerous business failures. The bankruptcy of Charles Eardley's large firm in 1818 was noteworthy and yet at the same time exceptional in that smaller firms increasingly seemed to bear the brunt of economic fluctuations. Persistent problems in calico printing also appear to have occurred in rather small, outlying firms.[69]

By contrast, the larger firms began to achieve a measure of stability. The largest enterprises in Stockport and Hyde in the late 1810s remained among the largest firms down to the early 1840s. It was these firms which cautiously began to increase the pace of innovation just before 1820. They concentrated on vertical integration, especially into the process of powerloom weaving. William Smith and Sampson Lloyd of Stockport and Thomas Ashton and Joseph Horsefield of Hyde began 'steam' weaving during this period, for example. By the early 1820s there were at least 17 firms engaged in powerloom weaving and the preliminary process of cotton dressing. There was also some tendency for larger firms to branch out into one or more of the finishing processes, as with John Ashton of Hyde, who began calico printing in about 1815. All of this, of course, required larger premises and increased power supplies, the latter almost invariably supplied by additional or larger steam engines. Inquiries to Boulton and Watt about rather large engines reflect this trend. Thomas Hope wanted details on a 40-50 hp engine in 1816, for instance, and John Bentley asked about a 24-30 hp engine in 1819. The Sykeses of Edgeley installed a

36 hp engine in 1816.[70]

Many of these expansive tendencies became more pronounced during the 1820s, especially during the first half of the decade. The second half turned out to be less buoyant because of a severe slump in 1825-6 and a lengthy strike in 1829 involving some 10,000 factory operatives. By contrast the period from 1820 to early 1825 could be characterised as a veritable boom period. A considerable amount of factory construction took place. A later survey indicated that 19 new factories or extensions were built during 1821 to 1825, while just seven had been built in 1815-19 and six in 1826-30. At one point in 1822 the editors of the *Stockport Advertiser* noted that eight factories were under construction. This, along with the numerous houses, churches, chapels and commercial premises which were being built, caused the editors to claim that 'more buildings have been raised in this town within the last 2 years than in the preceding 20'. The Hyde-Denton area likewise prospered. At Compstall Bridge, for example, various new cotton works helped to transform the former village containing 30 cottages into a town with thousands of workers. The amount of steam power simultaneously grew at a remarkable rate. The total steam power employed in the Stockport district by 1825 was nearly 2,000 hp – a fivefold increase since 1805, most of it installed after 1812. The average size of steam engines increased to about 30 hp. When the engineer Joshua Field visited a Stockport spinning factory in 1821, he could refer to its old 20 hp engine as 'rather a small one'.[71]

As at Manchester, these years were marked by significant structural changes in the Stockport district cotton industry. Before, from the 1790s to the 1810s, all evidence points to a 'steep pyramid' structure featuring a few giant enterprises at the top and dozens of small, and even tiny, firms at the bottom. Capital valuation for 64 firms in the mid-1790s, for instance, shows that the top four firms accounted for three-eighths of the capital valuation, while the bottom three-quarters of the firms accounted for one-quarter of the capital valuation. The Crompton census similarly reveals that the four largest firms owned three-eighths of the total spindles in the Stockport district in 1811, while the smallest three-quarters of the firms had one-quarter of the total spindles.[72] The various changes inaugurated just before 1820 resulted in a new 'bulging pyramid' structure during the 1820s and 1830s, with large firms still relatively few in number, medium-sized firms increasing in numbers, and small firms becoming less prominent (see Table 2.4).

Table 2.4: Distribution of Stockport District Cotton Firms in 1832–4

Size of Labour Force	Stockport and Suburbs	Hyde-Denton Area	Remaining Out-townships	Total
		Number of Firms in:		
Over 500	5 (25) [a]	7 (84)	–	12 (42)
151–500	33 (63)	3 (14)	3 (87)	39 (50)
1–149	30 (12)	1 (2)	2 (13)	33 (8)
Total	68 (100)	11 (100)	5 (100)	84[b] (100)[b]

Notes: (a) Figures in parentheses are the workers in each category expressed as a percentage of the total labour force in each column.
(b) Eleven firms of the total were derived from 1834 horsepower returns using as multipliers 6 persons per hp when total hp was below 100; 7 persons per hp when total hp was 100 or above.

Sources: PP 1831–2 (706) XV, Q 9409; PP 1834 (167) XX, D.1.; Andrew Ure, *The Cotton Manufacture of Great Britain Systematically Investigated.* 2 vols. (London, 1836), I, 334–42.

It was a complex process, but much of it can be explained by the stepped-up pace of technological innovation and vertical integration. Many firms shifted to 'long mules' beginning in the early 1820s. Whereas Stockport district mules at the time of the Crompton census ranged up to 216 spindles, by the early 1830s they often reached 300 and 400 spindles. Some small firms, especially those still using jennies, were driven out of business by this change. Others, however, became medium-sized as a result of installing the new machinery. In the decade after 1822, moreover, the number of firms engaged in powerloom weaving nearly tripled, while the number of powerlooms in use quadrupled. Since most of this activity occurred in firms already engaged in spinning, this type of verticalism might serve to upgrade some of the small spinning firms and thereby shrink the lowest part of the industrial pyramid in another way. The case of Thomas Ferneley, Sr, illustrates this phenomenon. A small jenny spinner in 1811, he was selling off jennies in 1822 to convert to mules. He also took up powerloom weaving, so that by the 1830s, with nearly 300 workers, his firm had become medium-sized.[73]

Some of the same patterns can be found among calico printworks in the 1820s. Smaller, outlying concerns lost the advantages that once accrued to the occupation of choice water-powered sites in close proximity to handloom weaving villages and hamlets. As in the 1810s, many of them faltered in the face of increasing competition, some of it from fairly large firms which made effective use of steam power, mechanisation of certain processes and economies of scale. The Daw Bank Printworks of Thomas Marsland was turning out 200,000 pieces of cloth per week in the mid-1820s and was said to be the largest of its kind in all of Europe. A few of the largest spinning and weaving firms followed the lead of the Ashtons at Hyde, integrated the finishing processes into their firms, and thereby achieved complete vertical integration of cotton textile manufacturing. Edward Hollins and the Peter Marsland family provide two cases in point.[74]

Structural changes of this kind naturally had far-reaching social ramifications. For one thing, occupational mobility probably became more circumscribed. The period from the 1770s to about 1805 had been noted for the ease with which shrewd, hard-working individuals like the Milnes, the Marslands and Oldknow had improved their situations. In calico printing it was much the same according to an 1807 pamphlet: 'It is a fact, that there are now many masters in the trade, and carrying on much business, who were enabled to begin by a capital they acquired by the good wages they earned while journeymen.'[75] While few could realistically expect to reach the apex of the industrial pyramid, becoming a small master posed few difficulties. With vertical integration not so pronounced as it was to become, a man might set up a firm exclusively devoted to carding or roving or spinning on a modest scale. Machines were still small and relatively inexpensive. One early jenning spinning workshop at Cheadle Hulme contained just five jennies, while another at Heaton Norris had 13 jennies ranging from 50 to 120 spindles each.[76] For machines which were not hand-operated, small amounts of power could be obtained fairly easily. There were numerous examples of factory owners leasing power (and space) to petty entrepreneurs. Such was the case in the Top o' th' Hill Mill in 1793, certain of the Carrs mills in 1795, Adlington Square Mills in 1797 and Stephen Joule's various premises in 1806. Dozens of tenants might occupy a single mill, with each employing perhaps only an average of ten employees.[77]

The result of these tendencies was that there were wide variations among masters and large numbers of small firms in which owners were still close to their employees culturally and perhaps also occupationally. As one worker later testified before Parliament:

Some of the master cotton spinners, so called, are little more than workmen themselves, keeping not more than a few children under them to assist them in working small portions of machinery, taking the more laborious part themselves; by degrees they increase the quantity, and get more, rising in this way gradually from one step to another, till they become possessed of large mills; thus in the small concerns they are scarcely separated from the journeymen, and cannot combine with the larger masters.

If comprehensive masters' organisations were impeded by the steep-pyramid structure of the industry, so too were workers' combinations. Operatives scattered in small firms under the close supervision of masters were less likely to become involved in combinations than those in larger factories despite the fact that there were many problems confronting workers in the smaller operations. The latter were often under-capitalised and notoriously unstable, for instance. They consequently might not be able to pay as much as larger firms and could not afford to keep workers on the payroll during economic downturns – assuming that the firm even survived. Lacking 'factory discipline' both masters and workers in smaller firms might take Saint Monday off (and perhaps also Saint Tuesday) and then work 'almost night and day', according to Peter Ewart, in order to catch up.[78]

Beginning with the crisis period from 1806 to 1812, it probably became much more difficult for an individual to enter the cotton industry in a small way.[79] After 1812, moreover, would-be petty entrepreneurs had to expect intense competition from established (and in many cases, expanding) medium- and large-sized firms. It could not have been an appealing prospect for ambitious workmen looking to improve their situations. The prominence and growth of factory unions beginning around 1818 was no doubt related to this phenomenon. With limited possibilities for social mobility in the cotton industry, with more workers employed in larger units of production and with more owners becoming rather remote figures (sometimes residentially as well as culturally), workers became markedly more determined to promote organisations which would enhance their standard of living as workers. This involved demands for 'uniform' wages, which must have seemed attainable as the disparities in factory size decreased; and for reductions in the long, regular, monotonous hours which affected increasing numbers of operatives as they moved from workshops to factories.

Structural changes in the industry also promoted strong, counter-vailing tendencies. With more masters controlling large- and medium-sized firms, there was greater homogeneity than before. Masters associations could, and often did, become more comprehensive and more effective. The increased size of firms after 1820 helped to foster greater stability, at least for the ensuing generation. This in turn led to improved work conditions in some cases and more regular employment, even during fairly substantial economic downturns. There were also increased opportunities for paternalistic control outside the workplace, as shown by masters' lavish patronage of carefully selected educational, religious and charitable organisations – something that the herd of small masters in the late eighteenth century could scarcely have considered doing. Many of these developments will be elaborated upon in subsequent chapters. Suffice it to note here that in the case of the structural changes underway in the 1820s, any resulting advantages for workers and their combinations were closely observed and, if need be, counter-acted by masters and their allies lest social harmony be disrupted and public order threatened. However slowly and haltingly, the social leaders and public persons of the Stockport district had learned at least some of the lessons of effective governance by the 1820s.

Constables and overseers had, in those days, a very straightforward way of doing business. On receiving an order, or even a direction less tangible from a magistrate or magistrate's clerk, it was forthwith carried into effect, – the magistrate was everything, – the rate-payers and vestry nothing, – and money was expended which was never enquired into afterwards. If the minister, or some one or two of the 'gentlemen rate-payers', put a question or so to the overseer when he met him, and the reply was, 'Oh, Mr A. or Mr B. the magistrate ordered it', all would be right, and nothing further would be said about the matter. – Samuel Bamford, *Early Days* (1849)

In the early decades of George III's reign Stockport district gentry seemed quite secure in their positions of power and prestige. A few families stood above all the rest. Individuals from three of the most prominent (the Warrens of Stockport and Poynton, the Ardens of Bredbury, the Leghs of Lyme)[1] even represented scattered constituencies in Parliament. Locally, Sir George Warren (1735-1801) was the most important gentry figure during the early Industrial Revolution. He held various parliamentary seats from 1758 to 1780 and again from 1786 to 1796. Ever mindful of his status, he chose the Rev. John Watson to be rector of Stockport (1769–83) primarily because Watson could provide him with a 'raked-up lineage'. When Warren was buried in Chester Cathedral, it was said that 'the procession was one of the most costly and attractive that has been seen for several years'. His daughter had married Viscount Bulkeley, and both then succeeded to Stockport and Poynton manors as Lord and Lady Warren Bulkeley.[2] In addition to the Warren, Arden and Legh families, the Isherwoods of Marple Hall, the Philipses of Bank Hall, the Hyde Clarkes of Hyde Hall, the Davenports of Bramall Hall, the Wrights of Offerton Hall and the Harrisons of Cheadle helped to fill major government offices, including those of sheriff and deputy-lieutenant of Cheshire county. Not surprisingly, many of these gentry families intermarried and were quick to co-operate with each other, as did the Warrens, Clarkes, Leghs and Davenports in an *ad hoc* scheme to stop poachers on their extensive estates in 1776.[3]

While the scions of gentry families dominated the magistracy, a few prominent attorneys also became JPs. Holland Watson (the Rev. John Watson's nephew) was raised to the bench in the late 1790s, as were two attorneys from the Newton family in the 1820s. Down to that decade, the rectors of Stockport parish usually served as magistrates, too. These 'rector-magistrates' and one or two other magistrates from the immediate vicinity of Stockport held weekly Petty Sessions, appointed clerks to help them in administrative matters and swore in special constables as the need arose. Only one industrialist, Peter Marsland, became a magistrate during the early Industrial Revolution. The number of active magistrates residing in the district ranged from an average of two in the 1770s to seven in the 1820s. They typically held commissions for both Lancashire and Cheshire, and their authority consequently extended into all 26 townships of the district.[4]

Attorneys who became JPs were the most notable in a profession which was relatively small and fairly close-knit. John Lloyd, for example, married the sister of Holland Watson; Lloyd's son, John Horatio Lloyd (also an attorney) later married Watson's daughter. The number of attorneys ranged from about three to five per 10,000 people, which was about the same as the total for the physicians and their less-esteemed colleagues, the surgeons. There were many more clergymen, who were ranged along a continuum from the respected Anglican ministers to the leaders of the new and sometimes ephemeral sects. Some of the latter clergymen even took the lead in radical political clubs and agitations.

It was usually the professional men, the major and lesser industrialists and the wholesale and retail merchants who held office in local government. Apart from the magistracy, the important governmental institutions were parochial and manorial.[5] The rector of Stockport parish (one of the wealthiest parochial positions in the country) was selected by the Lord of Stockport Manor. In turn, the rector appointed curates and presided over the vestry, which chose overseers of the poor, surveyors of the highways and a workhouse governor. The vestries of Cheadle, Manchester and Prestbury parishes had similar powers over the Stockport district townships which lay within their jurisdictions. The Stockport vestry was limited in one respect, however, in that the collection and expenditure of church rates was handled by churchwardens who were hardly responsible to anyone but themselves. This system grew out of a long tradition whereby churchwardens were appointed not by the vestry but by the four 'posts' of the parish – the lords of Stockport, Bredbury, Norbury and Bramhall manors.

Apart from this prerogative the lords of the various manors in the Stockport district had few notable legal functions except in the case of the Lord of Stockport Manor. Through his steward the Lord continued to hold regular meetings of the Stockport Court Leet until some years after the accession of Victoria. The Court had charge of installing two constables each year as well as three or four market inspectors and a host of lesser officials. It also heard misdemeanour cases arising out of offences committed at the Friday markets. All of those who held 'burgage' tenures in Stockport township were required, as burgesses, to attend the semi-annual meetings of the Court Leet. By a compromise made in Elizabeth I's reign, burgesses had the right to make the final selection for the largely symbolic post of mayor from among four persons nominated by the Lord of the Manor. When mayors finished their one-year terms of office, they automatically became aldermen.

At first glance the government of the Stockport district seems to have included a bewildering variety of officials with confused lines of authority. Yet for contemporaries the situation was somewhat simplified by the fact that certain individuals or families held many of the offices successively or simultaneously. Lords of manors might also be magistrates and deputy-lieutenants of the county. The Rev. Charles Prescot was rector of Stockport parish from 1783 to his death in 1820 and was a magistrate almost all of that time. His eldest son, Charles Kenrick Prescot, became rector (but not a magistrate) on his father's death and served in that capacity until his own death in 1875.[6]

I

If the institutions of government were as easily learned (and apparently as fixed) as the structure of society at the time when Lord North embarked on his long prime ministry, there nevertheless existed causes for dissatisfaction. During the 1770s and 1780s Stopfordians were expressing concern about the increase in crime, which by all accounts was out-pacing the growth in population. It might have been expected that from the first half of the 1780s to the second half, misdemeanour cases involving Stopfordians would have increased – demobilisation after major eighteenth-century wars frequently produced that phenomenon. Yet no one could have predicted that the number of such cases would nearly quintuple from one half-decade to the next.[7] Many local residents requested, and then demanded, such things as night watchmen, a larger prison and better street lighting.

Streets themselves attracted attention because some needed to be widened or repaired and most needed to be cleared of refuse on a more regular basis. The Market Place likewise needed to be enlarged, a suggestion which was often made in conjunction with complaints that market tolls collected by the Lord of the Manor were too oppressive. Many Stopfordians thought that since the common lands were no longer of much use for pasturage or fuel gathering, they should be sold or leased for their full commercial value with the proceeds to be used in ways which would reduce tax burdens. Problems in collecting small debts, especially if cases had to be delayed until the convening of Quarter Sessions, led some citizens to call for the establishment of a special local court to handle such matters. It can be seen that enactment of these proposals would have benefited urban tradesmen desirous of protecting their property and gaining the freedom to accumulate business profits as efficiently as possible. This was not so true of a final area of concern, the problem of assisting the poor to obtain the necessities of life, including adequate health care.

Leaving aside the problem of poverty, the commercial classes of Stockport agitated for piecemeal reforms in all of the above areas during the 1770s and 1780s. In 1775 they petitioned Parliament for the right to levy rates to light, clean and widen the streets because 'the Town of Stockport is very populous, and a Place of great Trade and Business...' Much the same language was used ten years later in a Stockport petition which requested, in addition to the aforementioned items, watchmen for the town, enlargement of the Market Place, establishment of a Court of Requests (for small debts) and the building of a new prison. All of this was to be paid for by proceeds from the sale of the common lands and, if need be, from the imposition of a local tax.[8]

If Stockport merchants gained few of their demands, it was largely because Sir George Warren opposed any fundamental change in local government, including the measures proposed in

1775 and 1785. Instead, he developed a policy which, if it had been pursued on the Continent, would be categorised by historians as a species of 'feudal reaction' – or seigneurial enterprise. Simply stated, Warren sought to maintain, revive or expand all of his traditional manorial rights at the same time as he exploited every significant new economic opportunity that came his way. Among other things, he tried to tighten up the collection of tolls and fees derived from the Stockport weekly market, from manorial mills and bakehouses, and from attendance at the Court Leet. He also collected fees from those who sought to make bricks from common-land clay while simultaneously enclosing numerous parcels of the common lands for his own profit. His building of Castle Mill and digging of coal pits at Poynton has already been mentioned. At the latter he installed a colliery steam engine but not one obtained legally from Boulton and Watt. It was, characteristically, a cheaper, pirated model made by Bateman and Sherratt of Manchester. A satire of 1779 unkindly (but unsurprisingly) referred to him as having 'the usurious complexion of the Jew, and the dangerous disposition of Sir Benjamin Backbite'.[9]

With Warren determined to maintain the *status quo* in most things (save his income) there were few novel departures in local government. The main features of Poor Law administration, for instance, remained undisturbed. On the basis of fragmentary information, it appears that assessments were kept quite low, generally at about 2s. on each pound of assessed value. Disbursements were also kept low. In Stockport township the ratio of disbursements to the total population in the mid-1770s and again in the mid-1780s was under 2s.[10] Official outlays were supplemented by endowed charities, the proceeds of which provided about £85 annually for the poor in Stockport township. This amounted to an equivalent of about 15-20 per cent of the official disbursements on the poor. As might be expected, many had been established by the Warrens, the Ardens and other prominent gentry families and thus served as continuing reminders of their wealth, status and paternalistic regard for the poor.[11]

In the absence of significant alterations in the institutions and processes of government, individuals and groups came to employ various unofficial, *ad hoc* measures to achieve their objectives. On one occasion, Roe and Kershaw, the master calico printers at Chadkirk, offered a reward for information leading to the conviction of those who had stolen some cloth from their printgrounds. After the theft of cloth from his Heaton Mersey bleachworks, Thomas Oldknow (Samuel's brother) not only offered a reward but also proceeded to install steel man-traps on his premises.[12] Associations for the detection and prosecution of felons were established at Stockport (1773, 1781 and 1785) and the Hyde-Denton area (1783). A 'Society for the Prosecution of Croft-Breakers' (1789) included at least two Levenshulme bleachers as well as others from outside the district.[13] Voluntaryism similarly characterised activities in other matters. The only street-lighting in Stockport was apparently that erected in the centre of the town by private subscription in the 1760s. To provide health care for the poor, James Briscall, a philanthropic surgeon, opened a cottage dispensary in the 1780s and ran it with his own funds.[14]

During a period when the provision for poor relief was not great and the forces of order were relatively weak, there existed considerable dissatisfaction among the middle classes over the outmoded institutions of government and the unwillingness of those in power (the imperious Lord of the Manor above all) to adopt measures of reform. On the surface, at least, this was a potentially explosive situation, especially during the depressed years of the War of American Independence (1775-83). That no major tumults occurred during the war can be explained by the continuing vigilance of the governors of local society (as during the spinners' agitations of 1779); by the departures of some of the most discontented from both the middle and working classes for more hospitable surroundings in America and elsewhere; and by the eventual creation of hundreds of new jobs in the cotton industry. In the decade after the war, all-but-unbroken prosperity probably helped to lessen the feelings of discontent, if not the demands placed on the harried officials and over-strained organs of local government.

II

Various reforms and improvements were finally instituted from 1790 to 1806. They may have been inspired by earlier reform movements elsewhere, including not only the steps towards 'economical reform' taken at the national level but also various movements to reduce crime, improve roads and aid the poor which had strong provincial roots, especially in the West Riding of Yorkshire.[15] In the Stockport district the fact that surging population growth was concentrated in the township of Stockport (and not spread evenly throughout the district) meant that matters were rapidly reaching a crisis point. Rather fortuitously, after about 1790 gentry families no longer maintained the tight grip on local government that they once had. In many cases, heirs to gentry estates chose to become absentee landlords. Such was the case with the Warrens. Sir George himself, while he acquiesced in some of the changes, generally became much less active in public affairs during the last decade of his life. When chosen to be county sheriff in 1797, he declined because 'my age and the state of my health would not enable me to discharge the duties of the office'. For two decades after his death in 1801 his successors spent little time at Poynton, preferring to reside at their homes in London or Anglesey. A recent study of Bredbury, Hyde and other parts of north-east Cheshire has likewise concluded that by about 1800, 'absentee landlords had taken the place of resident lords of the manor'.[16]

All of this provides some support for Harold Perkin's (and Thomas Carlyle's) notion of an 'abdication on the part of the governors'. One should note, however, that it may not have been a conscious or voluntary 'abdication' in all cases. Nor did it leave the Stockport district with a leadership vacuum. Many established gentry families remained, of course, and many cotton masters immediately stepped forward to claim positions of prestige and responsibility in local government. John Marsland, a dyer originally from Bramhall, became high constable of Stockport division in 1801-2, mayor of Stockport in 1803-4. Jesse Howard, a master cotton spinner, held the same posts in 1802-3 and 1808-9, respectively. William Howard was overseer of the poor (1802-3) and then mayor (1806-7), as was Joseph Lane (1803-4 and 1816-17, respectively). William Radcliffe proudly noted later in life that soon after he settled in Stockport in 1801, he became a commissioner for the property tax, a commandant for a troop of Volunteers, a turnpike commissioner, a trustee for the rebuilding of the parish church and, in 1804-5, mayor of the town.[17]

With the old guard becoming less visible and less intransigent as it simultaneously incorporated the most notable of the new industrialists into local government, changes naturally followed. A nightly watch was sanctioned by Quarter Sessions in 1790, and a handful of watch-houses was soon set up. Sources of financing are difficult to ascertain – watchmen may have been paid wholly or partly from voluntary subscriptions – but they were soon popularly referred to as the 'Stockport Police', indicating their official status in the public mind. A new jail was also built in 1790 on land donated by Sir George Warren with funds from Quarter Sessions and from private subscribers in Stockport and its suburbs.[18]

Law and order received additional support from purely voluntary organisations. The Reeves Association was active in 1792-3 in combatting Jacobinism. Many of the members of that Association then joined the volunteer movement. The Stockport Loyal Volunteers (250 men), the Cheadle Volunteers (65 men) and the Stockport Cavalry (30 men) were established from 1794 to 1798 to guard against a possible French invasion and also, explicitly, to suppress local political and labour agitations. In their first year of existence the Stockport Volunteers fought no French but did manage to suppress a disturbance by canal cutters in Disley, quell a food riot in Stockport and guard against a rumoured attack on the town by district colliers.[19] The Volunteers also functioned in more subtle ways to promote and exemplify social harmony. A drill in 1795 illustrates this point. It commenced with a ceremony in which the wife of the rector presented the troop with a set of colours donated by the wife of the Lord of the Manor. Captain Holland Watson then addressed the Volunteers and spectators, condemning 'the wicked attempts of those at home, who, by the industrious discrimin-ation [sic] of novel doctrines, have so insidiously endeavored to destroy the orders of civil society and spread anarchy and confusion over the land . . .' The Volunteers then marched to St Mary's, the parish church, to hear the Rev. Prescot speak from a text in Psalms 133, 'Behold, how good and joyful a thing it is, brethren, to dwell together in unity'. Many of the rank-and-file, it should be noted, were from the lower orders of society. Watson referred to them as 'persons of such description as cannot afford to give up much time . . .' He suggested that the government pay privates, but soon leading Stopfordians had established a local fund from which working Volunteers could draw.[20]

The Volunteers disbanded after the Peace of Amiens, but with the renewal of hostilities in 1803 enthusiasm for volunteer forces rose to new heights. Even the Stockport Theatre became involved by holding benefit performances for the Volunteers and featuring a new loyalist song, *The Female Volunteer*, as a musical interlude. Nearly one thousand Volunteers were enrolled in seven district groups. Incomplete listings show that they contained shoemakers, carpenters, tailors, leather breeches makers, a stonemason, a cooper, a hatter, a painter and a plumber. By 1804 Viscount Warren Bulkeley was consequently promoting another scheme to secure monetary compensation for the rank-and-file, whose service for King and country might otherwise cause them undue financial strain.[21]

In 1806 local merchants finally received their Court of Requests to speed the collection of small debts. Parliament gave it jurisdiction over Stockport and its Cheshire suburbs.[22] A year before that, the enclosure of the 125 acres of Stockport common lands had been sought again (as in 1785) in order to provide funds for the poor and for paving, lighting, cleaning and watching the streets. This objective was also achieved, although in the final Act, only aid to the poor was specified, probably because it was realised that the cost of extensive urban improvements would exceed the proceeds from enclosure. The support of the manorial government helped to speed the passage of the Stockport Enclosure Act. The names of Lord and Lady Warren Bulkeley headed the list of trustees, and their steward, James Antrobus Newton, testified in favour of the Act before Parliament. One of the two commissioners designated to oversee the enclosure process was Nathaniel Wright, a wealthy Marple resident closely associated with the Warren Bulkeleys by virtue of the fact that he leased coal mines from them at Poynton and Worth. The sales of the common lands occurred from 1806 to 1812 and simultaneously a new workhouse was erected at Daw Bank. When completed in 1812, it could accomodate 170 persons.[23]

Yet there were multitudes eligible for poor relief after 1790. The wars with revolutionary and Napoleonic France had the effect of exaggerating economic downturns, thereby creating more unemployment and underemployment. The war years also featured intermittent bouts of inflation which meant that a higher level of poor relief was required merely to keep recipients at subsistence levels. From 1782-5 to 1802-3 disbursements rose by over fourfold in Stockport township, by approximately the same rate in Stockport's suburbs, and by about twofold in the remainder of the district. Thus, in nearly all areas, poor relief expenditures were increasing at a faster rate than population growth. The average expenditure, when divided by the total population, generally increased from under 2s. *per capita* in the 1780s to over 3s. in the early nineteenth century. Added to such difficulties were the masses of ineligible poor – migrants having no settlement in the Stockport district and no claim on official Poor Law disbursements by Stockport district townships.[24]

Charities helped enormously in this situation, especially subscription charities. Endowed charities, by contrast, played a decreasing role in the overall provision for the poor. Only a few new ones were established in the generation after 1790. The amount expended on the Stockport poor from endowed charities was the equivalent of four per cent of the total disbursed to the poor from official funds in 1802–3, only one per cent in 1812-13. By the latter date, the impact of such charities in other townships of the district was minuscule.[25] During the same time, subscription charities became more popular than ever before. Whereas endowed charities were typically set up towards the end of a benefactor's life or after his or her death according to the formal dictates of a will, the wide array of subscription charities allowed for the possibility of making benefactions at convenient times throughout one's life. As a commentator stated in the *Manchester Mercury* in 1792, 'It was the fashion of past Times to abound in post-humous Benevolence; this Age is justly celebrated for Zeal and Activity in present Acts of Humanity'. Since subscription lists were often printed in newspapers, magazines and pamphlets, this type of charitable largesse could contribute directly to the prestige of those choosing to participate.[26]

Subscription charities had a further advantage in that they could be timed for maximum impact on the recipients and aimed at specific problems – clothing the poor in a harsh winter, for instance, or providing food to those ineligible for regular relief in times of dearth. Endowed charities, meant for the aged, were often aimed at the poor generally and provided fixed disbursements each week or month or year. Stopfordians established at least two subscription charities in 1792 to address specific problems. The Stranger's Friend Society was set up to help the ineligible poor, as has already been mentioned in the context of migration into the Stockport district. At about the same time a public meeting resolved to begin collecting funds for a new dispensary. A Manchester physician remarked not long after the meeting, 'The design has been pursued with great spirit, and a sum has been raised, sufficient for the Trustees to erect a building for the purpose'.[27] Probably more by chance than plan, both new subscription charities helped to mitigate the sufferings of the poor during the slump of 1792-3. Additional examples of subscription charities will be included in subsequent chapters. Suffice it to note here that the extent and timing of charitable relief had a significant impact on the course and outcome of certain workers' movements.[28]

During the period from 1790 to 1806 local authorities thus became better prepared to cope with collective disorders and crime in a number of ways. And, because they were engaged in a series of 'improvements' and charitable activities, they provided a less-than-satisfactory model for local Jacobins and other critics who tried to paint them into a picture of *ancien régime* corruption. Only a few of their improvements helped workers directly, however, and none addressed two kinds of grievances which emerged during these years. One type tended to be quite specific. How could calico printers cope with advancing mechanisation? How could handloom weavers survive as a trade in the face of severe economic downturns? Other grievances tended to be of a more general nature, concentrating on the notion that most socioeconomic problems, even those of a local or temporary nature, stemmed from national political incompetence and corruption. Even during its most progressive periods, however, Stockport government rarely offered a sympathetic ear to the demands of labour activists and Jacobin agitators.

III

After the Court of Requests was established in 1806, and for the succeeding 13 years, there were persistent expressions of concern or complaint, especially from the middling ranks of society, about the performance of local government. While a reform impulse of the kind found in preceding years was not absent, it was severely weakened by successive economic crises. Rampant inflation meant that the organs of government had to raise taxes or try to function on less real income. Both may have occurred simultaneously in various Stockport district townships, to the chagrin of local ratepayers. Economic setbacks also affected the personnel of government, which had been increasingly drawn from the ranks of local industrialists. Many of the latter, of course, went bankrupt during these years. After that pillar of local society, William Radcliffe, failed in 1807, he never again held a public office. Many of the more fortunate industrialists, though quick to voice complaints, were much less visible on lists of office-holders. Only one cotton manufacturer became mayor of Stockport under the Regency, for example.

Controversial issues seemed almost endless during those years.

Keeping the peace headed the list. The Rev. Henry Broughton, a rector of Cheadle who had also served as an active magistrate in the Stockport district for seven years, later stated that in terms of crime, Stockport and its vicinity was 'the worst part of Cheshire... half the prisoners at the sessions come from that neighbourhood'. Broughton himself helped to weaken the forces of order by leaving the district in 1813. By that time Holland Watson was gone, too. He had moved to Congleton soon after 1803, although he returned briefly in 1808 and 1817 to help beleaguered local authorities suppress tumults.[29] At the time of Peterloo, John Philips, the senior JP, was 84 and the Rev. Prescot was 74. As rector-magistrate, Prescot was the leading JP, but he was over-worked and consequently not so effective as he should have been. Testifying in April 1815 about an alleged incident of assault in December 1813, he had to admit to loss of memory: '...I have so many cases brought before me, that I cannot recollect the exact time; I suppose I have had not less than two hundred cases of assault before me since that time.' Peter Marsland's usefulness as a magistrate was limited due to his reputation for having introduced the hated powerlooms and due to continuing squabbles with John Lloyd.[30]

Conflict sprang up in other realms. Growing opposition to the Court of Requests resulted in a bitter controversy which began with a petition to the House of Commons in 1813. It stated that excessive court costs added considerably to an individual's original debt; that the Court regarded non-payment of taxes as a 'debt' which came under its jurisdiction; and that the Court seized goods even from those receiving poor relief in order to sell them and compensate creditors. The petitioners went on to condemn 'the violent, partial, and unjust proceedings of the said Court, and conceiving that, by the practice of it, the trial by jury is rendered nugatory, implore the House to repeal' the Act which had created it. When parliamentary relief was not forthcoming, the fight was continued for a time by Thomas Slaiter, a surgeon who also served as a commissioner of the Court. Slaiter not only failed in his objective but also ended up on trial himself on a series of related charges.[31] The enclosure and sale of the Stockport common lands brought in over £7,000 which was supposed to cover the cost of building the Daw Bank workhouse and to supplement regular expenditures on the poor. In fact, most of the proceeds from enclosure vanished. As far as is known, only a part of the cost of the workhouse came from enclosure funds, and none of those monies ever went towards the day-to-day relief of the poor. Those who might have wondered about these goings-on probably drew their own conclusions from the predominance of the manorial faction (the Warren Bulkeleys, their steward, their friends) in obtaining the Enclosure Act, supervising the sales of common lands, and in the end, purchasing numerous parcels for future development. No culprits were ever brought to justice, however.[32]

The episode must have rankled all the more during a time when closely-spaced economic slumps (1807-8, 1811-12, 1816-17) resulted in phenomenal increases in expenditures on the poor. It was the rare and fortunate township whose outlays on the poor peaked at a level only double that of 1802-3. Stockport's more than tripled, while 14 of the remaining 25 townships (many of them overflowing with destitute handloom weavers) fared worse. Increasing levels of taxation helped to trigger various complaints. Poor-rate assessments probably could not keep pace with the rapidly changing *de facto* values of industrial properties, which might be partly or wholly unoccupied for years at a time during economic slumps. Whatever the precise reasons, many Stockport district industrialists were appealing their assessments to Quarter Sessions from 1817 to 1819 – a step almost unheard of before that time.[33]

Church leys were also a source of conflict. An Act of 1810 allowed Stockport parish to assess all inhabitants (not just Anglicans) for the rebuilding of the parish church. The ill-will it caused was probably reflected in the increasing number of cases in which individuals simply refused to pay and in at least one appeal on the subject to Quarter Sessions. In Didsbury there was an extended and costly legal challenge to church leys in the 1810s. The curate, while opposing the dissidents, wrote privately: '...it must be admitted that taxation is ponderous, and that the middle class are like enough to fall into the state of the lower, and the lower into a state of starvation.'[34]

Despite all the protests, the legality of church leys was upheld. Indeed, it was only in the realm of law-and-order that significant changes in government occurred during these years. These changes can be seen in part as attempts to replicate the more placid situation of the 1790s in four respects: (1) by disseminating loyalist views; (2) by having a large number of volunteer 'infantrymen' at the ready to help keep the peace; (3) by having a body of reliable cavalrymen; and (4) by enhancing the effectiveness of the magistracy. Local loyalists encountered difficulties in all four areas. The Stockport

Reeves Association of 1792-3 was to a limited extent resurrected in the Manchester Pitt Club formed in 1812. Its original members included seven loyalists from the Stockport district, including the rector of Cheadle, the curate of Didsbury, two magistrates, two industrialists and John Lloyd. It reached its peak of activity early in 1817 when it distributed thousands of anti-radical pamphlets and handbills. At the time of Peterloo, however, there were still only 13 Stockport district members.[35] It is unclear what effect this small local representation had on an organisation whose headquarters lay in the cotton metropolis or, conversely, what effect the Pitt Club had on the Stockport district.

The effectiveness of volunteer infantry units was being undermined by a few volunteers who no longer supported such domestic peace-keeping activities as the suppression of the weavers' strike in 1808 and by rumours to the effect that many other volunteers secretly shared those views. The nationwide reorganisation of local military units during the last half of 1808 thus came as a welcome surprise. The various Stockport district volunteer corps were immediately disbanded. Many of their most loyal members were then re-formed into permanent local militia companies which were under closer government supervision than the old volunteers. If greater ideological purity was one result, less sensitivity to local needs was another. Despite the participation of Captain John Lloyd, the militia was rarely employed to stop or prevent local tumults. With the demise of the volunteers, Stockport authorities had unwittingly lost a major force for maintaining public order.[36] Their 'foot soldiers' increasingly became those master manufacturers, shopkeepers and artisans who would volunteer to act as special constables in times of crisis. Scores came forward to suppress the weavers' strike of 1808 and the Blanketeers' march in 1817. A weakness of the system surfaced at the time of the powerloom strike in 1818, when many of those who normally served refused to be sworn in, perhaps out of fear of retaliation from defiant crowds. The authorities' new cavalry was the Stockport Yeomanry, which loyalists established in 1814. It, too, encountered problems during the early years of its existence due in part to dissensions within the ranks. It was not really used to good effect until 1819 when, only weeks before the Manchester meeting on St Peter's Field, the Stockport Troop Club was established as an auxiliary organisation to help ameliorate conditions within the Yeomanry.[37]

In the 1790s the attorney Holland Watson had served as an

unusually active and effective clerk to the Rev. Charles Prescot. Watson's genteel background was only slightly less prestigious than Prescot's, but the two men's views were equally conservative. His effectiveness in government was somewhat circumscribed, however, by his conspicuous lack of sympathy for the lower orders of society. As one of his sons later put it: 'My father was a tory magistrate, full of the prejudices of his party, most violent in temper, opposed to all philanthropical measures, and almost dead to individual benevolence.'[38] John Lloyd was articled to Watson from 1791 to 1796. During that time he learned much more than the practice of law. He went on to take Watson's place as Prescot's clerk, to marry Watson's sister, and to use his memberships in the Orange, Pitt and Wellington clubs, the Stockport Permanent Militia and other groups to exceed his brother-in-law's record for zealous loyalism. His motto: *Non sibi sed regi et patriae.* Other quasi-official changes probably also helped to bolster the magistrates' power in the early nineteenth century. There appear to have been rudimentary attempts, for example, to place some offices on sounder foundations by reappointing capable and willing men to the same office year after year.[39]

The rise of Lloyd to a position of importance and the frequent reappointment of constables, overseers and other officials resulted in part from the reluctance of many industrialists to hold office or otherwise to concern themselves with public affairs from 1806 to 1819. These tendencies had several untoward consequences. It seemed as if local government was becoming more closed at a time when complaints about the activities and financial irregularities of government institutions were becoming more prominent. With the 'natural' leaders of society less willing to serve, those in positions of authority often had less distinguished backgrounds and were less likely to evoke voluntary deference. Lloyd, for instance, had neither a genteel demeanour, a distinguished pedigree, nor financial security. Indeed, lack of attention to his legal practice during the Luddite period nearly left him destitute.[40]

Yet while Lloyd was bluff, he was often compassionate as well, and always courageous – qualities which added considerably to the effectiveness of the local authorities. A poetic account of him composed by a staunch loyalist exaggerated his qualities only slightly.

> . . .generous Lloyd
> In whom no selfish act ever found,

A man dispensing every good around:
He serves the rich and poor alike, 'tis known,
Neglecting no one's int'rest but his own.

Lloyd personally knew many of the malcontents in the district and knew how to deal with them, whether with reason, cajolery or force. While he privately condemned the inaction of local industrialists, he frequently managed to compensate for their lethargy by his own vigorous actions. He often worked alone or with a few trusted officials and based his decisions on his personal judgement or the information of spies. Such was Lloyd's achievement at the time of the Luddite uprisings that the Rev. Broughton stated: 'We might about say, the town at this moment owes its existence to him.' Just after the powerloom riots of 1818 when a crowd started to become boisterous, Lloyd reported that he 'went amongst them in good time and by persuasion and threats I was able to keep the ground pretty clear'. The next night he dispersed another rowdy gathering.[41]

It is clear that from about 1806 to 1819 the desire for improvements and the will to impose order were not lacking altogether in the Stockport district but were much weaker than they had been in the years immediately before. Probably the major reason for this was the decline in active participation by leading industrialists who may have been disenchanted with certain local government activities, preoccupied with their own business interests, or frightened by the destruction which riotous crowds might wreak. This brought about not so much a collapse in the forces of order as widespread uncertainty regarding their ability to maintain the public peace in any given crisis. Workers who wanted to hold public meetings, even on trade union or radical topics, might have a chance of attracting crowds, stating grievances and finishing their business with little or no interference by the authorities. It was a gamble which was taken on more and more occasions with results which were satisfactory to the meetings' promoters. The ostensible success of workers' movements during these years thus can not be fully understood without taking into account the debilities afflicting the forces of order.

IV

The malaise proved to be transitory, however, and the trembling soon stopped. Lloyd thought he could already detect a stronger pulse on the morn after Peterloo. If that perception may have been somewhat premature, it was clear that local government was becoming more vigorous throughout the 1820s. Changes in the personnel of local government helped to alter the situation. After the death of her husband in 1822, Lady Warren Bulkeley seemed to spend more time at Poynton and take a greater interest in promoting district religious, educational and charitable schemes. At the same time the old ultra-loyalist clique vanished from the scene. The Rev. Prescot died in 1820; John Philips died in 1824; and John Lloyd left Stockport in 1822 to become Prothonotary for the Palatinate Courts in Chester. The ageing Holland Watson did not even make infrequent visits to the district anymore. The remaining Tory-loyalists shifted their primary attention away from shrill advocacy of law and order. Beginning in 1820 they could count on the aid of two companies of soldiers which were permanently stationed in barracks on a hill overlooking the town – but the military was seldom needed. Weakened and squabbling radical groups posed little threat to public calm for most of the decade. At the same time there was a pressing need for a host of reforms which had been long-delayed. With relative prosperity and deflation occurring simultaneously, it seemed as if the cost of government had reached acceptable levels once again. From 1815-19 to 1820-4 the average annual poor levy decreased by 44 per cent. Thus, new departures seemed not only necessary but also affordable. Industrialists consequently came forward once again to serve in various capacities (Thomas Marsland, Richard Sykes, George Talbot Knowles and Robert Hardy became mayors) and otherwise promote reforms, just as their fathers had done in the preceding generation.[42]

Important early changes were inspired by the Select Vestry Acts of 1818 and 1819. The system which emerged in Stockport in 1820 involved three stages of activity each year. First, at Easter a 'general town meeting' would select four overseers of the poor to serve for one year. Second, the overseers would call for a 'General Vestry meeting' of all ley payers which would: (1) review overseers' accounts for the previous year; (2) select salaried assistant overseers; (3) choose salaried deputy constables and supervise their accounts; (4) supervise the accounts of the nine-man fire brigade; and (5) elect a select vestry consisting of 24 substantial householders.[43] Third, during the course of the year the select vestry helped to oversee various aspects of local government, including poor relief, public order and civic improvements. Among other things, the select vestry suspended poor relief payments to six persons who participated in an illumination for Queen Caroline in 1820 and threatened suspension of relief to a hatter unless he could swear that he had not participated in a strike. In 1822 Heaton Norris also adopted a select vestry system featuring salaried assistant overseers and deputy constables.[44] These changes resulted in more effective local government and greater public scrutiny of financial accounts. Moreover, in Stockport and Heaton Norris at least, government was opened up to participation by larger numbers of local inhabitants.

Still, as before, many of the improvements of the early 1820s were the results of private initiative. The Heaton Norris fire brigade was financed from voluntary subscriptions. Sections of Stockport were first lit by gas in 1821 by a private firm which was capitalised at £10,000. Four years later, an act of Parliament gave this same firm permission to increase its capitalisation and extend its gas lines. Effluvium from gas production (and from textile finishing) often found its way into local rivers, streams and ground water and, along with continuing population growth, created problems in the supply of water for domestic uses. These were solved by Peter Marsland, who obtained an act of Parliament in 1825 to establish the Stockport Waterworks and provide Stockport, its suburbs and parts of four other townships with water from a reservoir he had constructed. It was primarily the supply of pure water, aided perhaps by improved scavenging efforts, which saved Stockport from a major outbreak of cholera in 1832. Just 66 cases were reported during that year, and of those, only 29 died.[45]

The Stockport Gas Act and the Stockport Water Act were followed, in 1826, by the Stockport Police Act. A half-century after Stopfordians first sought such a measure, Parliament granted them the right to levy taxes to repair, light and cleanse the streets and to better regulate the 'police'. The latter included a superintendent and three assistants who worked in conjunction with five private watchmen (possibly men occupying the positions established in 1790). They were all under the authority of the Stockport Police Commission, which consisted of local magistrates who met thrice weekly primarily to deal with local crimes of a petty nature. Plans to carry out the street-lighting clauses of the Act were being made before the end of 1826. A related improvement act had been obtained from Parliament in 1824. This provided for construction of Wellington Road and Bridge, a major two-year project which would ultimately divert travellers on the Manchester-London route away from the narrow, steep, congested Hillgate – and away from views of the ragged and impoverished handloom weavers who lived there.[46]

V

The needs, antagonisms and activities of the local middle and upper classes provided the basic framework for many of the significant local debates during the early Industrial Revolution. It was the complaints of these groups, moreover, which typically received the most solicitous attention from Quarter Sessions, the manorial government and parish officials. These groups saw their major concerns (protection of property, reduction of high tax levels, reform of ineffective organs of government) as primarily local matters which could be dealt with most easily through local institutions and networks of patrons, clients and friends. In some cases they had to look to Parliament. Yet Westminster was not normally seen as the relevant locus of power, and consequently appeals to Parliament or calls for its reform were not dominant themes in Stockport district government. Local officials (unlike radicals) probably questioned whether Parliament was really as corrupt as many were claiming. Did it not mirror their own local government in representing wealth, status and special interests? Furthermore, Stockport had *some* parliamentary representation even though it was not to become a borough until 1832. Sir George Warren, the Ardens and the Leghs looked after Stockport district interests in the late eighteenth century, as when Warren promoted a 1774 act against the emigration of skilled artisans in the cotton industry. Local forty shilling freeholders could participate in county elections, of course, and nearly all the large- and medium-sized industrialists would have belonged to that category. In 1806 Davies Davenport (a Whig) was returned for Cheshire county and, as an expert on the cotton industry and an advocate of free trade, appeared to fulfil every expectation of Stockport district freeholders. In 1818 over one hundred of the latter were urging him to run again. He did so and continued to sit for the county until 1830. For Cheshire's other seat, dozens of Stockport freeholders were supporting the candidacy of a Tory, Wilbraham Egerton, in 1812. He gained the seat and retained it until 1831, the year before Stockport obtained the right to elect two of its own representatives to Parliament.[47]

Locally, there was a perception that the gentry, the professional men and the major industrialists could work together to form institutions which were close-knit but never closed. Local government was thus poised ambiguously between an oligarchic elite and a government thrown open to talent and ambition. This gave it a measure of continuity, a collective memory of how institutions and relationships functioned in pre-industrial times, and a pragmatic notion that repression, charity and reform each had a place in good governance. Ambiguity of this sort also provided a sense that participation in government was a possibility for fairly large numbers of people – which should be distinguished from the fact that the average working man would probably hold no office during his lifetime and, if he did, he would probably serve one year in a lowly post (surveyor of the highways, market-looker, beadle) which would allow him little authority or influence. But in William Radcliffe, Stockport had its own version of the legend of Richard Whittington, and there were enough workers or former workers in office at any point to assure that local government could never be seen as monolithic in terms of the social status of its members.

It is perhaps understandable, therefore, that this socially variegated government was able to make effective use of public celebrations to promote a sense of civic solidarity. Rodney's victory over the French fleet in 1782 was celebrated in Stockport with a band and procession, the ringing of bells, bonfires, and ale provided for onlookers in the Market Place. Holland Watson sent an account of the festivities to the *Manchester Mercury*, which read in part:

Such was the Unanimity observed by all Classes of People in this populous and respectable Town, that numerous Meetings were held in different Parts of it, to celebrate the great Event, who [*sic*] vied with each other in shewing their unfeigned Zeal for the Honour of their Country, and Respect for the gallant Admiral, and the Fleet under his Command.

Similar celebrations at the time of George III's recovery in 1789 lasted for four days.[48] Although the festivities staged after Nelson's victory at Trafalgar were rather subdued, the Royal Jubilee of 1809 more than made up for it. At both Poynton and Stockport there were fireworks displays, cannon being discharged, and free mutton, bread and cheese for the assembled crowds. The Warren Bulkeleys gave their 200 Poynton colliers and labourers two quarts of ale each. One account states that at Stockport ' "Long life to the King" was drank [*sic*] with enthusiasm' and that

> the populace deserve praise for the decorum and spirit of loyalty manifested throughout the whole. Many gentlemen feasted their numerous companies of workmen with the substantial dinner of old English times.[49]

There were also special subscriptions for the poor on that occasion, a custom repeated four years later at the equally grand celebrations of the British victories over Napoleon. The coronations of 1821 and 1831 and the opening of Wellington Road in 1826 likewise inspired major celebrations in the Stockport district. Forty thousand people were said to have attended the latter festivities. After the coronation of George IV Stockport's mayor wrote to the Lord of the Manor: 'I can say without fear of contradiction the spirit and celebration of this day has done more toward suppressing the remains of radicalism than anything which occured [*sic*] for many years.'[50] As with radical meetings, one should always question whether the throngs of people that attended these proceedings did so out of strong convictions, moderate levels of commitment, or mere curiosity. Nevertheless, these rituals of social solidarity comprised a permanent feature of Stockport district life in the early Industrial Revolution, one which undoubtedly had a continuing impact on the consciousness of many working people.

The complex nature of this impact is perhaps best suggested by the fact that one of the most prominent local Jacobins, William Clegg, composed adulatory *Jubilean Lines* for the celebrations held in 1809.[51] He was willing, in other words, to help promote at least one of the civic festivities of local government. The latter, in any event, provided a rather poor target for the kind of sustained critiques needed by resident radicals to rally mass support. At the same time, local government furnished few significant opportunities for radicals to gain office and make fundamental changes. Clegg and other radicals did not force the issue and instead adopted a rather broad, national perspective. Petitioning Parliament, memorialising the King or Prince Regent, corresponding with national radical spokesmen, receiving emissaries from afar or sending out their own delegates probably gave them a feeling of accomplishment and importance which could not have been obtained so easily in the restricted local political arena. The final pattern is clear. Though open to criticism on many counts and obviously jerry-built, local government ultimately proved itself capable of withstanding the storms and stresses of early industrialisation.[52] The local organisations of radicals and workers, by contrast, encountered numerous (and at times, insurmountable) difficulties in defining precise goals, recruiting members, securing adequate funds and finding capable and dedicated leaders.

4   COTTON WORKERS

> . . .Next morning the weavers and cotton-mill folk held a
> meeting, and they, being skilled in the ways of committees and
> associating together, had certain resolutions prepared, by
> which a select few was appointed to take an enrolment of all
> willing in the parish to serve as volunteers in defence of their
> King and country, and to concert with certain gentlemen
> named therein, about the formation of a corps, of which, it was
> an understood thing, the said gentlemen were to be the
> officers. – John Galt, *Annals of the Parish* (for 1803)

The cotton industry furnishes a natural starting point for an
investigation of the growth of early workers' organisations in the
Stockport district. At any given time from the late 1780s to the
1820s, approximately 60-75 per cent of the population of the
Stockport district was supported by wages earned in this industry
– either as workers or their dependants. Slightly less than half of
the workers were involved in spinning and processes preparatory
to spinning, while a roughly comparable fraction was involved in
weaving, dressing and associated tasks. The finishing branches
(calico printing, bleaching and dyeing) employed under ten per
cent of the total, and miscellaneous specialties in the cotton industry
(engineers, machine repairmen, and so forth) employed less than
one per cent.[1] This chapter will focus on combinations and related
developments in many of these occupations, while Chapter 5 will
cover workers outside the cotton industry and Chapter 7 will deal
with the handloom weavers.

I

Scholars have lavished considerable attention on Hargreaves'
invention of the spinning jenny, Arkwright's invention of the water
frame and other technical breakthroughs in the spinning of cotton.
Already during the 1770s many of these new types of machines
began appearing in the Stockport district. Larger jennies were

gradually being introduced, for example, and by the end of the decade there were also cases of unauthorised use of Arkwright's patented carding and spinning processes.[2] Each of those innovations fostered grievances. The first small jennies had been intended for domestic use and meant that a person who formerly worked one spinning wheel could thenceforth operate a jenny and thereby increase his or her output by many times. But as the jennies grew larger – examples of over 100 spindles were noted by 1780 – they became too large for operation in the home and too expensive to be purchased by the average domestic worker. The larger jennies were, in fact, purchased by petty capitalists and installed in workshop 'factories'.[3] Thus, in this instance, the decline of a domestic industry was caused not by the introduction of a power machine but by the increase in size of the hand machine itself. Arkwright's power spinning machines did not compete with any hand spinning process, since no one had been able to perfect hand machines which made adequate cotton twist for use as warps. His carding process did, however, replace hand carding, and it seems to have been primarily for this reason (and the associated dread of working in large mills) that his factory at Chorley, Lancashire, was regarded with such hostility.

It is consequently not surprising that when the cotton industry became unusually depressed during 1779 Arkwright's Chorley factory and the large jennies of over 24 spindles were singled out for attack in Lancashire. Rioting occurred from 27 September to about mid-October. Crowds were most active at Bolton, Bury, Preston, Chorley and Blackburn – precisely the areas to the north and west of Manchester which had given birth to the new inventions and in which, presumably, their impact had been the greatest.[4] On 5 October a crowd near Bolton stated that 'their professed design was to take Bolton, Manchester, and Stockport in [*sic*] their way to Crumford [that is, Cromford, Derbyshire], and to destroy all the engines, not only in these places, but throughout all England'. Frightened authorities in various towns believed that crowds could easily keep their word and sweep right through Manchester and Stockport to Derbyshire.[5] Stockport manufacturers and tradesmen lived in daily fear of the approach of these northern crowds.

As a result, Stockport's rector-magistrate, the Rev. John Watson, requested troops from both Derby and Liverpool. One hundred militiamen arrived from Liverpool on 8 October, but in the end were not needed because Stockport 'gentlemen' were '*using every*

endeavour to defend themselves in a very spirited manner . . .',
according to one military commander.[6] Another source states that
'the Castle cotton works once more became a place of arms, and
the embrasures filled with Sir George Warren's cannon, which
commanded Manchester Hill, Stockport Bridge, and the ford of
the Mersey'.[7]

It is impossible to determine whether Stockport district workers
were overawed by the military and the voluntary law-and-order
forces or whether they simply felt less threatened by the new
machinery than did workers in some northerly areas. Whatever
the reasons, Stockport district workers played no prominent role
in the public disorders of 1779.[8] The movement as a whole was
channelled, during the first part of the ensuing year, into a
parliamentary petition to restrict the size of the new machines by
means of a tax. Here, too, it is unclear if Stockport district workers
participated. When the secretary to the Manchester Committee of
Trade expressed fears of renewed disturbances in the wake of the
1780 petitioning effort, he mentioned as potential trouble spots
only the areas in which riots had actually taken place in 1779.[9]

Grievances among Stockport jenny spinners appear to have been
directed instead towards trade union activities. By 1785 there was
a Cotton Spinners Friendly Society which had a committee and a
strike fund. It publicly called for an end to the strike then underway,
although no one was to return to work 'under the usual Prices'. It
seems likely that this was a jenny spinners' union, one of a number
which sprang up in Stockport in the late eighteenth and early
nineteenth centuries. Most did not last long, and some were brought
to an end by formal prosecutions. They were probably all based in
the new jenny spinning 'factories', which contained 20 or 30 men
working on hand-powered machines.[10] These were not true factories,
of course, but something more akin to artisanal workshops, even
with respect to their erratic patterns of work. As a former Stockport
jenny spinner stated in the 1830s, 'I have known the time with the
jenny-spinners in Stockport when it was the general practice to
begin at three or four o'clock in the morning, and they worked at
random, without any regularity'.[11]

It is important to keep in mind the autonomous development of
unions among the jenny spinners on the one hand and among mule
spinners on the other. In 1792 a friendly society for the latter was
established. There can be little doubt that like the 1785 jenny
spinners' society, this institution had trade union functions. The

mule spinners held large meetings in 1792 to gain support for their club and for their main objective, the prevention of wage reductions. The club also gave money to those who were fired by employers for objecting to reductions. Similar combinations were simult-aneously being established in other towns of the Manchester district. Oldham mule spinners had a club in 1792, and those at Manchester probably combined at about the same time.[12] Factory owners carefully observed the progress of these organisations and interceded in various ways. Many Stockport masters, for example, joined in sponsoring a massive new mule spinners' friendly society in 1795, soon after such societies became legal under Rose's Act. Masters saw to it that the society was registered at Quarter Sessions and that its printed rules contained prohibitions against assaults on factory managers, destruction of property and participation in riots.[13] This attempt to control workers' organisations by an informal association of masters probably helped Stockport to avoid the bitter labour struggles which occurred among Manchester mule spinners in 1795 and 1798. The formal registration of a Stockport jenny spinners' friendly society in 1797 perhaps indicates that a parallel effort to control workers' organisations was also underway in that trade.[14]

This form of control did not suffice to offset the nearby example of factious Manchester mule spinners, who were striking again in the winter of 1801-2. The issues involved were not clear, but Stockport mule spinners followed their lead in 1802, as did those at Bolton in 1803. The masters became especially alarmed at this phenomenon because workers used the technique of selective strikes in which some spinners would remain at work in order to support those who had turned out. Stockport masters responded with the technique of blacklisting to prevent striking workers from getting work at other factories, and with the establishment of a formal masters' association in 1802. Reputedly the first such association to appear in the cotton districts, it included only the largest of Stockport's master spinners. All of this was enough, however, to cause the collapse of the Stockport mule spinners' combination.[15]

It is clear that during those years, mule spinners focused not on establishing links with jenny spinners but on intra-trade grievances and, increasingly, on co-operation with mule spinners' unions in other towns. The strike of 1810 witnessed a revival of the same pattern. The primary goal of the strike was to increase wages in all localities to the slightly higher levels which prevailed in Manchester.

Regional co-ordination was in evidence. A central committee, or 'congress', consisting of 40 or 50 delegates from surrounding cotton towns (including Stockport and Hyde), directed the strike from Manchester. Strikes at Preston and Stalybridge during the summer were supported by contributions from non-striking towns. Stockport, for example, donated £10 to Preston strikers early in June (out of the total of £122 that Preston received at that point). It was an impressive show of strength, but the strikers had to return to work at the end of the summer without the wage increase they had demanded.[16]

Despite the outcome of the 1810 strike, the solidarity exhibited by the mule spinners probably helped them to secure certain benefits in succeeding years. As the cotton industry moved into another slump, masters in many areas neither reduced wages nor laid off men, as was customary, but decided simply to reduce the number of days worked each week by all employees. That is what the workers preferred. This scheme was in effect in various areas from 1811 to 1813 and was known to have been in operation in the Stockport district in 1812.[17] Many mule spinners apparently thought that the increased leisure time was more important than the reduced weekly income caused by short time. This attitude soon provided a major impetus to the short time movement. At Manchester a Short Time Committee was set up in 1814, immediately after factories began returning to longer hours. Sir Robert Peel introduced a Factory Bill incorporating short time in 1815, and a Select Committee met on the subject in 1816.[18]

The growing popularity of short time can also be detected among the jenny spinners. Instead of receiving short time in 1811, like the mule spinners, they suffered a wage reduction which triggered work stoppages and prosecutions. The reduced wage levels nevertheless remained in effect until 1814, when masters contemplated further reductions. The strikes which occurred on that occasion helped to convince masters to try the alternative favoured by the mule spinners, that is, reducing the number of hours worked per week. Soon after 1814 jenny spinners' hours returned to normal, and wages remained steady for a few years despite the onset of another slump in 1816. In the following year masters reverted to their old custom and reduced piece rates by one-third. No disturbances occurred initially perhaps because the reductions were thought to be temporary. By early 1818, however, jenny spinners were pressing for a return to the old, pre-1817 wage levels even if it meant that hours had to be reduced again. When the masters refused, 800 or more jenny spinners struck in May. After six weeks masters agreed to increase wages by half of the amount of the previous reduction.[19]

Thereafter, a degree of industrial harmony seemed to prevail in the jenny spinning trade. In times of distress, wages were reduced on occasion, but more typically, the hours of work were reduced. As a result, Thomas Worsley, one of the jenny spinners' spokesmen, could state in 1824 that 'there is more unity among them and the masters than among the fine spinners'. The jenny spinners officially formed a union at the end of 1824 soon after the repeal of the Combination Laws and at about the same time as wages were reduced by one-eighth. When the union asked for a return to the old wage rates at the beginning of 1825, the leading masters granted it. But the numbers of jenny spinners were dwindling. Worsley said that there were 500 in Stockport in 1825, of whom 200 or 300 belonged to the union. By the early 1830s only about 120 were left.[20]

The decline in jenny spinning in the dozen years after 1818 corresponded with the beginning of a new stage in the development of combinations among mule spinners and certain other factory occupations. There were many reasons for this heightened activity. Economic prosperity led to increases in the total number of factory workers and (as noted in Chapter 2) facilitated the multiplication of medium- and large-sized firms. With less of the workforce scattered in small jenny factories, the process of unionising was probably easier than before. Also, the precarious competitive position of many of the remaining small firms must have made it appear much less possible (and desirable) for an enterprising workman to establish a small spinning or carding business of his own. Such workers may have chosen instead to improve their positions in other ways, ways which involved concerted labour union activities. Mule and throstle spinners increased their numbers disproportionately since they did a growing share of the work formerly performed by jenny spinners. In a similar fashion, cotton dressing and powerloom weaving in factories grew with unusual rapidity while handloom weaving declined. This, too, tended to aid factory combinations. Whereas before, combinations and other organised activities were divided between domestic and factory workers, the trend by the 1820s was toward unified spinning, dressing or weaving combinations within the factories.

Mule and throstle spinners numbered in the thousands at the time of the last jenny spinners' strike in 1818. Like the jenny spinners, their primary objective was to obtain increased wages by returning to the higher wage levels which had prevailed before the 1816-17 slump. A few of the spinners supported additional demands for an end to payment in truck.[21] A larger number became involved in the agitation to support Sir Robert Peel's 1818 Factory Bill, which would have mandated certain limits and prohibitions on the labour of young persons. The Stockport short time movement reflects the fact that relatively high factory wages allowed for the possibility of many families to do without the incomes of their children under the age of nine or ten. It also highlights emerging popular views about childhood as a separate, special stage in human life and widespread concern about the health and education of children. Certain local professional people encouraged the Stockport Short Time Committee (STC). Thirteen Stockport clerygymen and eight medical men added their signatures to a short time petition which had been signed by operatives from 'all the cotton spinning factories of Stockport'. The presentation of this petition in April 1818 provoked Sir James Graham to utter one of the most vicious and ill-considered outbursts to be found in all the factory debates. Among other things, he called the Stockport petitioners 'a set of idle, discontented, discarded, and good-for-nothing workmen . . .' This rodomontade could hardly apply to the professional men who signed the petition, much less to the seven sympathetic factory masters who also affixed their names. These seven were probably among the minority of local masters who were soon voluntarily abiding by the hours specified in the proposed Bill. Most of the Stockport district masters, however, petitioned against short time and, by working longer hours than indicated in the Bill, made it difficult for short time factories to compete. Meetings on the subject of short time continued for the remainder of the year, but when the Factory Act of 1819 was passed, the movement quickly faded from view.[22]

Although that campaign seems to have gained more support from operative spinners in 1818 than did the anti-truck movement, it was hardly the most prominent agitation of the day. That distinction belonged to the 1818 effort to raise wages, which was led by William Temple, a spinner in William Smith's Heaton Norris factory. Temple led a group which sought to have Smith bring his wage rates up to those prevailing in the area. When Smith refused,

21 spinners quit their jobs. Smith promptly put their names on a blacklist which he sent around to other employers. Temple responded with no fewer than eight legal actions against Smith, but none was pursued. To the Stockport disturbances were added strikes in Manchester during June and in Wigan and Burnley during July. The violent Manchester strike lasted nearly three months and was said to have idled 20,000 spinners at its peak. The Mancunians were striking both for higher wages and shorter hours, the latter demand probably having been stimulated by the example of the reduced work-week in the early 1810s.[23]

In July two other groups of Stockport factory workers – cotton dressers and powerloom weavers – also went on strike. Dressers comprised about ten per cent of the workforce of a typical powerloom factory and were usually adult males who earned wages comparable to those of fine spinners. Powerloom weavers were often adolescent males and females ranging in age from about 15 to 20.[24] They earned about half as much as the dressers did. Earlier, in the winter of 1816-17, weavers had been forced to accept wage deductions for the provision of artificial light. When threatened with further deductions in the ensuing winter, the powerloom weavers of one factory turned out in what was apparently the first powerloom weavers' strike in England. The master brought 23 of them (including twelve females) before a Heaton Norris magistrate, John Philips, who ordered them out into the yard to determine what they would do. The weavers decided not to work if the further deduction was enforced, whereupon Philips sentenced them all to a month's imprisonment.[25]

Added to powerloom weavers' grievances over deductions and prosecutions was the common complaint that wages had not risen with the return of prosperity. At the beginning of July 1818 many Stockport weavers gave notice of their intention to leave work unless they received a wage increase of one-third. The masters refused. Cotton dressers joined the strike, which proceeded without incident until one master, Thomas Garside, brought in some female 'blacklegs' (as strike breakers were sometimes called by contemporaries) from Burton-on-Trent. Garside's striking workers – John Lloyd referred to them as 'boys' – gathered with hundreds of others outside the factory on 14 July. They threatened violence, though none actually occurred at that point. The next evening a crowd again assembled and began an assault on the factory. Robert Harrison, a Cheadle magistrate, read the Riot Act and led a contingent of constables, special constables and Yeomanry Cavalry against the crowd but with inadequate co-ordination and little success. Harrison and some others were wounded in the affray, and the crowd dispersed, more by choice than on account of fear of the authorities, at about midnight. The forces of order were better prepared the following night when a crowd again assembled and began another attack on Garside's mill. The authorities dispersed the crowd (although not without more injuries, including Lloyd's son) and took 20 prisoners. Minor disturbances occurred again on the evenings of 18 and 19 July.[26]

During the following week Garside's employees were requesting to be taken on again. He granted their requests on 25 July but without the sought-after wage increase. Other strikers (including those from the Sykeses', Howard's and Lane's) stayed out while the authorities braced for renewed disorders. One point of contention was the fact that on the last night of major rioting (16 July) the Yeomanry had fired shots into the house of a well-known Stockport radical. When the man who admitted firing the shots was acquitted of any wrongdoing on 4 August, a small riot occurred. On 8 August Lloyd reported that more of the powerloom weavers were going back to work without an advance because they could no longer support themselves. They had had a committee of four and a meagre strike fund, but Lloyd had surprised the committee in a public house on the previous day. When Petty Sessions committed the group to jail for three months on 10 August, other powerloom weavers turned out in protest. There were further disturbances during the last half of August when two of the Garside rioters were being tried at the Summer Assizes. Both were found guilty and received jail sentences of one and three years respectively. By that time, however, most of the impetus had gone from the powerloom strike. Nothing is heard of it after Lane's weavers returned to work on 22 August. It is known that Lane's dressers remained on strike after that date, presumably indicating that they had a separate union and strike fund.[27]

William Temple meanwhile continued his efforts to rouse support for the spinners. Contributions during July totalling £42 came from 464 individuals in 39 factories. Some of the money was sent to striking Wigan spinners, however, and local disbursements during July show that those stopping work in Stockport were apparently few in number. One disbursement went to the 21 on Smith's blacklist. Other funds went to 73 men and women. Although highly visible, this was not a mass industrial action like that occurring in Manchester and other urban centres, perhaps because wages at Stockport were not generally low for spinners and repression was always imminent. The spinners' accounts and papers were in fact seized by John Lloyd at the end of July. Smith brought an action against 15 of the ringleaders at the Lancashire Summer Assizes. Over at the Cheshire Summer Assizes, Lloyd secured indictments against five spinners for soliciting illegal contributions in Stockport. Temple was the only man charged in both courts. When the trials came up in the spring of 1819, the 15 Lancashire defendants pleaded guilty and were subsequently released. The five Cheshire defendants were found guilty, and all were imprisoned. Temple received a sentence of twelve months.[28]

The general pattern established in 1818 continued through the 1820s. Factory spinners focused primarily on wages – the maintenance or increase of prevailing wage levels, the prevention of decreases and the achievement of wage uniformity. The latter was invariably interpreted to mean that lower wage levels should be raised to the rates offered by the major firms. The strengthening of combinations was seen as the best means to achieve these goals. At the same time, masters and their allies among the local authorities retained their belief that every possible measure should be taken to prevent employees from dictating wage rates to employers. A dispute in 1822, another year of relative prosperity in the cotton industry, was perhaps typical. In July of that year a strike occurred against Marshall's of Portwood to bring wages up to the levels paid by the larger firms. This industrial action proved to be quite orderly. Eighteen employees gave notice of their intention to quit and were subsequently led out by William Salt. After a brief stoppage, Marshall met with Salt, who was then arrested along with six others. Each of the seven was sentenced by Petty Sessions to two months in jail.[29]

By the autumn of 1823 Stockport masters granted mule spinners the *de facto* right to meet as a trade union as long as wages were not discussed. The spinners organised along the lines of the 1792 combination (which they probably recognised as their forebear) and thus had many friendly society functions. Their ostensible objective at that time was the repeal of the Combination Laws. William Temple represented them on the repeal committee, the 'Committee of Artizans', which also included Thomas Worsley from the jenny spinners as its president. Both men were in contact with Francis Place in London, and both testified before Parliament during 1824. The Committee of Artizans continued to meet until 1826 in part to help conciliate the disputes which followed the repeal of the Combination Laws. Many factory workers viewed repeal as merely a means to an end – the latter being higher wages. Cotton spinners or dressers were striking for wage increases in at least ten Stockport, Heaton Norris, Portwood and Hyde factories during the winter of 1824-5. Masters at those factories blacklisted the strikers and even printed their names in broadside form for easier dissemination. Although the workers at Hyde stayed out six months, they failed in their objectives. The same was probably true of the Stockport strikers.[30] In the midst of all this activity, the short time agitation surrounding the passage of the 1825 Factory Act made little headway in the Stockport district. Another Stockport STC was established, but it did not even manage to prepare a petition for parliamentary consideration.[31]

The economic cycles of the late 1820s elicited rather familiar responses from the spinners. In the slump of 1826 many Hyde masters reduced hours and thereby avoided major disorders. That policy was not uniformly followed in Stockport. At one factory which reduced wages instead of hours, workers walked out and were consequently prosecuted for leaving their jobs without giving proper notice. As the economic situation improved in the two years after 1826 spinners attempted to keep hours somewhat reduced while enforcing uniform wages. Towards the end of 1828 there was a strike against one Portwood mill whose wages were below the standard rate. A lengthy and bitter strike occurred in 1829 at Stockport (but not Hyde) after masters announced that they were reducing wages by ten per cent.[32]

II

From the 1780s to the 1820s combinations in the Stockport district cotton industry made considerable headway but in no sense produced a united, militant proletariat of the kind Marx and Engels predicted would emerge. Certain reasons for this have already been adduced. Occupational distinctions within factories could not easily be overcome, and separate unions merely reflected those divisions. A strong Stockport masters' association opposed activities of combinations with regard to wage demands and strikes, and this naturally tended to limit the combinations' effectiveness. Workers had trouble forming all-encompassing unions, even within the confines of the Stockport district. By the mid-1820s combinations of Stockport jenny and mule spinners still contained only about half of the workers in their respective trades.[33] Hyde unions remained distinct from those at Stockport, while many isolated factories in the out-townships do not seem to have had combinations at all.

There were further obstacles. High turnover rates hindered the formation of strong unions. An oft-cited statistic indicates that turnover rates may have approached 100 per cent per year. George Smith of Stockport, for example, worked for five factories in about five years in the 1790s. When Jeremiah Turner testified before Parliament in 1819, he recalled only five of the (apparently numerous) factories he had worked in since 1790. Abraham Docker started working in about 1800 and was in his seventh factory by 1823. If some contributed to high turnover rates by going from factory to factory, others contributed by quitting factory work altogether, especially when they were between the ages of 20 and 30. Such people were apparently undeterred by the fact that wage levels in many non-factory jobs were lower than those in the factories. As one Stopfordian stated: 'I never knew any person in a cotton mill who would not get out of it if he could get into a situation of even less nominal value considerably.'[34]

Most of the turnover probably occurred among female workers who comprised around half of the factory workforce during the early Industrial Revolution. It has been suggested that single females in their teens and twenties regarded factory labour as merely a stage between childhood and marriage and that married women regarded intermittent factory work as a possible source of family income when financial exigencies required it or when child-rearing and household responsibilities allowed it. In either case, the common view among females that factory work was temporary would undoubtedly have diminished their interest in combinations. Moreover, because women worked in factory jobs requiring low skill levels, they received less pay than most men. Women were thus in a weak bargaining position because they could easily be replaced, and they had much less surplus income to allocate to labour organisations. Men kept women out of their combinations, perhaps due to fears that admission of lower-paid women would tend to drive men's wages down. It also provided a means of expressing male dominance in the workplace. The episodes of wife-selling which the *Stockport Advertiser* gleefully reported in the 1820s and 1830s indicate that the need for such demonstrations of masculine authority among workers was strong and enduring.[35] In any event, permanent combinations among women did not emerge in the Stockport district, leaving half of the factory workforce uncombined.

Another 15 per cent or so consisted of male children and males in their early adolescence who were not allowed into men's combinations and were unlikely to combine themselves. Men's unions nevertheless increasingly publicised the problems associated with child labour in the factories after 1815, partly out of a genuine and growing concern about the quality of children's lives. As already noted, it began to seem unnecessary, and even cruel, to have children working long hours in the factories with the results manifesting themselves in stunted growth, disease, limited educational opportunities, and so forth. These sentiments can be found in the parliamentary testimony of a sympathetic Stockport worker, who went on to state that 'it is general in Stockport to see fathers carry their children to mills in the morning on their backs', the young ones being unable or unwilling to walk to work so early in the day.[36] This new emphasis on children also emerged because it seemed to provide a potentially effective technique by which to win shorter hours and better working conditions for adults. Why, then, did it not serve to energise the men's unions and galvanise public opinion into mass support for their cause between 1815 and 1830? There is no simple answer. The workers themselves often seemed to view the 'factory question' as an issue of less importance than wages. That master spinners and others in the higher ranks of society were adopting numerous measures to change undesirable conditions, especially for factory children, must also have had a considerable impact in blunting the appeal of the early factory movement.

Concern about parish apprentices (who were often orphans) had a long tradition in the Stockport district. The London Foundling Hospital apprenticed girls to a Stockport silk mill as early as 1769 and later apprenticed many children to Samuel Oldknow. Hospital records show that it paid careful attention to its former wards. Jeremiah Bury's firm accepted hundreds of apprentices from London, Bristol and Bath and took exemplary care of them.[37] It is thus not surprising that the 1802 Factory Act was not a dead letter in the Stockport district, as it was in many other areas. Inspectors (mostly magistrates and Anglican clergymen) were duly appointed after the Act went into effect. At the end of 1803 cotton factory owners were publicly warned to register their premises if they had not already done so. Quarter Sessions records show that by 1810, specific lists of factories were being assigned to designated pairs of inspectors.[38]

Many industrialists were developing a paternalistic outlook not only towards their parish apprentices but also towards their regular wage labourers. Just as they were expected to fill public offices and volunteer for various peace-keeping forces, factory masters were also expected to take an interest in the day-to-day orderliness (punctuality, cleanliness, morality) of their workers. The *Annual Reports* of the Stockport Sunday School show this quite clearly. The 1809 *Report* linked combinations (like that which promoted the weavers' strike in the preceding year) to *masters'* conduct, especially in cases in which employees were 'treated with indifference or comtempt'. It noted that the more enlightened employers had, among other things, assisted their younger workers in obtaining Bibles and decent clothes. In 1814 masters were urged not to employ young persons unless they attended Sunday schools. In the midst of the tumults of the Peterloo era, masters were again chastised for being 'careless of the moral conduct of their work-people . . .'[39]

The *Annual Reports* of the Stockport Auxiliary Bible Society echoed those sentiments. The *Report* for 1820 stated that some masters had recently established Bible societies in their factories. Thomas Ferneley, Sr, had one in his Portwood factory, as did his son in his mill. The Bible society at the Heaton Mersey works already contained 300 members. The parent Stockport Bible Society expected other masters to follow suit.

> Their respectability as men, and the extensive influence they command over the working population of the town, justify such an expectation: and if these Associations had no higher aim than to exert a commanding influence over the morals of the people, where is the Master who would not sanction them?

Supervision of employees was probably easiest in situations in which factory masters owned some or all of the houses occupied by their workers. There were masters, however, who owned none of their workers' cottages but who nevertheless took seriously their paternalistic responsibilities. Thomas Ferneley, Jr, for example, not only helped his workers to obtain Bibles but also tried to enforce church attendance and strict morality. Thomas Robinson said of his employees that 'if I hear of any very immoral or improper conduct I take the first opportunity to dismiss them'. Francis Smith Clayton claimed that he did not try to control his employees' personal conduct but then confessed: 'I sometimes admonish them, when I hear of their behaving ill when off work.' A recent study of Marple concludes that paternalistic control there was strong and pervasive: 'No evidence has been found of workers' children having to bow or curtsy to the owners as happened at Compstall Mill, but when job and perhaps house could depend on the whim of the employer it was wise to conform.'[40]

Attempts to control the factory workforce coincided with efforts to ameliorate factory conditions. There is some evidence that the use of child and adolescent labour in the factories was decreasing during the early decades of the nineteenth century. In 1833 data from 36 factories, workers who were 18 years old or less comprised just 38 per cent of the workforce, which appears to have been a decline from earlier figures.[41] At the same time conditions for younger workers seem to have been improving. Joseph Mayer could favourably contrast the situation of factory children in 1816 with what it had been in the 1780s: '. . . their appearance is better now, their clothing is far better, their health is far better; and I am sure their morals are much better.' Corporal punishment of factory children was on the decline. According to Thomas Worsley, the overlookers and others who resorted to it were often fined or dismissed, while George Smith stated that 'punishment in the mills [is] less than among the same number of individuals engaged in other occupations'. By 1833 three-quarters of Stockport district factories forbade corporal punishment.[42]

There may have been a gradual, albeit modest, improvement in the health and well-being of factory workers in general beginning around the 1820s. There was a tremendous amount to be accomplished, of course. Long-term inhalation of cotton particles had to be dealt with. Horrible factory accidents were likewise all too common. The Stockport Dispensary treated 151 cases involving factory accidents in 1826-7, but the annual average for 1837-9, when the factory workforce was much larger, was only 113. This improvement was due in part to the enclosure of moving machinery, which was becoming increasingly common. It was done not only to avoid accidents but also, consciously, to reduce the amount of cotton dust in the air.[43] Although regularly-scheduled night shifts were unusual, factories were often in operation before sunrise or after sunset. That necessitated the use of hundreds of candles which polluted the factory air. Gas lighting constituted an improvement. During the 1820s and 1830s a large number of mills switched to the new type of lighting, and some even constructed their own gas works. It is possible, therefore, to give some credence to the results of a survey of 49 Stockport district firms taken in 1833. Only one proprietor responded unequivocally in the negative when asked if the health of the workers had improved during the preceding decade.[44]

In all such matters wide variations naturally existed. Little or no progress was made in certain factories or in improving specific conditions throughout the district. No efforts were made, for example, to diminish the incessant noise of the factories. Around 1818 Stopfordians began to voice criticisms about another matter, the pall of smoke which steam-powered factories created. But apparently only one company, that of Thomas Ashton in Hyde, made any advances in smoke abatement in the 1820s. By the mid-1830s an American visitor to Stockport remarked on a new, although not entirely satisfactory, 'solution' to the smoke problem.

As soon as one is outside of Manchester, where he can look off at a distance [to the south], his first impression is, that the entire environs and neighbouring villages are filled with *monumental towers*, running up towards the clouds from one to three hundred feet; but, as a black column of smoke is rolling from the top of them, he soon perceives they are connected with the manufactories.[45]

It should not be forgotten that for many decades after 1820, hideous accidents, physical deformities and cases of 'brown lung' disease continued to occur. Furthermore, many factory masters petitioned against the Factory Acts of 1802,[46] 1819 and 1833 in part because they disliked parliamentary intrusions into their relationships with employees. The opposition of the masters meant that certain provisions of the first two Factory Acts were not obeyed. During the 1820s witnesses who testified against transgressing masters were sometimes fired and then blacklisted. For their part, the workers seemed powerless to remedy the situation. They launched a new enforcement campaign in 1828 but achieved little. Thomas Ashton of Hyde claimed in 1832 that his firm (which was one of the most enlightened ones) and every mill at Stockport had contravened the Factory Acts at some point.[47]

None of this sufficed to forge a unified factory 'proletariat', however. The major concern of factory combinations was wage rates – but the wages of spinners, at least, appeared to be keeping abreast of prices. G.D.H. Cole published a series which showed that real wages of Manchester mule spinners actually rose from 1800 to 1830.[48] At the same time, some factory masters were taking well-publicised steps to improve conditions in their factories and reform the behaviour of their employees in order to make them more responsible, and perhaps even more respectable, individuals. In such a situation, it is to the credit of union organisers that they made even limited progress in a handful of factory occupations.

III

Trade unionism in calico printing and other cotton finishing trades grew up quite independently from combinations in spinning and related factory occupations. The finishing branches were distinctive in part because of the high levels of skill required and the resulting preponderance of adult and adolescent males in those trades. There were relatively few finishing tasks to be performed by women and children. Henry Marsland, who ran bleaching operations in Stockport's Park Mills in the 1820s and 1830s, later emphasised the welcome consequences of these distinctions. In bleaching, he stated, 'we get a superior class of hands . . .' who 'are a more moral class than the factory people are'.[49]

Combinations among nearly all of the finishing trades appeared at Manchester during the last quarter of the eighteenth century. Bleachers were apparently striking as early as 1777, while dyers and calenderers formed combinations in 1784.[50] In the Stockport district only the calico printers are known to have combined, although this combination may well have held sway over the lesser finishing branches. Printers of the district soon became associated with the strong regional Calico Printers' Union (CPU) whose history reflects much about Stockport district issues and trends. The CPU had two antecedents. One was the extensive tramping system which developed in calico printing during the 1770s. The focal point of the system was the individual print field, at which tramps would collect small sums of money as they travelled about in search of work. As in hatting, tailoring and certain other skilled trades, the tramping system had the ancillary effect of opening up channels of communication in the trade and providing a basis for concerted action at the regional and national levels.[51]

The other antecedent of the CPU was the venerable printers' association in the Metropolis, the birthplace of calico printing in England. Highly paid operatives from London were brought to Lancashire by Livesey, Hargreaves and Co. in about 1783 to work in their Mosney printworks near Preston. When Livesey discovered that these 'gentlemen journeymen' did inferior work while demanding their accustomed high wage rates, he set about introducing labour-saving print machinery and hiring cheap apprentice labour. In calico printing this marked the beginning of a classic pattern in which advancing mechanisation allowed masters to employ workers at progressively lower levels of skill and pay. Such tactics were to become points of friction in the trade for the ensuing three decades. In the short term, during the winter of 1785-6, Livesey's actions resulted in the Mosney turnout, the first calico printers' strike in the North. It revealed that links existed among the various printworks of the region. Money from printers in other establishments, apparently including that at Reddish in the Stockport district, helped to finance the strike. An anonymous threatening letter of January 1786 warned: 'Remember we are a great number sworn . . .'[52] When contributions from other works began to dry up after three months, the strike ended and the Mosney journeymen returned to work on Livesey's terms.

The seeds of combination were well-sown, however. Early in 1788 James Heald, one of the most prominent of Stockport's master printers, spoke of 'Ill usage from the Hands lately in his employ'. Four of his men had claimed that he was exceeding the customary maximum ratio of two apprentices to one journeyman, which would, of course, have the effect of inflating the labour force with low-paid novices and thereby tend to depress the wages of journeymen. The four men soon fled the area. Heald denied the allegation and vowed to prosecute any other master who hired the four trouble-makers since they were legally indentured to him.[53] A few months later, Livesey and Co. went bankrupt, an event which helped to spread and intensify the spirit of combination since other printworks absorbed all of Livesey's refractory workmen. Soon, workers at some of those firms had established 'sick funds', which were often really covert strike funds.

During the course of 1789, journeymen calico printers began holding meetings to agitate for three interrelated objectives: (1) more restrictive apprenticeship regulations, including a five guinea entrance fee to be paid to the local union either by the apprentice or the master; (2) an end to the introduction of machinery; and (3) uniform wages and hours throughout the trade. The main scene of activity in the Stockport district continued to be Heald's of Portwood. By September 1789 a group of his workers was striking and physically assaulting at least one of the non-strikers. A similar assault occurred in November.[54] The strike became widespread in Lancashire and Cheshire during 1790 and was soon exacerbated when various 'nobstick' masters hired strike breakers. Roe and Kershaw, whose works were on the Goyt river at Chadkirk, were guilty of this practice and received an anonymous threatening letter in the early summer of 1790.

NOBSTICK KERSHO

YOU damd Nobstick if you dont stop your copperplate machins and Nobstick shop and take all your old opprest gornemen and prentices and stop your low [wages?] We are sworn not to stop till we have destroyed both you and them so consider this in three Days from this 27th June.[55]

Some of the masters met in July at Manchester to condemn the combination and to state that the journeymen had high wages and full employment, with no attempt being made to reduce either. They gave the workers until 27 July to return to work, after which they said they would feel free to take on new hands and to commence prosecutions against the strikers. The final terms on which the strike was settled were said to have been unfavourable to the journeymen, a situation which, if true, was probably mitigated by the boom then occurring in the cotton industry.[56] Little is heard of the calico printers' combination during the subsequent dozen years of high wages, but there are indications of continuing union growth and activity. A Manchester calico printer stated in 1804 that the CPU had had a strike fund down to about 1800. Also in 1804 an anonymous writer condemned the journeymen calico printers for 'having been for a long time in a state of mutiny and insubordination'.[57]

The CPU had come into clear focus again during the preceding year when a long series of parliamentary petitioning efforts began.

An 1803 legal case against four journeymen calico printers of Dumbarton revealed that links had been forged among calico printers in England, Scotland and Ireland, links involving apprentices as well as journeymen. This loose association was probably behind the petition presented to Parliament on 21 February 1803 asking not for regulation of wages and hours but for Parliament

> to regulate the number of apprentices in their business, in the same manner as other trades, to such a number as will enable them, after they have served their apprenticeship to procure employ, and to make their indentures legal and binding to both parties.[58]

The masters, for their part, called a meeting for 1 March to decide how best to oppose the journeymen's petition. The result of that meeting was the formation of a masters' association which accumulated data on wages and hours at 14 major printworks. It showed that journeymen worked an average of 10.25 hours daily during the summer and from seven to eight hours daily during the winter. Annual wages ranged from about £52 to £103. The average weekly wage for the previous three years was said to have been £1 8s 3½d. This picture of moderate hours and high wages which was presented by the masters is impossible to verify and had nothing to do with the journeymen's explicit demands. In any event, the masters' propaganda efforts proved to be unnecessary. After collecting £500 in subscription money to pay for the petitioning campaign, the journeymen had to stand by helplessly while the petition was withdrawn from parliamentary consideration due to a technical error.[59]

No such error recurred the next year. The CPU (or the two agents it employed) had apparently taken a survey of its own from December 1803 to January 1804, which showed that there were 1,495 journeymen and 893 apprentices in Lancashire, Cheshire, Derbyshire and Staffordshire (probably the formal limits of the combination). Although the ratio of 3:5 between apprentices and journeymen was much better than the maximum ratio of 2:1 talked about some years before, it was still regarded as unsatisfactory. The journeymen sent up a new petition with 7,000 signatures, published a tract defending their position and, for the first time, obtained a parliamentary inquiry into their plight with the help of Richard Brinsley Sheridan, MP. The journeymen's forlorn tale was one of almost continuous decline since the early 1790s, a decline largely attributed to one cause: the inordinate use of cheap apprentice labour. Certain masters would hire apprentices in droves and employ them full-time, while journeymen could obtain work for only two or three days a week, if at all. Some masters would then proceed to discharge the apprentices on the very day their indentures expired. Heald of Portwood was hardly among the blameless. As of January 1804 he kept 16 apprentices while employing only nine journeymen, a ratio much worse than the regional average. With an abundant supply of cheap labour available, the journeymen claimed that their position *vis-à-vis* the masters could never be strong. Their wages tended to fall to the lower level of the apprentices, and these wages were sometimes paid in truck – damaged cloth goods in one extreme case. Also, the fact that they worked nearly naked in the scorching heat of the print shops and constantly breathed in the debilitating vapours of chemicals used in printing made them unfit for any sort of outdoor work. Thus they were determined to effect changes in perhaps the only trade for which they were physically fit.[60]

Despite the merits of their case and the precedent of the oft-cited Spitalfields Act limiting apprentices in the London silk industry, Parliament chose to do nothing. When two more petitions in 1805 (one to each House) failed to alter the situation, the CPU halted its annual petitioning campaigns.[61] But extra-parliamentary pressure seems to have continued, and Sheridan remained a staunch ally within Parliament. In July 1806 the Commons set up a committee to report on the situation. The committee noted the fact 'that the complaints of the Journeymen are loud and unremitting, has long been a matter of notoriety, and frequently mentioned in Parliament'. It proceeded to pose what was, for the age, a rather astounding question,

> whether it be quite equitable towards the parties, or conducive to the public interest, that on the one part there should arise a great accumulation of wealth, while on the other there should prevail a degree of poverty from which the parties cannot emerge by the utmost exertion of industry, skill, assiduous application, and may, at an advanced period of life, notwithstanding perpetual labour, be obliged to resort to parish aid for support of families. Is it just that such a state of things should be permitted to exist?

Yet the committee concluded that disputes should be left to the masters and men to settle, and it counselled inaction.[62]

In the following year Sheridan led a Whig faction in Parliament which again attempted to aid the calico printers. The group brought in a bill which would regulate the apprentice-journeymen ratio and prohibit the taking of apprentices without legal indentures, among other things. The 1804 and 1806 Select Committee Reports were also ordered to be reprinted at that time. This campaign elicited the unanimous opposition of the employers. Cheshire and Derbyshire masters joined together to petition against the measure, and Sir Robert Peel led the debate against it in the Commons. Opponents focused on the anachronisms of the apprentice system in calico printing. It was stated that in the early days of the trade, when division of labour was less prevalent, long apprenticeships were necessary. In 1807, however, a boy of 14 could 'in a few months, learn the whole business'. With such arguments, the second reading of the bill was effectively blocked.[63]

Between 1807 and 1813 the CPU was much less active than it had been from 1803 to 1807. Although some calico printers turned to violence in 1811-12, there is no indication that this comprised official union policy. The half-dozen years after 1807 were ones of acute distress in the cotton industry, years in which traditional union activities might be expected to wane. There is a report that many of the journeymen were simply tired of paying for strike funds and petitioning campaigns by 1807. At the same time the CPU was being vigorously opposed by the masters' association which had been established in 1803. The latter publicly announced a meeting in 1811 to elect a new committee and president, and it continued to exist for many years thereafter.[64] Its intransigence concerning all of the workmen's demands no doubt helped to foster the six years of relative quiescence.

The masters' association may also have promoted two tendencies apparent in the industry. The one was a decline in the number of apprentices, which was said to have begun about 1803 and was noted periodically over the next dozen years. This was, of course, a major demand of the CPU. The other tendency was for masters to introduce new machinery at a rapid rate. Between 1800 and 1815 the number of cylinder and surface machines (some printing in two, three or four colours) increased twentyfold. A new invention, the so-called union printing machine, was introduced in about 1807. So, the pressure for wages to advance in a restricted labour market was presumably offset (as far as the masters were concerned) by cheaper and more efficient modes of production.[65]

Given the pace of mechanisation, it is not surprising that the main issue of the next period of CPU activity (1813-15) was the introduction of labour-saving machinery into the print trade. In March 1813 the calico printers presented another petition to the House of Commons requesting a tax of 1½d. per yard on all goods printed by machines in order to bring their cost up to that of block-printed goods. They claimed that they had been without regular employment for a number of years 'as a great part of their trade is executed by an inanimate thing . . .' Later in the year the CPU, still claiming a following in Lancashire, Cheshire and Derbyshire, felt strong enough to publish its rules for general circulation. This prompted a meeting of 37 masters early in 1814, including Roe's of Chadkirk and other Stockport district masters. They saw the dispute as involving both the use of machinery and the hiring of apprentices and vowed to take legal action if the journeymen did not desist.[66] By the end of 1814 some 1,600 to 1,800 calico printers were striking for their demands amid rumours of plans to destroy machinery or emigrate *en masse* to France.

Masters continued to unite in opposition. They passed a series of resolutions against the workers' combination in late December, and early in 1815 they published a pamphlet condemning the workers' demands for control over which types of machines were used and which workers were to be hired. The masters told the journeymen that they were 'disgusted with your proceedings, and satisfied there was no permanent security for them, or for their trade, but in the total annihilation of your system . . .'[67] The journeymen immediately responded with a broadside claiming that the masters were dismissing workers who had not turned out so that there would be no printers to help support those on strike. Striking journeymen solicited loans or gifts from other trades with some success. London brushmakers answered their entreaties with a £10 loan in February and another in April. The Stockport hatters' union also contributed.[68] The final outcome of this regional strike is not known, but as in 1790 it probably ended badly for the journeymen. In July 1815 calico printers were again petitioning the House of Commons to redress grievances relating to machinery and apprenticeships.[69] The CPU suffered a blow later in that same year. Ten delegates from all parts of the United Kingdom were surprised and arrested at Bolton. The authorities seized their books and papers. The ten delegates ultimately received sentences of three months' imprisonment each, but the papers were of greater concern to the authorities. They revealed links between printers, hatters, weavers and shoemakers and evidence of support for calico printers from friendly societies. The documents also contained details on combinations in many branches of the cotton trade in the greater Manchester district.[70]

Little is known of the Calico Printers' Union in the Stockport district between 1815 and 1830. One historian of the trade concludes that the strike of 1814-15 marked a turning point and that afterwards machinery became supreme. Data presented to the Home Office in 1817 showed that advanced printing machines could produce the same amount of printed cloth as block printing techniques with over 90 per cent less labour.[71] Although Stockport district calico printers retained links with other areas and other trades after 1815, they took little concerted action.[72] This was probably due in part to the flourishing conditions in the trade during the ensuing decade and a half. With the rapid spread of the powerloom, calico printing businesses could hardly keep pace with the flood of cloth destined for printing. Prosperity provided the wherewithal for many forms of paternalist benevolence and control, even in some outlying firms. Recent commentators on Strines Printworks in Disley state that the proprietors 'supervised and encouraged the whole social and cultural life of the village, providing both Church and School . . .'[73] While economic booms were often conducive to union activities, the unprecedented prosperity in calico printing and the paternalistic good will it engendered perhaps allowed journeymen to win some of their demands without strikes or appeals for parliamentary intervention. Journeymen's agitations had already helped to achieve reductions in the number of apprentices before 1815. After that time, journeymen continued to maintain more or less absolute control over who was hired or fired and had control over fines levied for spoiled work. They also had some influence on wage levels, which remained high. Wage lists were in force before 1832, for instance, when a new list was proposed by the operatives.[74] Thus, as journeymen were being transformed from skilled artisans in large workshops to machine operators in print factories, they maintained certain powers but abandoned other demands (notably those regarding the introduction of machinery) which no longer seemed appropriate in changed economic circumstances. There is no evidence before the Chartist period, however, to link calico printers as a body, or any substantial numbers of them, to political reform agitations. They sought redress of sectional grievances through union activities and parliamentary pressure tactics.

IV

Early workers' combinations in the cotton industry developed along fairly rigid sectional or craft lines. This was true not only in the major branches, like spinning, dressing, powerloom weaving and calico printing, but also in the smaller specialities associated with factory and machine construction and repair. Thomas Ashton stated in 1824 that every craft was organised in the factories of Hyde and that each speciality jealously guarded its prerogatives. A millwright would not allow a carpenter to do his work; a filer would not allow a turner to do his. This trend was reinforced by the tradition that each major factory occupation have its own friendly society. By the 1830s Ashton's firm alone had separate societies for spinners, dressers, weavers and mechanics.[75]

By that time, some people were using the existence of different skill and wage levels to identify four 'classes' of cotton workers in the greater Manchester district. If one were to set the wage rates of the first class at 100, the respective rates of the other three classes would have been about 60, 30 and 15. When trade unions emerged, they nearly always included adult or adolescent males from the first and second classes. Occupations in the second, third and fourth classes which required little skill or were dominated by women and children had no known combinations at all (cf. Table 4.1). Where combinations did exist, their success in organising their whole trade was probably never complete. Calico printers seem to have fared the best, probably because of their high level of skill, but certain remote printworks never came under the sway of the CPU. There existed only limited co-ordination among different cotton trades in the same locality or even in the same factory. Jenny spinners did not strike when mule spinners did; cotton dressers continued to strike in one factory in 1818 after the powerloom weavers had returned to work; Hyde rovers refused to strike in 1824-5 when the spinners turned out; and calico printers pursued a course independently from all the other cotton trades. During the protracted strike of 1829, powerloom weavers returned to work weeks before the spinners.[76]

Table 4.1: Major Cotton Factory Occupations in the 1820s and 1830s

Occupations	Main Type of Employee	Approx. Weekly Wages in 1833
I. Mule spinners		
Cotton dressers		
Calico printers	Adult males[a]	18–30s.
Miscellaneous trades (mostly skilled)		
II. Weavers	Adult and adolescent	
Warpers	males and females	8–13s.
Throstle spinners		
III. Carders		
Cleaners	Adult females	6–10s.
IV. Piecers		
Scavengers	Children	3–6s.

Note: (a) 'Adult' in this context was generally applied to those 18 years of age and older.

Sources: PP 1834 (167) XIX, D.2., 127, 129; cf. PP 1830 (590) X, 4; *ST*, I (1820–3), 1395–8.

Sectionalism of this kind should not be obscured by the tendency of these trades to engage in strikes at approximately the same times, that is, during periods of relative prosperity. Jenny spinners and calico printers both struck in 1785-6; jenny spinners, powerloom weavers, dressers and mule spinners were striking at various points in 1818. Other strikes by mule spinners (1802, 1810, 1822) and calico printers (1814-15) likewise occurred during times of economic well-being. By the late 1830s, this seemed to be a universal pattern in the eyes of one dismayed Stockport industrialist. Factory operatives, he stated, somehow managed to discover owners' profit trends 'and depend on it, as soon as those profits become high, their hands would turn out for higher wages; aye, and would obtain their demands, too'.[77]

There was a slightly greater degree of co-ordination among similar organised trades in different areas. Calico printers again provide the best example. The regional CPU existed from the 1780s through the 1820s, and it was said to be in contact with calico printers in Scotland and Ireland. Mule spinners were also notable for their regional co-ordination, especially from 1810 onwards. Stockport jenny spinners, cotton dressers and powerloom weavers had no known contacts with their counterparts in other towns, probably because there were often few workers in those branches elsewhere.

Jenny spinning rapidly declined in most other areas after the 1780s, and powerloom weaving and factory dressing did not become widespread before the 1820s.

This examination of Stockport district cotton workers suggests the need for caution in accepting certain generalisations which have been made about the early factory 'proletariat'. Two extreme views seem especially untenable in this local context. One is the conclusion, first prominently advanced by Sidney and Beatrice Webb, that cotton factory workers' 'ephemeral organizations and frequent strikes were, as a whole, only passionate struggles to maintain a bare subsistence wage'. The Webbs further believed that factory workers alternated 'out-bursts of machine breaking and outrages, with intervals of abject submission and reckless competition with each other for employment'. In accepting this view, G.D.H. Cole also accepted the Webbs' claim that this situation was linked to the operation of the Combination Acts. Cole contended that persecutions under those Acts in the Lancashire-Cheshire cotton districts were 'far more brutal and systematic' than in London and most other parts of England.[78] James R. Cuca implicitly rejects this line of interpretation. He sees an angry and alienated factory proletariat united in its fight against enforcement of the Combination Acts. According to Cuca, all of this had additional ramifications by the 1820s: 'it appears that as workers under the factory system were militantly expressing their relations with the capitalistic-entrepreneurs, they were also being solidified as a class.'[79]

Neither of these views seems applicable to the Stockport district. Considerable achievements were made in organising particular cotton trades, and many of the combinations were long-lived. But differences in skill, pay, age, sex and location were inevitably reflected in differential institutional developments and, one would suspect, in disparate attitudes and forms of consciousness. There was, in any event, no unambiguous trend towards inter-trade solidarity. Nor was there a single pattern of conflict orientation or commitment to political radicalism which might have united these different cotton trades in a common struggle. None of the organised trades discussed in this chapter can be shown to have alternated industrial actions with political radicalism. None of these trades officially endorsed radical political programmes nor did significant numbers of individuals from these trades participate in radical campaigns or join radical clubs. Those workers with well-established trade organisations (which would have provided potentially good bases for radical activities) had the highest relative wages and the least fluctuations in employment. Like their brethren in other districts, they could increasingly obtain 'not merely the necessaries of life in food, clothing, and habitation, but also many comforts and some superfluities' and thereby 'pass through life with much of humble respectability'.[80] Thus, it can not be entirely surprising that they chose not to mount fundamental challenges to the political and economic systems in which their livelihoods were acquired.

5   THE SKILLED AND THE UNSKILLED

The origin of a Manufacturing town is this: a Manufactory is established, a number of labourers and artizans are collected – these have wants which must be supplied by the Corn Dealer, the Butcher, the Builder, the Shopkeeper – the latter when added to the Colony have themselves need of the Draper, the Grocer, &c. Fresh multitudes of every various trade and business, whether conducive to the wants or luxury of the inhabitants, are superadded, and thus is the Manufacturing town formed. – Richard Guest (1823)

Gerhart von Schulze-Gaevernitz claimed that Stockport in the 1830s was 'a town which was inhabited solely by cotton workers'. Friedrich Engels made a similar statement about Stockport in the 1840s.[1] Cotton workers certainly predominated in the town and its district in the early nineteenth century, as has been noted, but there existed a wide range of workers in other occupations throughout the period of the Industrial Revolution. The growth of trades not directly involved in the fabrication of cotton yarns or textiles was stimulated in various ways. The expanding contingent of cotton workers created increased demand for the output of shoemakers, chandlers, bricklayers and many other specialities. Moreover, the successful operation of the cotton factories themselves required the skills of many kinds of local craftsmen. It has already been noted that factory owners kept some artisans in their permanent employ. Among the 600 employees of Samuel Stocks, Jr, at Heaton Mersey in 1831, there were millwrights, mechanics, engineers, blacksmiths, joiners and sawyers (as well as carters and watchmen). Factory owners might also commission independent artisans for specific tasks. Besides the artisans found at Stocks' mill, these might include ironfounders, braziers, tin-men, clockmakers, carpenters and harness makers. The latter produced bands for carding machines, among other things, and their activities in turn stimulated the curriers' trade.[2]

It seems probable that most trades were expanding from the 1770s to the 1820s in terms of absolute numbers employed. The list of occupations of adult males given in the census report of 1831 (Table 5.1) gives some indication of the wide variety of trades. Leaving the cotton industry aside, hatters, shoemakers and tailors comprised the largest individual trades in the town of Stockport at that time. The history of Stockport hatters is unusually well-documented and will consequently be traced in some detail. After a brief examination of shoemakers, tailors and certain other trades, the self-help institutions which emerged in this period will be analysed with the object of determining to what extent they promoted inter-trade solidarity and a conflict orientation among workers.

Table 5.1: Categories of Adult Males in Handicraft Trades, Retail Trades or Agriculture in Stockport Township in 1831 (Cotton Workers Excluded)

Category	Examples	No.	% of All Adult Males
Clothing trades	hatter, tailor	551	9.2
Building trades	carpenter, bricklayer	369	6.2
Leather trades	shoemaker, currier	314	5.2
Metal trades	blacksmith, whitesmith	144	2.4
Food trades	butcher, baker	138	2.3
Wood trades	sawyer, cooper	75	1.3
Miscellaneous trades	clockmaker, printer	56	0.9
General retailers	food, fuel	367	6.1
Alcohol and tobacco	publican, brewer	139	2.3
Miscellaneous services	carrier, barber	87	1.5
Agriculture		109	1.8
Total		2,349	39.2

Source: PP 1833 (149) XXXVI, 68−9.

I

The felt hatting industry in the Stockport district dates at least from the seventeenth century, when limited production was intended, it appears, only for local markets. During the middle third of the eighteenth century, at a time when exports were expanding at a prodigious rate, the hatting industry in the town of Stockport began experiencing remarkable growth. The explanation for this phenomenon seems clear. London capitalists sought to establish or expand the industry in provincial areas, notably in the North and West Country where wages were lower than in the Metropolis. As one such entrepreneur stated in the early 1760s, '... In the North of England Labour is much cheaper; ... he had, on [that] Account, established his Manufactory there, as several other hatters of London had done'.[3] Because Stockport, Oldham, Manchester and other towns already possessed infant hatting industries, they must have seemed ideal locations for enterprising Londoners in quest of wider profit margins.

The spread of the hatting industry was accompanied by the spread of workers' associations. London journeymen probably had a continuous combination from the 1660s onwards. Combinations in the provinces may have arisen with the tramping system early in the eighteenth century. By 1753 it was claimed that 'this pernicious custom [of provincial combinations] hath long prevailed amongst the journeymen'.[4] Tramps could receive a living allowance at each provincial house of call (or turn-house) until they arrived at their destination or found work. The system lasted well into the nineteenth century. One hatter told Henry Mayhew of his experiences 'on the tramp' in 1828.

When I started from London, I needn't have gone if I hadn't liked it, if I'd exerted myself; but I wanted a change. I made for Lancashire. I had 1½d. a mile allowed then, and a bed at every 'lawful town.' Sometimes, if the society's house, which was always a public-house, was small, and full, I had half a bed – for other societies used the house, and I have slept with tailors, and curriers, and other trades on tramp.[5]

As in calico printing, the tramping system in hatting not only fostered links among different regions. A federation of more than a dozen towns emerged in 1771, for example. Hatters' 'congresses' were held in London in 1772, 1775 and 1777, but it is unclear whether these elicited more than regional representation. It was later stated by masters that the 1772 and 1775 congresses had agitated for – and received – wage increases.[6]

The first evidence of combinations at Stockport and Manchester coincided with the second London hatters' congress and with the beginning of a wartime slump in the export of felt hats. It seems likely that if the two northern towns did not belong to the London-based federation at that point, they were at least influenced by its demands in 1775 for a network of closed shops. The local controversy began at Manchester and focused on whether or not journeymen had to belong to the combination and whether or not there should be two apprentices per master as allowed by Elizabethan statute, or just one as necessitated by the exigencies of a depressed industry. Journeymen were thus concerned above all with regulating entry into the trade. Soon, the focal point shifted to Stockport where hatters employed by the London firm of Davies, Owen, Swanton and Evans turned out in order to enforce the one-apprentice rule. They were 'supported by many others employed by different Manufacturers'. This selective strike was answered by the threat from a dozen masters (eleven Manchester firms along with Davies and Co.) not to put out any work whatsoever after 11 December unless Davies' hands returned to work.[7]

As with so many early labour disputes, the outcome of the 1775 Stockport hatters' strike is unknown. But disputes certainly continued. Early in 1777 the Manchester masters published a newspaper notice reminding journeymen of the Act of 1749 (22 Geo. III, c. 27) against frauds in the industry and forbidding journeymen's combinations.[8] Conflict also took on national dimensions. As the London journeymen hatters met in congress for a third time, London masters pressed for a bill to regulate hours, wages and apprenticeship procedures. They were joined by masters from Manchester and its vicinity in their claim that an acute shortage of journeymen necessitated the loosening of apprenticeship regulations. Journeymen hatters saw the matter differently. Those from a dozen geographic areas petitioned against the new regulatory bill, but without effect. Journeymen from Manchester and vicinity claimed that

> the Journeymen hat or Felt Makers are so numerous, that unless the said Trade is in a very flourishing Condition, many Hundreds are, and often have been, obliged to go to any other Employment they could meet with, and which has many Times been the Cause of their travelling up and down the Kingdom in Search of Employ.

The Act which became law on 6 June 1777 allowed masters to take as many apprentices as they wanted.[9] In connection with this Act, Thomas Davies, the London entrepreneur whose Stockport branch was struck in 1775, testified that embezzling of materials was a major problem among his employees. Similar difficulties throughout the industry helped to gain inclusion of the hatting industry under the provisions of another act of 1777 to prevent frauds and abuses in certain trades (including cotton, silk, woollen and fustian trades as well as hatting).[10]

The two acts of 1777 may have had the temporary effect of checking the belligerence of the hatters' combination, but its continuing existence seems almost certain. In 1785 the wealthier masters of Manchester and Stockport were again airing their grievances in the newspapers. They expressed their opposition to: (1) the hatters' combination and its attempts to regulate prices, wages and hours; (2) the embezzlement of materials; and (3) the failure satisfactorily to finish work put out by masters. It is interesting that the large masters included in their strictures not only journeymen and apprentices but also the small or 'piece' masters (that is, makers and finishers). Because of their dependence on the large masters for raw materials and marketing arrangements, many small masters were becoming little more than wage labourers and were joining the hatters' union. Manchester and Stockport capitalists resolved to give preferential treatment to small masters and workmen who circumvented the union and also vowed to take joint legal action against the organisation. Such actions would otherwise be too expensive and time-consuming for a single large master. Three Stockport firms joined 14 others from Manchester and vicinity in this masters' combination.[11]

In spite of these actions, piece masters, journeymen and apprentices were striking at Stockport by September. Thomas Davies wrote rather sanguinely at mid-month to his Stockport agent:

I hope you have settled with the finishers to your satisfaction. If not, I would wish you at all events to endeavour to do it amicably. I should suppose you will be able to take them down a little in picking as well as finishing.

Two months later Davies' mood had changed. He had become desperate and was pleading for a quick settlement to avoid ruining the firm.[12] The ostensible issue in 1785 was not wages, since Stockport capitalists were prepared to offer higher wages than those in Manchester and Oldham. The main controversy was over apprenticeships and entry into the trade. The large masters argued that the dressing, dyeing, stiffening and finishing branches were legally 'free' and that they could therefore take into their dye and finishing houses as many apprentices as they desired. Twenty-two Stockport piece masters denied these claims in a public notice. They stated that wages at Stockport had fluctuated downwards as well as upwards in recent years and that apprenticeships should be strictly limited in all branches of hatting. The dispute continued for two more months. During that time, Stockport strikers were joined by hatters at Manchester, who sent an incendiary letter to four of the largest Manchester firms in December. As the dispute faded away in January 1786 the correspondence of Davies and Co. reveals that many new apprentices were being indentured.[13]

In sum, none of the issues debated in 1785-6 had been settled, and more disputes seemed inevitable. One did occur in Manchester from May to July 1791, when finishers struck to remove some hatters who had not served proper apprenticeships. Seven Stockport firms publicly pledged their support to the Manchester masters. But as with the calico printers, no major disputes seem to have occurred at Stockport in the early 1790s or for many years thereafter. One cause of this relative quiescence may have been the adoption of 'blanks' throughout the nation. These slips of paper certified that a hatter looking for employment was in good standing with the hatters' combination, especially with respect to his apprenticeship background. Blanks may thus have provided the long-sought after means to restrict entry into the trade at Stockport and other areas. Their use left the union at Stockport, Manchester and nearby towns in an unusually good position by the turn of the century. The strength of the Stockport Body of Feltmakers (SBF), as the union came to be called, may have been one factor in the decision of many London firms seeking northern bases to locate at Denton and Ashton-under-Lyne during the first quarter of the nineteenth century.[14]

Soon after the turn of the century, foreign competition (especially from the expanding American hat industry) caused severe reductions in orders for English hats. By all accounts, the SBF remained strong and influential none the less. Stockport hatters' wages remained high, perhaps the highest in the region. Eight Macclesfield hatters were prosecuted in 1806 when their local union pressed to bring wages up to the Stockport level. As the slump continued and dissensions revived, masters formed another association of their

own in January 1807. Their executive committee included two
representatives from Oldham, two from Manchester and four from
the important Stockport-Denton area. Operative hatters were not
intimidated – quite the contrary. In June 1807 the corpse of William
Williamson, a master hatter, was found floating in the Stockport
Canal. The SBF later took credit for the drowning, claiming that
Williamson had threatened to inform on it.[15]

On 19 September of the following year, the journeymen hat
makers and finishers of Stockport and vicinity held a general
meeting, or congress, which affirmed a set of 20 work rules. The
most extensive of these (rule no. 12) specified proper apprenticeship
procedures. To enforce the rules, the SBF launched selective strikes,
first against Thomas and John Worsley and then against Daniel
Cooper. In November Stockport masters joined in advertising for
journeymen to break the strike, but with little effect. Cooper became
a major target of the strikers perhaps because he was using 'Engines
for Making Hats', that is, labour-saving machinery.[16] In January
1809 Cooper sent a memorial to Lord Liverpool complaining of a
three months' strike, of threatening letters, and of combinations
among the thousands of employees in the hat trade in and around
Stockport which helped support those on strike by contributions
from those still at work. The economic pressure on Cooper became
so intense that by March he had to file for bankruptcy.[17]

Masters in other areas fared much better and seemed in fact to
gain the upper hand. Manchester and Oldham masters, for example,
instigated successful prosecutions against local unionists at the
April and July (1809) Lancashire Quarter Sessions. By contrast,
Stockport district masters appeared impotent in the face of the
SBF. As a premier centre for the northern hatting industry,
Stockport had gained the reputation for work of the highest quality.
A foreign visitor remarked in 1814 that 'the best English hats' were
made in Stockport and London.[18] This probably meant that
Stockport hatters could command higher wages and maintain tighter
control on entry into the trade than those in neighbouring districts.
The SBF formulated and printed specific regulations, used selective
strikes, and threatened (and was prepared to use) violence. Although
the events of 1812 properly belong to the complex story of Luddism,
the same themes clearly emerged during that period. Widespread
food riots led by hatters presaged new regulatory schemes involving
'Blue Blanks', which had the effect of reinforcing the strong regional
position of the SBF. As in 1807-9, Stockport masters seemed all but

powerless to protect their interests.

The situation began to change in 1816. The key incident was probably not at all unusual in the affairs of the union. James Green, a journeyman, went to George Pickford, another journeyman, to sell some hats he had embezzled from his employer. Green also tried to dispose of some embezzled monkey's wool to a third person, but this transaction was overheard by William Acton. Pickford and Acton went to the authorities, who secured Green's conviction at the Spring Assizes. The Stockport hatters' congress promptly fined Pickford and Acton five guineas each for informing on a fellow union member. Such was the power of the congress that both men quickly paid their fines. The incident would have been unremarkable if it had ended there. But Pickford and Acton told their story to John Jackson, one of the men on the masters' executive committee established in 1807 and an activist on behalf of his fellow employers' rights. John Lloyd, the magistrate's clerk, was also informed. Jackson and Lloyd prosecuted ten of the leading SBF members and secured convictions in nine of the cases at the 1816 Summer Assizes. Those found guilty received sentences of two years' imprisonment each. Lloyd secured two further convictions against hatters at the Spring Assizes of 1817.[19]

Repression in Stockport helped to shift the locus of union agitations to the Hyde-Denton area. Hatters from this and neighbouring areas met at Denton on 1 June 1818. They complained that wages had been depressed for the preceding five years, that wages were lower in that area than in any other part of the country, and that as a consequence, even industrious hatters were unable to support themselves without parochial relief. They also stated that some hatters had resorted to shoddy production, which was beginning to sap the confidence of hat buyers. The assembled hatters wanted a minimum wage and advocated that their brethren in each township 'form themselves into Friendly Societies or Sick Lists, to make a monthly or weekly subscription for their mutual assistance; in case of sickness, death, or when from a depression in trade, they are unavoidably out of employ'.[20] The latter suggests that hatters were tying to extend their combination at this point and trying to build up a large fund for special purposes, including, no doubt, strikes. Most of the master hatters in the Denton area quickly capitulated and agreed to a minimum wage rate. Denton hatters nevertheless continued to help those at Ashton, Oldham and Manchester to convince masters that they should raise wage levels. After a long, hard-fought campaign, 50 masters in Denton, Stockport and the other three towns finally decided in the spring of 1820 to raise wages by nearly one-third.[21]

These concessions were probably motivated in part by a change in the style of hats, which required more labour and, presumably, a higher selling price per hat.[22] Soon thereafter, Lloyd reported to the Home Office on 'another serious conspiracy . . . amongst the hatters, which was to be general'. Specifically, the SBF was continuing its practice of levying fines on those who refused to co-operate with union by-laws. Lloyd, in league with the master hatters, secured indictments against 18 journeymen.[23] Although the prosecutions were not proceeded with, the threat of prosecution seemed to be enough to preclude overt union activity for a few years. High wage levels probably also helped to lessen the necessity of industrial actions. The wage increase of one-third in 1820 was spoken of as being in effect as late as 1824. The unions at Stockport and Denton were still active at that time and remained dominant organisations in the whole region. In the spring of 1824 the regional combination of hat body makers published the sources of its income. The list showed that hatters in six Stockport district townships contributed about three-eighths of the total.[24]

The year 1824 marked a renewal of activity by various local hatters' unions. The SBF joined unions at Ashton and Manchester in petitioning for the repeal of the Combination Acts in 1824. At the same time, unions at the latter two places also launched successful legal actions against truck masters. It seems that some masters had resorted to truck payments in order to maintain the high 1820 wage level. But masters, in general, seemed receptive to the demands of their workers. At their 1827 annual meeting, masters resolved not to allow any wage reductions. Later in the year a dispute did erupt at Oldham, and it involved at least one Stockport district hatter who took out materials from the strike area. Yet within six weeks the dispute had been settled – and the journeymen were reported happy with the outcome.[25]

By the 1820s the hatters' combinations had achieved a high degree of comprehensiveness and had managed to gain control of entry into the trade. A list of journeymen and apprentice hatters in Stockport and Denton published in 1831 shows that the number of apprentices ranged from 10-15 per cent of the total, depending on the area. These figures were almost certainly low enough to satisfy union members.[26] Hatters were also able to maintain relatively high wage levels, with all that entailed. Denton hatters, for example, worked only five days per week, became noted for drunkeness, and took to hunting during the season with their own pack of dogs, the 'Oat-cake Pack'. While the hatters' achievements thus resembled those of the calico printers, the hatters exhibited additional strength. Unlike the calico printers, they achieved many successes in direct clashes with their masters, perhaps because the hatters were more concentrated geographically. Hatters were able not only to maintain their associations during economic slumps, which was no small feat, but also to agitate during such adverse periods to protect wage levels. The only hatters' strike to occur during a period of prosperity was that of 1818. In many respects, therefore, the hatters' combinations were the most successful of any in the Stockport district during the early Industrial Revolution.

II

To what extent did trades other than hatters combine in the Stockport district? The evidence on this question is fragmentary in the extreme. It might be expected that tailors and certain leather trades would have combined since such trades had tramping systems in the eighteenth century which helped to provide bases for national associations in the nineteenth century. And such trades were combined in large northern towns like Manchester and Liverpool.[27] Thomas Worsley was presumably citing Stockport evidence when he testified before a Select Committee of Parliament in 1834 that the 'awful' example of the declining handloom weavers had actually encouraged combinations in such trades as hatting, tailoring and shoemaking.[28]

The earliest mention of a tailors' organisation at Stockport was that of a journeyman tailors' friendly society in 1797. Since contemporaries believed that friendly societies which consisted of only one trade really performed trade union functions, this may have been the case with the Stockport tailors. In 1821, when they were the only trade to march in the local coronation procession, their ranks were preceded by a coach featuring the trade's flag and coat of arms. In the 1831 coronation procession, they marched at the head of other trades.[29] Shoemakers and curriers both had tramping systems in the eighteenth century. Both are known to have kept up correspondence among the major towns of England during the

1790s despite the various statutory prohibitions on such activities passed in that decade. With regard to shoemakers' combinations, it was stated at a York trial in 1799 that 'in every great town in the North combinations of this sort existed'. In 1801 the shoemakers, curriers, tanners and saddlers of Stockport and other towns were petitioning Parliament for protection of the trade in hides. A final piece of evidence on a Stockport shoemakers' combination comes from the following year, a prosperous time in which shoemakers were making demands (and causing official concern) in many parts of the country. In April 1802 some journeymen shoemakers of Stockport were convicted and sentenced to two months in prison for combining to raise wages.[30] Although there is no further documentation on local shoemakers' unions, periodic reports down to the 1820s confirm the existence of a national combination. As a Londoner lamented in 1817: 'If the *Benefit Societies* of shoemakers and tailors are not altered, I know that the country will be always harassed, *as it now is*.'[31]

Evidence on Stockport district coal miners is scarcely more enlightening. In 1804 Nathaniel Wright of Poynton complained that riots 'are not infrequent among the colliers'. He hoped that the successful intervention of the Poynton Volunteers would suffice to keep order. Indications of more organised activities appeared during the Regency period, when the rate of growth of output from Lancashire and Cheshire mines was decreasing and probably thereby eroding the position of highly-paid miners. A strike of 80 colliers from Poynton, Norbury and Worth collieries in 1810 revealed the existence of a colliers' committee and secretary. The committee may have been only a temporary body set up to deal with the immediate labour dispute, however. Nothing further is known about it.[32] Strikes recurred during the summer of 1818 after two years of wage reductions. They broke out not only at Stockport but also at Ashton, Oldham, Bolton and Manchester, and were directed by a central committee in the latter city. Only the disturbances in the Stockport district appear to have lasted into October, when John Lloyd helped to settle the conflict.[33] A coal miners' friendly society was established in Bramhall in about 1823. As with other colliers' societies in Lancashire at the time, it may have functioned as a trade union. There were disturbances in 1830-1 around Stockport and in other parts of the Manchester district. As in 1818 there were attempts to co-ordinate these activities over a wide area, but the schemes came to naught.[34]

If the evidence on individual combinations at Stockport is limited, so too are indications of 'trade unions' and inter-trade links. E.P. Thompson has made much of the temporary association of five or six Manchester trades to protest the passage of the 1799 Combination Act, but no such association can be found at Stockport. Thompson's further claims, that the Act triggered the formation of new combinations and caused Jacobins to unite with trade unionists, likewise lack verification from the Stockport district.[35] Contemporaries believed that the Combination Laws of 1799 and 1800 were largely ineffective against the skilled trades. Hence, there would have been little need for the kind of agitation which Thompson claims to have been widespread. In any case, as Dorothy George convincingly argued long ago, the two acts did not mark a new departure in official attitudes towards combinations but were the last in a series of statutes whose prohibitions were only sporadically enforced.[36] The Stockport evidence shows that in the ten or fifteen years after 1799, combinations of spinners, calico printers or hatters frequently acted to protect their sectional interests while remaining somewhat oblivious to, and largely unaffected by, the Combination Acts. Consequently, agitations to repeal the Acts generated little local enthusiasm.

The Stockport committees of trades in 1811-12 and 1816-17 were really not trades unions but rather weavers' clubs with radical political overtones. The Manchester Philanthropic Society established in August 1818 claimed to include numerous trades from most of the major towns of the Manchester district, including Stockport. Although delegates from the Society were active in the Stockport district during August and managed to gain the support of local radicals, the Society won few additional converts. Calico printers and handloom weavers steered clear of it and, at one point, it could claim fewer than 100 Stopfordians as members. Whatever its maximum strength might have been, the whole organisation collapsed at Manchester, its centre, within a few weeks.[37]

The Stockport Committee of Artizans established in 1824 was primarily concerned to secure repeal of the Combination Acts and assure that no further restrictions on combinations would be enacted. Its emergence was unquestionably helped by the official harassment of local trade unions which had occurred during the preceding decade and which grew out of ofttimes irrational fears of the dire effects of such combinations. A judge at the Cheshire

Assizes in 1817 reflected these sentiments when he stated that 'any master who should concede the demands of his workmen, who had struck for a rise of wages, ought to be considered as an enemy to his country!' Two Stockport workers' representatives blamed the resulting 'ill will' squarely on the existence of the Combination Acts.[38] Still, only three trades are known to have been represented on the Committee of Artizans – jenny spinners, mule spinners and handloom weavers. Even this indication of limited inter-trade solidarity is deceiving. Since the handloom weavers had no comprehensive organisation at that time, all that the Committee of Artizans gained was the support of certain members of the Stockport Weavers' Committee. The weavers finally sent up a separate petition to Parliament in March 1824. The jenny and mule spinners seemed to work more closely together, and their joint petition was also signed by 'other cotton mill labourers' of Stockport. Hyde factory workers sent their own petition. Stockport hatters ignored the Committee and sent up a separate petition in conjunction with hatters at Manchester and Oldham.[39] There may have been even less co-ordination in 1825, when jenny spinners prepared their own petition against the re-enactment of the Combination Laws. Separate petitions also came from tailors, from spinners and mill workers, and from calico printers – the latter being part of a combined petition from certain northern and home counties.[40] While one trade (the tailors) saw little reason to act in unison with the trades on the Committee of Artizans, two others (hatters and calico printers) saw more reason to co-operate with members of their own trades in different regions.

The repeal of the Combination Acts produced more cordial relations between masters and men in jenny spinning and, if the *Stockport Advertiser* can be believed, helped to promote general social harmony: 'Instead of the deep murmurs of discontent and disaffection [by the operatives], we have the cheering tones of loyalty and grateful attachment to their rulers.' At the same time, the Committee of Artizans was being rent by disputes. There were persistent rumours that Martin Blackett, one of its members, had abused his powers in various ways. Likewise, Thomas Worsley thought that Stockport's mule spinners 'would send me to hell if the[y] could and I relay [*sic*] do not know for what purpose'. William Longson, a weaver, suggested that Worsley's high-handedness in dealing with operatives was at fault.[41] The Committee of Artizans, in short, could not count among its achievements any significant increase in inter-trade solidarity or 'class consciousness'.

In the emergence of inter-trade links and in the formation of combinations themselves, effective and comprehensive organisations were difficult to establish. The unskilled, the semi-skilled and those in service occupations remained uncombined. This can not necessarily be blamed on lower skill levels and lower wages. In fact, the highest of the non-skilled workers might make about as much as the lowest of the skilled workers, as is shown in weekly wage figures for the greater Manchester district in 1814-16:[42]

Weekly Wages	Occupations
30–35s.	ironfounders, fine spinners
25–29s.	carpenters, sawyers, calico printers
20–24s.	hat finishers, tailors, bricklayers, masons
15–19s.	shoemakers, plasterers, unskilled labourers in building trades, porters

Many of the uncombined occupations were quite small, however, and were thus unusually susceptible to such things as employer control, the emergence of employee deference or, perhaps, the growth of a degree of camaraderie between 'master' and 'servant'. This was probably the case among the bakers, who were fighting in court for enforcement of traditional apprenticeship rules in 1801. It probably also occurred in the many service occupations which used the language of the Statute of Artificers well into the nineteenth century. In 1803 a Stockport ironmonger advertised for an apprentice, a hairdresser wanted two journeymen, and a grocer sought both a journeyman and an apprentice. Similar advertisements continued at least down to the 1830s but should not obscure the fact that successful respondents would become little more than wage-earning employees in Stockport's burgeoning service sector.[43] Domestic servants would have been in a comparable situation. Small in number (they comprised only two per cent of the district's population at the time of the 1831 census), they were mostly females who, no doubt, had to curry the favour of their employees in order to maintain a secure position in their respective households. Accounts from the outside of violent handloom weavers' demonstrations or defiant mule spinners' strikes must have seemed strange and threatening to many of them.

There remains the problem of the skilled trades which have left no record of combinations during the early Industrial Revolution.

One should recall that the types of extant evidence on combinations often relate to isolated disputes over wages and other matters in trades which were relatively large and which consequently posed threats to public order. The numerous smaller crafts, both within factories and without, which combined mainly to restrict entry into their respective trades or to carry out friendly society functions, would not typically appear in judicial records, Home Office files or newspaper accounts. Those groups may, in fact, have avoided major disputes because their control over traditional prerogatives remained strong, as was the case with Thomas Ashton's millwrights and turners. A high degree of artisan control over the workplace would help to explain why the issues of child labour and long working hours, matters which came to be significant among factory employees, rarely prompted skilled artisans to protest.[44] This phenomenon may also have been related to the relatively high level of real wages for many artisans. Elizabeth Gilboy has shown that the real wages of Lancashire artisans rose noticeably from 1770 to 1800. Artisans' wages at Manchester, Bolton and Macclesfield seemed to keep pace with prices during the wars with revolutionary and Napoleonic France.[45] If the somewhat euphoric testimony of a Cheshire man can be accepted, this may have been the case throughout the region.

> I never knew the country doing so well as when corn was selling at the high prices; all classes, all the little tradesmen in the towns, were doing so well there was no complaint from anybody; the farmers, if they could get money, would lay it out, and their daughters were fond of dressing, and the tradesmen were doing extremely well in consequence.

A comment of William Radcliffe likewise suggests that wages of non-weavers in Stockport kept pace with prices, at least during the years from 1802 to 1807.[46]

Still, one can only speculate on the reasons for the dearth of evidence on possible combinations in many of the skilled trades in the Stockport district. One observation can be made, however: none of the available primary documentation even hints that these rather shadowy trades were officially involved in inter-trade organisations or radical political movements.

III

It might be argued that important manifestations of broad-based 'working-class consciousness' lay in other types of institutions – for example, in the various self-help societies which began to appear in the late eighteenth and early nineteenth centuries. E.P. Thompson has suggested that some operated not only as benefit clubs but also as trade unions or covert Jacobin societies.[47] As will be demonstrated, however, these institutions can not be shown to have been major channels for the diffusion of class solidarity or a conflict mentality. Many sorts of workers' attitudes germinated in such organisations, but foremost among them was the desire for respectability and closer co-operation with the middle classes.

Friendly societies (or sick and burial clubs) provided a sort of insurance or savings scheme for workers and others to cushion the effects of sickness, old age or the expenses attendant on death. Some also allowed payments in cases of unemployment. Members' dues generally amounted to only a few pennies per week. Such societies first received legal sanction by Rose's Act of 1793 'for the Encouragement and Relief of Friendly Societies . . . by promoting the happiness of individuals and at the same time diminishing the public burthens'.[48] Friendly societies had existed at Stockport for nearly three decades before Rose's Act, however, beginning with the Charitable and Amicable Society established in 1765.[49] Ten additional Stockport district societies can be traced from the period before Rose's Act. Others probably existed and vanished without a trace or became visible in the records when they decided to register, whether in 1794 or thereafter. The Heaton Norris Society of Linen Weavers was established in 1773. At a quarterly meeting on 5 October 1793 the members decided to reprint the old articles, to add amendments, and to register them at Quarter Sessions. Its rules were allowed by Sessions on 22 July 1794. Stockport's Loyal Friendly Benefit Society was established in 1777, 'concluded' on 5 July 1794, and registered at Sessions on the same day. It was no doubt prudent for a friendly society to present itself as a new establishment rather than admit to a prior, quasi-legal existence.[50]

From 1794 to 1823 evidence exists concerning 125 separate friendly societies in the Stockport district, only ten of which were known to have been comprised of a single trade.[51] A single-trade society, like those among Stockport mule spinners, jenny spinners, hatters and tailors, might foster a conflict mentality by acting as a trade union and enforcing demands against masters in their respective trades. There is no intrinsic reason, however, why such friendly societies should promote inter-trade solidarity, and there is no evidence from the Stockport district that this occurred. On the contrary, the fact that single trades possessed their own friendly societies seems to have set them apart from other trades and to have enhanced their special, 'labour aristocratic' character. Multi-trade friendly societies probably did promote certain feelings of inter-trade solidarity, but their opportunities for fostering a conflict orientation were limited. In the industrial sphere, it is conceivable that a multi-trade club could instigate or help to support strikes in various trades. But there is no evidence of a friendly society acting as a sort of 'trades council' in the Stockport district before the 1830s.

For a number of reasons, it is probably safe to assume that few orgies of class vilification transpired in the back rooms of public houses on club nights. In the township of Stockport, one friendly society member in ten belonged to a female society at the time of an 1803 enumeration. There were 37 female societies in existence at some point between 1794 and 1823, or about one-third of the total. The female groups were not noted for their extreme views on either political subjects or industrial relations. There are examples of female societies in which all or nearly all of the members signed the society's charter with a mark. The two Denton female societies which registered in 1796 enlisted a male steward to oversee their affairs, as did a Heaton Norris female society in 1818.[52]

While supervision of the friendly societies and their funds by local authorities and others of the middle classes could never be complete, there exists considerable evidence that vigilance was exercised throughout the Stockport district. The example of the 1795 mule spinners' friendly society was mentioned in the preceding chapter. A Marple friendly society had over 100 members in 1808, including (at the head of the list) two scions of the Isherwood family from Marple Hall.[53] Other, less direct evidence seems to support this line of interpretation. The peak years of registrations of friendly societies in the Stockport district were 1794, 1797, 1806, 1808, 1812 and 1817. This pattern is not inconsistent with that which can be observed regionally.[54] The high level of registrations during the mid- and late-1790s is fairly easy to explain. From 1794 to 1799, society formations were widely encouraged, and many pre-existing societies came forward to register voluntarily. Many of the Stockport district societies composed of single trades registered during that period.

The first two decades of the nineteenth century deserve more careful examination, especially since peaks in society registrations occurred during periods of distress[55] – periods seemingly inauspicious for diverting any part of workers' incomes away from the basic necessities of life. It was also a time in which authorities' initial enthusiasm for friendly societies turned into suspicion and hostility. As early as 1799 a Stockport tract denounced the 'extravagance, drunkenness, idleness, and lasciviousness' found in some male and female societies. As one solution, it suggested that clubs hold their meetings in Sunday schools rather than in public houses.[56] In various parts of the greater Manchester district, it was believed that some friendly societies aided the weavers in their tumultuous 1808 strike. In the Luddite year of 1812 John Lloyd called Macclesfield 'a nest of illicit association . . . full of sick and burial societies which are the germ of revolution'.[57]

In other words, periods of distress coincided not only with peaks in registrations of friendly societies' rules but also with increased anxiety on the part of the authorities over the activities of the societies. One can surmise that in such periods, concerned officials tightened their control over friendly societies, forced unregistered societies to register, and in some cases compelled registered societies to re-register and thereby allow magistrates to scrutinise their rules and perhaps question their leaders. Cheshire Quarter Sessions issued a special order on the subject of friendly society registrations in 1807, and during the course of 1808, an unusually large number of Stockport district societies brought their rules before the bench.[58] Stockport district magistrates concurred in an abortive plan proposed in 1812-13 to require magisterial supervision of all friendly society functions, especially monetary disbursements which might be used for strikes.[59] In 1818 Lloyd was again trying to uncover abuses in local friendly societies. Among other things, he circulated a handbill warning about misallocations of society funds.[60]

At the same time, new types of friendly societies were being encouraged. There were at least seven which originated in religious institutions (the Methodist Chapel, the Stockport Sunday School, the Anglican National School).[61] Some of them were composed entirely of children and adolescents. In 1817-18 two prestigious Stockport friendly societies were established to promote loyalist views and perhaps to serve as conspicuous examples of how such self-help organisations should function. The Philanthropic Society had a distinguished list of industrialists among its officers, including Peter Marsland as president and Robert Parker as vice-president. It was avowedly patriotic, as was the Church and King, or 'Wellington' Club, which had as an explicit objective the dissemination of strict law-and-order views. By 1826 it could boast that it had a membership of over 600 'staunch Tories'.[62]

While some societies (female, juvenile, religious, loyalist) were unlikely to promote disorders and were often under the direct supervision of members of the middle classes, other societies became the objects of *ad hoc* investigations during periods of distress and public disorder. During the whole period under discussion, however, the authorities found only one society (the Artificers' Society) which, by its involvement with the weavers' strike of 1808, could be said to have acted improperly and perhaps illegally. Inquiries by worried Bolton officials in 1816 revealed a similar picture – there had been some friendly society aid to the weavers in 1808 but no known abuses since then.[63] Even allowing for the likelihood of unreported irregularities at both Stockport and Bolton, the limited membership of friendly societies must not be forgotten. Of the 26 townships in the Stockport district, ten had no friendly societies at all in 1803. A further six townships had only one society each, which comprised less than two per cent of the population of those townships in most cases. Nine district townships still lacked friendly societies in 1815. Friendly society membership in Stockport township (1797-1824) and in the district as a whole (1803-15) ranged from 11-16 per cent of the total population.[64]

Even if these figures must be augmented by the (usually unknown) membership totals of unregistered societies, it does not seem likely that conclusions regarding the development of 'class consciousness' would be altered. Probably the bulk of the unregistered societies were social clubs which made provision for the sickness and burial of their members but whose articles were laced with arcane rituals. Occasionally societies of this sort would come forward to register, as with the Stockport Knights Templars (c. 1820) and the United Free Gardeners (1808), apparently a lodge of the national Order of Free Gardeners.[65] Most such groups, including Masons, Druids and Oddfellows, remained unregistered in order to keep their elaborate rites secret. The earliest Masons' lodge in Stockport, established in 1760, included among its members a joiner, a plumber and a cabinet maker as well as many prominent professional men, manufacturers and tradesmen.[66] The Royal Arch Lodge of the Temple of Jerusalem contained a cordwainer, a butcher, a machine maker and others of a higher rank around the turn of the century. An 1806 petition to establish the Lodge of Concord was signed by a joiner, a tailor and a muslin weaver. The Masons' movement thus joined together working men with representatives of the middle classes in organisations conspicuous for their loyalty. Ten members of the Lodge of Benevolence served on the committee of the loyalist Stockport Reeves Assocation in 1792, for instance. Masons published a special patriotic *Masonic Song* for the Royal Jubilee in 1809. After 1820 these groups grew enormously upon the same broad social base. By 1831 the combined membership of Masons, Druids and Oddfellows was around 1,300 men drawn from both the middle and working classes. Ten years later the Stockport branch of the Manchester Unity of Oddfellows alone had over 2,000 members, including surgeons, policemen and shopkeepers as well as nearly every conceivable type of workman.[67]

Many other earlier trends were repeated after 1820. Relevant documents from 1824 to 1830 show the existence of another Anglican friendly society, another Wesleyan Methodist society, and two more associated with the Stockport Sunday School. A loyalist group formed the Stockport Royal Veterans' Society. There was, however, a much lower level of recorded activity than before. While an average of four societies had been established each year from 1798 to 1823, only about two were established annually from 1824 to 1830. This probably resulted in part from the establishment of savings banks which helped to diminish the need for separate friendly society funds. Stockport was hardly a pioneer in this undertaking because there existed a strong local prejudice against banks, especially those which (like the defunct Stockport Bank of the 1790s) issued banknotes. Despite parliamentary legislation in 1817-18 encouraging banks, favourable publicity on 'frugality banks' in the periodical press and the opening of a savings bank in Manchester, Stopfordians all but ignored John Lloyd's attempt to establish such an institution in 1818.[68] Four years later a correspondent to the *Stockport Advertiser* expressed surprise that the town still did not have a savings bank. Finally in 1824 a meeting of leading Stopfordians resolved to establish the Stockport Savings Bank. In lauding its opening, the *Advertiser* urged 'the mechanic and the working class generally' to deposit a shilling or two per week. Increasing numbers apparently did so. At the end of its first year, the Bank had about 500 depositors. In 1830 the figure had grown to nearly 900, the majority having accounts of £20 or less. Little is known of the early history of another savings institution established in 1824, the Stockport and Cheshire Bank, but it seems possible that it, too, had hundreds of depositors from the working classes.[69]

There were other reasons for the apparent decline in friendly society formations after 1823. Since data is based primarily on registrations, they may simply reflect declining official concern about potentially illicit friendly society activities. In the more orderly decade of the 1820s, in other words, there may have been less pressure on societies to register. After the repeal of the Combination Acts in 1824, moreover, workers probably established many unions which incorporated friendly society functions without being registered as such. Finally, the Friendly Societies' Act of 1819 made registration of friendly societies more difficult and may have had some impact on Stockport district figures. In the wake of the Act, many of those interested in taking part in friendly societies may have decided to join old ones rather than bothering to establish new ones.[70]

Other workers' self-help institutions of the period provided even less scope for the development of 'working-class consciousness'. There is evidence of only one co-operative in Stockport before the 1820s. Established by handloom weavers in 1800 to procure foodstuffs at wholesale prices for its members, it probably did not last for more than a couple of years. Co-operation in the late 1820s and early 1830s progressed slowly in the Stockport district. William Longson, a prominent workers' spokesman, offered one reason at the time when the first of the new societies was being established in 1827: '. . .in my opinion, the intelligence of the people, is far from that advanced state, which is requisite for to change the system of society from competition to co-operation'.[71]

At least seven building societies existed in the Stockport district before 1820. The earliest dated from 1788, involved the construction of 15 houses, and included two Heaton Norris attorneys on its list of members.[72] Little evidence survives concerning the numerous societies which sprang up during the 'building mania' of the early 1820s. The *Stockport Advertiser* referred to eleven building societies in 1823, but it is not known whether this figure includes the three societies associated with the Stockport Sunday School, the two associated with St Mary's Anglican Church or the single society associated with the Hillgate Wesleyans. In any event, the total number of workers belonging to building societies was small, and these societies did not provide a congenial organisational setting for the promulgation of radical ideas. Indeed, successful participation in a building society scheme meant that an individual accumulated a capital sum which was beyond the reach of all but the most persevering and highest paid workers. Ownership of a house, moreover, would set a worker above and apart from the majority of his fellows and can not be seen as contributing to an identity of interests among all workers.[73]

IV

Marx and Engels developed an analysis of combinations which has often been employed to gauge the relative strength of unionism at different times or in different regions. They emphasised that as the labour movement grew, it shifted: (1) from temporary combinations, such as those organised for a single strike, to more permanent institutions, with officers, treasuries, long-term objectives, and so forth; (2) from combinations consisting only of skilled workers to those which organised the semi-skilled and the unskilled; (3) from partial, local combinations, which included only a segment of a given trade, to comprehensive, national combinations; (4) from simple intra-trade organisations to those which focused on inter-trade alliances; and (5) from combinations concerned only with industrial matters like apprenticeship regulations, introduction of new machinery, wages and hours, to those with explicit political concerns like the formation of a workers' party and the acquisition of power in the state.[74]

Both Marx and Engels admitted, in statements made from the late 1840s to the 1880s, that there were numerous indications of weakness and underdevelopment in the English labour movement. It should come as no surprise, therefore, that the strongest combinations in the Stockport district before 1830 appear to have been relatively weak when judged by Marxist criteria. They tended to emerge only in trades which were wholly or substantially composed of adult or adolescent males and which were concentrated in factories, mines or sizeable workshops. Trades dominated by females or boys or pursued in small shops or domestic settings tended not to combine or encountered enormous difficulties in attempting to do so. In these patterns of development, there were no great distinctions between artisans and factory workers, despite the Webbs' assertions to the contrary.[75] When permanent institutions did develop in the Stockport district, they had problems in attaining comprehensiveness and were often merely local or regional in scope. Where regional or national links existed, they tended to be sporadic in nature or to focus on the traditional distinctions between 'foul' and 'fair' men. There is no evidence that the unskilled combined, that political concerns (whether traditional or radical) significantly intruded into the affairs of the disparate unions, or that notable inter-trade links were forged. The latter were impeded by the persistent wage differentials of those who did manage to combine. Wage levels ranged from those of the fine spinners down to those of the shoemakers and were 'high' only in relation to wages of women, children and the majority of the unskilled.

By the criteria of the workers themselves, however, many of their combinations fared quite well. If a combination managed to regulate entry into the trade, control the introduction of machinery or keep real wages relatively high, and by those means maintain or enhance their members' standard of living, what need did they have of help from other trades, from other regions or from the nostrums of radical political theories? In one sense, therefore, the most effective combinations of the early Industrial Revolution appear to be among the least developed according to Marx's criteria.[76] This paradox can be extended by noting a major trade whose increasingly sophisticated responses neither resulted from a position of strength nor indicated a growing degree of influence. The handloom weavers proved to be weak in their organising activities and largely unsuccessful in their strike actions. As alternatives, they vainly sought regional or national solutions, requested help from other trades, and embraced the radical political ideologies which were being disseminated in the Stockport district from the time of the Jacobins onwards.

6   THE RISE OF JACOBINISM

It is our labour that supports Monarchy; it is our labour that supports Aristocracy; it is our labour that supports the Priesthood; and it is our labour that supports ourselves. ...Our design is to shew, from incontrovertible facts, that we are of some service to the State; that we have Rights that have been long lost; and that we are not the '*Swinish Multitude*' Mr. Burke calls us. – Stockport Friends of Universal Peace and the Rights of Man (1792)

The formation of trade unions in Stockport and its district in the late eighteenth and early nineteenth centuries paralleled increasing local interest in 'Jacobin' ideologies and movements. Since 'Jacobinism' has rarely been defined with precision in the English context, it has long remained a rather ambiguous term. On the one hand, it clearly had ideological links to the Levellers and certain other agitators of the Civil War years, and to their successors (notably the Commonwealthmen) of the century after the Restoration.[1] On the other hand, Jacobinism helped to spawn numerous nineteenth-century 'radical' programmes and movements and provided a training ground for many radical leaders and spokesmen prominent from the time of the Westminster Committee of 1807 to the Chartist movement and beyond. In other words, the Jacobinism which appeared in the 1790s and the earliest years of the nineteenth century can be seen as a link between two 'radical' traditions. The earlier one, as defined by John Brewer, encompassed 'any position which, if fulfilled, would undermine or overturn *existing* political authority'. He includes in this category demands for annual or triennial Parliaments, demands which were made not only by Commonwealthmen but also by 'radical' MPs and country gentlemen who might publicly label themselves Whigs or Tories. Brewer shows that this broadly defined 'radicalism' developed in various ways during the 1760s, notably through revived demands for an extension of the franchise and a redistribution of parliamentary seats. There was also the establishment of a radical organisation in London, the Society of Supporters of the Bill of Rights, which gained support in many provincial areas.[2]

There is little evidence, however, that this early 'radicalism' had a substantial impact on the Stockport district or, for that matter, on the counties of Lancashire and Cheshire during most of the eighteenth century. Indeed, a prominent group of Stockport radicals during the War of American Independence exhibited little willingness to agitate for political reform. They spent most of their time trying to emigrate to America with smuggled machinery which, they were convinced, would make them rich and famous.[3] This is not to say that Stockport Jacobinism did not have important local antecedents within the earlier radical tradition. But a different analysis of radicalism, that formulated by Egon Bittner, has more relevance to Stockport district events and trends than the pattern advanced by Brewer. Bittner in fact ignores the earlier movements which form the basis of Brewer's discussion and instead concentrates on the Jacobinism of the 1790s as the first significant and enduring English radical movement of the eighteenth century. He stresses the following characteristics of Jacobinism: (1) Jacobins' democratic and anti-elite beliefs; (2) their small, locally based clubs; (3) their propaganda campaigns; (4) communications between clubs in different localities; and (5) the ability of small groups of activists to mobilise mass support.[4] Bittner's Jacobins thus differ from Brewer's radicals in the larger scale of the Jacobins' activities, in the degree to which they functioned outside of elite circles, and in their ability to establish long-lived provincial clubs.[5] An analysis of Stockport district Jacobins and their proposals can thus serve not only to provide a case study of the wider Jacobin phenomenon but also to help understand the roots of later radical movements in the area.

I

The Stockport Friends of Universal Peace and the Rights of Man was established on 25 August 1792 and was soon in contact with the London Corresponding Society (LCS) and Jacobin corresponding societies in the North. It is not an easy matter to determine why a provincial town of 10,000 or 15,000 inhabitants should have provided an appropriate setting for an early English Jacobin club. Certainly Stockport's tradition of opposition or 'country' politics played a role. Its inhabitants had supported Parliament in the Civil

Wars and had evinced a rather independent spirit throughout the eighteenth century, notably in the Cheshire election riot of 1734 (on the occasion of the last contested county election before 1832) and the militia riot of 1757. Closely linked to political opposition was Stockport's strong Dissenting heritage, which also dated from the seventeenth century. It is not surprising that in the autumn of 1792, Nonconformist tradesmen and manufacturers were believed to have been ardent supporters, if not members, of the Stockport Jacobin club.[6]

Certain other long-term antecedents are important for an understanding of Stockport Jacobinism. Better communications during the eighteenth century meant that Stopfordians could learn a great deal about various reformist and revolutionary causes. Manchester newspapers and magazines, in particular, furnished accounts of John Wilkes and his supporters, the revolt in the American colonies, English Nonconformists' efforts to gain increased toleration in the 1770s and 1780s, and the storming of the Bastille and subsequent revolutionary events in France.[7] Stopfordians may not have needed to rely on the Manchester press to hear of urban reform movements and protests closer at hand. Various events at Manchester, Liverpool and Chester, for instance, paralleled Stockport's own protracted efforts to loosen the control of the Lord of the Manor over market tolls and to establish an independent urban improvement commission.[8]

Such long-term conflicts merged with short-term difficulties in the early 1790s, a time when, among other things, winters were said to have been especially severe in the English North-west. Against this background, it is not surprising that the passage of the Corn Law of 1791 triggered numerous protests in the greater Manchester district. The new Law favoured landed interests by encouraging exports of grain while placing duties on imports. It took effect at a most inopportune time: the harvest of 1792 proved to be so deficient that corn exports had to be halted by a special order of the Privy Council.[9] The years 1792 and 1793 also marked the beginning of a long decline for that numerous and increasingly vocal body of workers, the handloom weavers. And the Nonconformist issue remained unsettled. After Parliament defeated the Nonconformists' bid for toleration in May 1789 Nonconformist clergymen of the Manchester district held meetings for nearly a year in order to redouble their efforts to secure toleration. After another defeat in March 1790 some of the Manchester merchants and manufacturers active in the campaign shifted from religious to political agitation and formed the Manchester Constitutional Society.[10]

The same type of shift from religion to politics occurred elsewhere. In 1790, 1792 and 1793, Whigs at Westminster were introducing motions for parliamentary reform, while 'Jacobin' reform clubs were springing up all over the country. The Sheffield Constitutional Society, the most vigorous of the provincial clubs, was set up in November 1791. In London, the LCS was formally established on 25 January 1792; the Society for Constitutional Information revived in March; and the Friends of the People was founded in April. Two Workmen's clubs, the Manchester Patriotic Society and the Manchester Reformation Society, began in May and June, respectively. By the beginning of August, more than a dozen additional provincial societies had appeared in England and Scotland.[11] A flood of radical literature accompanied these formations. Tom Paine's *Rights of Man* (two parts, 1791-2) not only attained the greatest renown nationally but also achieved considerable popularity in Stockport.[12] While the LCS printed and distributed pamphlets of its own during 1792, the *Manchester Herald* (established in March) and the *Patriot* of Sheffield (established in April) disseminated radical views on a regular basis in the North.

All of these examples and influences, though undoubtedly affecting the attitudes of some Stopfordians in the early 1790s, had an especially profound effect on John Andrew, a young man who resided east of the Stockport district at Matley in Mottram parish. He was apparently from moderatly well-to-do yeoman stock. Although only in his twenties, he had read widely in history and philosophy and had been converted to the Enlightenment ideas of liberty and equality. He had been further inspired by the early issues of the *Patriot* in April and May of 1792, issues readily obtainable at a Stockport bookseller's shop.[13] Andrew highly recommended the Sheffield paper to all his acquaintances and claimed that by October it was in 'general circulation' in the area. The *Patriot*'s accounts of the establishment of various reform clubs gave Andrew the idea of founding such a club in north-east Cheshire. He drew up a declaration and took it to a populous centre near Matley (possibly Gee Cross or Newton) but was frustrated there by the timidity of the would-be Jacobins. He next circulated the declaration among friends at Stockport for some weeks before the decision was made to form a society there at the end of August 1792.

Andrew's declaration was embodied in the formal address issued at the inaugural meeting of the Stockport Friends on 25 August. The address was then printed as a broadside and reprinted in the *Manchester Herald*.[14] The first meeting consisted not only of manufacturers, mechanics and labourers, according to the address, but also of yeomen and farmers. The text of the address presented a fairly standard Enlightenment view of people being born free and equal; stated that the liberty of the press was inviolable; favoured religious freedom; condemned wars; and advocated such political causes as annual elections, suffrage for all taxpayers and equal representation. The small society went out of its way to dissociate itself from public disorders. Its members said they were not levellers, much less Burke's swinish multitude. 'We abhor and detest all riots and tumults; we are the friends of peace; our only armour is reason . . .' The society specifically praised the *Patriot*, whose editors later publicly thanked the group. The address was signed by N. Hibbert of Mottram parish as president and John Andrew as secretary.

The formation of the Stockport Friends was mentioned briefly in the *London General Evening Post* of 8-11 September 1792. This prompted the LCS to authorise its secretary, Thomas Hardy, to write to the infant provincial society on 13 September and to send it some LCS literature.[15] The Stockport Friends were not entirely pleased with the LCS contact. They wrote towards the end of September that the LCS pamphlets 'hardly rise to that height which we expect from men sensible to their full claims to absolute and uncontrollable liberty . . . . Would not all the evil be done away at once by the people assembled in a convention?' The Stockport Friends also hinted that their mail was being watched. The LCS responded on 11 October that 'our sentiments are expressed in as strong terms as prudence will permit . . .' Yet it did mention that it planned to communicate with the French National Convention and wondered if Stockport objected to this potentially treasonous plan. The Stockport society, in its last known letter to the LCS, responded on 3 November that it wholeheartedly supported the plan. It also repeated its claim that the LCS letters were being intercepted. Although the LCS resolved to answer the Stockport letter, the response may never have reached its destination.[16]

When the Stockport Friends discovered in late September that they were not entirely in accord with the cautious policies of the LCS, they resolved to make contacts elsewhere. The editors of the

Sheffield *Patriot* had sent the Stockport Jacobins a congratulatory letter on 5 September. A month later, John Andrew responded belatedly on behalf of his comrades. He spoke of local difficulties and asked for advice on how to spread the idea of reform in hopes that the Stockport Friends could become 'both numerous and respectable'. The implication was, of course, that the society was small and did not have enough members drawn from the 'respectable' elements of Stockport district society. Andrew said that even tradesmen had held aloof, although many tacitly supported the goals of the club. The *Patriot* editors responded sympathetically. They reprinted the Stockport Friends' declaration in their periodical, and they replied to Andrew in a letter filled with practical advice.[17]

One of Andrew's proposals with which they concurred was the idea of sending delegates out to rural areas to promote reform. Andrew wrote, 'I know several very populous villages and country places where great majorities are for reform, and yet they sit still and are silent'. Some missionary work was subsequently accomplished. Andrew himself went to Newton, just to the north-east of the Stockport district in his native Mottram parish, and helped to turn a Guy Fawkes celebration into a meeting to establish a Jacobin club. By mid-December there was a 'liberty and equality' society at Bullocksmithy. There are also hints that Jacobin sentiment may have been evident in other parts of the district.[18]

The spread of Jacobinism in the Stockport district led to increased efforts by local Church-and-King loyalists to thwart the Jacobin cause. During the summer, Stockport gentry, clergy, merchants and manufacturers had sent a loyal address to the King supporting his 21 May Proclamation against sedition.[19] Soon after the formation of the Stockport Friends, the authorities began intercepting their mail (as the Friends had suspected) and managed to introduce a spy into their meetings. Not all the loyalist efforts were covert, however. Holland Watson, the clerk to Stockport's rector-magistrate, carried on a public debate with the Jacobins. He countered their notice in the *General Evening Post* of London with his own notice in the London *Evening Mail* of 21-24 September. He said that a handful of mechanics, cotton spinners and labourers had met two or three times – hardly the equivalent of the 'inhabitants of Stockport' being committed to Jacobinism. He claimed that Hibbert was an old, illiterate, idle pauper, that Andrew was a cotton spinner, and that both men were from outside the town. He ended by claiming that Stockport Nonconformists 'are, in general, admirers of Mr. Paine, and perhaps, may secretly wish for a change in the Government, yet they certainly have not openly joined this association'. Watson added that he did not know any persons of 'respectability' who belonged to the Stockport Friends.[20] This public criticism of the Friends coincided with various repressive measures taken during its first month of existence. Constables put pressure on innkeepers to deny a meeting place to the Friends and 'by oaths and horrid imprecations', according to John Andrew, 'resolutely declared that if ever they discover when another meeting takes place they will (to use their own language) "blow them up"'.[21]

Watson was answered by the anonymous pamphlet, *Rod for the Burkites* and by 'Tyrtaeus', a schoolmaster. The author of *Rod*, apparently a Stopfordian, called Church and King supporters 'hair-brained bigots'. He castigated the social structure based on wealth and heredity in rather scathing terms:

> Some of the wise-acres of Stockport imagine they oppose us when they tell us we should honour and esteem our superiors. We know that. But the term superior is in our opinion a word of construction. If by it we are only to understand one who has five hundred or a thousand a year, or a man with a large wig or a big belly; a haughty strut, or a significant stare; an imperious voice, or of a domineering dictatorial temper, we shall not hesitate but utterly refuse to give him the least reverence whatever.[22]

The author of *Rod* also denied that Andrew was a cotton spinner and that Hibbert was idle, a pauper, or illiterate.

'Tyrtaeus' the schoolmaster made similar observations in the *Manchester Herald* of 20 October. He stated that Andrew was the son of a respectable freeholder and was a young man of 'large pecuniary expectations'. 'Tyrtaeus' confirmed that the Stockport Friends were comprised mostly of country people but otherwise condemned Watson's inaccuracies. Watson, he said, had behaved similarly in a recent religious dispute, this perhaps referring to the Nonconformists' campaign for toleration in 1789-90. Watson defended himself as best he could in the *Manchester Mercury* of 23 October, a defence notable for the reaffirmation of his belief that local Nonconformists preferred a republican form of government. 'Tyrtaeus' continued the debate in the *Herald* of 10 November, but the last word came in a broadside dated 6 December and presumably written by Watson. The sheet stated, among other things, that Hibbert *had been* a pauper, which was, as near as can be determined, the truth.[23] By this time, however, Watson was more concerned to set up loyalist associations to oppose, in a collective and organised fashion, the Jacobin menace.

One inspiration for this shift in emphasis was the establishment of the London Association for Preserving Liberty and Property against Republicans and Levellers on 20 November. Founded by John Reeves, a former Newfoundland Chief Justice, the London 'Reeves Assocation' encouraged the formation of branch associations throughout England. A new Royal Proclamation against seditious literature (1 December) also spurred on provincial loyalists. On 7 December, moreover, the Treasury Solicitor and his assistant wrote to Watson and another Stockport attorney, Robert Newton, asking them to act as agents to gather up potentially seditious materials.[24]

This chain of events stimulated both voluntary and official actions in Stockport. Watson and Newton took part in a meeting to set up the Stockport Reeves Association on 10 December. They also served on the Association's committee, which was headed by the Rev. Prescot, the rector-magistrate. As its first activity, the Association sponsored a declaration of loyalty to the King and Constitution which received 1,070 signatures immediately and over 4,000 signatures by 21 December. Stockport Wesleyan Methodist congregations publicly supported the address in a statement issued on 14 December. Innkeepers likewise expressed their loyalty, although probably not without renewed coercion. One innkeeper was tried for seditious expressions allegedly uttered on 16 December. The innkeepers' loyalist declaration appeared on 17 December.[25]

Given its composition, it is not surprising that the voluntary Reeves Association worked hand-in-hand with the local officialdom. The magistrates of Stockport Division met on 17 December to discuss how best to effect the recent Royal Proclamation. It was decided to swear in special constables, 70 of whom took the oath on the spot. According to Robert Newton, when the magistrates' meeting was over everyone moved outside to the Market Place where a 'mob' burned Tom Paine in effigy – one of the earliest of such ritual burnings which were soon to become a familiar sight in Lancashire and Cheshire. The Stockport Reeves Association helped with the prosecutions of prominent local Jacobins beginning with James Hartley, a bookkeeper who had been distributing Paine's works at Stockport since September. The Association also distributed loyalist tracts obtained from the London branch.[26]

The exertions of Watson, Newton and other loyalists had the desired effect. In the latter half of December Watson wrote that seditious literature could scarcely be obtained. Newton stated that 'since the last proclamation, [Stockport Jacobins] have changed their tune and have dwindled to nothing, and I fancy we shall hear no more of them'. In January 1793 London Jacobins sent a circular letter to Stockport requesting subscriptions for Thomas Spence, who had recently been arrested. Stockport authorities intercepted the letter at the post office, and little else was heard of Stockport Jacobins for the remainder of the year. When the LCS tried to revive its correspondence with the Stockport society during August, its efforts were without apparent success.[27]

Nonconformists probably helped to nurture certain Jacobin ideas at Stockport and Bullocksmithy during those difficult months. Not only were they cognisant of the fact that political reforms could lead to greater religious toleration, but they also probably supported (and may have identified with) Jacobins' initial attempts to achieve respectability. In any case, early Stockport Jacobinism had close, if informal, ties to Nonconformity. Holland Watson refused to act formally and publicly as an agent to the Treasury Solicitor because, as he stated, 'I have already rendered myself very unpopular with the dissenters by holding up to ridicule, in some of the public papers, the Jacobin Club established here (a circumstance which will not soon be forgot)...' Watson exercised extreme care in deciding whether or not to circulate a loyalist tract entitled *Britannia's address to her People* out of fear that it might offend a Presbyterian sect (probably the Unitarians).[28] And, apart from the conservative Methodist leaders, Stockport district Nonconformists were not intimidated. They published a declaration in the radical *Manchester Herald* on 12 January 1793 pledging support for the Glorious Revolution settlement and opposition to public disorders. But they continued: 'We declare ourselves to be friendly to, and desirous of, an impartial representation of the people. For if representation is of importance, the more pure and equal it is, the more likely will it be to produce the end desired.' The declaration was signed by ministers or trustees of seven Nonconformist congregations in the Stockport district and by others in nearby townships.

II

Over the succeeding five years local supporters of Church and King managed to maintain the upper hand, in part because Nonconformist sects became increasingly sceptical of Jacobin ideas as the war intensified and the revolutionary events in France became more horrific. Local Nonconformists never again endorsed Jacobin programmes or activities. They remained discreetly aloof, for example, when Jacobin fortunes revived after the high-spirited meeting of the 'British Convention' in Edinburgh beginning on 29 October 1793. By December the inflammatory rhetoric of that body prompted Scottish authorities to arrest the two LCS representatives as well as a number of Scottish delegates.[29] Also during December, Stockport constables rounded up three persons and charged them with sedition. At the beginning of 1794 there appeared the famous pamphlet, *Rights of Swine, an Address to the Poor*, written by 'A Friend to the Poor'. This 'Friend' was reportedly a Stockport Methodist preacher formerly from Nottingham. The text was dated 'Stockport, Jan. 5, 1974', but no printer was given. It seems likely that it was first printed at Manchester or Sheffield.[30] Its author discussed the prevailing economic distress, especially that afflicting the handloom weavers of the greater Manchester district whose wages had allegedly dropped 50-60 per cent since 1792. He condemned public subscriptions and charitable schemes and blamed the distress on 'great men' who supported foreign wars while raising rents at home. Finally, the author called for universal suffrage and annual Parliaments (the objects sought by the Edinburgh Convention) with a stirring invocation: 'Awake! Arise! arm yourselves – with Truth, Justice and Reason – lay siege to Corruption; and your unity and invincibility shall teach your oppressors terrible things!' Neither his own Methodist congregation nor any other Nonconformist sect responded to the call.

Continuing Jacobin activity during early 1794 elicited renewed vigilance on the part of the authorities. During May an anonymous Stockport Reeves Association member informed William Pitt that the Methodist author of *Rights of Swine* acted as an agent for Yorkshire and London Jacobins. This informer also learned from James Hartley, the former distributor of *Rights of Man*, that Thomas Hardy and the LCS had written again, this time to find out whether there was any sympathy for the French in Stockport. As early as February 1794, Stockport's *Rights of Swine* had found its way into an LCS divisional meeting where it was read aloud to the assembled membership. Stockport was clearly becoming part of a reinvigorated Jacobin network.

When the LCS met at Chalk Farm on 24 April to discuss the convening of another British Convention, Parliament reacted by suspending *habeas corpus* in May. A national round-up of Jacobins quickly ensued.[31] The first action taken by Stockport authorities under the Suspension Act was to apprehend a suspicious Frenchman named Barbier.[32] Although the Home Office saw no reason to detain him, his arrest in June proved to be the prelude to more arrests in July. The names of several more Stockport district Jacobins were mentioned at that time. At Stockport there was a middle-class element represented by Barbier and the two Jacobin 'gentlemen' who secured his bail. There was also a representative from the cotton spinners and a faction drawn from the weavers with whose plight *Rights of Swine* had recently sympathised. The Jacobin coterie seems to have been small and close-knit. The known Jacobin weavers, for example, all had some relation (whether by blood, marriage or employment) to one man, Joshua Gordon, Sr. He was chosen to be prosecuted for sedition. The occupation of another Stockport Jacobin, James Hyndman, was not recorded, but his background deserves mention. Born in Scotland, he spoke with a French accent and had lived in the Stockport district only three years. He nevertheless served as a high official in the Stockport Jacobin club. The only Stockport cotton spinner named as a Jacobin at this time had links to Jacobin cotton spinners at Bullocksmithy. Two of these, William Holdby Atkinson (who called the King a 'Hanoverian butcher') and John Baxter (who thought there should be no king) were singled out for prosecution and were ultimately sentenced to two years in jail. They had agitated for reform with Abraham Cheetham, a Bullocksmithy surgeon whose son Thomas was to carry on the radical tradition at Stockport in the early nineteenth century. Atkinson, Baxter and Cheetham opposed the war and were reported to have solicited money for imprisoned Scottish reformers.[33]

There were further problems for local authorities at the end of 1795 when the passage of the repressive 'Two Acts' helped to rouse local Jacobins. The Acts made criticisms of the King and Constitution capital offences and prohibited all meetings of more than 50 persons. Middle-class Manchester reformers held a meeting on 7 December to protest the Acts. One of the requisitions for the meeting was signed by John Mitchell, a reform-minded Stockport physician. A Stockport druggist was gathering signatures for the Manchester protest petition the next day when he was taken into custody and his signature list seized. A Stockport meeting against the Acts on 8 December was dispersed by the Volunteers. These incidents resulted in angry petitions to the House of Lords[34] and vitriolic correspondence in the press. 'V', a loyalist in the Stockport Volunteers, wrote to the *Sun* of London and the *Manchester Chronicle*. 'V' may have been Holland Watson defending the loyalist cause in 1796 in a less conspicuous fashion than he had before in 1792. As Major Watson, he commanded the Volunteers. 'V' was opposed editorially by the new *Manchester Gazette*. Although nothing resulted from the public arguments and protests to the Lords, the incidents serve to show how repressive Stockport authorities could be in the face of any public demonstration in favour of reform. They were in fact over-zealous. After they had detained two men at this period for seditious words, they found that the evidence against them was so flimsy that no charges could be brought against them.[35]

After the excitement over the passage of the Two Acts had subsided, there was little trace of Stockport Jacobin activity for a full year. The Jacobins did not disappear, of course. William Clegg, a Stockport schoolmaster and Jacobin, composed an anti-war sonnet for the *Manchester Gazette*. When John Thelwall, the London radical, visited Stockport during the early autumn of 1796, he was probably entertained by the small Jacobin coterie of which Clegg was a member.[36] Still, the major events and trends within local Jacobinism during the year are simply not known. Perhaps as at Manchester, the decline in the Jacobin presence could be attributed to disputes between 'gentlemen' and 'mechanic' adherents. Yet Manchester Jacobins revived during the course of 1796 due in part to the exertions of a Yorkshire organiser and in part, no doubt, to the vigorous anti-war campaign being waged by the *Manchester Gazette*. By the winter of 1796-7, Manchester Jacobins had been introduced to the United Englishman's oath.[37]

The only evidence of such activities in the Stockport district dates from the spring of 1797 and reveals the existence of four related groups. At Stockport and Heaton Norris, United Englishmen met in small classes and collected membership fees of one shilling per person. During April both branches were actively swearing-in members – primarily cotton spinners. Their oath consisted of a promise of secrecy with respect to the existence of this new Jacobin organisation and its goal of radical change in the British government aided by rebellion in Ireland, invasion by the French and domestic revolution.[38] Such explicit talk of revolution was new to Stockport Jacobinism in 1797, but it amounted to little more than intimidating rhetoric borrowed from Irish radicals who were becoming increasingly prominent in the Stockport district. In other words, there is almost no evidence of revolutionary plans being actively pursued in the Stockport district at this time. The one known exception involved James O'Coigly, an Irishman who travelled between Dublin and Paris in an effort to promote French-aided risings in the British Isles. He probably passed through Stockport on numerous occasions. After one such trip in June 1797 at which he met with Stockport Jacobins, he wrote from London requesting money. A subscription of nearly £4 was collected at Stockport and taken to the Manchester society where it was added to other subscriptions and sent to O'Coigly. During the nationwide wave of repression in the first half of 1798, O'Coigly was arrested, tried and executed for treason.[39]

Besides the Stockport and Heaton Norris groups, a third group emerged at Gee Cross. The only known document from the group, probably dating from 1797, relates to a visit by delegates from the Manchester United Englishmen to the Gee Cross Jacobins. The latter approved of the United Englishmen's rules and objectives and voted to become part of the organisation.[40] This provides a further indication that the United Englishman's oath was simply superimposed on local, pre-existing Jacobin societies or informal circles of men committed to political change.

A fourth group consisted of a small number of atheists gathered around James Davies, a Stockport tailor. The group was probably inspired by Paine's *Age of Reason* (two parts, 1794-5) which was already provoking a pamphlet war in Stockport by 1796. After reading it in that year, a local Presbyterian minister was moved to write two refutations, one for each part. A rising young Stockport industrialist joined the fray with a work which was sympathetic to deism and to religious toleration in general.[41] James Davies went further. During 1797 he was in contact with a Liverpool carpenter named Brighouse who headed an atheistical Jesus Christ Club. Davies and Brighouse hoped to establish an atheist corresponding society and to print and disseminate atheist tracts. Davies himself wrote a blasphemous pamphlet, *Scripturian's Creed*, which circulated at Stockport, Liverpool and Bolton, much to the disgust of local authorities. Another pamphlet by Davies, *Philanthropic Reasoning*, was scheduled to appear in the spring of 1798, but no copies seem to have survived, if indeed it was ever printed. The Bible burning and mock rituals of the Liverpool Jesus Christ Club soon alienated both local Jacobins and deists. At Stockport, though Davies claimed that there was a 'crowd' of Jacobins, he found only five or six fellow atheists. He did, however, make further contacts in the surrounding district. But Davies was soon prosecuted and imprisoned for his *Creed*, and nothing more is known of his tiny atheist circle.[42]

By the early months of 1798 fears were growing at all levels of British government about a French invasion, an Irish rebellion, and the effects either event might have on disaffected persons in the manufacturing districts. This helped to produce 'Pitt's Reign of Terror', a concerted move by government officials against Jacobins, including those in northern industrial towns. A Bolton magistrate wrote on this occasion that a Stockport man was active in planning an Irish invasion and that Stockport was 'a place very notorious for these pernicious principles'.[43] The man in question, John Cockin, a cotton slubber, had been active at Stockport since the preceding April. Stockport authorities soon found out about him and about another man with a similar record, a cotton spinner named Charles Radcliffe. He had often acted as an officer of the Stockport United Englishmen and in February 1798 administered the Englishmen's oath to a fellow cotton spinner in Portwood. When the latter informed the magistrates, Radcliffe was arrested, convicted and sentenced to be transported for seven years.[44]

III

Repressive actions against the United Englishmen in 1797-8 marked the end of a period in which self-confident Church-and-King advocates could easily marshall public opinion against Jacobin theories and, if need be, assemble special constables, Volunteers or urban crowds to oppose Paine's disciples. This change led to increasing trepidation on the part of local authorities, if the tone of their letters to the central government can be used as a guide. The shift was a subtle one. It did not result in the depths of official despair which would be exhibited during the Regency, nor does it alter the generalisation that from about 1790 to 1806, local authorities held the upper hand. Nevertheless, the years 1797-8 marked the beginning of a period in which talk of reform by Jacobins was supplemented by discussions of revolution and foreign military intervention. The alarums sounded within the local ruling classes were thus not without some justification. When taken together, this complex web of events, intentions and anxieties contains a sufficient number of ambiguities to leave recent historians somewhat perplexed.[45] In order to clarify the local situation, four tendencies should be mentioned at the outset: (1) the continuing influx of Irish included some who, like O'Coigly, did not shrink from introducing the rhetoric of rebellion into the Stockport district;[46] (2) Jacobin societies or loose circles of reformers continued to exist in Stockport (as in most other towns in the region) and became visible from time to time in agitations to end the war or to reform Parliament; (3) societies of handloom weavers appeared during the spring of 1799 to agitate for various industrial objectives; and (4) the Jacobins attempted, with only limited success, to infuse the weavers' sectional movement with wider political goals. Part of the confusion among historians arises from the fact that a few prominent Jacobins were weavers and vice versa. This has led some commentators to assume that the movements were inter-changeable, that political and industrial objectives were used alternately by the same activist group. For the events in Stockport, this does not seem to be an acceptable explanation.

The weavers' societies were newly created in the spring of 1799, a period of rising grain prices and falling piece rates. Their organisation resembled that of the United Englishmen (and the Methodists) in being based on local classes and town and regional meetings. There is evidence that this Weavers' Association declined in strength during the summer due partly to the fact that its agitation to end the export of twist was co-opted by master manufacturers. The Association may also have lost some members to a new Jacobin organisation established in July. This Jacobin revival resembled that which had occurred in the greater Manchester district during 1796-7 in that it was said to have originated in Sheffield and to have spread to Manchester, Stockport, Bury and other towns. The Jacobin organisation was based on local class meetings and had certain industrial objectives which weavers probably found appealing. The Jacobins hoped to secure repeal of the Combination Laws, for example, and they opposed the export of twist. They even talked about a plan to burn spinning factories which exported their goods:

'The mode, meant to be adopted is, by one of their society wiping off the oil, in one or more of their spinning machines, and inserting, *emery*, – It will very soon burst into a flame.'[47]

Spies at both Manchester and Sheffield were certain that Jacobins were behind the agitation against the Combination Laws and that they had combined industrial grievances with politics in order to gain as large a following as possible. At Manchester this tactic showed some signs of success. A meeting of anti-Combination Law activists in late October had representatives from calico printers, shoemakers, fustian cutters and machine makers. A similar meeting a month later also had representatives from the cotton spinners. There is additional evidence that weavers participated in certain phases of the agitation. The movement quickly faded away, however, due in part to repression by magistrates who had received reports of impending disturbances over food shortages and consequently intervened.[48]

At Stockport it is doubtful if the Jacobins managed to gain a foothold in even as many as six trades at this time. There was concern, none the less, that the local branch of the Weavers' Association was being swayed by Jacobin ideas. Three Stockport division justices joined other Manchester district magistrates in condemning this tendency in November. William Radcliffe, a master manufacturer active in the Stockport anti-twist export movement, also noted the trend: 'until the year 1800,' he wrote, 'the weavers as a body were as faithful, moral, and trustworthy as any corporate body amongst His Majesty's subjects.' But by the end of 1799 or the beginning of 1800, he recalled, some weavers were supporting the Jacobin anti-war stance.[49] Still, there was little immediate cause for alarm. The Stockport weavers devoted most of their time and energy to industrial concerns over the next four years, leaving the Jacobin core at Stockport without a base of widespread workers' support.

General dearth and the consequent adulteration of food from 1799 to 1801 caused problems of a different sort for the authorities. A riot in the Stockport Market Place in February 1799 motivated the Rev. Prescot and Holland Watson to issue a printed circular assuring farmers in the area that they would be protected from rioters in their future trips to market. Despite such assurances, the scarcity of food in Stockport became worse. During the winter of 1799-1800, when the Oldham market began featuring nettles on sale at 2d. per pound, Stockport authorities set up a soup charity in an effort to forestall disorders. They also issued another circular letter to farmers promising protection, but to no avail. A riot occurred on the last Stockport market day in January 1800, and crowds attacked numerous corn mills in the out-townships the next day. Watson noted that 'under such extremities, even against rioters, everyone feels unwilling to proceed hastily to extremes . . .'[50] These events proved to be only a prelude to the sporadic disturbances over the price of food which continued for the remainder of the year. It came to be widely believed that food shortages, radical politics and the weavers' movement were – or would somehow become – merged into a broad-based revolutionary campaign. The Rev. Prescot voiced these sentiments in a letter to the Home Office in September. Although the military had managed to disperse hungry crowds up to that time, Prescot feared that the disaffected '(especially *if* also acted upon by politics) *may* do more mischief than it will be in their [the military's] power to stop or prevent'.[51]

Such fears increased at Stockport towards the end of the year. It was learned that 'one Moorhouse from Stockport under the pretense of selling a pamphlet of his own composition is supposed to be an agent of correspondence among the fraternities . . .'[52] James Moorhouse, an auctioneer until his bankruptcy in 1812, was later mentioned as a member of the Stockport Jacobin committee. There were also reports (usually unsubstantiated) of large meetings outside of town and of plans to seize the weapons of the Stockport Volunteers in preparation for a revolution. Consequently, when there appeared a Royal Proclamation and Home Office injunctions urging action by local authorities, Stockport magistrates were eager to comply. They arrested a labourer for saying, 'Damn the King', on 12 November. They also tried to arrest John McGee, an Irishman apprehended in Manchester during the repression of the United Englishmen in 1798. He had promoted revolution since moving to Stockport in July 1800. Attempts to take him at his lodging house and to seize his papers failed, however.[53]

During the early months of 1801 popular discontent decreased somewhat in the wake of repression, gradually falling grain prices and expanded charitable schemes. Stockport's soup charity, for example, was supplemented by government shipments of rice and corned herring.[54] Reports to the Home Office reflect this change. One suggested that areas to the south of Manchester did not exhibit a strong spirit of disaffection. Macclesfield and Congleton, for instance, were believed to harbour none of the carriers of Jacobinism, although Stockport was 'far from being free from the contagion'. Strongholds could be found at Manchester and the satellite towns stretching from Bolton and Rochdale to Oldham and Ashton. The St Patrick's Day arrests of Jacobins at Manchester and the locales of meetings held during early 1801 confirm this pattern. A large protest meeting was to have been held near Rochdale on 3 May, but it was moved to 'Buckton Castle', a hill near Ashton, in order to foil the authorities. Manchester dragoons nevertheless managed to find and disperse the crowd of 5,000 many of whom were said to have been from Stockport.[55]

The Buckton Castle meeting probably helped to energise Stockport Jacobins and their 'Union Society'. In May 1801 a spy reported that Stockport was the site of a delegate meeting which allegedly debated the best time for a rising. There is evidence that a Jacobin society existed in Gee Cross at this time. And during the summer of 1801 a new model organisation and a new oath were being introduced. Delegates from Oldham, Royton and Stalybridge established a new society based on the revised oath at Marple Bridge in July. The new model was believed to have been created in London and to have spread to the provinces through Sheffield. But it is unclear how it differed from the old model, and it may have been devised simply to attract attention to the Jacobin cause. It is known that the two systems were causing debates within Jacobin societies and that these quarrels caused a temporary check in Jacobin growth during the winter of 1801-2. By the spring of 1802, however, Ralph Fletcher, the tireless Bolton magistrate, reported that committees had been reorganised, contributions were increasing, and sedition was expanding.[56] At the same time, one of Fletcher's spies, John Mellish ('D'), managed to get lodgings in Stockport at the same house as one of the Stockport Union Society's Irish members. He immediately began to send informative reports to Fletcher through an intermediary.[57]

The leaders of the Stockport Union Society consisted of 'several persons above the lowest rank both as to property and ability', according to Mellish. Prominent among them was William Clegg, the schoolmaster who had proved as indefatigable in his proselytising as he was cautious in recruiting new members. His caution, though it may have served to hinder the expansion of the Society, also probably helped to keep Stockport out of the Home Office reports during most of the previous year. Besides Clegg, there was Moorhouse the auctioneer; McCabe (with whom Mellish lodged), an Irishman who dressed like a gentleman and who spread the doctrines of the United Irishmen among the Irish workers of the town; a man by the name of Winn about whom little is known; and possibly Sergeant Henshall, with whom Mellish had served in the infantry. The Society flourished through the summer of 1802, a time of growing support for parliamentary reform throughout the region. In July Mellish reported that Stockport and its vicinity contained 574 (presumably sworn) Jacobins. The missionary work of Clegg and McCabe were probably supplemented by Clegg's teaching activities. Besides such practical subjects as arithmetic and navigation, he used his classroom to lecture on the British Constitution. The Society also used printed materials to help gain adherents. John Philips, the senior Stockport magistrate, was circulating William Cobbett's anti-Jacobin *Democratic Principles* (1798) in the Stockport district at about this time. Clegg answered it with *Freedom Defended*, a scathing attack on monarchs of the past (especially Louis XIV) and a ringing defence of the 'democratic' regime of Napoleon.[58] Late in June a correspondent from the West Riding complained to the Lord Lieutenant of Yorkshire about the influx of seditious literature which he believed came from Stockport.[59] All of those tracts were apparently reprints of older publications. Included were a four-page edition of *Rights of Swine* and the *Address to United Britons*, which urged its readers not to petition Parliament but to join union societies.

During the spring and summer of 1802 communication among radicals and radical groups continued. On 27 March an Irish delegate named Macginnis passed through Stockport and called on Moorhouse, who gave him letters of introduction to Buxton and Leicester. Mellish reported that 'he travelled in post chaises and appeared genteely dressed in black'. The Stockport Society sent Winn as a delegate to the National Committee which met in Soho Square, London. By 3 April he had returned with instructions for the Stockport group and plans for further correspondence between the two societies.[60] In July, Mellish reported that the union societies were in regular correspondence and that several delegations (some presumably from Stockport) had been sent into Staffordshire. The activities of Irish radicals also continued apace. Two went from Liverpool to visit an Irish group in Mottram. A fashionably dressed young man named William Putnam McCabe, a friend of Lord Edward Fitzgerald's, made various trips to the National Committee in London. While *en route* he was entertained in Stockport on at least three occasions by Moorhouse.[61]

Little can be learned about the Stockport Society after Mellish left for Nottingham in the autumn of 1802. It probably continued to exist for another year or so, that is, until after hostilities with France began anew. In October 1803 Mellish (by then in London) learned from his old colleague Sergeant Henshall that Stockport Jacobins had adopted a new oath 'to succour all Frenchmen who landed, and to use their utmost endeavours to form a new government'. In the meantime, movements of the disaffected scarcely diminished. Fletcher's spy 'B' reported from Manchester on three suspicious French travellers and on a stream of Irish delegates.[62] As a Chester magistrate complained, 'so many sloops arrive weekly from Ireland that it is an easy matter for any traitor to escape by this means from thence; or the disaffected may go from hence thither'. Even as late as August 1805 there was a report that a Dubliner was in correspondence with a Stopfordian named Bibby concerning the long-awaited invasion of Ireland by the French.[63]

After 1803, however, the Stockport Union Society faded from view. William Pitt, the inveterate anti-Jacobin, came back to power in 1804, and soon there were Stockport sedition cases appearing at the Cheshire Assizes. In December a complaint was lodged against Hugh Davies, a small master cotton spinner, for uttering various seditious expressions. He had apparently called King George a madman and said that Napoleon was better able to rule the English. Davies was indicted and found guilty at the Spring Assizes in 1805. Recognisances were taken in two sedition cases during the ensuing year, but neither case reached the indictment stage. As in the middle of the preceding decade, individual Jacobins continued to voice support for their cause. In 1805 William Clegg published another rousing tract, this one criticising the war and the Pitt ministry.[64] Yet by all appearances, co-ordinated Jacobin activities were on the wane. Even Col. Fletcher of Bolton was wondering at the end of 1805 whether he should continue to hire spies, since 'at present from the reports lately received it appears that there are no regular meetings of the disaffected in any part of this county nor I believe in the great county of York adjoining'.[65]

IV

Evidence of early radicalism in the Stockport district is not so abundant as one would like, and this relative paucity gives the impression of somewhat haphazard expansion and contraction, of short-term activity and inactivity. Historical reality presumably lies hidden behind this rather angular façade. It would be stretching the evidence beyond its proper limits, however, if one were to insist upon the existence of permanent organisations of an elaborate sort. Small, informal circles of Jacobin friends at Stockport and in certain nearby villages remained in contact with each other, but it may have been difficult to maintain (and justify) a complex organisation divided into classes and districts at times when support dwindled. The long-term trend in Jacobin fortunes was, nevertheless, one of modest expansion. The early Stockport and Bullocksmithy clubs of 1792 probably contained total memberships of only a few dozen men each. Although Bullocksmithy's Jacobins dropped from view after 1798,[66] Gee Cross had already appeared as a district Jacobin centre. The report of the spy Mellish that such Jacobin clubs contained 500 or 600 members in 1802 may have been exaggerated, but its suggestion that around one per cent of the district's population belonged to a Jacobin society at that point may be taken as a probable maximum figure.

From among this group a handful of well-educated, determined adherents carried Jacobin traditions into the new century. John Andrew is not known to have been active in any political organisation after 1792. But the famous infidel Richard Carlile visited him twice in the late 1820s and found this 'rural philosopher', now in his sixties, to be 'a man of extensive reading, deep philosophical thought, well versed in mathematics, and possessed of a fund of original idea' [*sic*]. Since early-nineteenth century *devins du village* were regarded with some esteem,[67] it seems likely that Andrew was able to win at least a small audience for his Enlightenment views in the hills of north-east Cheshire. Other early Jacobins remained more visibly involved in radical affairs. William Clegg, for example, was a prominent figure at Stockport reform meetings in 1816-17 and spoke at an anti-Corn Law meeting in 1826.[68] Abraham Cheetham's son Thomas became a leading radical in the 1810s and 1820s. James Moorhouse was especially active in radical circles in 1818-20 and was arrested for his role at Peterloo.

These early Jacobins confronted many of the internal contradictions found in later Stockport radicalism. The restoration of ancient constitutional rights within the framework of a tolerant but Christian polity co-existed with a rational republicanism which was often laced with deism or atheism. Many tactics can also be discerned, including: (1) self-help, which might involve formal classroom education, expanded knowledge of the course and meaning of current affairs, and other pursuits; (2) peaceful agitation, which encompassed propaganda campaigns of various kinds, petitions to Parliament or King, and meetings to co-ordinate such activities; (3) intimidation, which involved verbal threats of violence, the formation of clubs in which violent actions were discussed, and the conscious use of public meetings to frighten local or national authorities; and (4) violent confrontation, which could involve making or purchasing weapons, drawing up specific plans for violent actions and participation in violent episodes. Clegg and the other early adherents to the Jacobin cause never bothered to resolve these various contradictions in ends and means.

The organisational strategies of the early Jacobins likewise caused little debate and in fact, provided a ready-made pattern for later radical activities in the Stockport district. Like later clubs, Jacobin societies down to about 1805 were organised on the basis of small classes. They quickly established links with other like-minded groups in the Manchester district, the West Riding, the Metropolis and elsewhere. And Jacobin societies attempted to convert important Stockport district trades to their cause just as later radical clubs would try to do. Weavers' and spinners' complaints during the years from 1792 to 1802 certainly grew out of (and, in turn, contributed to) the same climate of discontent that led to the formation of the Stockport Friends, the Stockport United Englishmen, the Stockport Union Society and similar groups. Since weavers and spinners comprised the largest occupational groups in the district, it is not surprising to find some of them involved in Jacobin activities from time to time. Evidence of mass Jacobin support from among these groups is lacking, however. Spinners were concerned with narrow sectional problems during those years and were preoccupied with establishing, expanding and protecting their combinations. Efforts by Jacobins to win the official support of various trades in 1799–1802 by opposing the Combination Acts were without any known success in the Stockport district. Jacobin attempts to win over weavers *en masse* also failed. Around the turn of the century weavers were deeply involved in setting up their own industrial organisation and in seeking redress for their sectional grievances. These findings are in accord with those of the leading authority on English Jacobinism, who has found it 'impossible to detect, at this period, any trace of the nineteenth-century consciousness of the identity of interest between working men of different occupations . . .'[69]

It can be said, therefore, that the failure of Stockport district Jacobins to gain mass support before 1806 was related to their failure to win the allegiance of any large trade. By the same token, later advances by the radicals resulted primarily from the intermittent support of one increasingly impoverished body of workers, the handloom weavers.

[Weavers'] present pleasures soon will fade,
This every sense confirms;
Anon, the gaudy butterfly,
Must rank among the worms.

– Gas-Light (1818)

Accounts of Stockport district trade unions and Jacobin societies obviously remain incomplete without a careful examination of the handloom weavers. This group furnishes an example of a large trade which was only sporadically successful in employing the techniques of trade unionism but which became (perhaps as a direct result) intermittently involved in radical politics. The story of handloom weaving also has an intrinsic interest for any study of labour in the early Industrial Revolution because of the tumultuous and protracted character of the decline of this once-flourishing cottage industry. The story must begin with the structural problems which faced the weaving branch in the late eighteenth and early nineteenth centuries. A discussion of the means by which weavers initially but ineffectually reacted to these problems will then provide the background necessary to understand the more violent responses which followed.

I

The rise of handloom weaving has been well-documented. A fundamental technological breakthrough, Kay's flying shuttle, was introduced in the 1730s, but it gained prominence only in the 1760s and thereby provided a direct stimulus to the spinning inventions which soon followed. The next logical step, that is, further improvements in the weaving process, lagged behind. Although Edmund Cartwright attempted to perfect a powerloom in the 1780s and 1790s, it was not until the early years of the new century that significant advances were made. This meant that during the last three decades of the eighteenth century and the earliest years of the nineteenth, when the spinning jenny, water frame and mule were becoming commonplace, weaving constituted the major technological bottleneck in the burgeoning cotton textile industry. The result was an immediate and growing demand for handloom weavers, a demand easily filled because of certain characteristics of the trade. Except for the highly paid fancy and fine work, weaving was easy to learn. Looms were inexpensive, and the prices of looms seems to have declined substantially over time. There is a case of a Stockport weaver buying three looms for only £14 in 1799, but it was possible by that time for those lacking capital to rent looms.[1] In the Stockport district there seem to have been few of the 'weaving sheds' in which dozens of handloom weavers were gathered together under the watchful eye of the master manufacturer or his foreman. Weaving was thus almost wholly a domestic industry with little or no overhead beyond that which would accrue to the normal maintenance of a household.[2]

The attractiveness of handloom weaving was enhanced by the high wage rates which resulted from the growing demand for labour. As a consequence, men left off other trades or migrated, sometimes from great distances, to join the weaving branch in the Stockport district. Women and children also crowded into the trade, which they could use as a lucrative replacement for that rapidly disappearing occupation, domestic spinning. Commencing in 1793 a further impetus appeared when the French Wars began draining off adult males to serve in the army and navy. Mary Bealey of Stockport (born around 1770) married a weaver and had a total of 17 children during the period of the war. When she was interviewed as an old woman in 1841, she stated that she had brought up *all* of her children as weavers because weaving was 'a better trade when she was young than now'. From the 1790s onwards, English men, women and children were increasingly joined by Irish migrants. Ultimately, large numbers of weavers could be found in every one of the 26 townships of the district. Cotton weaving predominated in most areas, but in southern townships like Bramhall, Woodford and Disley, weaving on silk materials put out from Macclesfield may have been more important. The key distinction is said to have been between town and country weavers, with the latter often having small farms. They probably fared better than their urban counterparts in times of high food prices during the war, but ultimately they suffered more when weaving wages became so low (and poor rates so high) that they could not pay their rents. Town weavers by contrast could organise more easily to seek relief and switch more readily to alternative occupations.[3]

Despite the dazzling expansion of the weaving branch in the latter decades of the eighteenth century, the trade is most noted for the long decline that ensued. This decline can be traced in various piece rate series, which seem to have passed through stages. Each stage (after the first) was introduced by a sudden, precipitous drop in wage rates. Each of the last three stages, moreover, was characterised by piece rates at a distinctly lower level than the previous stage–the highest level in a given stage rarely exceeded the lowest level in the previous stage.[4] There were five such stages.

Stage A (1770s–1787). Although little detailed wage data are available for this period, George Unwin estimated on the basis of Stockport evidence that weavers' wage rates rose by about 50 per cent.[5] This is certainly not inconceivable, since the period witnessed the diffusion of the new spinning inventions and the growing demand for labour in the weaving branch.

Stage B (1788–1802). This period corresponded with William Radcliffe's 'golden age' and contained instances of wage levels at extraordinarily high levels, as in 1791–2, and 1802, and at least one lesser peak in 1796 or 1797. This period seems equally notable, however, for the first major buffetings of the trade cycle. Slumps occurred in 1788, 1792–4 and 1799–1801. Samuel Oldknow's weavers were earning about 50 per cent less per loom in 1794 than in 1786–7. A Stockport weaver testified before a parliamentary committee in 1800 that there had been a continuous decline in piece rates since 1795. He received 41 per cent less in 1798 than he had received in 1795 for weaving one variety of muslin; and 50 per cent less in 1800 than in 1799 for weaving lappets, another variety of muslin. Decreases of such proportions were probably not typical, but they serve to indicate the weakening position of some handloom weavers even during the 'golden age.'[6]

Stage C (1803–1815). Wages never exceeded the levels found in Stage B. This stage is also notable for its troughs (1804, 1808 and 1811–12). Although the peak in 1805 was significant, those in 1809–10 and 1814 were extremely short-lived.

Stage D (1816–25). This stage began with another major trough in

1816–17, followed by a brief upturn in 1818 and a trough in 1819. But thereafter the wage rates more or less stabilised at a level one-half to two-thirds below the 1814 level. The most notable fluctuations in 1819–25 seem to have been in employment–that is, in weavers being fully employed, only partly employed, or completely unemployed. The mass exodus from the trade began during this stage.

Stage E (1826–1830s). There is little direct evidence for Stockport piece rates during this stage. One estimate from the mid-1830s shows that total weekly earnings were three-fourths lower than they had been in 1814. This conforms to an available series of piece rates for 'Lancashire calicoes' which suggests that wage levels during Stage E were usually 70–85 per cent below the 1814 peak. The latter series also indicates slumps in 1826, 1829 and 1837; a minor peak in 1828; and a peak of fairly high wages in the mid-1830s.[7] But the exodus from the trade had reached such proportions that by the time of the latter prosperity, there were no longer many handloom weavers left in the Stockport district.

These piece rates did not, of course, translate directly into weekly wages for a given weaver. As Duncan Bythell has pointed out, weekly wages were dependent on: (1) locality, since wages were higher in and near towns and higher especially in and near Manchester; (2) the quality of the work, with fine, fancy and patterned goods fetching higher wages than coarse plain goods; (3) the individual weaver's strength, skill and application; and (4) the wage rates offered by a given firm, since rates often varied from five to 15 per cent in the same locality for the same cloth. An example of the latter can be found in the piece rates paid by Jeremiah Bury for middle grade cambric from 1802 to 1808, rates which typically differed a little and sometimes as much as one-third from those paid by John Bentley for the same cloth.[8] An individual weaver could hope to increase his weekly income by switching to a higher paying firm, moving to a different locality, working on a different sort of cloth or working longer hours. He could (and often did) add to family income by securing employment for other family members, especially in high-paying factory work. Differing options and incomes led some observers to speak of distinct 'classes' of weavers. At the time of the 1808 weavers' strike, for instance, one source mentioned three such classes, with the first earning as much as 18s. and the third as little as 7s. per week. Richard Guest stated in 1823 that the existence of a wide range of opportunities during the earliest years of the Industrial Revolution had a further effect: it produced in weavers 'a spirit of freedom and independence, and . . . a consciousness of the value of character and of their own weight and importance'.[9] Both the intensity and the content of weavers' agitations in the early nineteenth century indicate the survival of that spirit long after conditions for the weavers had begun to deteriorate.

What were the reasons for the long and occasionally tumultuous decline of the handloom weavers? A primary cause was the conflict with France (1793–1815) and the disruptions in trade and wildly fluctuating patterns of supply and demand that it engendered. For nearly a quarter of a century the spectre of war bedevilled the plans of masters and men alike. But already in the 1790s master spinners had found a way to circumvent some of these uncertainties by exporting twist, which provides a second reason for the handloom weavers' decline. Twist was the strong cotton yarn used for warps, the product of Arkwright's water frame and later of Crompton's mule. Continental countries had large weaving contingents of their own which were fully capable of using the twist to weave cotton cloth. By selling twist abroad, master spinners (some of whom were also master manufacturers) could avoid having inventories pile up in their warehouses as demand for cotton cloth declined. Twist was usually easier to market than cloth. And, as exporters were always quick to point out, there were not enough British weavers to work up all the domestically-produced twist into cloth anyway.

A third reason for the decline of the handloom weavers was what might be called the 'unresponsiveness' of the labour force to conditions in the trade, a process sometimes referred to as 'industrial involution'.[10] People did not give up handloom weaving to the extent that would have been expected by the increasingly depressed state of the trade. Some may have been inspired to continue weaving under adverse conditions by tales of the 'golden age' in which a man like William Radcliffe rose from the status of a simple weaver to that of a major industrialist and mayor of Stockport. There were, of course, numerous early examples of successful petty capitalists who controlled three or four looms and further cases of weavers who rose in the domestic system to the rank of warehouseman or putter-out.[11] For women and children, there may have been another reason to continue weaving. If they did not weave, they might have no remunerative employment whatsoever. Any supplemental income they could earn for their families was better than no extra income at all. This naturally tended to drive down the wages of adult male weavers.

Another reason for decline was the persistently small-scale organisation of the trade. Some masters, of course, stood at the head of large regiments of weavers. Oldknow had 300 in 1786–7, while William Radcliffe and John Swindells each employed 1,000 weavers in the first decade of the nineteenth century. The largest known figure for the Stockport district was that of around 1,500 employed by Jeremiah Bury in 1807.[12] But there were far more 'small masters' who might have a few dozen or just a handful of weavers working under them and who might also work as operative weavers themselves.[13] Bury blamed these small capitalists for causing the slump of 1807–8:

> Of late a custom had crept in the trade, which is, that a number of men getting into the trade without capital, these men have been encouraged to increase their trade beyond the real natural demand, their goods have been sent to Commission Houses in London, on which they have been permitted to draw to the full amount, which has enabled them to continue their trade till it has ended in bankruptcy.

Radcliffe observed that these small masters had suffered most during that slump because they did not have sufficient capital to hold back cloth from glutted markets until prices began rising.[14]

Finally, in a situation already made bleak by war, twist exports, oversupply of labour and deficient industrial organisation, the introduction of a workable steam loom in the early nineteenth century provided fatal competition for the handloom weavers. Because of the inventions of Radcliffe, Marsland and Horrocks, Stockport remained an important centre of powerloom weaving for many years. Of the four powerloom factories in England in 1806, two were at Stockport.[15] By the latter half of the 1820s, considerably more than half of the cloth produced in Stockport was woven by powerloom. The spread of the powerloom in the Stockport district thus provides a classic example of the triumphant factory mode of production contributing to the agonising decline of a once-prestigious domestic industry.

II

Weavers' responses to this decline were influenced by a long tradition of organised activity in the region. Combinations and strikes at Manchester, Oldham, Royton and Ashton have been traced from the 1740s and 1750s. A 'Stockport Weavers' Club' was in existence before 1771, and the Heaton Norris Society of Linen Weavers was established by 1773.[16] Clubs of this sort may have participated in the widespread agitations of the early 1780s which sought to enforce seven-year apprenticeships and to gain wage increases despite the wartime economic slump. When Stockport magistrates committed several striking weavers to the Middlewich House of Correction in 1781, they learned in a letter from 'Gamaliel Goodadvice' that '500 men were bound by an Oath, under a curse, that if the said [House of Correction] Keeper detained the said Persons till the time of their [the oath-takers'] coming, they would pull down the House of Correction'. By the end of 1782, weavers were taking some of these disputes to court. A masters' group, the Manchester Committee of Trade, vowed to do whatever it could to put a stop to these prosecutions. It probably succeeded in this objective less because of its own actions than because of the expansion of the cotton industry which occurred during the decade after 1782, a decade in which men, women and children flocked to the weaving trade in such large numbers that strict enforcement of apprenticeship regulations became an impossibility.[17]

There exists some evidence of combinations during the slump of the early 1790s. The broadside parody *Death of Calico Jack; or the Weavers' Downfall* first appeared at Stockport around 1792. It linked weavers' distress to the decline of the republican spirit which had characterised Oliver Cromwell's rule. In 1794 weavers in various parts of the Manchester district were trying to organise a strike.[18] But signs of solidarity among weavers became more conspicuous in the late 1790s when weavers suffered from increasing exports of twist,[19] competition from Irish immigrants, severe economic fluctuations exacerbated by war and demands for greater productivity by masters. Disputes over the latter became especially contentious and helped to break down the 'sort of familiarity . . . which in those days was the case between all *masters and men*', according to William Radcliffe.[20] During the mid-1790s masters had increased the customary length of a piece of cloth with no commensurate increase in the piece rates. In one case the increase was 20 per cent, that is, from 20 to 24 yards. Disputes came to a head in the spring of 1799 when Stockport masters published a notice condemning weavers who

> defraud the manufacturers of their property by purloining or embezzling the weft, or exchanging it for others of an inferior quality, or destroying it in a wasteful and careless manner; altering, removing or destroying the marks on their warps and stretching them to an unusual and extraordinary length to obtain large fents [*sic*]; taking part of the breadth of their warps and putting them in coarser reeds; and such like practices.[21]

For their part, operative weavers were complaining of capricious wage abatements which could not be tolerated in a period of falling piece rates.

The direct consequence of this conflict was the establishment of the Association of Weavers during April 1799 in Stockport, Bolton, Manchester and other towns. The hierarchical structure of the Association was to rest on numerous small groups or 'societies' of weavers, which chose representatives to a weavers' committee in each town. Delegates to regional meetings of the Association of Weavers were often chosen from these weavers' committees. The objects of the Association were threefold: (1) to fix wages at a moderate level which was not to be altered without the mutual consent of masters and operatives; (2) to specify more clearly wage rates on the basis of the length and breadth of the cloth; and (3) to end twist exports. The first delegate meeting appears to have been that at Bolton on 13 May 1799, with representatives attending from 13 towns, including two from the Stockport Weavers' Committee. Discussions centred on a fixed minimum wage linked to the exact size of the cloth woven. Since this in effect amounted to a wage increase, weavers urged that it be financed by an increase in the selling price of cotton cloth. Delegates also expressed their attachment to 'King and Country' and denied any contacts with Jacobin societies–a disclaimer consistent with the limited impact that Jacobins were making at that time in the Stockport district.[22]

During the summer of 1799 the Association temporarily shifted its main focus to the prohibition of twist exports. Since the campaign against twist exports was increasingly dominated by master manufacturers, the Weavers' Association must have appeared redundant. It lost support and nearly terminated its proceedings before sharp wage reductions in the autumn helped it recapture its original impetus and return to its initial concerns.[23] By the end of October the Association was planning to petition Parliament, 'that Tribunal, from which alone we expect relief' and was asking weavers to keep records of abatements and fines. A delegate meeting on 16 December published a handbill with examples of wage reductions between 1792 and 1799 ranging from 25 to 60 per cent. The text of the handbill stated that typical reductions during the period were about one-fourth or one-third.[24]

The weavers' petition was presented to the House of Commons on 5 March 1800. Weavers prayed for relief and blamed the distress that had occurred since 1792 largely on the deleterious activities of a combination, or union, of masters. This view notwithstanding, some masters simultaneously petitioned for relief of the weavers, stating that they desired a system whereby the payment of wages could be regularised and incessant disputes thereby ended. A Select Committee soon met and heard testimony from a number of Manchester district weavers, including Thomas Beaumont of Stockport. He agreed with the other witnesses that wage disputes were poorly handled. If a master and a weaver could not agree, the dispute would be taken to a magistrate. The latter, feeling himself unqualified to judge, would frequently ask the opinion of another master, who could hardly be expected to be objective. Further appeals to Quarter Sessions were usually prohibitively expensive and time-consuming for operative weavers. The result of this inquiry was the Arbitration Act of 1800. It provided that in a dispute over wages or fines, each party would choose an arbitrator to decide the issue. Only if the arbitrators could not agree would the case be submitted to a magistrate, whose decision would be final.[25]

The Cotton Arbitration Act did not in any sense work effectively. At the beginning of 1802 weavers were again petitioning Parliament, calling the Act 'totally inadequate'. They requested an act which would not simply set up arbitration procedures but which would regulate wages by statute. Masters meanwhile met at Manchester to oppose any enlargement of the Arbitration Act. In the end, they set up a committee to agitate for the Act's total repeal.[26] Dissatisfaction on both sides continued through the bountiful year of 1802 and into 1803. Weavers' delegates from 16 towns met at Bolton on 7 February of the latter year. After they elected the representative from Stockport to preside, the delegates resolved to continue to press for a strengthened Arbitration Act. Just nine days later, masters of Cheshire, Lancashire, Yorkshire and Derbyshire presented a petition to the Commons against the Act. On 21 March Stockport merchants and manufacturers sent up a separate petition urging total repeal. They stated that

> the said Act has been the source not only of vexation and oppression to the Master, by involving him in frivolous disputes with the restless and discontented part of his Servants, but also of serious injury to the Weaver, by the additional loss of time he has been obliged to submit to in bringing his disputes to a decision, and to both parties has been productive of much animosity, as well as of fruitless and expensive litigation.

On 15 June Stockport merchants and manufacturers sent up still another petition, this one opposing a parliamentary manoeuvre simply to amend the 1800 Act.[27]

In the meantime a new Select Committee had heard evidence on the matter. Perhaps the most interesting testimony came from James Wilson, a weaver of fancy and plain muslins at Stockport for 15 years. During the previous three years he had acted as an arbitrator for operatives in some 20 cases. About half were settled by the two arbitrators in favour of the weavers. The other half were appealed (always by the masters' arbitrators) to the local magistrates, and all of those cases were also settled in favour of the weavers. Wilson mentioned specific cases involving complaints against such large manufacturers as William Radcliffe and John Bentley. The Select Committee also heard from Joseph Gee, a master from Romiley. He testified that he had had no disputes before the 1800 Act but had six arbitrations after its passage and many more disputes not arbitrated. Like other Stockport district masters, he complained about the loss of time involved. Most of his cases were settled in favour of the weavers, but here, as with James Wilson, the influence of a tough, popular arbitrator may have been responsible. Gee claimed that a man called Henry Allen, 'an Irish Deserter, and a Man of bad moral character', was employed by the weavers in the Romiley area as a standing arbitrator and was paid half a guinea for each arbitration.[28]

It seems clear that due to the consistent use of forceful arbitrators, weavers were winning disputes with their masters, and the masters wanted to put a stop to it. The Select Committee Report, which was not printed until 1804, concurred. It stated that the Arbitration Act had not had the good effects intended and suggested that either magistrates or magistrates' nominees settle all future disputes. The new Arbitration Act of 1804 which resulted from this Report empowered magistrates to nominate two or three possible arbitrators for the master and two or three for the weaver. Each side was then to choose an arbitrator from among these nominees. It is not clear how the Act of 1804 functioned in the Stockport district, but John and Barbara Hammond stated that it 'seems to have been practically inoperative' in general.[29]

From 1799 to 1810 Stockport district weavers focused most of their attention on wages and directly related issues. Down to 1804, they believed that an equitable arbitration scheme might suffice to regulate piece rates. After 1805, they increasingly supported the direct regulation of wage levels by government, possibly by means of a statutory minimum wage. Many master manufacturers at first supported an arbitration measure as a means of controlling widespread abuses on the part of weavers. When they realised that the Arbitration Act of 1800 worked in favour of their operatives, masters sought to repeal the Act and simultaneously to deflect weavers' energies towards a budding movement which both masters and men could support. This was the agitation to halt the export of cotton twist and, so it was argued, thereby end the transfer of Englishmen's jobs to their Continental rivals. Master weavers like William Radcliffe, John Bentley and William Bradshaw may have regarded this movement as a means by which they could be seen supporting a measure potentially beneficial to their operatives while simultaneously opposing vexatious arbitrations. A greater supply of twist on the domestic market would also have tended to reduce their costs. Master calico printers and bleachers, like William Sykes of Edgeley, probably also joined the movement in expectation that their costs would decline. Peter Marsland and other large spinners naturally opposed the agitation since they sold much of their output overseas.

Parliamentary returns of the period understated the true amount of twist exported. Nevertheless, one series showed that while 7,051 cwt. of twist were exported in 1798, the figure rose to 30,815 cwt. in 1799 and to over 50,000 cwt. in 1800. Another return indicated that the latter figure had doubled by 1804-5.[30] These alarming increases inspired a flood of pamphlets and broadsides[31] and prompted the convening of two Manchester meetings during the spring of 1800. A contingent of Stockport industrialists participated in the meetings and supported the resulting anti-export memorial sent to the Lords of the Treasury. They subsequently held a meeting of their own in Stockport. But opponents of the anti-export faction, notably the representatives of the large spinning houses, rallied support at a separate Manchester meeting on 6 May.[32] This fundamental division within the cotton trade itself helped to assure that little would be done to limit twist exports. It was during this debate that an anonymous writer in the *Manchester Mercury* of 6 May advocated that weaving be mechanised in order to help resolve the deadlock. William Radcliffe was soon at work on his powerloom in part to provide the means to manufacture more twist in Britain.

Although thwarted in 1800, the opponents of twist exports did not give up. It has been claimed that the anti-export faction promoted the restrictions on work-hours in the 1802 Factory Act in order to limit the output of cotton twist and yarn.[33] Amid another flurry of pamphlet literature the main debate revived in 1803 just as the Arbitration Act was again becoming a matter of parliamentary concern. An especially compelling argument emerged from the spinning faction that a limit on British twist exports would hurt the domestic spinning industry while stimulating foreign (and above all, French) spinning interests, which had been growing at a prodigious rate.[34] While William Radcliffe remained the Stopfordian most visibly opposed to such views, William Horrocks, an MP for Preston, emerged as the movement's national leader. Early in March 1803 Horrocks invited Radcliffe and some others to Preston for a parley on the issue. Later in the month Horrocks introduced a bill in the Commons and spoke on behalf of the cause. But Prime Minister Addington would have nothing to do with it because he believed, incorrectly, that the export of twist from Britain was negligible.

Little else happened until the following spring. In March 1804, while Radcliffe was in London taking out one of his powerloom patents, masters and weavers held a meeting in Stockport and resolved that the export of twist was the chief reason for their distress. They decided to petition the Commons to tax twist exports and eventually gained 10,000 or more signatures in support of the measure. The president and secretary of the meeting were John Bentley, a master, and William Bradshaw, a master who sometimes acted as an arbitrator for other masters. Both men had been involved in bitter arbitration disputes.[35] They immediately sent a message to

Radcliffe asking him to find out from Addington whether Horrocks' 1803 bill was to be proceeded with or not. The result was a meeting between Addington and Radcliffe. The Prime Minister reiterated his contention that the amount of twist exported was relatively small and requested that petitioning on the subject be halted. Radcliffe presented a rather spirited defence of the anti-export movement. He claimed that four-fifths of the 'piece goods' exported each year were really twist in falsely labelled packages. As a result of such practices, moreover, fewer looms were at work than two years before, and 'those still at the loom are very much distressed indeed'. Wages had been reduced by one-half during that same period. However sympathetic he might have been, Addington was forced from office within a few weeks after this meeting and, once again, the whole effort came to naught.[36]

After the defeat of the anti-export initiative and the passage of the new Arbitration Act in 1804, weavers were said to have concentrated their energies on two specific programmes. The first came to the attention of the Home Office through the spy 'B' who was strategically located at Manchester, and from 'B' through Col. Fletcher of Bolton. The story was one of a 'new' weavers' organisation, which, in its inter-urban links, closely resembled the Association of Weavers. Fletcher learned that the object of this new organisation was to protect weavers from their masters. Hence, it seems to have been a direct consequence of the new Arbitration Act. Fletcher nevertheless lumped it together with a second programme involving subscriptions and petitions against the Corn Law of 1804.[37] It is unclear to what extent Fletcher's analysis held true for the Stockport district. Stockport's anti-Corn Law petition, which was presented to Parliament in February 1805, complained that the 1804 Corn Law 'has contributed to cause the advance in the price of Corn and Bread Flour, and if the same should continue in force, it will perpetuate this grievance, whereby many branches of Manufactures will be transferred from Great Britain to other nations'.[38] The tone is that of the anti-twist export forces; the petition is stated to be from 'manufacturers' and others of the town and neighbourhood of Stockport. It is not known whether operative weavers joined masters in this agitation, which may have been another effort to divert weavers' attention away from the issue of wage arbitrations. In any case, the movement was not long-lived. The ensuing year passed with hardly a sign of activity from the anti-Corn Law forces, from the weavers, or from their covert association.

III

By the end of 1806 there were signs that another slump in the cotton trade had begun. During that winter the weavers of Cheshire, Lancashire, Yorkshire and Derbyshire again launched a petitioning campaign for wage regulations throughout the trade. In the petition presented to the Commons on 26 February 1807, weavers complained that wage reductions caused them to work longer hours and produce more cloth, only to glut the market further. But weavers' complaints did not stand a chance of gaining statutory redress after master manufacturers publicly opposed any regulatory measures at a Manchester meeting on 12 March. A few months later Radcliffe took the opportunity to renew his campaign against twist exports. He prepared a paper entitled 'Remarks on the Evils of Exportation of Cotton Twist', for the Chancellor of the Exchequer. The document concisely rehearsed most of the arguments advanced from 1799 to 1804.[39] Yet while many weavers had embraced the masters' anti-export campaigns in 1799 and 1804, they now ignored Radcliffe's proposals. They perhaps sensed that even in the best of circumstances, a decline in twist exports would not provide an immediate solution to the problems of Stockport district weavers. Furthermore, if all the twist spun in Britain were also woven in Britain, it would only increase the glut of finished cloth, which many observers thought to be a major part of the problem. There was, in any case, little chance that a prohibition of twist exports would gain parliamentary approval in the face of stiff opposition from master spinners throughout Britain.

Most weavers wanted some sort of wage regulation, although this objective was temporarily combined with political agitations fostered by Stockport's radical coterie. The latter seems to have been aroused from its lethargy by the advent of the Ministry of All the Talents after the death of Pitt in 1806; by the elections of Sir Francis Burdett and Lord Cochrane to Parliament from 'radical Westminster' in 1807; and by the concomitant parliamentary reform agitations which occurred in both London and the West of England. When these agitations took root in the North, however, they were transformed into an anti-war movement. The editors of the *Manchester Gazette* explained that political reform could not be a practical objective while the war dragged on. This focus on opposition to the war gained some support from weavers, to whom wartime trade disruptions must have seemed a more logical cause of distress than did constitutional defects.[40] During the winter of 1807-8 an anti-war movement emerged at Stockport and many of Manchester's other satellite towns. William Clegg, the Jacobin schoolmaster active since the mid-1790s, served as secretary at an Ashton delegate meeting on 23 November at which it was decided to petition Parliament to end the war. A series of local meetings followed, including one held in Stockport on 11 January 1808 against the wishes of the local magistrates. Although attacked in print by the curate of Didsbury,[41] among others, the petitioners were publicly supported by Lt. Col. Joseph Hanson, a former commander of the Manchester Volunteer Rifle Corps who had resigned his post in part because of his anti-war sentiments. Hanson's *Defence of the Petitions for Peace* was in its third edition by March 1808, and was circulating at Stockport, Bolton and other towns.[42] The republican *Death of Calico Jack* was also circulating again as it had been in the early 1790s.

Over 12,000 weavers and spinners allegedly signed the Stockport petition for peace which was presented to the Commons on 26 February. Fletcher, the Bolton magistrate, perceived that at that point, the anti-war movement became detached from the weavers' agitations.[43] This was probably an accurate portrayal of the situation at Stockport, where a small group of radicals continued proselytising while the mass of weavers shifted its support from the anti-war agitation, which seemed to have little hope of success, to the minimum wage agitation, whose prospects seemed unusually bright.

From 1805 to 1808 piece rates paid for most types of weaving in the Stockport district fell by approximately 50 per cent. In parliamentary testimony given in the spring of 1808 William Radcliffe stated that some weavers were working 18 hours a day in order to survive.[44] It is thus understandable that even as they were signing the radicals' peace petition, weavers were preparing another, quite different petition on the subject of wages. The supplication of the journeymen cotton weavers of England, presented to Parliament on 19 February 1808, was more desperate in its tone than the petition they had presented a year earlier. The weavers noted that while increased wages in other trades 'correspond with the increased prices of provisions', weavers' wages had fallen behind. They consequently requested a universal minimum wage in weaving to alleviate their mounting distress.[45]

Manchester district masters (including representatives from Stockport) met ten days later to discuss the proposal. Out of that and subsequent meetings emerged an unprecedented decision by certain masters to support a minimum wage. Jeremiah Bury, one of Stockport's most compassionate manufacturers, gave three reasons for this decision before a Select Committee: (1) a minimum wage would prevent weavers from going on the parish rates; (2) it would tend to prevent over-production; and (3) it would make wages uniform in different regions. He complained about the long hours weavers had to work and stated that 'there was never a time before the present when the Workman could not live by his trade'. Bury also included with his testimony a letter from other Stockport masters who were somewhat sceptical of the minimum wage proposal. It was signed by John Bentley, William Bradshaw, Robert Parker, Jr and John Swindells.[46] Thus, as before, there existed a group of local masters who thought that there should be no government interference between masters and men in the determination of wages.

The response in the House of Commons to a minimum wage bill overwhelmingly reflected the latter sentiments. When George Rose requested leave to bring in such a bill on Thursday, 19 May, one MP reasoned aloud that the weavers' distress resulted not from low wages but from the fact that wages had once been too high and had lured too many people into weaving. Sir Robert Peel argued that the loss of foreign markets, not wages, lay at the root of the problem. With others rising to speak along the same lines, Rose finally saw fit to withdraw his motion. News of Parliament's rebuff reached Stockport over the weekend. In a year far worse than 1803 or 1804, and worse too than the disastrous year 1807, the weaver's last remaining chance for relief had been taken away. Coming as it did when the prices of flour and oatmeal were soaring, Parliament's rejection left Stockport weavers without a minimum wage and with the prospect of not having enough money even to buy basic provisions.[47]

Early on the morning of Monday, 23 May, a large crowd of weavers made clear what their response would be. They gathered at Edgeley, the Irish weavers' enclave, and then moved to a spot close to the Lancashire Hill factory of Jeremiah Bury. There, some Irishmen set forth what was to become the pattern of strike activity for the following three weeks. They 'proposed that no more work should be done without an advance in wages and that the weavers should continue such meetings with a view of frightening the masters into a compliance'.[48] The crowd then moved south into Stockport carrying a standard, groaned and hissed as they passed John Bentley's warehouse, insulted the magistrates in the Market Place, and moved out of town before a troop of dragoons arrived from Manchester. True to their word, the weavers assembled the next day and vowed to meet in ten times greater numbers the following day at Manchester.

That Wednesday marked the climax of the early phase of the weavers' strike. At Stockport weavers again assembled on Lancashire Hill, where they were told by William Dawson (a sympathetic master manufacturer like Jeremiah Bury) to persevere in their demands but to remain peaceable. The magistrates were fully prepared for the proceedings and quickly arrested Dawson, who was later sentenced to 18 months in prison. The magistrates also called out the dragoons to put a stop to the crowd's intimidation of men trying to work in factories. Some of these weavers probably helped to swell the ranks of the Manchester meeting on St George's Field later that day. The meeting attracted 10,000 or 15,000 people, with the Irish foremost among them. Joseph Hanson, the ex-commander of the Manchester Rifle Corps, spoke with evident emotion to the throng: 'Your cause is good, stick to your cause. I will support you as far as £3,000, and if that will not do I will go further.' A delegate was then sent to meet with the boroughreeve and town officers, but the latter refused to treat with an unlawful assembly and soon arrived on the scene with dragoons. According to *The Times*, the people cried, 'we have nothing to eat; and unless our wages are raised, we might as well play and starve as work and be famished.' Their cries went unheard. In a scene prefiguring the events of Peterloo, dragoons moved relentlessly through the crowd, wounding at least a dozen people with their swords, shooting dead an Irishman who threw brick-bats and severely wounding another.

The magistrates had their sights on the ringleaders. Hanson was arrested, found guilty at the ensuing Lancashire Assizes for aiding the rioters, sentenced to six months imprisonment, and fined £100. Stockport weavers did not soon forget him. They helped to subscribe the forty thousand pennies used to purchase a special commemorative cup for Hanson, and on his release from Marshalsea Prison in November 1809, they greeted him as a returning hero:

> On his approaching Stockport, the multitude rent the air with shouts of joy at beholding him; . . . his horses were taken out, and preceded by an excellent band of music, colours flying, &c. the

populace drew him from thence to the top of Manchester Hill . . . .

This same contemporary account adds that people 'literally lined the road from Stockport to Manchester'.[49]

The debacle on St George's Field failed to intimidate Stockport weavers. On the next day, 26 May, they again assembled on Lancashire Hill where they were joined by many of their fellow weavers from the countryside. The magistrates heard from weavers' delegates that the purpose of the meeting was merely to assure the crowd that their masters intended to redress their grievances and that no further meetings were needed. Everything proceeded peaceably, and after being addressed by a weaver named Wright Sixsmith, the crowd dispersed. Despite a warning notice published by the magistrates, an even larger meeting was held on the same spot the following day. Stockport magistrates responded by repeating the two-pronged attack (against the weavers' leadership first, then against the crowd) which had been so effective two days before. At the first hint of a meeting, they arrested Sixsmith and convicted him at Petty Sessions for an illegal combination. Sixsmith later appealed to Quarter Sessions, but Stockport magistrates agreed to drop the prosecution if he would enter into a six-month recognisance for good behaviour.[50] The crowd assembling on Lancashire Hill again contained many country weavers, some complaining that they had been forced to attend by their neighbours. Magistrates proceeded with regular troops and Volunteers to disperse them and then to break up a throng in the Market Place. On Saturday, several weavers assembled at six o'clock in the morning to prevent workers at Spencer, Haigh and Co. (successors to the bankrupt William Radcliffe) from going to work at the new powerlooms, but constables and dragoons prevented violence.

It had been a turbulent week. The Rev. Prescot and another magistrate reported to the Home Office on the same Saturday that the town and neighbourhood

> have been under continual alarm and terror, owning to great bodies of weavers being assembled for the purpose of obliging the manufacturers to raise their wages, and in the meantime neither working themselves, nor suffering others to work, and of course their families starving. . . .

Their additional remark, that 'the evil seems to be spreading at present into the neighbouring towns and country . .',[51] reflects the urban-to-rural shift in the gradually widening strike. In the face of widespread and constant pressure, the masters of the greater Manchester district decided to form another committee to try to redress the weavers' grievances. More than 300 masters met on 31 May and decided to offer increases averaging 20 per cent, although no guarantees could be given regarding full employment.[52] Whether consciously intended by the masters or not, this offer helped to break down the tenuous sense of unity achieved by the weavers during the preceding week. The combination had been fragile from the start, with many weavers, especially those in outlying areas, showing reluctance to join the strike. At this point, even many of the striking weavers decided to abandon the cause and accept the proposed settlement. In so far as they could avoid the harassment of their fellow weavers, they began to return to their looms.

Stockport weavers planned to meet and discuss the wage offer on 1 June. While there is no evidence regarding the meeting, it is clear from subsequent events that there existed a dissident faction which was determined, like similar factions in other towns, to remain on strike. On 2 June the dissidents circulated a handbill which denied that any agreement had been reached and stated their own demands for an increase in wages of one-third and payment by the yard according to length, breadth and strength of the finished cloth. Over the next ten days they held scattered meetings, but these were generally smaller than before. Stockport, like most of the greater Manchester district, was assuming a fairly calm appearance. Wages had gone up, grain prices had fallen, and Richard Farington, the Didsbury magistrate, could write to the Home Office that 'all serious apprehensions have subsided. We have reason to believe that the numbers inclined to work are daily increasing.'[53]

Despite the prudent watchfulness of the authorities, tensions suddenly heightened a few days later. On 13 June there was a large meeting near Stockport, and that same night, work in the looms of a weaver at Stockport and of another at Edgeley was destroyed by oil of vitriol. The next day a crowd collected by shouts at Edgeley and marched off to Cheadle Heath. There, a young stranger addressed the assembly and assured it that all work had stopped at Chowbent, which was presumably his home township. The weavers were now demanding a 20 per cent wage increase agreed to by *all* the masters. Later cross-examinations revealed that most of the people attended on 14 June to see whether an agreement had finally been reached. In the meantime, all work was to cease. The crowd moved from Cheadle to Gatley in Stockport Etchells and finally to Cross Acres Green in Northenden Etchells, by which time it numbered over 200 persons. Along the way small detachments visited weavers and forced them to stop work and join the crowd. One case was reported of a shuttle being confiscated to prevent further weaving.[54]

All this time the magistrates had been assembling a band of special constables and Volunteers to follow the trail of the crowd. They caught up with them at Cross Acres Green and took 62 persons into custody (including one errant member of the Stockport Volunteers)[55] plus three more persons on the road back and one in Stockport. These latter four had loudly urged the captives to resist. Of this quartet, a Dissenting minister from Gatley and a fairly substantial weaver from Stockport were prosecuted at the Summer Assizes for conspiracy. Of the 20 others from the main group of protesters who were committed, only the Volunteer and eleven others were ultimately prosecuted. The authorities were clearly continuing to make some attempt to select for prosecution those who would serve as the best examples.[56]

The next day proved to be similarly productive for the forces of order. Stockport weavers held a meeting one mile outside of town along the banks of the Goyt river at Thatcher's Wood, a spot selected to foil any use of the cavalry which had proved so effective against them the day before. About 100 of them discussed their grievances without interruption, but they were met on the way back to town by pistol-wielding special constables, who managed to surround 59 of the weavers and take them into custody. Nine were finally prosecuted at the Summer Assizes, making a total of 23 prosecutions arising out of the events of 14-15 June.[57] Although the authorities remained vigilant and the Volunteers continued on duty until early July, all impetus was taken from the weavers' strike in the Stockport district by these arrests and by the continuing improvement in the cotton trade. The latter was aided by the Spanish rebellion and the consequent opening of the South American and Iberian markets and by the relaxation of the Continental System by a France preoccupied with the deteriorating Peninsular situation.[58]

IV

Richard Farington informed the Home Office that secret committees directed the strike at such satellite towns as Bury, Rochdale and Ashton. Was this true of Stockport? Available evidence suggests that it probably was. The strike was characterised by a precise plan of action, by strict discipline and by an absence of violence.[59] The guiding plan (presented to the crowd assembled on Lancashire Hill on the first day of the strike) seems to have encompassed the peaceful enforcement of the strike through frequent public meetings at which leaders would dictate future actions and exhort the weavers to stay out; and through the use of roving bands to stop work in the outlying townships. Besides 'frightening the masters into compliance', these tactics comprised ingenious responses to the problems facing a strike in an industry dispersed in cellars and cottages over dozens of square miles.

It is obvious that the major strike meetings were planned in advance. On 13 June while taking out warp, a weaver and his wife were stopped by a group of weavers who told them to return the warp and attend a meeting the next day to find out the proper prices for weaving. The two periods of most fervent activity (23-31 May and 14-15 June) both began with a crowd collecting at Edgeley. The Crown Brief prepared for one of the prosecutions suggests that a similar plan was used for the 15 June meeting:

> The manner in which [the 15 June meeting] was convened was observed – district delegates or active individuals of the weavers went to the different parts of the town to give notice of the time of such meetings and small groups were soon going from every quarter of the town towards a place called Thatcher's Wood . . . .[60]

Since this Brief was made up not of spies' reports but of depositions of constables and other local observers, its accuracy on this point can probably be accepted.

There was also a financial problem facing local organisers: how could an impoverished workforce afford to strike? Farington reported rumours of 'a considerable fund' to be used by strikers, but its source was unknown. Such a fund apparently did exist at Stockport. When a weaver was forced to stop work on 14 June at Cross Acres Green, he protested to the crowd that he had to support his family. The crowd's leaders told him that there was a subscription to help unemployed weavers and that he should apply to it. By 9 June Farington received news that such funds were dwindling and that 'applications are making for assistance from the funds of friendly societies, but these I think must prove as fruitless as illegal, for there are few if any consisting wholly of weavers'. This conjecture proved faulty, and five days later he reported to the Home Office:

> In some instances I learn the weavers have drawn money from their friendly societies' funds. Several of these in this neighbourhood have not their rules inrolled [*sic*] at the Sessions, and of course are not under the cognizance of the magistrates.[61]

Of special interest in the Stockport district was the Artificers' Society, which had met at the Joiners' Arms in Stockport since at least 1777. Its rules were re-examined and approved by Quarter Sessions on 10 July 1808, but this document has a further endorsement: 'delivered by Mr. Lloyd of Stockport for examination, 5 October 1808'. This Society was clearly of interest to the authorities, and a perusal of the membership list suggests the reason. Among the 60 names were James Wilson, a long-time weavers' spokesman, and William Torkington – both of whom were tried at the Summer Assizes for their leading role in the weavers' strike. At least one other member of the Artificers' Society, William Wood, can be identified as a member of the 1808 crowd.[62] Here then is a club which could have been a centre for the direction of the 1808 weavers' strike at Stockport.

There is further evidence that the weavers had a recognised set of leaders. Owen Coyle of Edgeley attended the first weavers' meeting on 23 May and may have been one of the Irishmen to address the crowd on that occasion. He was observed at many meetings thereafter, was finally apprehended at the 14 June meeting, and was one of the handful chosen to be prosecuted. Three more of the latter choices – James Wilson, Thomas Chadwick and Robert Green – had previously attended a 10 June meeting at Wood's Moor and had promised not to meet again. A fifth person apprehended on 14 June, James Jervis, also had a record of activity. On 25 May he had been reported to the magistrates as having led 100 weavers on strike against Robert Parker, a master known to oppose minimum wage demands. Two magistrates convicted Jervis on 6 June and sentenced him to three months in Chester Castle.

But Jervis gave notice of an appeal to Quarter Sessions and remained at liberty – hence his continued activity and his re-arrest on 14 June. He ultimately had the strike conviction quashed and escaped prosecution on the later charge.[63]

Jervis, Thomas Chadwick and others active in 1808 continued to participate in workers' movements for years thereafter. Jervis, for example, spoke at the massive political meeting held in Stockport in the summer of 1819 and had his son baptised by the radical Parson Harrison in the following spring. Chadwick participated in reform meetings in 1816-17, was identified by Samuel Bamford after Peterloo as a long-time friend to radicalism and, as a member of the Stockport infidel club in 1821-2, frequently contributed to collections for the imprisoned freethinker, Richard Carlile.[64] William Wood was visible in Stockport radical circles in 1818-20, when he was described as an 'old committeeman'. According to a spy, he was advocating revolution immediately after Peterloo, but he fell in with the Stockport infidels during the 1820s. Joseph Sherwin, to give but a final example, served on the Stockport Weavers' Committee from about 1811 to 1824 and in that capacity supported Luddism and many subsequent radical campaigns.[65] Individual weavers had participated in Jacobin activities for short periods during the 1790s and early 1800s. But from 1808 onwards, there existed a cadre of weavers whose careers in radical movements can be traced for a number of years. Although this group probably supported the Stockport anti-war petition of 1808, it was not able to divert weavers' attention from their primary concern over wages for any length of time. Furthermore, the radicals failed to attract the official public support of the Weavers' Committee or the unofficial support of significant numbers of weavers for anti-war or parliamentary reform movements for many years thereafter. In other words, the existence of a radical faction among the weavers in 1808 should not be taken as proof that the mass of the weavers in the Stockport district embraced radical ideologies at that time.

The weavers had nevertheless made important advances in a period of downward cyclical fluctuations in piece rates and real wages. Before 1799 there had been combinations at Stockport and other towns, but there seems to have been little co-ordination among the various towns. Such co-ordination became the rule during the years from 1799 to 1808, probably in part to compensate for organisational weaknesses within local jurisdictions. In 1809 there was evidence of inter-regional co-operation. Specifically,

Scottish weavers joined with those of Lancashire and Cheshire in petitioning Parliament for a minimum wage. During the early nineteenth century, British weavers may also have had formal contacts with weavers in Ireland.[66] Two minor themes also characterised those years. The first was the growing prominence of Edgeley and of its Irish weavers, especially in the strike of 1808. The other theme involved the increasingly visible role which women played in the weavers' struggles, if a *Times*' comment can be accepted:

> The women are, if possible, more turbulent and mischievous than the men. Their insolence to the soldiers and special constables is intolerable, and they seem to be confident of deriving impunity from their sex.[67]

If this were so, then it must not have been surprising to contemporaries when the female image played an important role at a climactic moment of the Luddite upheavals.

...1812 opens with a gloom altogether so frigid and cheerless, that hope itself is almost lost and frozen in the prospect. – *Manchester Gazette* (4 January 1812)

One of the most vivid memories of my childhood is hearing [my grandmother] tell how her mother received the news that the mills had been set on fire and the mob was making for the house. The old coachman hurried the family into the carriage – and as they drove over the brow of the hill, they looked back to see their home in flames. – Lillian Baylis, great-granddaughter of John Goodair (1926)

The spectacular outbreaks of Luddism in the Stockport district comprised a part of 'Lancashire Luddism', a regional phenomenon involving activities besides machine breaking, or Luddism in its narrowest sense, and activities in east Cheshire as well as Lancashire. Recent historical work on Lancashire Luddism has been characterised by a considerable degree of perplexity. E.P. Thompson has correctly emphasised the problems involved in dealing with a number of different movements and types of public disorders which 'took place simultaneously, sometimes spontaneously, and often with no direct organizational connection with each other'.[1] At the opposite end of the ideological spectrum, Malcolm Thomis has written in the same vein, concluding that 'of all the areas associated with Luddism, unquestionably the one which poses the most difficulties for the historian is Lancashire...'[2]

None of the available accounts has provided a systematic treatment of Luddism in the Stockport district despite the fact that one writer has called it 'the centre of the agitation' and another has observed (probably accurately) that 'the impulse for the adoption of violent tactics seems to have come initially from Stockport'.[3] With a massive body of handloom weavers threatened by mechanisation, Stockport and its district would seem to provide an ideal case study for analysing conflicting interpretations. Two viewpoints may be treated briefly at the outset. There is no evidence from the

Stockport district that Luddism was the product of government spies and *agents provocateurs*, which is in keeping with findings in most parts of the cotton districts. The Hammonds' contrary view, based largely on the activities of John Stones at Bolton, is no longer widely accepted as an explanation for most of the disturbances. It is true that the government spy 'B' (William Bent, a Manchester cotton waste dealer) occasionally visited the Stockport district and submitted rather exaggerated accounts of what was occurring there. But those who emphasise indigenous workers' agitations can find much more support from the Stockport district than those who would stress the role of mercenary *provocateurs*.[4]

Religious conflicts played a role which was only slightly more important. Two episodes deserve mention. In 1811 Lord Sidmouth tried to secure new regulations for Dissenting ministers which would have been especially restrictive for itinerant ministers of the kind found in most branches of Methodism. Nearly all Dissenting groups opposed the suggested legislation, and two of the leading opponents were familiar figures in Stockport. Stockport Dissenters also had another grievance at this juncture, the rebuilding of the parish church under a special 1810 Act of Parliament. The Act outraged the local Dissenting interest because it authorised the taxation of both Anglicans and non-Anglicans throughout the parish. Included among the trustees carrying out the Act was William Radcliffe, a subsequent target of the Luddites.[5] Still, there is no evidence of a Dissenting chapel acting as a Luddite command post or furnishing significant numbers of recruits to the Luddite cause. Contemporaries did not note a Dissenting strain in Stockport district Luddism nor can one be recovered from the available names of local Luddites. Many Dissenters probably shared the confusion and fear that one Methodist expressed in an April 1812 diary entry:

> Such times as present I believe none now living upon earth
> ever knew, the people of lower orders are relinquishing their
> employments, breeding tumults, and committing
> outrages . . . what will be done I cannot tell but something
> terrible is expected . . .[6]

Religious disputes in 1810-12 contributed to a sense of local discontent. And they may have added to the reluctance of many Dissenters to help the predominantly Anglican forces of order.

Peter Marsland, a prominent industrialist, a JP and a Unitarian, was not at all involved in quelling Luddite disturbances, for example. But religious differences did no more than to help set the stage. They can not be regarded as direct causes of Stockport Luddism.

Other approaches to the subject require more careful scrutiny. For the purposes of analysis, it may be useful to distinguish four interpretive foci which are neither mutually exclusive nor directly translatable into 'schools of thought'. As already indicated, contemporary observers and subsequent commentators often combined parts of two or more interpretations with the result being that there exist about as many 'schools' as there are interpretive combinations. Malcolm Thomis, for example, seems to have arrived at a four-part causal hierarchy with general economic distress being the most important, and criminal depredations, industrial grievances and co-ordinated political activities following in descending order.[7] To be sure, few if any accounts of Lancashire Luddism have omitted economic conditions. The price of provisions was extremely high in 1811-13, leading to food riots in many parts of Lancashire and east Cheshire.[8] At the same time, decreased exports of cotton goods caused great economic distress in the cotton districts.[9] It is unclear, however, to what extent economic trends could have dictated the timing or the forms of public disorders. Other explanations must also be taken into account.

Some have emphasised the role of criminals and other marginal men as central to the Luddite phenomenon. According to this view, robbers and arsonists used the prevailing distress and the cloak of Luddism to intensify their criminal activities. Thomis views Luddism as part of a veritable 'crime wave'. The Irish have also been singled out as leading instigators. In February 1812 John Lloyd stated that 'the bad spirit is kept up by some few desperate characters from Ireland . . .'[10] The implication of these views is that Luddism had a limited following with limited and selfish objectives. A third line of interpretation focuses on the role of specific grievances in certain occupations. The declining wages of the handloom weavers during a period when powerlooms were being introduced nearly always figures prominently in discussions of Lancashire Luddism. G.D.H. Cole concluded that Luddite disorders 'were never more than incidents or auxiliaries of strike action.' His student, E.J. Hobsbawm, has expanded upon this theme, calling Luddism 'collective bargaining by riot' and asserting that it contributed to a sense of 'working-class' solidarity.[11] By contrast, Malcolm

Thomis and Frank Darvall have questioned the extent to which industrial outbursts were well-organised or conducive to long-term growth of class feeling.[12]

Both Thomis and Darvall extend their doubts to a fourth area of controversy, the political dimensions of Luddism. There is evidence that Luddite objectives ranged from obtaining parliamentary reform to fomenting insurrection, which in turn necessitated drilling, arming and a high degree of planning and co-ordination. Debate continues on the subject of how widespread and organised Luddism really was. One contemporary source characterised it as merely a 'vague spirit of misrule and insubordination'. Major General Thomas Maitland, in rejecting general economic conditions as the primary cause of Luddism, came to believe that there existed a specific 'combination to overcome all Legal Authority'. But he was convinced that the combination was neither so large nor so effective as many believed. J.R. Dinwiddy claims, on the contrary, that Luddism elicited more support from northern workers for political agitation than any previous movement in the Industrial Revolution. John Foster characterises Luddism in Oldham as a 'political strike by the weavers and a full-scale attack on the yeomanry' which, though unsuccessful, amounted to a veritable 'guerilla campaign'. E.P. Thompson has concentrated on the seemingly large degree of co-ordination among different Luddite activities (political agitations and machine breaking, for instance), among different trades and among different towns and regions. Noting that 'sheer insurrectionary fury has rarely been more widespread in English history', he comes to regard Luddism as a true rising of the people.[13]

I

Even a cursory examination of the available secondary literature shows that Stockport district Luddism contained representatives of the economically distressed, marginal men, industrial protesters and political radicals ranging from peaceful reformers to 'intimidationists' to revolutionaries. No acceptable account can deny the complexity of motivations and goals. It may, nevertheless, be useful to begin by examining the occupational group most in distress, the handloom weavers. Nominal piece rates for weaving in the Stockport district peaked at relatively high levels in late 1809 or early 1810 and again in 1814. In 1812 they were in a trough about one-quarter or one-third lower than either of those peaks. At the same time prices of provisions were increasing at rapid rates, especially in late 1811 and early 1812. Weavers' real wages consequently plummeted, perhaps by 40 per cent or more from 1809 to 1812. Some sense of the weavers' relative position can be obtained from a petition presented to Parliament by Stockport industrialists who stated that 'for some years past, the Wages of that very numerous, useful, and ingenious [*sic*] class, have averaged less by far than those of the lowest species of day-labourer . . .'[14]

Weavers could already sense the downward pressures on piece rates during the course of 1810. Rather than embark on another big strike like that which had only partially succeeded in 1808, weavers chose at this juncture to convince masters to keep wages up. The main target was one of the largest maufacturing firms, John Swindells and Son. Two leaders of the weavers, Thomas Bentley and Samuel Brooks, published an anonymous handbill, *Plain Facts,* in July 1810. In it they claimed that the Swindells were almost invariably the first to lower wages and that they had tried to lower wages as early as February 1810 but were pressured into rescinding the abatement by fellow manufacturers. In May they had reduced wages with more success. Bentley and Brooks finally called for a work stoppage by Swindells' one thousand weavers in order to gain higher wages. The Swindells' countered with a libel suit at the Summer Assizes directed against *Plain Facts.*[15] Neither side could claim victory in the struggle, since the legal suit was never brought to trial, the strike apparently never materialised, and wages remained depressed. Interestingly enough, weavers did not espouse radical programmes at this time despite the fact that the radical Thomas Cheetham acted as one of two sureties for Bentley in the libel suit.

From the autumn of 1810 to the summer of 1811 diminished trade prospects in both South America and the restricted Continental markets continued to force one manufacturer after another to lower wages and lay off employees. The Stockport Weavers' Committee directed efforts locally to solicit relief and co-operated with committees in other towns to devise additional measures. The Manchester Weavers' Committee was especially active, announcing in November 1810 its finding that unemployment had reached one-quarter of the total populations of such towns as Stockport, Blackburn and Preston.[16] Early in 1811 the Stockport Weavers' Committee formally applied to the magistrates for increased relief measures. The magistrates demurred but suggested that the weavers apply to the national government, a tactic the weavers were probably already considering. A petition was drawn up and signed by Thomas Bentley 'on behalf of about 8,000 weavers'. It stated that many weavers had been forced onto the poor rates because of the rapid decline in wages during the preceding six months and that the direct intervention of the Prince Regent was needed. The petition was taken up to London in April by Joseph Sherwin (a participant in the 1808 strike) and another weaver. They gained an audience with the Home Secretary, Richard Ryder, who urged them to 'have patience'. The petition was then forwarded to the Board of Trade, but the Board decided 'that it was unaware of any measures that could be taken to relieve the weavers . . .'[17]

The degree of co-ordination observable in 1810–11 leaves little doubt that delegates from weavers' committees in different towns met to plan future actions.[18] There is no evidence, however, of a parliamentary reform movement somehow concealed within this system despite the fact that, as Ralph Fletcher of Bolton stated, widespread unemployment furnished radicals with 'great opportunities of instilling disaffection into the lower orders'. His misgivings prompted him to obtain Home Office permission to hire spies to infiltrate workers' groups throughout the greater Manchester district. Among them was the infamous 'B'[19]

II

From the autumn of 1811 to about the middle of March 1812 outbreaks of public disorders seemed a distinct possibility, especially at the beginning and the end of the period. The deficient harvest of 1811, further declines in handloom weavers' wages and a diminution in the amount of work available to weavers helped to create an explosive situation. While weavers saw virtually no prospect of relief emanating from Westminster, beleaguered Stockport manufacturers likewise offered little solace. One of the most active, William Radcliffe, renewed his foredoomed campaign to limit the export of twist and simultaneously sought to speed up the introduction of powerlooms. He hoped thereby to convince the major spinning firms to have their twist woven in England. This must have seemed peculiar, if not reprehensible, to distressed handloom weavers who felt directly threatened by powerlooms. In other words, the situation had changed since 1809 when weavers had affirmed that 'the well-intentioned part of the Master Manu-facturers have long lamented, and done their utmost to ameliorate the situation' of their distressed employees.[20] In the autumn of 1811, by contrast, no immediate help seemed to be forthcoming from that quarter.

Schemes for radical reform consequently gained some ground. The *Manchester Gazette,* a newspaper especially popular among the weavers, continued its long-standing editorial campaign for peace but after 1808, increasingly linked it to demands for parlia-mentary reform. Certain steps had already been taken by London radicals who sensed that the time was ripe for another reform campaign. A City of London petition for parliamentary reform reached the House of Commons early in 1811. Formation of the genteel Hampden Club was proposed in the spring, and one of its supporters, Sir Francis Burdett, called for county meetings to discuss reform. Another supporter, Sir Charles Wolseley, tried to stimulate support in his native Staffordshire. George Wilbraham of Delamere Lodge, Cheshire, probably did the same in his home county. Around this time, the less prestigious London Union for Parliamentary Reform was established, with Henry Hunt and William Cobbett among its early members. Hunt proceeded to hold a county meeting in Somerset on the subject of reform, while *Cobbett's Political Register* trumpeted the call for reform throughout the nation.[21]

By late 1811 reports began reaching the Home Office of a 'secret committee' at Stockport and of meetings in the Stockport district and surrounding areas. 'B' reported on a meeting at Mottram in early October consisting of about 140 people who chose a delegate to determine sentiments in Nottingham, Sheffield, Leeds and other major towns of the North and Midlands. It was possibly at the Mottram meeting that 'B' was shown a letter from a man called O'Donovan (or Cannovan) to Maclure of the secret Stockport committee. O'Donovan wrote from Whitby that he was employed to gain the sentiments of the people in English seaports and that from Yorkshire he planned to return to Ireland via Glasgow. About this time, too, 'B' claimed to have learned the master plan of the group: to press for parliamentary reform and, when refused, to commence 'the work' – a co-ordinated national rising.[22]

Events at Manchester suggest a partial model for what was occur-ring at Stockport. The Manchester Weavers' Committee had led a relief effort in the spring but was not prominently active during the summer. Then, in a handbill of 21 October addressed to

'Manufacturers, Mechanics, Artizans, and Others',[23] this Committee publicly declared itself to be in favour of parliamentary reform. It planned to form a Committee of Trades which was to campaign among all the trades of the greater Manchester district. The Manchester Committee of Trades thus represented not so much a merger between radicals and various organised trades (including weavers) as an acceptance by the Manchester Weavers' Committee of radical programmes with the hope that rank-and-file weavers and other trades would join them in their agitation.

Maclure's secret Stockport committee probably consisted of those members of the Stockport Weavers' Committee who had decided to press for radical solutions to the weavers' distress by forming a new organisation which would collect money, co-ordinate activities with reformers in other regions and seek help locally from other trades. There exists scattered evidence that members of this Stockport 'Committee of Trades' talked of insurrections and administered secret oaths and thus could be categorised as 'intimidationists' if not full-fledged revolutionaries. That the new Committee did well financially for a time probably indicates that it was attracting some support from non-weaving trades. But this early progress received a setback around early November. Maclure and another man absconded (supposedly to Dublin) with the treasury of the Committee in the amount of £61. 'And,' as 'B' put it, 'they knowe that no one der [dare] to make clame of it' to the authorities. But 'B' recognised that 'it as [has] done a deal of good as some of them declare thay never will subscribe any more . . .'[24]

Accounts differ as to the pattern of subsequent events. The Lord of the Manor, Viscount Warren Bulkeley, wrote of delegates from Nottingham on 21–22 December but saw the situation as otherwise calm. 'Till this happened,' he wrote in an early report, 'everything here has been very quiet . . .' Within a week he could write, 'I fancy the storm, if there was any, has blown over . . .'[25] His reports were somewhat inconsistent with those of the spy 'B' who wrote that the Stockport radicals managed to overcome the Maclure debacle and by the beginning of December were again holding regular meetings and expanding their membership. They gained one hundred converts in a three-week period, according to 'B', but they were too weak to stage public demonstrations. Moreover, they no longer solicited subscriptions because weavers were too poor to pay. The radical weavers nevertheless had plans for a demonstration in a month's time if wages did not increase and, meanwhile, the work of proselytising continued. To their contacts at Gee Cross and Romiley, Stockport radicals added bases at Pott Shrigley, Rainowe and other points outside the district. They also sent a delegate to travel through Yorkshire. At Leeds the Stopfordian emissary found the people split into reformers and revolutionaries, but they promised to correspond with Stockport once a month.

The true situation probably lies somewhere between this account of 'B' and that of Warren Bulkeley. The radical organisation established in September and October probably did not vanish but also probably did not revive so quickly as 'B' claimed. The stabilisation or slight improvement of the economic situation in December 1811 and January 1812 may in fact have hindered the revival. The Maclure theft probably stifled the inter-trade links that were being formed and left weavers at the helm of the shrunken Stockport Committee of Trades. When the Nottingham delegates visited Stockport in late December, they had a meeting with 'some delegates of the weavers', according to Warren Bulkeley. 'B' mentioned only Stockport weavers when he wrote on 23 December of a rising which was to take place 'in the Cors of a month'.[26]

By February a new phase of the agitation was definitely beginning. The Manchester Committee of Trades made renewed efforts to extend its influence. On 3 February it divided the surrounding country into districts and sent out delegates, ostensibly to gain petitions for peace and reform. Although oaths of some sort had surfaced in the latter part of 1811, many claimed that the 'Luddite' oath first appeared on 3 February. It undoubtedly became more widespread after that time. Consisting as it did of a simple promise not to reveal who was on the 'secret committee', it could have been used in reference to the radical Committee of Trades in Manchester as well as to similar committees in surrounding towns. While the words of the oath say little, the context of oath-giving tells much about its purpose. The oath was almost always administered amidst talk of violence, often centring on the destruction of powerloom factories. It was thus reminiscent of the oaths taken exactly 20 years earlier by workers who had burned Grimshaw's powerloom factory in Manchester.[27] As 'twisting-in' continued, the Manchester Committee chose Humphrey Yarwood, a weaver, as its secretary at a meeting on 19 February. Bent, the spy 'B', became treasurer, overseeing dues of a penny per week. A permanent executive committee of three was also soon established. It consisted of an Irishman, a Yorkshireman and a former Stopfordian—John Buckley, a weaver and preacher who became its leading member. The executive committee, and Buckley in particular, appeared to be quite receptive to the calls for violence emerging from the Stockport Committee of Trades at that time.[28] In February and March, in short, it is clear that there existed a new boldness on the part of Manchester activists, a determination no doubt prompted by deteriorating economic conditions and by vows made at the end of December to do something after a month's time.

Responses to this new spirit of determination took different forms in different parts of the cotton districts. At Bolton and Preston a campaign for peace and reform went forward, with Bolton radicals preparing petitions for both the House of Commons and the Prince Regent on 21 February. At Manchester violence occurred within a week after the Luddite oath became prominent. On 9 February Haigh and Co.'s Manchester warehouse was set on fire, and about the same time there was an attempt to set fire to Peter Marsland's Oxford Road factory. Haigh may have been involved in the Spencer, Haigh and Co. factory at Stockport which was picketed by striking weavers in 1808. The latter company was the temporary successor to the powerloom king, William Radcliffe, who had filed for bankruptcy in 1807. Marsland– 'Peter the Great' – was not a Mancunian at all but was the most opulent of the Stockport cotton manufacturers and was, like Radcliffe, an early innovator in the field of powerlooms.[29] It seems like more than a coincidence that these incidents having links to Stockport businesses should occur just as John Buckley was rising to prominence in Manchester and also while the increasingly militant Stockport Committee of Trades still found it difficult to win support for its views in its home territory.

Stockport authorities sensed the mood of growing discontent but observed that it was channelled neither into campaigns for peace and reform, as at Bolton and Preston, nor into co-ordinated violence, as at Manchester. Instead, Stockport experienced widespread, albeit empty, threats of violence against the numerous powerloom factories during February and most of March. John Lloyd wrote to the Home Office in early February about anonymous letters sent to the Rev. Prescot threatening to destroy the powerlooms; and about subscriptions solicited locally to help Nottingham rioters who had been arrested.[30] At the same time Joseph Mayer, a manufacturer of Heaton Norris, stressed the pitiable plight of weavers trapped in a situation where 'an *honest industrious fellow* by *hard labour* cannot get bread much less clothes for himself and children... Nothing but an advance [in wages] will do...' He conjectured that Stockport people had thus far avoided the 'hub-bubs' because of their superior education. He also confirmed Lloyd's reports of threatening letters and nocturnal meetings attended by delegates from Nottingham, Carlisle and Glasgow.[31]

Mayer's observations contain much truth. The Stockport Committee of Trades did remain in touch with weavers and/or radicals in other areas. In late February or early March, two Stockport delegates introduced the Luddite oath to Bolton. One of the Stopfordians reportedly said that 'since government would give them no satisfaction it became necessary to take the means into their own hands...' It may have been these Stopfordians who went to Preston to promote the destruction of powerlooms there. One of the members of the Stockport Committee, Thomas Whitaker, a weaver, was administering oaths near Huddersfield about this time. An anonymous Stockport weaver stated on 3 March that the disaffected 'have accounts from one to another and districts'. He confirmed that they were little interested in the radicals' campaign for peace, since it seemed to offer no immediate solution to the problem of over-production. He talked vaguely of a rising but mentioned only one specific target: 'they are determined to do away with those Steam Looms'.[32] But unlike Manchester, Stockport experienced no 'hubbubs', indicating that the Stockport Committee of Trades probably still had a limited local constituency, even among the weavers.

The official Stockport Weavers' Committee was, in fact, involved with something else altogether. During the second week of February weavers' leaders requested that the Rev. Prescot supervise negotiations between weavers' delegates and masters on the subject of wages. Negotiations ensued and continued for over a month, a sign of conciliation in an atmosphere constantly threatened by violence. At the same time weavers met frequently in small secret conclaves and on at least one occasion (24 February) in a big public meeting followed by a procession through the streets of Stockport. The same tactics were being pursued at Bolton to 'frighten' masters into raising wages. 'B' showed some insight into the situation at Stockport in his report of 23 February: 'I am afraid something would be done at Stockport. Mr Prescott [*sic*] is in favor with the people but Mr Peter Marsland is not. These are the two magistrates and if any man can satisfy the weavers it is Prescott, as he is mild with them.'[33] During March Stockport masters finally agreed to raise weavers' wages by 20 per cent. Stockport district weavers must have been jubilant but, as it turned out, without good cause. After consulting with other masters at Manchester, the Stockport masters decided to rescind their offer. Joseph Sherwin, a member of the Weavers' Committee and eventually also of the Committee of Trades, later recounted what the masters said: 'They told me, that they were only making game of us; they said one thing in the presence of the magistrates, and another when they met themselves.' Violence quickly ensued.[34]

III

Attacks on factories, the best known variety of Luddism, lasted from 20 March to 14 April. They were succeeded by 'rural levies' of food and money which evolved into raids for arms throughout the Stockport district. In much of this, there are indications that the Stockport Committee of Trades helped to incite the disturbances. During May and June the raids diminished in most areas excluding the north-eastern townships, where a different pattern was emerging. In those townships food riots had broken out on 21 April. That hatters played the most active part in these riots was probably the result of intra-trade grievances which were only gradually resolved during the ensuing weeks. The unsettled state of the north-east townships consequently provided fertile ground for the continued growth of Luddism. Hatters and weavers took oaths in that area, meetings were held, arms raids intensified, and nocturnal drilling commenced and lasted into the summer.

The first attack occurred on 20 March at what must have seemed an obvious target to the handloom weavers–William Radcliffe's powerloom factory. Even though a determined effort was made to set fire to the factory by as many as 500 men using torches of pitch, tar, oakum and turpentine, little damage was done. The details of the arson attempt suggest that it was planned well ahead of time, thus providing implicit confirmation of earlier rumours. Two weeks later, during the night of 4–5 April, eleven slugs were fired through the windows of John Goodair's house. The windows of two other manufacturers were also broken that night.[35]

Stopfordians played a leading role not only in carrying out local violence in late March and early April but also in promoting violence elsewhere. During those two weeks there were reports, for example, that a Stockport delegate was administering the Luddite oath in Manchester. On 5 April at a Manchester meeting of delegates from Stockport, Bolton, Ashton, Oldham and other towns, deputies discussed (one account says 'planned') the destruction of power-looms. The next day Thomas Whitaker was administering the Luddite oath at Gatley in Stockport Etchells. He also collected dues of one or two pennies from each man amidst a general discussion of the destruction of powerlooms and the necessity of arming. About 20 Gatley men were twisted-in on that occasion; all of them were weavers. When Whitaker was arrested two weeks later, he had a piece of paper in his pocket addressed to the president and Weavers' Committee of Stockport from the Bolton Weavers' Committee.[36] If there were doubts before, it was clear by April that the Luddite system and the Luddite oath were being promoted in the Stockport district by men connected with the official weavers' organisation. Although riots at Stockport and Bolton were delayed, violence recurred at Manchester. On 8 April a crowd was assembled by the broadside *Now or Never*, and it proceeded to pass radical resolutions before wrecking the Manchester Exchange. John Buckley may have been a leader of the riot, which the *Gentleman's Magazine* thought was carried out primarily by weavers. *Now or Never* soon turned up in Stockport along with other inflammatory placards.[37]

Another delegate meeting on 13 April preceded the most violent Stockport riot by one day. As usual, local authorities were alert to the potential for disorder, but they were also justifiably apprehensive about the conspicuous weakness of their forces. The magistrates had been swearing in special constables for some weeks but had difficulty getting them to act. For some unexplained reason, the Sheriff would not convene a meeting to put the Watch and Ward Act into effect. Hence, the main burden of peace-keeping fell on the military, which believed its responsibility lay in keeping order in Manchester and in avoiding a division of its forces by making sorties throughout the district. Moreover, that active peace keeper, John Lloyd, was away at the Cheshire Quarter Sessions on 14 April, and the major tradesmen of the town left early in the morning for the Tuesday cotton market at Manchester. The stage was perfectly set for the appearance of 'General Ludd's wives'.[38]

The action began at about ten o'clock on the morning of 14 April when two men dressed as women led a small crowd to the

Edgeley house of John Goodair and began pelting it with stones. They then marched through Stockport where they gained hundreds of followers and broke windows at Marsland's, Radcliffe's,[39] John Bentley's and Hindley and Bradshaw's. While in Stockport the crowd also stoned Thomas Garside when he urged them to disperse, although the attack was cut short on the command of one of the crowd's leaders. The crowd then moved back to Goodair's house and factory in time for the noon bell and (with the Goodair family fleeing before them to the Sykeses') set about destroying the powerlooms, burning the factory and then setting fire to the house. A shout of 'Now to Sykes' arose, but before the crowd could proceed, the military arrived, divided the crowd, and forced the scattered groups out into the countryside. Two men were seized in the melee, one a 19-year-old cotton spinner and the other, Charles Hulme, a weaver who had also been arrested during the 1808 weavers' strike. Three days later, Joseph Nadin, Manchester's deputy constable, arrested Joseph Thompson, a weaver originally from Preston who was in possession of the silver which had been taken from Goodair's in the confusion of the riot. Three other members of the crowd, all of them weavers, were subsequently arrested.[40]

The events of 14 April marked at once the climax and the virtual end of public disorders in Stockport and Edgeley. Almost immediately the activities of General Ludd's wives passed into local folklore, to be told and retold for generations to come.[41] The pattern of victimisation on that eventful Tuesday has never received much attention, however. Bentley, Bradshaw, the Sykeses and Radcliffe were probably targets in part because they had led the opposition to various weavers' demands over the preceding decade, notably the weavers' repeated calls for a minimum wage. Radcliffe, Marsland and Goodair must have seemed especially obnoxious for pioneering the introduction of powerlooms. They had, of course, been victims of the crowd in previous weeks. Marsland had the further stigma of being an unpopular JP. Goodair, for his part, owned a powerloom factory which stood incongruously in the midst of the Irish handloom weavers' enclave at Edgeley. Moreover, he was an outsider—a London muslin factor since about 1799 who seems to have acquired his Stockport factories in 1808. Although he maintained a house at Edgeley, he was in London at the time of the Luddite attack, and he continued to reside there until his death in 1832.[42]

If violence ended in Stockport and Edgeley after the Goodair riot, threats of violence continued. Two days later, for instance, a

factory owner who used dressing machines of the Radcliffe type
(and who leased space to Thomas Garside, a victim of the crowd's
ire) received a letter from 'General Justice'. The letter threatened
to burn his factory in seven days unless he removed the dressing
machines. It also stated a broader goal.

> We are fully determined to destroy both dressing machines and
> steam looms let who will be the owners. We neither regard those
> that keeps them nor the army for we will conquer both or die in
> the conflict.[43]

Threats such as this were not unique to Stockport. They presaged
violent activities throughout the Manchester district during April.
The Manchester Exchange rioters of 8 April went on to attack a
factory. On 20–21 April a powerloom factory at Middleton was
destroyed. On 21 April looms were smashed at a factory in
Tintwistle, Mottram parish. And on 24 April, after repeated
attempts, Luddites demolished a powerloom factory at Westhough-
ton, near Bolton.

These violent episodes helped to spark acrimonious debates in
Manchester between the three-man executive and the Committee
of Trades. The three activists of the executive, along with Humphrey
Yarwood, continued to favour oath-taking and machine-breaking
as part of (or a prelude to) insurrection. They were apparently
supported in this by the Stockport Committee of Trades and those
committees in a few other towns which had only limited support
from non-weavers. At the same time, the spinners, tailors and
other craftsmen of the Manchester Committee became increasingly
reluctant to contribute additional money to the cause, probably
because they thought they had little to gain by being linked, however
indirectly, to the destruction of powerlooms. At a delegate meeting
held on 20 April the Manchester Committee consequently threatened to dissociate itself from the committees of other towns, and
the spinners and tailors refused to contribute any further money
until the next delegate meeting. John Buckley saw to it that those
two trades were excluded from that meeting which was held at
Failsworth on 4 May, by which time the breach was irreparable.
Buckley himself was allegedly marked for assassination. Within a
month he and the other two men of the executive had fled to the
Stockport district where they sought work as weavers and possibly
played a part in the meetings and disturbances of the early

summer.[44]

In the face of such dissensions many Manchester radicals followed those at Chorley and Chowbent and took the advice of Major Cartwright to turn discontents 'into a legal channel favourable to Parliamentary Reform'.[45] John Knight and other Manchester radicals established a new organisation, held two reform meetings in May, and attempted to promote the agitation in other towns. At a third reform meeting on 11 June, 38 delegates were surprised and arrested by the authorities for being involved in administering oaths. The 'Manchester Thirty-Eight', all of whom were ultimately acquitted, contained 23 Manchester delegates, four from the Stockport district and eleven from ten other towns. The occupations of the Manchester delegates show that, as usual, radical campaigns in the cotton metropolis could elicit support from individuals in a wide variety of trades. Weavers acted as delegates from most of the other towns, however. The Stockport district was unusually well-represented, but its delegates came from just two north-eastern townships—two hatters from Hyde, two weavers from Denton. As in February and March, in other words, the radical agitation for peace and reform gained little apparent support from most parts of the Stockport district.[46]

Nor were there further attacks on Stockport factories after 14 April. It seems as if there were a conscious decision on the part of the Stockport Committee of Trades to limit collective disorders in Stockport in order to avoid confrontations with the military. Instead, activists on the Committee appear to have taken charge of the 'rural levies' or 'robberies' which had begun to appear during the second week of April. In these, crowds or small bands solicited voluntary contributions from well-to-do gentry and farmers, thereby acting out the traditional notion that the rich had an obligation to aid the poor in times of distress. The first levy occurred around 9 April when four men 'robbed' Henry Mayer's house a mile or two outside of Stockport. On 14 April a crowd in Wilmslow parish demanded money from three separate men.[47] The next day a crowd led by two crofters moved north from Wilmslow, picked up some weavers and others at Handforth, and proceeded to ask for money at the houses of at least nine gentlemen and substantial farmers, mostly in Northenden and Stockport Etchells.[48]

Also on 15 April (the day after the Goodair attack) a crowd met on Cheadle Heath near Edgeley and then broke up into two small bands. One group of about ten approached the house of John

Parker, Esq., of Etchells and demanded money. Its spokesmen falsely claimed that the Rev. Broughton of Cheadle had given them 5s. Parker gave 7s., but just then a small force headed by Broughton and Lloyd arrived and apprehended seven of the suppliants. Six of the men were weavers–three Irish and three migrants from Lancashire. One of the Irish weavers resided in Edgeley and had been seen in the Goodair attack.[49] On 21 April the Rev. Prescot wrote to the Home Office that a master calico printer in Disley had requested help in suppressing groups which were 'robbing' farmers in his area.[50] Two days later Thomas Chadwick of Stockport and a band of six other weavers solicited money at Bagguley, a town some miles to the west of Stockport. It was later learned that they had also been as far afield as Ashton-under-Lyne. Chadwick, it should be noted, was on the Stockport Committee of Trades and had been accused of administering oaths.

Prescot wrote to the Home Office on 27 April that robberies and burglaries were increasing. No one knew where the 'associated banditti' would strike next. That same night authorities braced for an attack on the Stockport gaol, but nothing came of it. They then began observing a system of rockets and blue lights which lit up the night skies and which probably signalled rural raiders as to the movements of the military billeted in Stockport. By this time the rural levies had little resemblance to the daytime requests for charity out of which they evolved. They had been transformed into nighttime raids by disguised and armed intruders calling themselves 'Ludd's men' who took money, food, clothing and arms from isolated farm houses. Such was the case with John Temple, who was captured on 10 May after an evening raid at Adlington. He was a weaver then residing at Edgeley but originally from Londonderry *via* Scotland and Manchester.[51]

Later confessions by Thomas Whitaker, though partly self-serving, give further insight into the Stockport district Luddite system.[52] Whitaker spoke of two distinct groups, the Stockport Weavers' Committee, which was merely trying to raise wages and relieve distress through legal channels, and a secret committee bent on using violence, especially against factories. He claimed to have been active in the former group as a member and delegate but not in the latter group. He also claimed that the idea of a secret Committee of Trades and oath taking came from a mysterious Manchester man. At the base of the Committee of Trades there were supposedly groups of ten men, each under a sergeant, with every ten groups under a captain. Whitaker mentioned 16 men as active in the Luddite system at Stockport (Table 8.1). This listing

Table 8.1: Men Active in the Luddite System at Stockport According to Thomas Whitaker

Name	Occupation	Activities: Weavers' Strike 1808	Committee of Trades 1812	Arms Raids 1812	Oath Giving 1812	Radical after 1812
Thomas Chadwick	weaver	X			X	X
William Fenton	weaver		X			X
Thomas Greenhalgh [a]	weaver?		X	X		
Hamer [b]	weaver?			X		X?
Hyde	spinner				X	
Makin [a]	weaver?			X		
Thomas Massey [c]	weaver			X		X?
McCracken	?			X		
Thomas Miller	weaver		X			X
John Mitchell	?		X			
Robert Patten	?		X			
Rhodes [d]	weaver?	X?	X			X?
Sampson Robinson	hatter				X	X
Joseph Sherwin	weaver	X	X			X
John Temple	weaver			X		
Joseph Thompson	weaver	X		X		

Notes: (a) Member of the Edgeley gang, strong suspicion that he was a weaver.
  (b) Possibly John Hamer, Stockport weaver, active in radical affairs from the 1810s to the 1840s.
  (c) Possibly the Thomas Massey who was described as a 'farmer' when he was active in Stockport radicalism in 1818–19.
  (d) Possibly John Rhodes, Stockport weaver, who was active in both the 1808 weavers' strike and in radicalism in 1816.
Source: HO 42/123, Whitaker to the Governor of Chester Castle, Chester Castle [c. 29 May 1812].

shows the relationship between weavers and the Committee of Trades, and between at least one member of the Committee and nocturnal arms raids. Whitaker, a weaver himself, should also be taken into account. Like Sherwin, he was on the Weavers' Committee and was probably on the Committee of Trades. He was an oath giver, knew the names of other oath givers, and knew some of the leaders of the arms raids. In other words, Whitaker's list and his own career seem to confirm what has already been suggested, that the Luddite organisation in Stockport was predominantly a handloom weavers' organisation. Lloyd was not far wrong when he sent a copy of the Luddite oath to the Home Office under the title 'Oath or Engagement of the Weavers'. One certainly can not accept E.P. Thompson's assertion that this was 'an incipient secret trades council' consisting of officially deputed members of 'many' trades.[53]

The two main types of public disorders discussed thus far (factory attacks and rural levies) often had links to men from the town of Stockport or its suburbs. A third type of disorder, food riots, found less support in the urban core of the district. Most of the activity occurred in the district's north-eastern townships. On 21 April a crowd collected in the forenoon at Denton and moved to Hyde, where it attacked the mill of John Ashton and distributed flour–first at reduced rates, then free of charge.[54] Meanwhile, a crowd rose up at nearby Gee Cross and attacked various provision shops in that village. A local minister witnessed some of the events.

> I saw a large mob attacking a shop opposite our garden gate, and I saw the meal and flour brought out and distributed to the people, chiefly women, who received it into their aprons, hand-kerchiefs, caps, old stockings, or anything else in which they could carry it away. One man named Walker, for a frolic, had put a paper round his hat with *General Ludd* written on it, but it cost him dear, for he was transported as a ringleader, and died at the hulks.[55]

Walker, a collier, and others from Gee Cross then joined the main Denton crowd on its march through Butterhouse Green to Harden Mill, Bredbury. There the distribution of food was interrupted by John Lloyd leading a contingent of cavalry. Six men were taken into custody and the rest were dispersed by gunfire.

At least one contemporary account regarded the food riots of 1812 as 'unconnected' with other types of public disorders.[56] In one sense this is correct. While weavers played prominent roles in the factory attacks and rural levies, hatters played the leading part in the food riots at Hyde, Gee Cross and Bredbury. The hatting industry had been depressed for a number of years. A defender of machinery blamed it on hatters' backwardness in adopting improved technology and stated that they 'have already in part, lost, and are intirely [*sic*] losing, the Trade to Foreign Countries'.[57] Also aggra-vating the hatters' situation was the flood of journeymen who obtained 'blanks' or work certificates from 'foul' establishments which did not adhere to the rules of the hatters' union. The problem was national in scope, with both Manchester and Stockport local unions consulting with the Glasgow union on the matter. Negotiations came to a head in May, soon after the suppression of the food riots, when it was determined that after 1 June, only Stockport, Manchester and Rochdale could issue blanks for hatters in the greater Manchester district. Blanks from such places as Oldham, Bury, Ashton, Newton Moor, Gorton, Marple, Romiley, *Denton* and *Gee Cross* would no longer be honoured. Presumably these had been places where the influx of illegal workmen had been especially large, and the damage to the trade had been unusually severe as a result. Thus it appears that industrial grievances in a single trade combined with the extremely high price of food provided the major causes for the food riots in the townships to the north-east of Stockport.[58]

In late April the authorities could not have known that food riots and factory attacks would not recur or that rural levies would quickly subside in most areas and become concentrated in the north-east townships. Sensing danger on all sides they tried to redouble their efforts to maintain order. They had already obtained £200 from local industrialists as a reward for information about the men who had attacked Radcliffe's mill on 20 March. A month later they hurried the Watch and Ward into effect for both Stockport and Cheadle Bulkeley, the township containing Edgeley. County meetings were held in mid-May in both Cheshire and Lancashire to discuss the possibility of calling up the militia, a move feared by a few of the authorities who thought that some militiamen were Luddites.[59] Such activities coincided with anti-Luddite propaganda campaigns in Stockport and Hyde which were aimed at defending the introduction of new machinery and condemning unlawful oaths.[60]

Perhaps the most important deterrent measure was the holding of Special Commissions at the end of May and beginning of June to try Cheshire and Lancashire Luddites. The Chester Special Commission, convened on 25 May, tried 27 men who were either from the Stockport district or were accused of committing 'Luddite' crimes there (Table 8.2). The occupations of those indicted supports what has been said with respect to weavers and the Luddite system. The inclusion of two colliers who joined the food rioters was meant to serve as an example, since colliers were highly paid and, the authorities believed, had no reason to riot.[61] In general those indicted were carefully picked to serve as examples. The names of

18 Gatley oath takers were known to the authorities, for instance, but only four were indicted along with Whitaker, who had administered the oaths. The only two men hanged, Joseph Thompson and John Temple, had been involved in what was regarded as an especially egregious sort of crime, house robbing (Thompson at Goodair's, Temple at Adlington).[62]

Table 8.2: Occupations of Stockport District Luddites Tried at the Chester Special Commission in May 1812

Activity	Weavers	Hatters	Colliers	Spinners	Total
Secret oaths	5				5
Factory attack	5			1	6
Rural levies	15	1			16
Food riots		3	2		5
Total	25	4	2	1	32

Source: PRO, KB 8/90, Cheshire Special Commission, 1812.

Almost simultaneously, expanded relief measures were begun. The Association for the Relief of the Manufacturing and Labouring Poor was established on 23 May in London. It immediately engaged in correspondence with the northern manufacturing districts to see where aid was most needed. Stockport district correspondents reported that some master manufacturers continued to employ weavers in spite of the fact that they had enormous stocks of cloth already on hand. Even so, a Disley man reported in July as follows: 'Necessities of the poor urgent and extreme. It is known to the neighbourhood that many families have sought sustenance from boiled nettles and wild greens without salt.' By 1813 the London Association had contributed £100 to Stockport and £20 to Marple. Although seemingly insignificant amounts, the Association noted that such grants often stimulated local charity, sometimes at the ratio of £10 for every £1 of Association money. The exact extent of contributions in the Stockport district is not known, but already by June 1812 a fairly complex system had emerged in which the poor were being supplied with bacon, peas, rice and herrings at reduced prices.[63] Thus, as in previous seasons of distress, local charitable activities were probably not without considerable impact.

The relative calm in Stockport, its suburbs and most of the

remainder of the district during that time can be explained by the amount of repression which was being exerted in those areas,[64] by charitable relief efforts, and by the sophistication which had already characterised the secret organisation and the public outbursts. It was not a question of having failed at a traditional form of protest (like the food riot) which could then be replaced by something more novel like 'twisting-in'. By the beginning of the summer, workers in those areas had been thwarted in the use of all such tactics. This may account for the increase in out-migration which occurred. Jeremiah Bury testified before Parliament in May that many weavers had left the district. The practice of the Stockport Sunday School to indicate in its registers those of its scholars who had 'left town' (presumably with their respective families) furnishes evidence that departures during the second half of 1812 were higher than in any comparable period in the preceding five years. Lt. Col. Nelthorpe, the military commander at Stockport, thought that some of these movements were quite purposeful and that 'many have fled the country'.[65] Officials in Ireland were warned in August to watch for fleeing fugitives. At least one suspicious weaver from Stockport (apparently a relative of John Knight, the famous Manchester radical) was discovered in Dublin on 16 August, having gone over six weeks previously.[66] With many of the Luddite leaders apprehended and many sympathisers apparently helping to swell the high out-migration figures, it is little wonder that such large areas of the Stockport district quickly became pacified.

Yet the north-east sector became fertile ground for oath taking and radical-insurrectionary plans beginning in May and June, that is, after the failure of the food riots. One of the Hyde hatters included among the ranks of the Manchester Thirty-Eight stated that he had taken the Luddite oath from a Haughton weaver in May and that he himself subsequently twisted-in 20 or 30 people.[67] By June crowds numbering in the hundreds were roaming around the north-eastern townships and delegating bands of ten or twelve to approach houses and demand arms. The raids were not notably successful. On 13 and 14 June, for example, five separate raids at Hyde and Werneth netted only six guns. There were reports of crowds engaging in nightly military drills. These groups supposedly had spies to watch soldiers' movements and thereby elude capture.[68]

It was in this context that Lloyd suggested 'a measure beyond the law' to the Home Office. He wanted military and civilian authorities to begin searching for arms in private houses. Already by 19

June Nelthorpe could report that such searches had been undertaken and that many arms had been confiscated as a result. His reports continued in an optimistic vein. On 24 and 25 June he wrote that the arms seizures seemed to be deterring nocturnal activities by the disaffected and that 'the state of the county within our quarters has materially improved within the last few days . . .' Lloyd had no further reports of disaffection to make through the end of June.[69] The following month passed with hardly any reports of arms raids or violence in the north-eastern townships.

It is interesting to learn of the simultaneous reports 'B' was making to Col. Fletcher of Bolton. The spy claimed that Luddites in the neighbourhood of Stockport had large caches of arms, were familiar with military discipline and planned a rising to occur perhaps after the hay harvest. Unless 'B' is to be dismissed as an inveterate fantasiser, his reports seem to indicate that there was a hard core of radicals who still believed in the imminence of revolution. This notion seems to have been fostered by delegates' visits. On 16 July a London delegate reportedly visited Stockport and 'told his friends to keep up their spirits, for things were going on well; they had many friends both in Scotland and Ireland'. But nothing resulted from this incident, nor from the visit of two suspicious strangers and a person 'known' to be a delegate whom Lloyd reported on two weeks later. The last major activities of the Luddites consisted of a pair of Sunday meetings. The first, on 24 July about two miles outside of Stockport, was held to collect money for the Manchester Thirty-Eight. The other meeting, advertised throughout the town of Stockport to be held on 2 August near Hayfield, Derbyshire, may have been intended for the same purpose.[70]

IV

The continuation of voluntary charitable efforts and of high (perhaps increasing) levels of migration out of Stockport and its district probably helped to ease tensions somewhat during the second half of 1812. Clemency offers undoubtedly helped, too. By the beginning of August 1812 the magistrates of Stockport division were preparing to put into effect an Act passed on 9 July (52 Geo. III, c. 104). It increased the penalties for oath taking but offered clemency for those confessing before 9 October to having taken illegal oaths.

Clemency was also unofficially extended to oath givers who came forward before the deadline.[71] The confessions did not really begin, however, until 22 August–the day on which the widely-circulated *Manchester Gazette* explained the provisions of the Act to its readership. It was also Petty Sessions day in Stockport. Prescot reported that 25 people arrived from Mottram (just to the north-east of the Stockport district) to confess and then take the oath of allegiance.[72] The trickle soon became a torrent: by 25 August 200 had taken the oath of allegiance and by 29 August the figure exceeded 500. George Hyde Clarke, a magistrate at Hyde, wrote on 28 August that he had sworn the oath of allegiance to 95 men and that he expected to swear in 50 more the next day. He was still at it in the second week of September. Nearly all of the thousand individuals who finally took the oath were from the townships to the north-east of Stockport town. Indeed, north-east Cheshire seems to have been the single area in the whole region where people in any numbers took advantage of the clemency offer.[73]

Edgeley, Gatley and other early strongholds of Luddism and oath taking did not figure in these proceedings. The situation at Manchester presents a similarly puzzling picture. No Mancunians came forward to take the oath of allegiance before 11–12 September, when the number amounted to a mere 58. On 2 October, a week before the expiration of the clemency offer, Richard Farington (the Didsbury JP) expressed disappointment at the small turn-out.[74] The Hammonds attributed the forwardness of the north-east Cheshire townships to the harassment of the military in the area. Two additional explanations must be considered. The one was expressed in a Manchester handbill of 22 September urging oath takers to confess.

It is to be feared, that several of them have been deterred from so doing, under an Apprehension (excited or encouraged by designing Characters) that the Declaration they are required to make, will, on some future Occasion, be used to their Prejudice.[75]

Rumours such as this may have spread more easily in towns like Manchester and Stockport than in rural areas like north-east Cheshire. The other explanation is that the oath takers of the latter area felt more apprehensive about being caught simply because they had taken the Luddite oath not long before (May, June and possibly July) whereas the main period of oath taking in Stockport and Manchester occurred from February to May. The few Manchester confessions seem to have been from those who had taken the oath comparatively recently. By the early autumn of 1812 those who had taken the Luddite oath as much as six months before probably felt themselves unlikely to be detected.

Social tensions were also lessened by the substantial harvest of 1812 and the resulting fall in grain prices during the third quarter of the year. Oat prices then continued their downward course through the fourth quarter but rose moderately during the first half of 1813. Handloom weavers' wages unfortunately paralleled this trend, falling slightly in the last half of 1812 and rising slightly in the succeeding six months. Although their real wages remained almost unchanged as a consequence, the amount of work available to handloom weavers seems to have gradually increased. Such had been the strain of the previous disorders that even slight or temporary economic advances were seized upon as sure signs of the return of prosperity. In October the *Manchester Gazette* exulted over 'the rapid improvement of every branch of manufacture in this country . . .', while Lloyd wrote about the 'very happy change in the dispositions of the people in and about Stockport'. Yet the overall economic situation remained unsettled, especially for the handloom weavers. Prescot was warning the Home Office of possible repercussions of low wages and high prices in November 1812, and the Lord Lieutenant of Cheshire echoed his sentiments early in the following year.[76]

Despite the gloomy reports, the main activity of the weavers during this period was neither oath taking nor machine-breaking nor rioting. Nothing further was heard of a Christmas rising. Instead, weavers returned to their more traditional demands for a minimum wage. Bolton weavers had discovered in the spring of 1812 that the Elizabethan Statute of Artificers provided for wage-fixing by magistrates but only at the Easter Sessions. Their discovery was made too late for action in 1812, but weavers throughout the Manchester district were prepared to act in 1813. Unfortunately for them, Parliament began the process of repealing the Statute of Artificers, beginning with the wage-fixing clauses, in February of 1813. Weavers from Stockport, Bolton, Manchester, Preston and other towns petitioned against the repeal, but to no avail. It received the Royal Assent on 15 April.[77]

In the meantime, the small radical circle in Stockport gained encouragement from John Cartwright, 'the good, grey Major'. In August and September 1812, he went on a provincial tour to promote parliamentary reform. He visited Manchester to help the Thirty-Eight and possibly visited Stockport. He definitely stopped in Stockport on a second tour in January and February 1813.[78] E.P. Thompson has claimed that Cartwright left behind a chain of 'incipient' Hampden Clubs after these tours–the implication being that the old reformer accomplished something new and significant. In the case of Stockport, at least, Cartwright appears merely to have energised the small, pre-existing radical group which included, among others, Thomas Cheetham the surgeon. By the spring of 1813 these radicals had prepared a petition for parliamentary reform.[79] It would be surprising if it had not gained the signatures of some handloom weavers–the occupations of the petitioners is lacking, however–but weavers' support for radical proposals at that time should not be overemphasised. When reporting their anxieties during the winter of 1812–13, none of the local authorities mentioned political designs by the weavers. It seems likely that they were focusing their attention once again on a narrow sectional issue, the campaign for a minimum wage. A similar pattern had occurred in Stockport in the winter of 1807–8, when large numbers of weavers signed a radical petition for peace but seemingly abandoned it after its presentation to Parliament in order to concentrate on minimum wage agitations. The radical coterie and its parliamentary reform campaign met with little support from weavers or any organised trade from the summer of 1813 through the year of 1814, a time of high piece rates in weaving and low prices for provisions. The need for a sweeping reform of the nation's political institutions must have seemed less urgent in times such as those.

Stockport district Luddism involved significant participation by only a small number of different trades which often operated in separate geographic areas and sought distinct objectives. A brief examination of cotton finishers, another trade group active in 1811–12, scarcely alters such conclusions. Calico printers, bleachers and dyers had long-standing grievances over apprenticeship regulations and the introduction of labour-saving machinery. Their activities involved various scattered disorders and threats of violence during the Luddite period. On the night of 13–14 December 1811, for example, the calico printworks of Thomas Andrew and Sons at Compstall Bridge (Werneth township) were plundered and then burned. Although generous rewards were offered, the incendiaries were never caught, and their precise motives were never known. In late January a cart belonging to Thorpe and Son, a Reddish calico printing firm, was stopped at night by four men. Presumably looking for machine-printed cloth, they let the cart pass when they found only dyestuffs.[80] In the *Manchester Gazette* of 11 April journeymen dyers inserted 'A Caution to Master Dyers' which warned against hiring boys and young men who had not served a full seven-year apprenticeship. Some workers from the bleachworks and printworks along the Handforth-Wilmslow border took part in the 'rural levies' of 15 April. The rector of Cheadle parish, who also served as a magistrate, wrote that calico printers met among themselves on 26 April and sent delegates to their masters the next day. The operatives wanted the new printing machinery to be removed and printing to be done solely by means of hand blocks. The rector was amazed at their demands since they were 'well off'. He concluded that they were 'in a complete revolutionary system now pervading the whole part of this country. The object of destroying machinery is, no doubt, to throw all the lower classes out of employ and thereby increase the discontents.' He may have thought his suspicions confirmed a few months later. On 12 September a Cheadle printwork belonging to John Thorpe, a relative of the Reddish Thorpes, was burned to the ground.[81]

Yet it is unlikely that the calico printers were integrated into the Luddite system. None of them is known to have served on the Committee of Trades. Moreover, there is no evidence of oath taking in the trade, nor does the pattern of activities among calico printers correspond to the main patterns of Luddism in the Stockport district. Their grievances over apprentices and machinery had been articulated for years, often by the strong Calico Printers' Union. It seems likely that they took advantage of the disturbances in 1811–12 to press once again for goals narrowly confined to their own trade by using violence, the popular tactic of the day. In 1813–15, they were seeking the same objectives through parliamentary petitions and strikes.

V

The complex events of Stockport district Luddism clearly can not be reduced to a simple formula. None of the four major interpretations mentioned at the beginning of this chapter can be accepted without qualification, and none can be rejected altogether. Economic conditions undoubtedly helped to create a milieu in which

Luddism could flourish for a time. While economic fluctuations did not determine the myriad forms in which the discontent manifested itself, economics had some influence on the timing of the disturbances. Disorders became most pronounced starting at the end of the first quarter of 1812 just after grain prices had been rising at their fastest rate (even if they had not yet reached their highest absolute levels). In this sense, economic distress was not only a pre-condition but also a trigger for mass actions.

'Marginal men' played a significant role in Luddite activities at Stockport and Edgeley. Over and over again, Luddite leaders appear to have been either Irish or migrants from other areas. These men often found work weaving the cheapest types of cotton cloth. Hence, they were probably more 'desperate' than other weavers because they received the lowest wages, were likely to be discharged first in a slump and were not eligible for poor relief since they had no legal settlement in the Stockport district. The presence of outsiders was mentioned by Jeremiah Bury, who thought that the weavers (and the spinners) had been well-behaved, 'especially the resident weavers'. His comments would seem to call into question any interpretation which holds that the great majority of handloom weavers was integrated into the Luddite system.[82]

With regard to industrial grievances, three fairly separate series of events can be discerned. First and foremost came the activities of the handloom weavers who tried industrial pressure in 1810 and entreaties to local and national authorites in early 1811. When these tactics had failed, some weavers turned to the radical political solutions which had long been espoused by the radical coterie in Stockport. Yet before agitation for political change could become mixed up with machine breaking, weavers tried once again to bargain with masters, only to be duped. The factory attacks of late March and early April can thus be regarded as reprisals for the poor treatment previously accorded the weavers and the beginning of a new insurrectionary stage of the agitation. In the latter sense, the rural levies which merged into robberies and arms raids during April, May and June can be seen as furthering insurrectionary goals.

A second group of occurrences took place primarily among hatters in the north-east townships of the Stockport district. There, the reaction to distress took the form of food riots on 21 April. Subsequent struggles to reduce the influx of hatters into the trade coincided with the appearance of the Luddite oath in the area and arms raids. These activities seem to have died out in July, and soon many from this area were taking the oath of allegiance.

A third series of events occurred among calico printers who mixed violence with collective bargaining in 1811 and 1812. Their objects were to try to stem the number of apprentices entering their trade and to halt the introduction of new print machinery. These demands, though resembling the hatters' desire for labour restriction in their trade and the weavers' for an end to the use of powerlooms, had been long-standing grievances with the calico printers and were to appear again in subsequent years. The demands had no direct relationship to the demands formulated by other trades at this time, nor did calico printers' activities in 1811–12 have any known relationship to the Luddite system.

Luddism nevertheless figures prominently in accounts of those who attempt to trace the formation of an English 'working class'. Harold Perkin believes that Luddism and similar activities were 'the inevitable accompaniment of the first stage of class development, above all in traditional dependent occupations'. John Dinwiddy refers specifically to Lancashire and Yorkshire Luddism of 1811–13:

> These years are . . . important, it may be suggested, as a stage in the process whereby working men came to regard democratic control of the state as an essential means to the improvement of their condition.[83]

In the Stockport district the actions of coal miners on behalf of distressed hatters during the food riots of April indicates the presence of a degree of inter-trade solidarity. Handloom weavers likewise gained some response when they tried to elicit inter-trade support through the Committee of Trades. Yet all of this pales into insignificance when one recalls the aloofness of the spinners and related factory occupations, the building trades, the metal trades, the wood-working trades, the semi-skilled and unskilled in most non-factory and service occupations, and so forth. There is thus limited evidence at best that workers' solidarity was significantly expanded during the Luddite period.

Moreover, the political reform movement was not important in the Stockport district during most of this time. The Stockport Jacobin/radical coterie appears neither to have been interested in insurrection nor to have been involved with the Committee of

Trades. Radicals' proposals for parliamentary reform really gained support only after the main period of Luddism was over. Earlier intimidationism had been fostered not by the radical coterie but by the Committee of Trades. There had been widespread talk of risings over many months, and the Luddite oath itself may be taken as an implicit threat to established law and order. When one turns to concrete plans for revolution, one discovers a much more limited phenomenon. Arms raids and drilling had begun only in April and May and had largely ceased by the end of June. While some thousands took the Luddite oath, probably only a few hundred practiced marching and participated in arms raids. In other words, revolutionaries did exist but their comparatively small numbers lead one to think less in terms of Thompson's 'rising of the people' than of Foster's scattered and defeated 'guerillas'.

9 WEAVERS, RADICALS AND THE MARCH OF THE BLANKETEERS

My mother comed out o' Oxfordshire, and were under-laundry-maid in Sir Francis Dashwood's family; and when we were little ones, she'd tell us stories of their grandeur: and one thing she named were, that Sir Francis wore two shirts a day. Now he were all as one as a parliament man; and many on 'em, I han no doubt, are like extravagant. Just tell 'em, John, do, that they'd be doing th' Lancashire weavers a great kindness, if they'd ha' their shirts a' made o' calico; 'twould make trade brisk, that would, wi' the power o' shirts they wear. – *Mary Barton*, ch. 8

The years between 1812 and 1816, brightened as they were by a brief period of prosperity in 1814, proved to be relatively quiet for the workers of Stockport and its district. Local radicals managed to attract little support despite the continuing efforts of Major Cartwright and Sir Francis Burdett to promote petitions for parliamentary reform. Pacifist pamphlets circulated by the local Quaker printer James Lomax similarly failed to elicit any public stirrings of anti-war sentiment. The 'general spirit of combination' detected by authorities at Manchester and Bolton in the winter of 1813–14 appears to have affected Stockport only slightly. Apart from the calico printers' disputes (1813–15), the Stockport district experienced no major strikes until 1818.[1]

In the meantime the economic situation rapidly deteriorated both within the Stockport district and throughout the nation. The economic slump of 1816–17 was made worse in the English North-west by acute food shortages and soaring grain prices. Average contract prices paid in Cheshire by the commissariat for the supply of troops reflect these trends:[2]

	Oats (per 100 lb)	Bread (per 4 lb)
25 April–24 Oct. 1816	8s. 5½d.	6⅗₀d.
25 Oct.–24 Dec. 1816	9s. 6d.	7d.
25 Dec. 1816–24 June 1817	13s 6d.	11¼d.

194

| 25 June–24 Oct. 1817 | 12s. | 8d. | 11¼d. |
| 25 Oct.–24 Dec. 1817 | 8s. | 6d. | 8 d. |

Two aged Stopfordians interviewed in the 1880s recalled that the non-wheaten bread that they were consuming around this time was 'nearly black'. Francis Place quoted a Manchester manufacturer as saying in reference to the working classes after Waterloo that 'the sons of bitches [have] eaten up all the stinging nettles for ten miles round Manchester and now they [have] no greens for their broth'. A ten mile radius would have included nearly all of the Stockport district.[3] It should not be surprising that shortages of food in 1816 were linked to the political machinations surrounding the passage of the restrictive Corn Law of 1815, and more generally, that economic distress was again thought to be associated with political corruption. At the same time, local authorites had to worry about returning soldiers who were unable to find employment, unwilling to resign themselves quietly to their plights, and capable of infusing workers' movements with more discipline and better organisation than ever before.

I

Beginning in May 1816 there were various manifestations of workers' discontent. The *Death of Calico Jack* was again circulating as it had been in earlier periods of distress. Lloyd wrote to the Home Office on 13 May, 'They speak here of Ludditism being revived . . .' He blamed the slump in the cotton industry on the spirit of speculation and abuse of credit but could still claim that Stockport was not so badly affected as other towns. A week later Joseph Sherwin and Simon Lilly of the Stockport Weavers' Committee asked the Rev. Prescot to sanction a public meeting for the purpose of petitioning Parliament. They presented data which suggested that weavers' wages had declined to between one-quarter and three-fifths of the 1814 levels. The data probably reflected only the worst cases, but Sherwin and Lilly nevertheless hoped that such evidence would help them to obtain minimum wage legislation and an end to the export of twist.[4]

Prescot persuaded the two weavers' leaders to forego a public meeting and instead simply to send a petition to Wilbraham Egerton, one of the Cheshire MPs. The weavers agreed to comply with this request, and their petition was presented to the House of Commons on 23 May. A mere three days later both Cheshire MPs concluded that there was no chance of obtaining parliamentary relief.[5]

In the meantime Prescot and Lloyd had continued to exhibit generalised concern about the mounting distress and the disorders it might engender. Prescot reported that 'many families are in a starving condition, numbers are and more will soon be out of work. They are about driven to despair. The symptoms of intended rioting are stronger than I recollect they were previous to the breaking out of the Luddites.' Lloyd worked to assure that no local opposition would be offered to the weavers' petition since 'there are bad spirits amongst the weavers and some of the lower orders here, that no pretext should be given to'.[6] With the news that the weavers' petition had failed to gain its objectives came more rumours of illegal combinations and delegate activity. Yet leading Stopfordians soon set about promoting specific measures—an end to twist exports and alterations in the poor relief system—which diminished the possibility of public disorders through most of the summer of 1816. William Radcliffe had renewed his personal crusade against twist exports in 1815 by distributing copies of his 1811 pamphlet, *Letters on the Evils of the Exportation of Cotton Yarns*. In the following year, which saw twist and yarn exports increase by 77 per cent over 1815 levels, Radcliffe went to London to talk with Treasury officials about the problem. This prompted renewed efforts at Stockport, Bolton and elsewhere to try to prohibit twist exports altogether. It seemed ironic even to four Deputy Lieutenants of Lancashire that while the cotton weaving and finishing branches were suffering, the spinning branch was flourishing as never before due to twist exports. Talk of a memorial advocating prohibition occurred as early as 25 June at Stockport, and a printed copy of the memorial was prepared by 17 July.[7] Radcliffe claimed that it ultimately gained the signatures of 8,000 Stockport district weavers in addition to all of the master manufacturers, bleachers, dyers, calico printers and merchants of the area. Some ten or twelve master spinners also signed. On 29 July Joseph Sherwin sent the memorial to Viscount Warren Bulkeley, Lord of Stockport Manor, who then forwarded it to the Prince Regent. Radcliffe and some of his friends then ran a series of letters on the twist export controversy in the *Manchester Gazette* beginning on 28 September and continuing for nearly half a year. Already by September, however, the thoughts of some weavers had turned to more radical solutions to their distress.[8]

During Radcliffe's campaign many leading Stopfordians, including the major spinners and John Lloyd, continued to oppose efforts to limit or end the export of twist. Lloyd reasoned that spinning employed between one-quarter and one-half of Stockport's population and that disruption of twist exports would not only hurt them but also induce foreign nations to perfect twist-spinning machinery of their own. The alternative adopted by this faction of Stopfordians was to support and supplement the poor relief system. As early as 20 May Lloyd (expecting the parliamentary petition to fail) was urging people to help weavers obtain relief from their native townships.[9] Those without a legal settlement in Stockport would not, of course, be eligible for relief from Stockport overseers of the poor. Lloyd was instrumental in convening a public meeting of Stockport 'gentlemen' on 20 June to see what could be done to relieve suffering weavers. They decided to set up a Committee of Gentlemen to investigate the weavers' distress and identify specific cases deserving immediate relief. Weavers' delegates aided the Committee by gathering data on the numbers engaged in weaving and the number of looms unemployed (Table 9.1). These data show that for Stockport, Edgeley and Heaton Norris, three-fifths of the looms were unemployed in the summer of 1816. The Irish enclave at Edgeley had the greatest unemployment of looms (69 per cent) and the least favourable position in regard to poor relief. Whereas weavers and dependents in Stockport comprised only 17 per cent of the total population and those in Heaton Norris 15 per cent, weavers and dependents at Edgeley comprised 37 per cent of the population of Cheadle Bulkeley township. These data also indicate that families were already working three looms each in order to survive. The higher average at Edgeley (3.4 looms per family) may indicate that average wages were lower there than in Stockport and Heaton Norris, or it may simply reflect the larger family size at Edgeley which would require greater income. Indeed, with large Irish families probably weaving the cheapest plain calicoes, both factors may have been operative.

Whatever the situation in Edgeley, Lloyd and the Committee of Gentlemen were primarily concerned with Stockport township. Dificulties plagued their earliest efforts, not the least problem being that the weavers themselves, or at least the 'meddling part' of them, to use Lloyd's expression, were more concerned with relief of some sort from Westminster. Nor were the respectable classes

Table 9.1: The Weaving Branch in Stockport, Edgeley and Heaton Norris in June 1816

Township or Hamlet	(a) Total No. in Weavers' Families	(b) Looms Employed	(c) Looms Unemployed	(d) % Looms Unemployed	(e) Looms per Family
Stockport	3,410	775	1,117	59	2.8
Edgeley	1,070	208	475	69	3.4
Heaton Norris	913	254	241	49	2.7
Total [for (a) − (c)] or average [for (d)−(e)]	5,393	1,237	1,833	60	2.9

Note: Column (e) is based on 5.0 persons per family in Stockport and Heaton Norris, 5.3 for Edgeley. These are the average of family sizes in the census reports of 1811 and 1821.

Source: PRO, HO 42/151, Lloyd to Beckett, 25 June 1816.

themselves united. William Dawson, a master silk manufacturer and prominent supporter of the weavers during their 1808 strike, publicly opposed the Committee's scheme of investigation and selective relief. He favoured the weavers' own programme of agitation for a minimum wage and an end to twist exports. In any case, Lloyd and the Committee soon discovered that a voluntary subscription adequate to aid the large number of those in distress would be impossible to collect. The Committee then decided on an alternative approach, the promotion of more efficient collection and distribution of the poor rates. Lloyd foresaw great problems there, too, especially with the

> overseers of the poor, who cannot collect the rates sufficiently to answer the extra demands thus brought upon them. And I anticipate the greatest vexation from their conduct, for their humanity is not *natural* and when they are not in my office, they are very untoward and agravate [*sic*] the distresses of the poor.[10]

With characteristic energy, however, Lloyd endeavoured to surmount all such difficulties. In early July he could report that the poor rates were increased and that another sort of subscription was to be undertaken for the poor. It was to be used not for direct relief but rather to buy materials to be distributed by the overseers to the eligible poor, who would work them up for sale at a profit (or so it was hoped). At that time the fund was increased by money from the London Association for the Relief of the Manufacturing and Labouring Poor, a group similar to that active in 1812–13. In a broadside of 26 August explaining these developments, Lloyd stated that materials would be given out immediately. What became of this scheme is unclear, but since other plans were bruited in December, it is probable that the Stockport Committee's initial plans for setting the poor to work did not succeed.[11]

Thus, both major attempts to aid the weavers ran into difficulties. Radcliffe, Dawson and the opponents of twist exports tried pamphleteering, persuasion at the Treasury, memorialising the Prince Regent and finally, in September, a publicity campaign in the *Manchester Gazette.* Lloyd and other opponents of Radcliffe's faction contemplated charity subscriptions, helped tighten up the collection and disbursement of poor rates, and tried to set the poor to work. Both the agitation against twist exports and the Gentlemen's Committee gained some support from operative weavers and, after the failure of the weavers' parliamentary petition, probably helped to keep the large weaving population quiet for a time. But Radcliffe's hopes for success in his agitation to end twist exports effectively came to an end the moment Warren Bulkeley forwarded the Stockport memorial to the Prince Regent on 12 August. And despite Lloyd's relentless activity, the poor relief schemes proceeded in fits and starts and seemed to have achieved little success by the beginning of autumn. It is not surprising, therefore, that fears of a revival of Luddism should reappear in August and grow in strength through the autumn and into the winter months.

II

For a brief time, eruption of the most violent sort of Luddism seemed a distinct possibility. At Preston a crowd rioted on 13 August and broke windows at the house of a prominent powerloom manufacturer. A crowd of 1,000 Prestonians assembled again on the following day. On the night of 16 August a fire started in Peter Marsland's Park Mills at Stockport. It did extensive damage to the corn mill, destroyed Marsland's powerloom factory and razed an adjoining factory and warehouse which belonged to a London capitalist. Lloyd felt confident that the fire had started accidentally and that it had nothing to do with the Preston riots.[12] Still, the mood of Stockport weavers was clearly becoming more militant. On 26 August they met to requisition Prescot for a public meeting to discuss the worsening distress. One speaker roared:

> Damn the Rector. We have as much authority to call a second meeting as we had to call this. We may wait for ever if we wait for him. He will order us soup!

The meeting proceeded to divide Stockport into six districts, each to have three delegates to a committee which was to meet on the following night. Lloyd tried to subvert the new system with a broadside warning against unlawful assemblies and reiterating his belief that the distress was not so bad in Stockport as in other places where factory spinning was not so important. Small meetings continued nevertheless. On 29 August two weavers formally applied to Prescot for a public meeting to petition the Prince Regent. Prescot brought them to Lloyd, who gave them a copy of his latest cautionary broadside. The new workers' committee met again that evening and sent three more delegates to Prescot the next day for the same purpose. Prescot again referred them to Lloyd, who flatly refused their request. He explained his uncompromising (and in this case, successful) obstructionism in a letter on 1 September: 'I suppose they will begin upon cotton yarn–and end in ordering a reform.'[13]

Although seemingly inconsequential, the events of late August and early September marked a shift from a narrow weavers' movement to one encompassing other trades and advocating wider political changes. Lloyd noted that the furtive meetings from 26 August onwards included some poor inhabitants who were not weavers, although weavers predominated.[14] Since the weavers already had an organisation of their own, the new committee and district divisions were probably designed to recruit non-weavers into the agitation and to revive formal links between weavers and the local radical coterie. In fact, this new organisation can be said to have constituted the beginning of Stockport's Hampden Club, or Union Society. While a few such societies had been established earlier in July and August, the inspiration for the formation of many provincial clubs was the 21 August meeting of the Mayor, Aldermen and Liverymen of London promoted by the London Hampden Club and dominated by Sir Francis Burdett. The participants called for parliamentary reform and urged every county, city, town and parish to assemble and work for this goal. The promoters of the 26 August meeting at Stockport had read of the London meeting in the *Statesman* newspaper and had assembled in part to endorse the Liverymen's resolutions. Lloyd was perceptive in his simultaneous observation that the topic of twist exports would have to share the stage with parliamentary reform.

By 3 September William Fitton, a Royton radical, could write that union societies had been reported in many of Manchester's satellite towns. Some talk of revolution—a harbinger of things to come—accompanied the formation of these societies. Stockport radicals were in contact with their counterparts in other towns of the Manchester district and in London, a fact which helps to confirm that the new Stockport Union Society comprised a link in the chain of Hampden Clubs. Lloyd wrote on 18 September that Cartwright's agents of reform were at work on 'low men who are flattered by a correspondence with a man they consider of consequence'. This comment was probably made in response to Cartwright's widely circulated call in September for a national reform meeting, the meeting ultimately held in London on 22 January 1817. Cartwright also circulated printed petition forms praying for parliamentary reform.[15]

While local radicals could not manage to stage a large public meeting during September, they appeared to grow in strength while continuing to meet in small groups to prepare a second memorial to the Prince Regent on the subject of the weavers' distress. On 18 September Prescot and Marsland thought it advisable to request that the Home Office station cavalry in Stockport. Soon thereafter, Prescot sent the second Stockport memorial (signed by 10,000 persons) to Warren Bulkeley for presentation to the Prince Regent. The document is apparently not extant, but Prescot's remarks indicate that it urged the government to take decisive action to lessen the economic distress, perhaps by buying up surplus cotton goods and thereby relieve the glut. The Stockport radical committee met again on 23 September, a meeting attended by the spy 'B'. He reported that the committee was still planning to hold a public meeting, and if its next requisition were refused, it would convene one anyway. 'B' also spoke of a 'National Committee'—presumably the London Hampden Club—and of three delegates who attended various provincial meetings.[16]

The Stockport committee presented another request for a public meeting to Prescot on 29 September, a document signed by (among others) Thomas Cheetham the surgeon and James Swindells, a draper. Their request was again promptly refused. The following day the committee printed a broadside announcing a parliamentary reform meeting on 7 October. Lloyd countered with a broadside declaring (incorrectly) that such a meeting would be illegal. The radicals then circulated another broadside announcing that the meeting would discuss the prevailing distress. Lloyd, at least, was not deceived by the change in topics. With obvious reference to men like Cheetham, he wrote: 'There are a set whose characters I am acquainted with that have been active agents in sedition throughout their lives that will take care the original subject is not abandoned whatever becomes of the distressed.'[17] Lloyd observed the meeting of 7 October through a telescope. He learned that the speakers used revolutionary language and declared that there had to be a change in government or no government at all. Resolutions were passed proposing that Parliament be convened immediately to deal with the distress, that sinecures and the standing army be ended and, as Lloyd had predicted, that Parliament be reformed. The latter resolution held

> that the failure of several applications which have been made to Parliament, for upwards of fifteen years, in aid of the Manufacturers of this town and Neighbourhood, may be attributed principally to an unequal, and consequently inefficient Representation of the People, in the Commons House of Parliament.

Thirteen men were on the platform of this meeting. Six were weavers. Three 'agents of reform' were from out of town: John Knight from Manchester, Joseph Mitchell and Mr Davies, both of Liverpool. The others included such veteran local radicals as William Clegg, Sampson Robinson (a hatter) and Joseph Bertinshaw (a cobbler).[18]

No further public meetings of the radicals were held in Stockport before January 1817, although meetings were held in other parts of the greater Manchester district to the increasing alarm of the authorities. New of delegate conclaves also continued. One was scheduled for 24 November at Stockport. 'B' claimed that the working classes in the western and southern parts of the Stockport district, that is, at Cheadle, Handforth, Woodford and Bullocksmithy, were more radical than those at Stockport. Radical adherents in those areas were especially critical of the extravagance of the Prince Regent and thought that he should be forced from the throne. At Bullocksmithy, in particular, 'B' found that 'the people pretends to be very religious but you may reloy, the[y] are a dangerous set as the[y] cloak their actions by it and instruct their children in it also. It is one of the forwardis places I know of . . .' 'B' 's comments serve to emphasise the extent to which radical ideas had spread into many corners of the Stockport district. At least one event lent some support to allegations of this type. Rumours circulated that there was to be a rising on 2 December, the day of a second Spa Fields meeting in London. Nothing happened on that day in Stockport, but at the village of Denton (and in Newton, Lancashire) weavers stopped working, 'exciting a great sensation throughout the whole of this neighbourhood . . .'[19]

The apprehensions raised by these events helped to stimulate new efforts to aid the poor. The Stockport Dorcas Society was established at this time as a voluntary charity with no formal links to Stockport's governing authorities. Lloyd, by contrast, continued to regard charity as merely a part of larger official schemes to maintain order. On 11 December he called a meeting of gentlemen to revive efforts to help the poor and to take steps to defend against revolution. As a result of this meeting the able-bodied poor were set to work levelling a large tract of land near the town. Lloyd was checking with the surveyors of the highways to see if the poor could next be put to work repairing roads. The meeting also advocated outright charity which would especially benefit those without a legal settlement in the town. Voluntary subscriptions financed this effort, which involved the purchase of soup, coal and clothing for the poor. Out of the 11 December meeting there also emerged a loyalist asociation made up of those Stopfordians who had taken the special constables' oath. They were to arm themselves with pistols and were to assemble immediately at the Castle Inn and await the magistrates' orders in cases of riot. A great many men came forward during the subsequent month to take the oath of membership in this para-military organisation.[20]

III

Radical activity meanwhile increased and became centred at Middleton, where Samuel Bamford was a leading figure. Delegates from 14 union societies, including Stockport's, met there in an abandoned chapel on 16 December. The meeting had been called by a broadside which announced that the London Hampden Club had set 2 March as the day for presenting petitions to Parliament. Delegates from 21 societies met again at Middleton on 1 January. Out of these meetings there emerged a renewed commitment to promote parliamentary reform and to alter the Corn Laws. Delegates at Middleton also decided to write to Cartwright and Burdett on these subjects.[21] A wave of public meetings ensued. Stopfordians may have attended the meetings at Manchester on 23 and 30 December and were certainly well-represented at the Macclesfield meeting of 2 January. Denton radicals held a meeting on 4 January.[22] Stockport radicals requisitioned the Rev. Prescot on 9 January for a meeting of their own. When he refused, they circulated a broadside announcing a meeting for 13 January without official sanction. True to form, Lloyd responded with a broadside critical of the meeting's promoters. The meeting took place anyway, with special constables and the Stockport Yeomanry at the ready. It dealt largely with parliamentary reform and the Corn Laws, but few attended, perhaps because of an unexpected, albeit temporary, surge in the cotton trade which occurred around that time.[23]

Fearing the worst nevertheless, leading citizens in various urban centres began to hold anti-reform meetings. The first such meeting, which coincided with the Stockport reform meeting of 13 January, was held in Manchester.[24] Yet Lloyd's reports during this time show that Stockport did not need to defer to Manchester in the matter of vigilance. Stopfordians were already busy expanding the functions of the loyalist association formed on 11 December. Lloyd himself was distributing loyalist posters, which were having a salutary effect, he thought. As a member of the Stockport Orange Lodge, he also attended a general Orange meeting at Manchester on 28 January at which delegates resolved that Orangemen should actively support the authorities in cases of public disorder. Local loyalist schemes received further stimulus when the Prince Regent's carriage window was broken on his return from opening Parliament on 28 January, an event which precipitated the suspension of *habeas corpus*. Meetings in both Stockport and Heaton Norris on 5 February congratulated the Prince Regent on his escape and gave additional publicity to the loyalist cause.[25]

The start of the anti-reform meetings also coincided with a third delegate meeting at Middleton on 13 January. Among the numerous topics discussed was the idea of sending representatives chosen by local union societies up to London with the reform petitions which had been collected. The Stockport Union Society acted favourably on this suggestion. Lloyd reported that its representative was James Swindells, 'a petty draper . . . of *the least* consequence either in point of talent or property'. There were also delegates from Denton and Hyde. This trio formed part of the majority at the 22 January London meeting which voted for universal manhood suffrage (Henry Hunt's proposal) rather than householder suffrage (the measure favoured by Cobbett, Cartwright and Burdett). Despite the vote tally, this disagreement left the parliamentary reform movement at somewhat of an impasse. A speaker at Stockport's next reform meeting (10 February) informed the crowd, with considerable ambiguity, that their reform petition had to be withdrawn for 'revisions'. Other speakers at the meeting proceeded to suggest a whole new array of radical schemes. One advocated exclusive dealing, the buying of goods only from friends of reform. Calicoes were to be purchased solely from James Swindells, for example. Another speaker by the name of Bradbury (probably the radical Manchester stone cutter of that name) told the crowd to go to the overseers of the poor *en masse* to demand relief. Petitions for reform, he said, should be carried up to London in groups of ten–the first hint at Stockport of what was to become the abortive Blanketeers' march. He also echoed Spencean agrarian dreams when he pointed out that there were six acres per man if divided up. A third speaker, a 'shabby' young minister, then 'made many shocking and blasphemous alusions [*sic*] to the Deity, which had a tendency to lead the people to question the *Justice* of the Almighty'. Lloyd, from whose letter these accounts are drawn, thought that Bradbury, at least, had received his instructions from the 'Grand Committee at Middleton Chapel'. The other proposals may likewise have emanated from Middleton or, perhaps, from the Metropolitan radical circles so recently visited by the Stockport district's three delegates.[26]

From late January to early March there were rumours of arms being made and insurrections being planned. Secret meetings occurred at all the major urban centres of the Midlands and the North. A parliamentary Committee of Secrecy concluded in mid-February that from the network of secret clubs, 'which are composed of the lower order of Artizans, nothing short of a Revolution is the object expected and avowed'. The tactic most in favour in the

Manchester district, however, was that of marching in groups of ten to London to 'undeceive' the Prince Regent. Samuel Bamford, who opposed this plan, mentioned as leading supporters 'two young men, named Bagguley and Drummond who had recently come into notice as speakers, and who being in favour of extreme measures, were much listened to and applauded'. John Bagguley, a Manchester apprentice, was just 18 years old at the time. Samuel Drummond, a Manchester reedmaker of Irish parentage, was 24. It was Bagguley whom the Manchester radicals sent to persuade Stopfordians to attend a meeting in Manchester on 3 March against the suspension of *habeas corpus* and in favour of a march to London. Such a march must have seemed increasingly attractive to many in the Stockport district during the following week. The reform petitions finally presented to the House of Commons on 3 March from Stockport, Denton, Hyde and Offerton were showing absolutely no sign of achieving their stated goals.[27]

Not surprisingly, therefore, some people from the Stockport district joined others from outlying areas at Manchester on 10 March for the famous Blanketeer meeting. To one JP, female radicals seemed especially prominent in the crowd of some 12,000.

The women of the lower class seem to take a strong part against the preservation of good order and in the course of the morning of the 10th, it was a very general and undisguised cry amongst them that the gentry had had the upper hand long enough and that their turn was now come.[28]

Bagguley and Drummond were the orators of the day, proposing a Blanketeers' petition critical of: (1) excessive government spending and high taxes, the latter allegedly having quadrupled during the war; (2) high rents which were said to have doubled during the war; (3) the Corn Law of 1815; (4) the Libel Laws; (5) the suspension of *habeas corpus*; and (6) the Prince Regent's ministers, whose dismissals the petition demanded. When the meeting was broken up by magistrates and military, Bagguley and Drummond were among the 27 arrested on the spot.

The march to London to present the petition had meanwhile begun, and Holland Watson, the magistrate formerly of Stockport but now of Congleton, played a leading role in suppressing it. With a handful of Yeomanry, he dashed to Stockport's Lancashire Bridge and stopped the leading party of marchers, 48 of whom he was able to take into custody with the help of military reinforcements. Other marchers avoided a confrontation with the military by wading across the Mersey. In Stockport this group was joined by a few marchers from the neighbourhood who had not attended the Manchester meeting but who wanted to take part in the trek. Thousands of others came out to observe the goings-on. One account stated that 'the streets of Stockport were literally wedged full of the inhabitants of the vicinity'. As Watson and the troops moved into Stockport to aid the Yeomanry and special constables, more marchers swarmed across the now-unprotected bridge. About 170 were finally apprehended in the Market Place and taken back' to Manchester, with 28 more held by Lloyd in Stockport for further questioning. Four or five hundred marchers reached Macclesfield in small groups, while less than 100 continued on to Leek and Ashbourne with their blankets under their arms.[29]

Manchester weavers comprised the vast majority of those arrested. No Stopfordians were arrested at Manchester, while only a few district weavers were taken at Lancashire Bridge and in the town of Stockport. Moreover, the real involvement of this handful of men seems to have been slight. Charles McAlman, one of the weavers taken at Lancashire Bridge, was a 16-year-old lad who lived with his parents and claimed he had merely been trying to find work at Manchester on 10 March. The authorites apparently believed him, and he was discharged. James Schofield, a Haughton man arrested at Ashbourne, had attended the Manchester meeting and set off on the march with one shilling in his pocket and little apparent knowledge of the objectives. 'I had no concern in petitions,' he stated. 'I do not know what they were going for.' He, too, was discharged from custody. One might compare this with a general account given in a Stockport Sunday School publication:

> Our labouring poor demeaned themselves with a propriety of conduct well-according with their situation. The patient and silent resignation with which they sustained hunger and nakedness, even in the face of a rigorous winter, amidst declining wages and the advance of provisions is fresh in every recollection.[30]

All the evidence, in short, points to the fact that active participation in the Blanketeers' march by workers of the Stockport district was minimal.

Exactly one week after the Blanketeers' fiasco, another delegate meeting was held at Middleton. Although Bamford claimed that spies caused all the talk of armed insurrection in the weeks immediately after the march, there can be little doubt that detailed plans were proposed by Manchester district delegates themselves at this meeting, plans which became the foundation for the 'Ardwick Conspiracy'. The target was to be Manchester – the army barracks, the New Bailey Prison, the Police Office, the magistrates' houses. There was also talk of seizing the Leghs' cannon at Lyme Park just to the south-east of Stockport, but nothing further was to be done until the rising could be co-ordinated with Birmingham and Nottingham.

As with the Blanketeers' march itself, few Stockport district inhabitants were involved in the post-Blanketeer plots. The only Stockport man in attendance at Middleton on 17 March was a weaver named Richard Flitcroft who had not previously been prominent either in weavers' agitations or in the reform movement. He probably saw the delegate meeting as an opportunity to make a name for himself in radical circles and volunteered to act as a radical missionary to the Potteries and Birmingham. One reason he gave was that the Potteries were already in correspondence with Stockport. His eagerness to volunteer nevertheless provoked mounting suspicions about the degree of his commitment to radicalism. While he received money for the trip and set off on 21 March, on his return to Stockport and Manchester a week later he found himself ostracised by the radicals. As a consequence he probably did not attend the secret meetings held on 28 March in Ardwick. By that time rumours were rampant of a rising planned for Sunday, 30 March. According to the various stories, weapons were being made, the rising was to be signalled by a small rocket, and Leicester and Sheffield had been added to Birmingham and Nottingham as radical centres preparing for revolt. The Stockport Yeomanry were called up on 29 March, but the weekend passed without incident. The only Stopfordian implicated in the plotting, it seems, was Flitcroft. On 5 April the Home Secretary, Lord Sidmouth, issued a warrant for his arrest on suspicion of high treason.[31]

Flitcroft was the sole Stockport district man to be sought under the 1817 suspension of *habeas corpus*. He was apprehended at Stockport on 13 April and was immediately sent up to London. Sidmouth examined him on 15 and 22 April and again on 29 April along with Samuel Bamford. Bamford was released after this examination; Flitcroft was committed to Chelmsford Gaol. By 7 May he indicated that he wanted to give information in order to secure a pardon. This gave rise to his 'Narrative' of 23 May, which, though extremely informative on the Stockport Union Society, failed to help Flitcroft. He remained incarcerated until 12 November.[32]

Flitcroft stated that he was a handloom weaver in his early thirties who had served for 15 years in the Lancashire Militia in Ireland (c.1800-15). After being discharged, he lived in Bolton for a month and then migrated to Stockport where he found work. He said that he had belonged to the Union Society for less than a year and that its secretary was William Ogden, a weaver. The Society met weekly (apparently on Mondays), had dues of a penny per week, and had terminated its affairs before the Blanketeers' march. This could help to explain the seeming indifference of the Stockport radicals to the march and to later plans for revolt – and to the sudden rise to prominence of a comparative unknown like Flitcroft.[33]

With Flitcroft in prison and the Union Society disbanded, Stockport radicalism entered a period of seeming inactivity. Repression was a primary cause. The energy of local loyalists both before and after the Blanketeers' march had been reinforced by restrictive acts passed by Parliament, notably the suspension of *habeas corpus*. As Lloyd wrote in a fulsome letter of 17 May, 'The excellent measures that my Lord Sidmouth has pursued has left me nothing to communicate.'[34] Also in the spring of 1817 the campaign against the export of twist started up again, this time with London becoming the initial focal point and Stockport following its lead. William Radcliffe sent copies of his 1811 pamphlet to every MP on this occasion. A Stockport parliamentary petition of 6 June blaming all the weavers' and finishers' problems on the export of twist was signed by 'manufacturers, weavers and others'.[35] As with previous Stockport petitions in the same vein (1799, 1811, 1816), it no doubt gained the support of numerous operative weavers who were impressed by the spectacle of so many master manufacturers working for an objective of mutual benefit. Handloom weavers may have been content to embrace a peaceful anti-export campaign for other reasons. Food prices were beginning to decline, and the cotton trade improved markedly throughout the remaining months of 1817 and beyond.[36] Although the latter did not lead to increases in average wage rates, it substantially decreased the unemployment

and underemployment which had made the twelve months beginning
in May 1816 such intensely miserable ones for Stockport district
weavers.

IV

In certain general respects the events of 1816-17 paralleled those
of 1811-12. In both cases weavers' distress (resulting from varying
combinations of low wages, lack of employment and high food
prices) played the major role in stimulating public disorders. In
both, *ad hoc* poor relief measures and agitations against the export
of twist probably helped to diminish support for radical programmes
at key junctures. Moreover, certain patterns of activity were
repeated. Humble requests to local authorities and peaceful
petitioning of Parliament gave way to demands for fundamental
changes in the nation's political structure and to threats of violence.
In each case an important point of transition was the formation of
a new institution – the Committee of Trades in 1811, the Stockport
Union Society in 1816. Finally, with Luddism in April 1812 and the
Blanketeers' activities in March 1817, the two periods of discontent
reached their respective climaxes.

Beyond such parallels, it is possible to view the events of 1816-17
from three perspectives, that is, in terms of sectional weavers'
complaints, the political radicalism of the Hampdenites and the
more extreme radicalism of the Spenceans. While there were
thousands of weavers willing to petition for redress of sectional
grievances, there were probably only a few hundred members of
the Stockport Union Society and only a few dozen extremist
Spenceans. When the weavers were voicing their complaints in the
spring and summer of 1816, London Hampdenites were trying
(with limited success) to promote parliamentary reform agitations.[37]
They succeeded only at the end of August when their Westminster
meeting finally stimulated the formation of typically short-lived
provincial clubs like the Stockport Union Society. Meanwhile, the
Spenceans renewed their activities. Thomas Spence, a prophet of
land redistribution and violent revolution, had died in 1814. His
leading disciple, Thomas Evans, thereupon established the Society
of Spencean Philanthropists (SSP). The SSP seemed to attract the
attention of the Home Office only in 1816, when it became the
topic of spies' reports. In that same year, Evans wrote a tract

announcing that the world was on the threshold of a new era, one which would feature the communal holding of land. By the winter of 1816-17, he was preaching revolution.[38]

It has been claimed that certain union societies (like those at Norwich and Bath) shifted from Hampdenism to Spenceanism during that same winter. Such societies were perhaps inspired by the impressive Spa Fields meetings in London on 15 November and 2 December 1816, both of which had Spencean support.[39] To what extent did events in the Stockport district depend on such national events and trends as these? While they influenced Stockport district affairs to some extent, the inner dynamic of local discontent was probably more important. In a situation of worsening distress, when peaceful, limited requests were refused or even ignored, more far-reaching demands were voiced and coercive measures were threatened or employed, particularly by weavers. This was the pattern observable in 1811-12 and also in 1807-8. It occurred again in 1816-17 but with modifications which deserve closer scrutiny.

In both 1807-8 and 1811-12, there had been undercurrents of parliamentary reform agitations. In both cases, however, the major source of discontent remained the weavers. Consequently, when illegal actions were taken, such actions involved objectives (like higher wages for weavers and destruction of powerlooms) which were of narrow concern to the weaving trade. The situation in 1816-17 was perhaps different *because* of this, because two specific mass actions had been tried and had failed in the recent past. Weavers' leaders were not so foolish as to advocate a strike or machine-breaking spree again at this time. Thus, when they renewed formal contacts with the local radical coterie, weavers' leaders seemed determined that peaceful parliamentary reform agitation was going to be the limit of their exertions. This presumably applies to William Ogden, the weaver who served as secretary to the Union Society, to Simon Lilly, and above all to Joseph Sherwin. Sherwin had participated in the abortive strike of 1808 and had been on both the Weavers' Committee and the Committee of Trades in 1811-12. But he (like Ogden and Lilly) became less and less active as the Blanketeers' march approached and had no known role in the post-Blanketeer conspiracies.

When the parliamentary reform agitation of the Stockport Union Society became intertwined with measures reminiscent of the extra-legal tactics of the recent past, the weavers' leadership abandoned the agitation and returned to narrow sectional concerns. The radical coterie, though not willing to abandon the goal of parliamentary reform, was willing to dismantle the Union Society. Three individuals were probably typical of the latter group. Sampson Robinson the hatter had been active on the 1812 Committee of Trades. William Clegg the schoolmaster had been active in Stockport Jacobinism since the 1790s. Thomas Cheetham the surgeon had been involved in Stockport radicalism since at least 1810. All were associated with the Union Society of 1816-17, but none was ever known to advocate violence, Spencean reform, or a march to London.

This is not to say that Stockport did not have some disciples of the more extreme forms of radicalism. Richard Flitcroft was one, and so was another newcomer to the town, a Scottish weaver named Henry Rose. He was active in the Stockport meetings of 7 October 1816 and 13 January 1817 as well as that at Denton on 4 January. He had been active in Scottish Jacobinism earlier in his life and was one of three Glasgow delegates to the Convention held in the spring of 1793. In January 1817 he was advocating 'sweeping' reform, not merely parliamentary reform. He also claimed to despise the Hampden Clubs, presumably because of their limited objectives. At the 10 February Stockport meeting he advocated exclusive dealing as part of a programme (enunciated by his fellow speakers) of some sort of deism or atheism, equal division of land and a march on London. Yet as a few prominent individuals like Rose (and at Manchester, Bagguley and Drummond) became increasingly zealous, the more cautious radical leadership withdrew from the agitation. The Union Society disbanded with the approach of the date for the Blanketeers' march, an event some linked to a national convention or a rising upon arrival in London. An MP who was in touch with Lancashire radicals noted later: 'This foolish proposal was objected to strongly by the generality of those, who, from their superior intelligence and activity, were regarded as their leaders.'[40] Lacking the approval of weavers' leaders and established local radicals and without institutional support, the Blanketeers' march could gain only modest support from the inhabitants of the Stockport district.

John Belchem has stressed the crucial importance of the Blanketeer epoch as a stage in the development of workers' solidarity and the 'mass platform'.[41] Yet his conclusions are perhaps too heavily influenced by the patterns and experiences of the Metropolis to possess much interpretive value for the North-west. Mass petitions, mass meetings, the advocacy of 'intimidationist' tactics and the perception of a linkage between economic distress and corrupt politics were not new in 1816-17, either in the Stockport district or most of Lancashire. Likewise, the coalition between Hampdenites and Spenceans which was notable in London had only faint reverberations in the North. The *Manchester Political Register* (22 February 1817) was not precisely correct when it denied the existence of any connections between the two groups. Still, the introduction of Spencean ideas into Lancashire, far from enriching and enlarging workers' agitations, seemed to be part of a process by which workers' objectives were multiplied and their movements thereby diminished. As in 1811-12, widening agitations led to greater internal diversity and lack of cohesion. Advocates of advanced deism and outright atheism, for example, were regaining prominence for the first time since the late 1790s, much to the chagrin of Christian reformers. The Rev. Prescot overheard the following in a public house in 1816: 'There is no God, for if there was a God, he would take care that the rich did not oppress the poor. Therefore they must take care of themselves [and] kill the magistrates . . .' A government spy thought that most of the reformers were deists, but Samuel Bamford and others denied that accusation.[42]

It is not merely the existence of such centrifugal impulses that should serve as a caution against easy generalisations about 'stages of growth' in popular movements. The origins and content of divergent goals point to the same conclusion. Weavers and other workers continued to be attracted to various reform proposals advanced by local manufacturers and merchants. That Peter Marsland and William Radcliffe led the respective campaigns against the Corn Laws and twist exports illustrates this phenomenon. The Stockport elite's near-obsession with high taxes was likewise echoed by delegates at Middleton and speakers at the Blanketeers' meeting, among other individuals. The new silver coinage of 1816-17 shows the same pattern. It caused immediate anxiety among Stockport's shopkeepers because of its possible inconvenience. It subsequently provoked concern among some local radicals who read *Theory of Money* and Cobbett's *Paper Against Gold* and learned about the potential of the new coinage to retard economic growth.[43] Econometricians may some day be able to determine whether masters or operatives would have benefited more from such measures as Corn Law repeal, a ban on twist exports, tax cuts or currency reform in 1816-17. Suffice it to say for the present that one would err in suggesting that these agitations in the Stockport district comprised parts of a singular 'working-class movement'. Indeed, it would prove to be a difficult and complex task for successive workers' leaders and institutions to comprehend and harness such divergent aspirations.

The absence of collective radical activities for many months after the spring of 1817 did not mean, however, that radicalism died away. Certain lines of continuity can be traced. For example, on 7 June 1817 a radical delegate visited Stockport from Honley, near Huddersfield. He contacted William Perry, a weaver who had been arrested during the 1808 weavers' strike. This delegate warned that the rising now scheduled for 9 June (and presumably known to some Stockport radicals) was to be postponed because Birmingham and Sheffield were not ready. The delegate returned to the West Riding on 8 June. On that night the Huddersfield district witnessed the 'Folly Hall Rising', and on the night of 9 June the famous Pentridge Rising occurred in Nottinghamshire.[44] The unprepared towns obviously could not restrain the districts and villages which were ripe for insurrection. At about the same time efforts to expand the Stockport Yeomanry met with difficulties. Tradesmen who had previously lent horses to the Yeomanry now refused to do so, fearing the hostility of the radicals. This suggests that exclusive dealing by the radicals was having some impact. Lloyd received word of a secret club meeting on Mondays which was made up of 'disaffected characters – some of them from the time of republican principles being first imported from France'. This was surely the regrouping of Clegg, Cheetham and Stockport's radical coterie.[45]

Continuity could also be found in the increasing volume of workers' handbills, pamphlets and periodicals. Stockport's radical weavers made frequent use of handbills from the reappearance of *The Death of Calico Jack* in May 1816 onwards. In addition to this, radical literature poured forth from Manchester presses. William Hone's satiric *Political Catechism* went through four Manchester editions before the end of 1816. A pamphlet advocating parliamentary reform (*Petitioning Weavers Defended*) appeared in Manchester early in 1817. Such pamphlets undoubtedly circulated throughout the Manchester district, distributed by men like Joseph Mitchell, a Liverpool pamphlet seller. Mitchell spoke at the Stockport meetings of 7 October and 13 January and travelled extensively in the North until his arrest on 3 May. Hone's *Political Litany* (including the *Political Creed*), which included gibes at both religion and parliamentary corruption, circulated from Manchester as far as Macclesfield. There, a bookseller was arrested on a charge of blasphemy for selling it on the day of the Blanketeers' march. The *Manchester Political Register*, a short-lived radical newspaper which first appeared on 4 January 1817, probably also circulated throughout the region.[46]

Added to this profusion of local radical literature were London publications of various kinds. Walter Fawkes' *Englishman's Manual; or, a Dialogue between a Tory and a Reformer* went through three editions in 1817, some of which made their way to the North-west. So did some of the Whig/radical periodicals, like the *Statesman*, the *Independent Whig* and, beginning in November 1816, a two-penny pamphlet version of *Cobbett's Political Register*. The impact of the cheap *Register* was judged to be immense, even by its critics. One of the latter called this publication

the most malignant and diabolical that had ever issued from the English press. These were hawked up and down the country poisoning the minds of the poor and ignorant; and perplexing the magistracy, who knew not how to deal with the novel and detestable trade in sedition.

Bamford's famous remark that the writings of Cobbett 'were read on nearly every cottage hearth in the manufacturing districts of South Lancashire' attests to the popularity of Cobbett in the greater Manchester district. The first pamphlet in Cobbett's new series, *Address to the Journeymen and Labourers*, may indeed have provided the inspiration for the Stockport loyalist broadside, *To the Journeymen Mechanics & Labouring Poor*, which urged workers to 'unite the spirit of Christianity with that of patriotism . . .'[47]

Other radical periodicals with national circulations soon followed Cobbett's 'Two-Penny Trash' into the Stockport district. In May Lloyd arrested a man for selling the *Black Dwarf*, *Sherwin's Political Register* and Southey's *Wat Tyler*. In August 1817 and March 1818 Lloyd was still complaining that *Sherwin's Political Register* was being circulated in Stockport. The stream of printed materials scarcely abated thereafter. William Blackshaw was claiming in 1829 that he had sold political and anti-religious publications at Stockport continuously since 1817.[48]

The radical press supplemented radical clubs and the tactic of exclusive dealing as a means of sustaining interest in radicalism at

Stockport in the year or so after the Blanketeers' march and Ardwick Conspiracy. The plight of the weavers also helped to provide continuity, for although theirs was a trade doomed to extinction, the path to extinction was not uniformly downwards. In the two decades before 1817 wage rates and availability of employment had both fluctuated wildly. From 1817 onwards, wage rates remained extremely low and fluctuations occurred mainly in employment, with full employment being required for most weavers to maintain themselves at bare subsistence levels. When employment fell off, as it did from the summer of 1818 through the summer of 1819, the weavers were again ready to mingle industrial grievances with the radical politics advocated by various periodicals and nurtured in secret local clubs.[49]

I saw an angel standing in the sun and he cried with a loud voice
saying to all the fowls that fly in the midst of heaven come and
gather yourselves together unto the supper of the Great God,
that ye may eat of the flesh of Kings and the flesh of captains
and the flesh of mighty men . . . It comes, it comes, the
dreadful storm comes rolling on. – The Rev. Joseph Harrison
(August 1819)

I

Stockport radicalism was already undergoing a modest revival
during the first half of 1818. John Lloyd complained about the
circulation of 'seditious trash' during these months, and he had
good reason to complain after the first appearance of the highly
popular *Manchester Observer* on 3 January. The *Observer*'s reports
of local radical news and its uncompromisingly radical stance caused
its weekly circulation to soar into the thousands during its first
three months of existence.[1] In the premier issue its proprietors
called for renewed parliamentary reform agitations, which the
Observer was to support with unrelenting energy over the next
three years. It also carried detailed stories on what was to become
the first major radical issue of the year, the financial assistance of
those who had been imprisoned under the suspension of *habeas
corpus*.

The only Stockport man so imprisoned, Richard Flitcroft, played
no part in those proceedings. Lloyd had told him that the Court of
King's Bench would discharge his recognisance and that he did not
need to journey to London. But the role of four Manchester men
(Bagguley, Drummond, Johnston and Knight) was significant
because of their subsequent participation in Stockport district radical
affairs. John Bagguley and Samuel Drummond had been the fiery
young orators at the Blanketeers' meeting. John Johnston was a
Manchester tailor. John Knight had been a small manufacturer,
but by this time his radical lectures and writings seem to have
provided most, if not all, of his income. The four left Manchester

on 21 January to appear under their 1817 recognisances before
King's Bench in London. After tedious and frustrating proceedings,
their recognisances were finally discharged. The whole affair – the
initial imprisonments and the expense and inconvenience attendant
on discharging the recognisances – put London radicals in an
uproar. Various Hampdenites, including Burdett, Cochrane and
Cartwright, launched a subscription to relieve all sufferers under
the Suspension Act, especially the Spencean Thomas Evans.
Bagguley ('a young man of respectable appearance' according to
The Times) and Johnston spoke at the inaugural meeting of the
London Relief Committee.[2] The Manchester men thus probably
came into contact not only with those espousing moderate Hampdenite
programmes but also with the more extreme Spenceans. A London
Relief Committee meeting of 6 February resolved that local
committees and subscriptions be set afoot, but already on 7 February
Lloyd reported that such a subscription was going forward at
Stockport. When the petitions of Bagguley, Drummond and Knight
were presented later in the month, however, Parliament took no
action whatsoever.[3]

These proceedings can only have served to strengthen the radicals'
resolve to obtain their fundamental objective, parliamentary reform.
Discussions of precise goals and tactics probably figured in the
'debates' Stockport radicals held in a room they rented in February.
The subject of tactics certainly emerged prominently at the first
reform meeting of the year, that held at Manchester on 9 March.
The main speakers derided petitioning, which had failed a year
earlier, and instead advocated the formation of reform societies.
They also endorsed the proposal they found in *Sherwin's Political
Register* to resist the payment of taxes. Bagguley, Drummond and
Johnston were among those on the stage at that meeting.[4] From
March through July an average of about three reform meetings
was held each month in greater Manchester district towns, with
the peak coming in April when Stockport radicals had their meeting.
The Rev. Prescot as usual turned down their requisitions for a
meeting, but seven householders, including Cheetham the surgeon,
announced the meeting in the *Manchester Observer* anyway. Joseph
Bertinshaw, the old radical cobbler, took the chair on 13 April,
with William Perry (a vendor of radical literature), Bagguley,
Drummond and Johnston as principal speakers. The last three
spoke in such violent terms and so roundly denounced Lloyd that
the magistrate's clerk became 'determined that they shall not prevail.

They have goaded me to a decided opposition of such proceedings which before I viewed with contempt and indifference and directed a forebearance which I now regret.' The meeting's resolutions resembled those passed at Manchester a month before, with support for annual Parliaments, adult male suffrage, the formation of reform societies and resistance to taxation being most notable.[5]

There followed a few months of relative calm,[6] but the situation changed during the third quarter of 1818 owing to the emergence of new leaders in Stockport radical circles and to heightened industrial tensions. Some time during the first half of 1818 Bagguley decided to move to Stockport, the home of his uncle, a tailor. Johnston maintained his residence and tailoring shop in Manchester, and Drummond probably continued to live there, too, but both frequently joined Bagguley in Stockport. Bagguley proceeded to set up a day and evening school or lecture room in an old Edward Street windmill around the beginning of July. Although it may have simply been the successor to the debating club discovered by Lloyd in February, this school seems to have provided a more public, and hence stronger, focal point for radical affairs than did the semi-clandestine club. Bagguley's fellow teacher at the school was the Rev. Joseph Harrison, a dynamic Presbyterian minister who was new in Stockport and was now active in radical politics for the first time. The son of a Whiggish Yorkshire minister, Harrison had been at Essex and had recently taught at Glossop, Derbyshire, but was forced to leave, Lloyd found out, 'for improper liberties taken with his young female scholars'.[7] He was to gain great regional fame and some national attention during the ensuing months.

The radicals' hand was also strengthened at the beginning of July by their open espousal of the powerloom weavers' struggle, especially after the introduction of blacklegs (see Chapter 4). The authorities were convinced that Bagguley, Drummond and Johnston had actually helped to incite the powerloom rioters.[8] Radicals denied these charges and claimed in response that the authorities had used excessive brutality during the clashes. Two incidents were guaranteed to win public sympathy for the radicals – the firing of shots into Thomas Cheetham's house by local authorities and the fatal beating of an aged pauper by a band of soldiers. Bagguley used the Cheetham episode and derision of the Yeomanry (one of whom, he claimed, had fled up the Hillgate crying, 'murder! murder!') as the basis of a scathing letter to the *Manchester Observer* soon after the riots. When the Yeoman who fired the shots into

Cheetham's house was officially absolved of any wrongdoing on 4 August, Johnston helped to instigate a public demonstration.

The lingering death of the old pauper (William Reek) became the subject of a second Bagguley letter to the *Observer*. Soldiers had apparently dragged Reek from his lodging house in the Hillgate because he was suspected of throwing brick-bats from a window. Although there is little doubt that he died from their beating, the coroner's jury enraged the radicals by concluding that 'he died a natural death'. Bagguley immediately published a broadside, *Oh! Horrible! Horrible! most Horrible!*, calling for a meeting on 10 August to discuss the Cheetham and Reek incidents and the riots in general. Lloyd said the meeting was 'attended by about 1000 ragamuffins'. With Bagguley as the main speaker, the meeting resolved that 'the late unjust and unprincipled outrages . . . are not surpassed even in the annals of barbarity . . .' and that resistance to oppression (as legitimised by Lockean social contract theory) was now necessary. Those present planned to begin a subscription to help individuals who had suffered as a result of the riots.[9]

The next day the radicals held a political reform meeting but only 200 attended. Another meeting was scheduled for a fortnight later. It must have been apparent to the radicals that the programme of reform by itself would not attract large audiences unless linked to a case of obvious injustice or to industrial grievances. It was at this juncture that Bagguley addressed a Stockport weavers' meeting and urged them to arm in preparation for their confrontation with the master manufacturers. It was also about this time that 'Parson' Harrison addressed striking spinners in Manchester. Although the reform meeting on 24 August quickly broke up at the arrival of the Yeomanry and military, Bagguley and James Sims, a watchmaker, planned another meeting for 1 September to coincide with the first day of the weavers' strike.[10]

On that day the official group of striking weavers paraded the streets and avoided the reform meeting just as they had been shunning Bagguley for the preceding week. Hundreds of others attended Bagguley's meeting, however, and they were joined by 500 Manchester spinners and 300 people from Ashton. Such a large assembly following so soon after the fiascos of 11 and 24 August must have had as intoxicating an effect on the speakers as did the gin from which they 'drank pretty freely' during their four or five hours on the platform. Parson Harrison acted as chairman and Bagguley, Drummond and Johnston were the main speakers.

Bagguley urged arming as one means to force Parliament to support reform. He also mentioned the establishment of a National Convention – a Spencean proposal – as another means. Drummond seconded the call to arms. Johnston threatened to blow out the brains of Castlereagh, Sidmouth and Canning and urged weavers and spinners to steal rather than work for low wages, advice some Stockport district weavers would soon be following in order to gain enough money to emigrate. Johnston's appeal to weavers and spinners suggests that they may have comprised the bulk of his audience and thus indicates the continuing, conscious effort of the small group of radicals to attract the support of large occupational groups.

Although the meeting dispersed peaceably amid showers of rain, Bagguley, Drummond and Johnston were soon arrested because of the seditious language they had used. Bail for each was set at nearly £2,000. These enormous sums were sufficient to assure that the trio remained imprisoned until their trial in the following spring and that a significant gap was left in the leadership of the Stockport radicals.[11]

II

From the summer of 1817 to that of 1818, when nearly full employment prevailed in the weaving trade, Stockport district weavers had exhibited little public enthusiasm for either trade unionism or radical politics. This behaviour corresponded with the period early in 1818 when Stockport radicals tried to launch a new parliamentary reform agitation with a notable lack of success. When the weavers became publicly active once again in July, August and September, radicalism seemed to advance. Radicals' support for the powerloom strike and especially for the attacks on the powerloom factories gained the sympathy of many handloom weavers. The handloom weavers' activities during the summer of 1818 thus deserve careful examination in the context of the radical affairs discussed above.

As with nearly all trades, the modest boom of 1817-18 induced weavers to believe that wages could and should be raised. On 18 July – only a few days after the powerloom strike had erupted into violence – Stockport handloom weavers were planning their own strike for wage increases. If the powerloom strike provided a local stimulus, the immediate trigger for strike plans came when one Manchester district firm dared to *lower* its handloom weavers' wages by 1d. per yard. Other weavers were joined by masters in protesting that the step was wholly unwarranted, the masters naturally fearing that they would be undersold. Yielding to the torrent of criticism, the errant firm not only reinstituted the previous wage rates but proceeded to raise them an extra 1d. per yard. This provided tangible evidence for the handloom weavers' belief that with the return to prosperity, wages did not have to be as low as they were.[12]

During July, therefore, Stockport district weavers renewed their contacts with others in the region and in Scotland. A Stockport weavers' deputy attended a delegate meeting at Prestwich in mid-July. The Stockport Weavers' Committee soon called for a meeting on 3 August 'to take into consideration the depressed state of the trade'. In the meantime another regional meeting of weavers' delegates was held at Bury on 27 July with a Stockport delegate known to have been in attendance. The delegates found prosperity increasing but weavers starving and decided to ask masters for an increase of 7s. in the pound.[13]

When delegates returned to their localities to request the 35 per cent increase, they met with mixed reactions. At Ashton, Oldham and Leigh, masters promised the full increase if masters elsewhere followed suit. At Bolton masters promised a 15 per cent increase. The offer of the Stockport masters is not known, but as at Bolton, the Stockport masters' offer probably fell below the 35 per cent level. Faced with a lack of uniformity in wage offers, Manchester district weavers held a third delegate meeting on 11 August at Manchester. Masters met simultaneously nearby and sent two representatives to the weavers to offer the desired wage increase in instalments: 20 per cent on 7 September, the other 15 per cent on 1 October.[14] Stockport weavers met on 19 August and adopted a hard line when apprised of this offer. They formally resolved to strike if the full 35 per cent was not met. On 22 August at Bury a fourth delegate meeting was attended by men from Stockport, Burnage and Levenshulme, among others. This meeting took a position similar to that taken at Stockport. Weavers were to wait until 31 August for the masters to decide on the wage increase. Weavers would then meet, and if the full increase had not been granted, they would begin a strike on 1 September.[15]

As the date for the strike drew near, the main body of Stockport weavers took steps to dissociate themselves from radical politics and radical politicians. Around the beginning of August, they replaced their secretary, a radical sympathiser and convicted felon, with a man who had no discernible links with the radicals. Bagguley addressed their 19 August meeting and urged them to arm. There was probably also talk on that occasion of the strikes in other trades that had occurred during the early summer and of the need for solidarity among trades. A trades union called the Philanthropic Society was being formed that very day at Manchester. Stockport weavers would not have anything to do with the Philanthropic Society, however, and Lloyd reported that weavers refused to listen to Bagguley's reform rhetoric. They chose instead to focus their main attention on narrow sectional grievances.[16]

Thousands of weavers paraded through Manchester on 31 August only to learn that a uniform 35 per cent wage increase would not be granted. Stockport weavers struck promptly on 1 September. By Lloyd's count 1,222 men and 355 women marched through Stockport streets that day with banners and music. They carefully avoided Bagguley's simultaneous reform meeting. The *Manchester Chronicle* reported that the next day a large body of Stockport weavers 'with many women' marched to Manchester, again with music and large banners, one of which read 'Seven Shillings in the Pound and no less'. The leader was a man who bore on his shoulders a reed and a heald draped in black crepe, emblematic of the well-known message in the broadside, *Death of Calico Jack*. On 3 September 1,500 weavers from Newton Lane, Manchester, reciprocated and joined thousands parading through the streets of Stockport. The next day Stockport weavers joined those from other towns marching to Ashton for similar parades and demonstrations.[17]

At Bury on 5 September, a fifth weavers' delegate meeting reviewed the week's activities in the light of continued intransigence by many masters. The majority of delegates resolved to return to work and accept the wage increase by instalments previously offered. A few delegates, including those from Stockport and Manchester, urged a continuation of the strike but had to be satisfied with a clause ordering weavers not to work below the agreed-upon instalments. These resolutions were circulated in a handbill signed by the meeting's three leaders.[18] As in 1808, one segment of Stockport weavers seemed determined to continue the strike no matter what the others decided. Lloyd wrote during the following week that a partial strike consequently went forward at Stockport supported by a system whereby some of the working weavers were billeting strikers. But at the end of the week Lloyd could report that an agreement had been reached and that the weavers were going back to work. The agreement was apparently the same as that offered by Lee's of Stockport – a ten per cent increase each month until the requested advance of 35 per cent was reached. Lee's own men, in fact, refused to work under such an agreement and were reported still striking on 19 September. With rumours of nocturnal open-air meetings by weavers accompanying the waning strike, Lee reportedly declared, 'They want a *Revolution*!'

It was at that point that the three signatories of the 5 September Bury resolutions were arrested. Repression occurred simultaneously at Stockport. On 20 September a Scottish weaver in a pub with some of the strikers shouted 'seditious' gibes at two soldiers. Lloyd had the Scotsman arrested and later secured his conviction and a sentence of six months in jail. Although there were reports of weavers' meetings for an additional week, there was no indication of even a partial strike after 20 September. There is only a little documentation on the weavers for the rest of the year. Joseph Sherwin stated some years later that the various prosecutions had had a chilling effect on the weavers and had convinced them that 'they are doomed to starvation; and without legislative enactment, they are afraid they never shall rise like other trades'.[19]

III

Thus, during September both radicals and weavers had reached impasses. Radicals were quick to regroup, however. The leadership vacuum left by the three arrests was filled by Parson Harrison with the assistance of John Knight, the Manchester cotton manufacturer, and Joseph Mitchell, the Liverpool pamphlet seller. Both Knight and Mitchell had been imprisoned under the suspension of *habeas corpus* and both had previously been guest speakers at Stockport radical meetings. By this time they could be characterised as full-time radicals. That they both gravitated to Stockport at this juncture provides a commentary on the effect of Bagguley, Drummond and Johnston's outspoken radicalism in putting Stockport at the centre of Manchester district radical affairs. The three arrests in turn became a regional, and eventually national, rallying point. As a Manchester magistrate wrote, 'The Chester prisoners are represented as martyrs in their cause'.[20]

Stockport radicals claimed that the speeches of 1 September had been misinterpreted and asked the magistrates to allow another meeting to discuss the arrests, methods of procuring bail and parliamentary reform. The meeting, unsanctioned as usual, was finally held on 28 September. Harrison acted as chairman, and both Knight and Mitchell spoke. The meeting voted to begin a subscription which was to be collected by a committee of ten Stopfordians (with Harrison as secretary and Cheetham the surgeon as treasurer) and also by individuals at Manchester, Oldham, Birmingham and London. Knight spoke against the Corn Laws, paper currency and high taxes. On the issue of parliamentary reform, the meeting resolved 'never more to petition that body called "the House of Commons"...', and instructed Harrison to draw up a petition for the Prince Regent. The meeting also claimed the right of each person to carry his own petition or remonstrance to London, a plan still popular among the Spenceans and reminiscent, of course, of the Blanketeers' march.[21]

The meeting in late September occurred amidst far-reaching organisational changes in local radicalism, alterations which would result in the formal establishment of the Stockport Union for the Promotion of Human Happiness in October. This institution deserves careful analysis because of its alleged impact on radical unions throughout the country and because of its startling success. From December 1818 to April 1819 an average of over 900 people contributed to the Prisoners' Relief Fund each week. After the three prisoners' convictions a total of 4,550 persons signed a petition requesting a new and fairer trial. The spy 'B' claimed that there were 4,300 'armed' men in the Stockport district in the summer of 1819 and 4,653 adherents to the radical cause in January 1820.[22] The Sunday school of the Stockport Union contained about 2,000 scholars at its peak. These figures suggest that the Stockport Union may have held as many as ten per cent of the district's inhabitants under its sway in the first year and a half of its existence, thereby making it the most successful radical organisation Stockport had ever known. The following features of the Stockport Union can help to explain its rise: (1) its basic organisation; (2) its ideologies; (3) its emphasis on religion; (4) its emphasis on education; (5) its toleration of infidels; (6) its impact on the outlying townships of the district; (7) its recruitment of women; and (8) its solicitous attitude towards handloom weavers.

At the core of the Stockport Union were 'classes' with a maximum of twelve members. Their weekly meetings, as described by a Union member in 1819, consisted of oral readings for about thirty minutes, interrupted by questions on difficult passages. About thirty minutes of general conversation followed 'when each member states his opinion and ideas of government, etc. etc.' Dues were a penny per week, the sums taken by class leaders each Monday to the Union Committee where he received the week's instructions. The town was divided into twelve districts, and members of each district elected two persons to sit on the Committee, half of which was newly elected each quarter. The Committee appointed its president and vice-president each week by rotation but appointed a secretary and treasurer to hold office at pleasure. Harrison became permanent secretary, and Thomas Cheetham seems to have been installed more or less permanently as treasurer. The Windmill Rooms in Edward Street, Sandy Brow, served as Union headquarters and also contained a reading room.[23]

The key positions of leadership remained largely in the hands of men from the lower-middle classes. A couple of surgeons were prominent, but Parson Harrison remained pre-eminent. His charisma, patience and skill as an orator–the result of many years in schoolroom and pulpit–contributed immeasurably to the Union's growth. He also exhibited considerable deftness as a writer and propagandist, as when he compiled and published an account of the 28 September meeting and sent it to the *Black Dwarf* and *Sherwin's Political Register*. The national attention this publicity generated soon produced tangible results. On 3 December Sir Charles Wolseley, one of the founders of the London Hampden Club, passed through Stockport and inquired whether he and Sir Francis Burdett could post bail for the three prisoners in Chester Castle. Although the magistrates refused his offer on the grounds that neither he nor Burdett resided in Cheshire, Wolseley later joined with William Greathead Lewis, a radical Coventry journalist, to retain an attorney for the prisoners. Six weeks after Wolseley's visit, Henry Hunt visited Stockport on his way to the Manchester reform meeting of 18 January 1819. According to Lloyd, Hunt 'gave audience to all the ragamuffins in the town . . .'[24]

The visits of Wolseley and Hunt to Stockport serve to highlight the local shift from the strident radicalism of Bagguley and company, which was intensified by contacts with London Spenceans, to a moderate radicalism more in keeping with the tenets of the London

Hampden Club. The full extent of the connections between Spenceans and Stockport radicals will probably never be known in full. Lloyd reported on 7 October that the notorious Spencean James Watson was busy collecting money at Stockport for his petition-and-Convention scheme but that the people were wary of him. Soon thereafter Stockport radicals chose the imprisoned John Bagguley as their delegate to march to London with the petition drawn up by Harrison. The choice assured that Stockport's role in the scheme, which proved unpopular anyway, would be negligible.[25] This was perhaps the inevitable result of a situation in which a small, dedicated radical coterie was expanding to include thousands of members, many of whom favoured speedy radical reforms but were reluctant to support armed confrontation. The objects of the Union were thus to be those of Major Cartwright–the acquisition of universal manhood suffrage, annual Parliaments and vote by secret ballot–not land redistribution, the inauguration of a republican state, a mass march to London, or any of the more extreme measures then in vogue. This moderate tone can be discerned in a letter to Hunt written by G.L. Bolsover, a Stockport surgeon and Union member, early in 1819:

> Our object being to obtain a great and positive good, viz. equal rights, equal laws, and equal justice; and our weapons being reason, discussion and persuasion, it follows that we shall obtain our object without either anarchy or confusion.[26]

Parson Harrison was willing to accommodate shifts of this sort, at least temporarily. After it was clear that Bagguley would not be bailed and would not therefore be able to bring Stockport's petition up to London, Harrison sent it to Henry Hunt for delivery to the Prince Regent. In other words, he chose Hunt, whose sympathies lay more with the Hampden Clubs, rather than James Watson or any of the other Spenceans.[27] As another indication of this tendency, the London agent chosen by Stockport radicals to handle Metropolitan subscriptions to the Chester prisoners was Thomas Cleary, secretary to the Hampden Club.[28]

Religion figured prominently in the Stockport Union, which its own rules referred to as 'Christian in the truest and fullest sense of the word'. Soon after Bagguley's arrest, Harrison started using Bagguley's school for Sunday religious services. The fact that one Sunday congregation in 1819 contained 400 or 500 persons suggests that Union-style religion achieved considerable popularity. Harrison probably laced his religion with contemporary politics,[29] a conclusion supported by the fact that Knight and Mitchell helped conduct the services during September and October 1818. Harrison admitted that he regarded religion and politics as the twin pillars of his life, saying on one occasion that he was 'fond of two kinds of meetings, the one for the acquirement of his rights and liberties as an Englishman–the other for the salvation of his immortal soul'. Harrison took his religion seriously. After civil registration of vital statistics began in 1837 and local registers of all sorts were being called in to London by the Registrar-General, Harrison sent in the carefully preserved baptismal register of his radical congregation.[30] He labelled the congregation 'Independent' and stated it had been formed in 1817 (presumably the time he arrived at Stockport), although the first baptisms occurred only in August 1818, and no more occurred until January 1819. Baptisms stopped in 1820 when Harrison was imprisoned but revived briefly in 1823–4 after his release. Of a total of 61 different families mentioned in 1818–24, 50 were from the Stockport district and nine were from the Oldham area where Harrison had many friends.

It would be wrong, however, to assume that many other political unions had similarly strong religious orientations. Those who have claimed this[31] have misunderstood the use of the term *protestant* in the titles of many such clubs, a use which suggests the importance of the Hull Political Protestants as a model. The Hull society was formed many months before the Stockport Union 'for the purpose of sincerely *protesting* against the mockery of our indisputable right to a real representation . . .', and seems to have had no religious functions at all. Indeed, it is difficult to find formal religion as a truly significant element within any of the political clubs of this period except Stockport's. A Lancashire magistrate who investigated union schools in his area found that 'at more than one of them their master had publicly burnt the Bible before them; and that some of the speechifying Radical ladies of these latter meetings he knew to have placed children in these schools in order to have these opinions taught to them'.[32] A report from Oldham's union, in which religion seems to have intruded more than in most political clubs, states merely that 'we have occasionally a gratuitous sermon'– –a sermon not inconceivably preached by Parson Harrison himself. Harrison's mixture of politics and religion was not without at least one recent parallel. In 1816–17 the Middleton Hampden Club (not far from Oldham) featured politics on Monday and Saturday evenings and interdenominational religious services on Sundays. Samuel Bamford probably did not exaggerate in his account of the Club's fame:

> The proceedings of our society; its place of meeting–singular as being the first place of worship occupied by reformers . . . together with the services of religion connected with us–drew a considerable share of public attention to our transactions, and obtained for the leaders some notoriety.

A spy's account further suggests that the famous Middleton model greatly influenced Harrison.[33]

If Harrison's brand of radical religion can be regarded as a merely localised phenomenon in 1818–20, his educational programmes must be accorded more significance. At the Union Rooms Harrison presided over: (1) a day school for children with instruction in reading (for 4d. weekly), writing (6d.), arithmetic (8d.) and grammar and geography (10d.); (2) an evening school for adults featuring basic education, lectures and debates; and (3) a Sunday school. The day and evening schools were simply continuations of Bagguley and Harrison's institution set up in July 1818. The Union Sunday School, the first of its kind in England, resulted from Harrison's increasing contempt for the large, interdenominational and unquestionably loyalist Stockport Sunday School (SSS). At the 28 September meeting he urged scholars at that institution to resist loyalist indoctrination and to be 'determined reformers, or give up their work of *ill-bestowed charity*, and their labour of *misconstrued love*'. This triggered conflicts within the SSS, an ensuing 'paper war' according to Lloyd, and ultimately the resignations of a few SSS students. As John Knight later told a Blackburn crowd:

> Soon after the arrest of Drummond, Bagguley and Johnston, the doctrine of passive obedience and non-resistance [was] so disgustingly inculcated and enforced in the old established Sunday-School, at Stockport, that the more intelligent part of the scholars could no longer endure it, but absented themselves and applied to the Political Reformers requesting they would commence a Sunday-School and they would join and assist them therein; and . . . this was the history of that highly valuable Institution.[34]

When Henry Hunt paid a visit to the Stockport Union Sunday School, he found that scholars were '*taught* on the *basis* of true *Christian morality*, and the spirit of genuine liberty'. Writing books contained 'short abstract sentences of general political application'. The school's combination of religion and politics proved to be enormously successful for a time. Prescot, the rector of Stockport, reported to the 1818 educational survey that it already contained 1,000 children. By August 1819 it allegedly contained twice that number.[35] Whilst 'Stockport led the way' in this according to the *Manchester Chronicle*, the idea of radical Sunday schools rapidly caught on. Similar schools sprang up at Manchester, Oldham and Bury during the first half of 1819, for example, and others were formed later on.[36]

Many such schools, and the institutions which spawned them, gained reputations for infidelism. It was claimed that scholars at the Stockport Union Sunday School were taught to burn Bibles and that, in general, local radicals were unbelievers. There is some basis to those claims. William Perry, a leading figure in the Union, was an infidel, for example. Some of the Union's Irish members and some of its honoured guests, like William Fitton of Royton, likewise embraced infidelity. It may have been the case that in some of the Sunday school classes derision and desecration of Bibles occurred. Yet infidelity was not the dominant theme in Stockport radicalism in 1818–20. Christian reformers, like Parson Harrison, held the upper hand and apparently tolerated the infidels in order to avoid rancorous internal debates and thereby to increase popular support for radical causes.[37]

Little is known about the precise techniques by which these varieties of radicalism spread from major urban centres to smaller towns and villages, although one can assume that the circulation of radical printed materials and the activities of radical 'missionaries' played their accustomed roles in this process. It appears that after the public revival of radicalism occurred in the town of Stockport in 1818, radical ideas soon filtered out into the district and gained (or regained) adherents to the cause. By the first half of 1819 moderate progress had been made. Radicals at Bullocksmithy, Denton and Strines in Disley contributed to the Prisoners' Relief Fund, for instance. In June 1819 Gee Cross sent a representative to an Oldham delegate meeting. Yet Gee Cross appears to have had the only formal Union Society outside of Stockport in 1818–20. As before, the town dominated the district, and the Stockport Union remained the predominant institutional locus for miles around.[38]

At the same time, radical ideas made headway among an important segment of the population, urban women. Although women had been prominent at the Blanketeers' meeting, Bamford claimed that the trend really began at a Lydgate (Saddleworth) reform meeting– probably that of 4 May 1818–when women were allowed to vote on the proposed resolutions for the first time. He stated that women voted at every reform meeting thereafter. Articles such as the 'Rights of Women' in the *Black Dwarf* helped to stimulate female participation in radical affairs.[39]

Women were active on the fringes of the Stockport Union from the very beginning. Harrison allowed females to receive instruction at his schools and of course to become members of his congregation. But the Union apparently did not allow them to become formal members in the sense of belonging to a weekly class. Harrison, nevertheless, seems to have been receptive to the idea of women's rights. He baptised the children of three Stockport women who could list no husband in the baptismal register and of two more who had different surnames from the fathers of their children. One of the latter, an Edgeley woman, had offspring by two different men. A magistrates' report draws a direct correlation between radical ideologies and the increasingly obvious female sexual licence: 'The women have adopted the doctrine [of following the 'irresistible laws of nature'] and enjoy the bliss of having their minds and bodies free.'[40]

Male radicals applauded the growing prominence of women reformers. At a radical dinner on 15 February 1819 a toast was offered to 'The Female Reformers of Stockport'; Bagguley addressed a letter from Chester Castle to the female reformers during June; and the big Stockport meeting of 28 June passed a resolution praising the town's female reformers.[41] Separate meetings of Stockport female reformers began on 1 July when 36 women divided themselves into three classes. At the second meeting on 5 July there were five classes, with two more being added a week later. At this latter meeting (12 July) the Stockport Female Union was officially established. There were permanent officers (a secretary and a treasurer), a committee of twelve and dues of a penny per week. The organisation, in short, was modelled closely after that of the male Union, and the avowed purpose of the females was to be like Spartan women and aid the men in their struggles by whatever means possible. Accounts of these activities were sent to the *Manchester Observer* with the remark that 'it is a very rare thing now a days for Stockport to be second in anything that relates to reform . . .', but that Blackburn females had led the way by organising a union on 18 June. At their meeting of 18 July the Stockport females embarked on their first project, helping the male Union support Bagguley, Drummond and Johnston.[42]

Female reformers at Stockport and elsewhere quickly gained widespread notoriety. In August 1819 local loyalists felt constrained to circulate a broadside denouncing them:

> We have lately witnessed a new contrivance for the ruin of society: Female Establishments, for demoralizing the rising generation: Mothers instructed to train their infants to the hatred of every thing that is orderly and decent, and to rear up Rebels against God and State. Hitherto, this diabolical attempt has been confined to the most degraded of the sex; and it is to be hoped, that no woman who has a spark of virtue or honor remaining in her character, will engage in a scheme so disgusting and abominable.[43]

As with the spread of radical ideas into small towns and villages, the appearance of organised female reformers clearly added to the momentum of the radical movement.

So, too, did the handloom weavers. During the summer of 1818 they had chosen to handle industrial grievances through sectional means, that is, by engaging in collective bargaining and by launching the strike which collapsed in September. Soon after, wages began to fall again as unemployment rose. A Stockport weaver reported in February 1819 that some wage reductions had already occurred and that others were contemplated. Further reductions did occur in the summer, prompting the *Manchester Gazette* to complain that weavers' wages outside Manchester were below subsistence levels.[44] Three distinct but ultimately convergent patterns of activity among Stockport district weavers occurred during those months. First, although it was undoubtedly the case that some weavers favoured radical political solutions even during the strike, many more decided to become associated with the Stockport Union afterwards. This is suggested (but, of course, not proved) by the prominence of weavers among those calling for reform meetings (Table 10.1). Second, some weavers followed the lead of the Stockport Weavers' Committee and traditionalists elsewhere in seeking to obtain a minimum wage and an end to twist exports. This movement became prominent in Bolton, Bury, Burnley, Blackburn, Preston and Carlisle during the spring and summer of 1819.[45] Joseph Sherwin and Simon Lilly of the Weavers' Committee favoured those proposals and hoped that they would be taken up at a weavers' meeting held on 21 June immediately after another wage reduction occurred at Stockport. The assembled weavers had other ideas. They rejected proposals for charitable subscriptions, soup shops, turning-out for a wage increase, 'and as to petitioning government, that thought turned sour upon their stomachs'. Sherwin and Lilly finally had to present a memorial to the Rev. Prescot which stated that the Weavers' Committee now endorsed parlimentary reform.[46] In contrast to 1816, when leading weavers participated in the formation of the Union Society, the tardy (and in the cases of Sherwin and Lilly, reluctant) adherence to the radical cause in June 1819 seemed to assure them of a negligible voice in radical affairs. A similar lack of decisive leadership would continue to plague the Weavers' Committee during the 1820s. Third, many weavers began thinking about emigration. On New Year's Day of 1818 the Black Ball Line had commenced regular monthly sailings between Liverpool and New York, thus facilitating departures from the manufacturing districts.[47] The chief promoter of emigration at this time was John Knight, whose *Emigrant's Best Instructor* appeared in May and went into a second edition before the end of the year. In August he brought out the first series of *Important Extracts from Original American Letters*, with a second series following soon thereafter. Finally, on 7 November, he brought out the short-lived *Manchester Spectator* in the first issue of which he strongly recommended emigration. It is probably not coincidental that Knight was closely identified with Stockport radicalism in the latter part of 1818 and that Lloyd first reported Stockport weavers planning to emigrate in December, in some cases with money derived from embezzled raw materials.[48]

Emigration remained an object of weavers' hopes throughout the first half of 1819. A letter to the *Manchester Observer* (29 May 1819) from 'A Poor [Stockport] Weaver, On the verge of Despair' urged weavers to petition the government for aid in emigrating. His object was 'to make us all transports, rather than be as we are'. In theory, the issue of emigration was not one which could be readily endorsed by political radicals, for however much they might like to see their corrupt government weakened by a drain on population and industrial skills, they still wanted as many workers as possible to remain in England marching in the legions of reform.[49] In practice, such questions rarely arose. Knight himself was a leading spokesman for both emigration and parliamentary reform. And at Stockport, the radical Union became involved in its own emigration scheme to an area long before made famous by Sir Walter Raleigh. Substantial land grants were being made on the Orinoco River in Venezuela, a land of 'perpetual spring' according to an advertisement. The fare, however, was ten guineas per person plus provisions, which would have cost the better part of a year's wages for a Stockport district weaver. James George Bruce, for a time an associate teacher in Parson Harrison's school, was the Union member in correspondence with the scheme's Liverpool agent.[50]

Table 10.1: Occupations of Persons Calling Reform Meetings at Stockport, 1818–19

Occupation	(1) 1 Sept. 1818	(2) 28 Sept. 1818	(3) 15 Feb. 1819	(4) 28 June 1819
Weaver	9 (38%)	19 (73%)	4 (50%)	9 (60%)
Spinner	2	1	-	2
Shoemaker	3	3	-	1
Tailor	-	1	1	-
Hatter	-	-	-	1
Pattern drawer	1	1	-	-
Cabinet maker	-	-	-	1
Schoolmaster	1	1	1	-
Bookseller	-	-	1	-
Surgeon	-	-	1	-
Farmer	1	-	-	-
Unknown	7	-	-	1
Total	24	26	8	15

Sources: (1) *MO*, 29 August 1818; (2) HO 42/180, Prescot to Sidmouth, 23 Sept. 1818, enclosing requisition; (3) *MO*, 30 Jan., 6 Feb. 1819 (two lists combined in table above); (4) *Public Meeting at Stockport* (Manchester, 1819), pr. s.sh.

However unrealistic the Orinoco venture may have been, it serves further to illustrate the process that was occurring. In the late summer of 1818 some weavers, despairing of industrial action, began to support the radicals. In June 1819 the Weavers' Committee gave up its commitment to a minimum wage and an end to twist exports and also joined the radicals. And by July the only other significant option open to the weavers, emigration, was being co-opted by the radicals. The *Manchester Observer's* reference on 3 July to 'the weavers of Stockport [who are] very numerous, and most of them radical reformers . . .', was not mere hyperbole. Harrison concurred as to the main source of radical strength while remarking on the chief difficulty inherent in building a movement out of impoverished workers. 'The weavers are the best givers,' he wrote, 'but alas, they have nothing to give now. As the cause of reform advances, it becomes more and more expensive, and the means more and more circumscribed . . .' Later evidence supports these indications of strong connections between weavers and radicals. William Longson, a Stockport weaver, testified before Parliament in 1834 and explained Peterloo in the following way: '. . . that celebrated affair in 1819, I do not believe it would ever have taken place if it had not been for the distress of the weavers; those politics you denominate radical originated amongst them and the publications in which they are conveyed were first sold to them, and thus handed to other members of the community . . .'[51]

Because of its complex organisation, the Stockport Union has been judged by some historians to have had an immense impact at both the regional and national levels. E.P. Thompson refers to the Union as the 'important' and 'impressive' Stockport model, while Donald Read states that 'the rules of the Stockport Union had given a lead to Radicalism throughout the country'.[52] In stressing the Stockport Union's influence and innovativeness, these historians have perhaps gone too far. The 'Rules and Resolutions of the Political Protestants' of Hull, drawn up on 20 July 1818, appeared in the *Black Dwarf* of 19 August. The *Dwarf* was circulating at Stockport throughout this period. On 9 September its editorial urged that societies similar to Hull's be set up in all parts of the country. The Stockport Union was formally established about a month later. Moreover, the organisation of the Stockport Union resembled the Hull society's structure of weekly classes and periodic meetings of class leaders with dues of a penny per week. All such organisations, of course, harked back to the Hampden Clubs of 1816–17, to even earlier political societies and, ultimately, to the Wesleyan class structure. Even Stockport's pioneering Union Sunday School was not enough to convince Parson Harrision of the distinctiveness of the 'Stockport model' of political unions. He wrote early in 1819 that Unions were of two types, those on the London plan and those on the Hull plan. The former was probably a reference to clubs like the exclusive London Hampden Club or Liverpool Concentric Society, while the latter referred to more inclusive, proletarian societies with weekly classes inspired in 1818 by the Hull Political Protestants. The Stockport Union for the Promotion of Human Happiness was clearly one of the latter.[53]

IV

The size and strength of the Stockport Union soon became evident in its public activities, which showed some of its members to be not only confident but also militant in the best Bagguley tradition. Local authorities responded by redoubling their efforts to maintain order, often with a lack of success which only increased their frustration, anger and desire for revenge. At the same time, there were hints of discontent within the Union, although Parson Harrison, with his usual patience and tolerance, managed to control his flock with considerable success. These themes emerged in the context of the various reform meetings held during 1819, climaxing with Peterloo in August.

The Stockport Union readily joined other towns in the reinvigorated reform agitation advocated by the *Manchester Observer* on 2 January 1819. It was also probably about that time that Stockport radicals began wearing white (undyed) hats in emulation of Hunt and in visible, daily defiance of Stockport loyalists.[54] Local radicals proceeded to hold a reform meeting on 15 February. Chaired by William Fitton, the Royton radical-infidel, the meeting passed a remonstrance almost identical to one passed a month earlier at Manchester. It called for parliamentary reform, support of Bagguley and company, and repeal of the Corn Laws. The basic themes of the day were expressed in two prominent banners which read, 'RIGHTS OF MAN' and 'NO CORN LAWS'. When a cap of liberty was hoisted, the Stockport Yeomanry and special constabulary moved in, but the exuberant crowd dispersed *them* (and in the process, assaulted John Lloyd's son) in a scene reminiscent of the powerloom riot of the preceding summer. The meeting then continued. When the speakers retired to the Windmill Rooms for dinner, the crowd followed them. The magistrates read the Riot Act at the Windmill and again at the Market Place when the crowd began reassembling there. It dispersed gradually but rallied once more to clash with the authorities as the Riot Act was read a third time. Finally, the crowd dispersed of its own accord, triumphantly singing the popular song, *Millions Be Free*.[55]

The confrontation on Sandy Brow immediately became a cause for radical self-congratulation throughout the greater Manchester district. Various poems celebrated the proceedings and their aftermath. Samuel Bamford, in his *Fray of Stockport*, ridiculed the attempts by Lloyd, Birch and the Stockport Yeomanry to intimidate the 'Gruntin herd' (swinish multitude) and lauded the actions of the 'Stopport lads'. The anonymous author of *Sandy Brow Fight* likewise revealed the feelings of pride engendered by the episode:

> Then helter skelter sticks and stones,
> From every side flew at the drones,
> And drove them all away;
> Wigs, stays and wiskers [*sic*], took their legs,
> And Dandy stunk with rotten eggs,
> Still Pudding's now hangs on pegs,
> For Britons rul'd the day.[56]

It was only at that juncture that the Stockport Union decided to print its rules for general distribution with George Bolsover the surgeon in charge of the project.

The authorities became alarmed after the 15 February tumults and listened to all sorts of informers' tales, notably those having to do with secret oaths and the manufacture of pikes. Although the stories probably had little basis in fact—no pikes were discovered at that time—they did serve to put Lloyd and his colleagues on guard. Even the cotton manufacturers, who were often loath to become involved with matters of public order, were calling for the suspension of *habeas corpus*. On 27 February Lloyd apprehended the two rioters who had roughed up his youngest son. He secured indictments against them at the Spring Assizes in April. Lloyd also obtained an indictment against a Stockport man accused of using seditious language in a pub. He drew up another indictment for the Spring Assizes, this one against Parson Harrison, but for some reason chose not to present it. By May he had spies at work in the Stockport Union. In that same month William Birch, the deputy constable, joined two special constables in disrupting one of Harrison's Sunday sermons.[57] If the authorities could not prevent a riot by the radicals, then they would harass them as much as possible.

The *esprit* of the radicals remained high despite these repressive measures and the outcome of the Bagguley trial at the Spring Assizes. Radical supporters had made strenuous efforts to procure bail for the three prisoners since September. By early January contributions had been received from Manchester, Oldham, Hull, Glasgow and other towns and also from Sir Charles Wolseley and T.J. Wooler, editor of the *Black Dwarf*. Public meetings dealing in part with the subject of bail ensued but all to no avail. The prisoners remained in Chester Castle until their trial on 15 April. Then, with Wolseley, Harrison and many Stockport and Manchester radicals looking on, the defence lawyer claimed inadequate preparation time and called no witnesses whatsoever. Bagguley, Drummond and Johnston were consequently found guilty and each received a sentence of two years' imprisonment. Four days later radicals staged a demonstration at Stockport and secured thousands of signatures on a petition for a new trial. When confronted by constables, the radicals, repeating their aggressive behaviour of February, pelted them with stones. In later correspondence to the *Black Dwarf*, both Harrison and Johnston supported the conduct of the defence attorney. That, and the publication of an account of their trial in separate instalments, assured that the Chester prisoners would not be forgotten.[58]

If the militant Chester prisoners provided a convenient rallying point, their tribulations also served as a focus for dissensions within the Stockport Union. As early as December 1818 many members objected to the fact that the committee to relieve the militant prisoners had become barely distinguishable from the leadership of the 'moderate' Union. Both groups, for example, had Harrison as their secretary. Lloyd reported that the Union was 'splitting' over the issue, but on 23 December it issued a broadside proclaiming that a new, independent subscription committee had been set up. The new committee again included Harrison and Cheetham, but a weaver presided. Not so radical as Bagguley and friends but more radical than many of the Union's rank and file, Harrison later wrote with a tinge of bitterness: 'I succeeded in obtaining support for these unfortunate men [the three prisoners], when violently opposed by an association called the Stockport Union . . .' Discord did not end there. By April, amidst further publicised disputes, a branch of the Union had opened at London Place.[59] It seems plausible (admittedly on the basis of later evidence) that London Place sheltered those who were opposed to the pattern of confrontation advocated by Bagguley and endorsed by some of the Windmill radicals. It may also have been the case that infidels found a more congenial atmosphere at London Place than at the Christian Windmill. Yet Harrison saw to it that no schism occurred: London Place was a branch of the Stockport Union, not an independent radical club.

After the Bagguley trial, agitations focused on the presentation of the Stockport and Manchester remonstrances approved at public meetings earlier in the year. In May Lloyd noticed that the Stockport Union was 'very busy'. Members from the Union probably attended the 23 May delegate meeting at Oldham, by which time Henry Hunt had the two remonstrances in his possession. On 26 May he presented them to Lord Sidmouth to be forwarded to the Prince Regent. Three days later Hunt learned that the remonstrances would not be forwarded at all. At this affront, Hunt vowed to 'find some other means of making the prayers and petitions of the suffering people known to the Prince Regent'.[60]

Such interference with an Englishman's right to petition clearly gave the radicals not only a new grievance but also a new problem: what tactic was to be adopted after petitioning and remonstrating had failed? The representatives of the 28 Union societies who met at Oldham on 7 June offered no clear answer. While the delegates passed resolutions favouring parliamentary reform and repeal of the Corn Laws, their stated mode of achieving these measures was simply to draw up another address. Harrison and Cheetham represented Stockport at the meeting and may have shared with others a sense of futility at the prospect of yet another radical declaration. In any case, the Stockport Union soon became intimately involved with the propagation of certain new measures, notably the convening of some sort of national union, political meeting or convention. The immediate inspiration for this proposal may have been the reviving London Spenceans, whose Committee of Two Hundred was active in promoting a convention about this time. Whatever the source, the proposal solved certain problems for Harrison. It appealed to moderate Union members who saw a national meeting as an appropriate means to advance reform; it also appealed to extremist Union members who saw it as a militant act —as convention *qua* revolution; and it provided a new programme for the Union at a time when its political agenda seemed moribund. Harrison served as chairman at an Ashton meeting on 14 June at which the national convention scheme was formally presented by a Stockport delegation headed by Wright Sixsmith. At the Blackburn meeting of 5 July, the Stockport proposals (presented by Harrison) inspired at least one of the Blackburn resolutions, that having to do with a national meeting in London. Between the Ashton and Blackburn meetings there occurred what one historian has called 'probably the greatest of the Radical meetings in the area in 1819 apart from Peterloo itself'–the Stockport reform meeting of 28 June.[61]

Lloyd thought that about 4,000 attended this meeting on Sandy Brow; the *Manchester Observer* put the figure at 20,000. There were people from various parts of the Stockport district and also from Ashton, Oldham and Royton. Sir Charles Wolseley journeyed north specifically to chair the meeting, which also included James Willan of Dewsbury (a leading exposer of Oliver the Spy), William Greathead Lewis and a Mr Goodman both of Coventry. Violence was expected. The Union had issued a broadside calling for peaceable behaviour but simultaneously stirring up feelings against 'a most diabolical Plot' allegedly including *agents provocateurs*. On Wolseley's arrival in Stockport, a radical delegation went directly to Prescot to ask for protection at the meeting. Prescot refused. The delegation then asked for Prescot's attendance. The *Observer* recorded his reply: ' "No, no," says the Rector, "fine talking, when stones and sticks are flying, to think that it is in the power of two or three individuals to stop the torrent!" ' Isaac Murray, a man later wounded at Peterloo, greeted the occasion with a defiant poem, which reads in part:

> And Stockport's sons shall by thy van,.
> thy country's rights to save.
> Should Tyrant's vengeance thee assail,
> thou'lt Stockport's courage prove;
> She'll safe from harm her Wolseley keep,
> wrapt in his country's love,
> Their base designs should they this day,
> attempt as they have said,
> E'er they thy sacred person Touch,
> THEY'LL CLIMB O'ER ENGLISH DEAD.

The June meeting thus promised to be as tumultuous as the meetings in February and April. But with the exception of an incident in which the crowd removed a Manchester constable from the scene, no violence occurred–not even when the cap of liberty was hoisted at Wolseley's request. A major explanation for the absence of conflict was the fact that the forces of order were not able 'to muster *ten men!*' according to Lloyd, who exclaimed: 'We are forever disgraced . . .'

The major themes of the speeches (nine men spoke, some of them twice) involved a condemnation of Parliament as totally unresponsive to the people and a condemnation of the Home Office, whose head (Lord Sidmouth) had committed a 'crime' by interfering with Stockport's right to petition. The solutions proposed were to convene a national delegate meeting in London to agitate for parliamentary reform and to begin a national subscription 'to enforce the law' against Sidmouth. William Fitton of Royton spoke on currency problems, using as his text Cobbett's pamphlet, *Paper against Gold*. Parson Harrison spoke on the topic of parliamentary reform and on the uselessness of petitioning the Commons again. Only the Lords or the Prince Regent should be petitioned, he declared, adding that a petition presented to the Prince Regent 'would decide a point in many unbelievers, whether the seat of royalty was or was not occupied by a pig or a man'. The general themes discussed at the meeting were embodied in 'An Appeal to the Nation by the Inhabitants of Stockport and its Neighbourhood', which was endorsed unanimously by the crowd.[62]

The great assembly at Stockport climaxed a month of reform agitation in the region and occurred when the effects of a short-term economic slump were becoming manifest. Joseph Johnson, a Manchester radical who had spoken at Stockport, later described the situation rather melodramatically:

> Trade here is not worth following. Everything is almost at a stand still, nothing but ruin and starvation stare one in the face. The state of this district is truly dreadful, and I believe nothing but the greatest exertions can prevent an insurrection.[63]

Lloyd wrote early in July of rumours (not unfounded, as before) that pikes were being made and of shopkeepers being afraid to oppose the radicals so as not to lose profits, presumably because exclusive dealing was being practiced. 'The working classes,' he wrote, 'are become more independent and insulting, expressing their confidence of soon having the rule and power.' On 7 July Sidmouth sent a circular letter to the Lords Lieutenant to go to their counties and have their Yeomanry in readiness. But even before that, Lloyd determined to try once again 'to spring up the better people to loyal association'. He had a loyal address printed up for signatures on 7 July. He promoted and became a member of the Stockport Troop Club which was established on 12 July as a sort of loyalist infantry adjunct to the Yeomanry Cavalry. And he helped to secure indictments against Harrison and Wolseley at Quarter Sessions on 13 July.[64]

Wolseley soon arrived at the Knutsford Quarter Sessions, pleaded 'not guilty' and posted bail with the help of two Stockport men (a grocer and a shoe-clog-patten dealer) as sureties. Of the two sureties, the *Manchester Observer* soon remarked that 'the lower and middle class [sic] seem to vie with each other which shall crowd their shops most to purchase the respective articles in which they deal'. Harrison meanwhile had gone—fled according to Lord Castlereagh in a subsequent Commons' speech—to London to meet with the Spencean Committee of Two Hundred and to join Hunt in speaking at the 21 July Smithfield meeting. Along the way, Harrison promoted the national convention scheme at Sheffield and Leicester and was a principal speaker at the Nottingham reform meeting of 19 July. In *The Times'* words, 'Parson Harrison seemed to be the grand pivot for giving motion to the machine' at Nottingham. Other meetings at Birmingham (12 July) and Leeds (19 July) discussed the scheme, with Birmingham going so far as to elect Wolseley 'legislatorial attorney' to 'advise' Parliament on its duties.[65]

As the reform movement was gaining a wider national audience, the forces of law and order were becoming more active in the greater Manchester district and especially at Stockport. The latter can be seen in the quick apprehension of Harrison. Lloyd sent William Birch and another constable to London with a warrant for the Parson's arrest, a warrant enforced only moments after Harrison had addressed the Smithfield throngs. The threesome immediately began the journey back to Stockport, which took the customary two days. When they arrived on the evening of 23 July, a crowd formed around Birch's house, in which Lloyd had begun questioning Harrison. Birch remained outside. Three men approached him, and while one of them talked to Birch, one of the others fired a shot at the constable. In the confusion that followed, the wounded Birch managed to flee. It was soon learned that the bullet had lodged in his breastbone but that no further ill-effects were to be expected.[66]

Lloyd quickly launched an intensive search for the three assailants.

Early attention focused on James George Bruce and William Pearson, who were arrested the next day. Bruce, 'a little deformed man', told Lloyd that he had been born in London but had taught school for many years in Ireland. He had arrived in Stockport only in March 1819 and had become an assistant in Harrison's school, also lodging with Harrison. Soon, he had opened a 'Radical speaking-school' of his own and took charge of the Stockport Union's South American emigration programme. He said that he, Pearson and another teacher in the Union had been the three who approached Birch with the unnamed teacher doing the firing. Pearson, a weaver active in radical circles for at least a year, disclosed in a series of statements over a period of weeks that it was two Irish brothers who in fact had joined Bruce in the shooting. On 5 August a broadside appeared and offered £300 for apprehension of the gunman and £50 for each of his accomplices. Suspicion finally fell on James and especially Jacob McInnis, both from Warringstown, county Down, both immigrant weavers at Edgeley, and both in their early twenties. Pearson continued to give information which led to the discovery of Jacob McInnis on 23 August hiding in county Down in his aunt's bed with a woman's cap on. He was arrested and conveyed to Chester Castle.[67]

The radicals of Stockport must have expected a wave of adverse public opinion, for they spread tales that one of Lloyd's sons had shot Birch, that Birch had only been shot with wadding, or that he had not been shot at all. The full effects of the Birch shooting on Stockport opinion is irretrievably lost in the heightened pace of reform activity after the Smithfield meeting and Harrison's escorted return to Stockport. The radicals' object in late July and early August seems to have been to expand and reinforce radicalism on a regional level, and in this Stopfordians again led the way. The day after he preached a Sunday sermon at Stockport (25 July), Harrison brought the gospel of reform to Rochdale, a town not previously noted for advanced radical sentiments. Another such town, Macclesfield, had looked to Stockport for leadership and direction in June. When it held a reform meeting on 31 July, it was led by Joseph Swann, a former Stockport hatter and seller of political pamphlets; Joseph Bertinshaw, the old Stockport cobbler; William Buckley, a Stockport weaver; and a Stockport female reformer, Mrs Hallum. Another indication of the rudimentary state of the radical movement at Macclesfield was that the speakers at the reform meeting were often interrupted by shouted insults.[68]

On the same day as the Macclesfield meeting, Manchester radicals announced a meeting for 9 August to discuss parliamentary reform and the election of a 'representative' to Parliament. The magistrates met immediately and declared that such a meeting would be illegal. The *Manchester Observer* printed this declaration on 7 August along with a notice that the meeting had been rescheduled for 16 August, the topic now ostensibly limited to parliamentary reform. The radicals became daily more buoyant, the authorities more frightened. In inviting Hunt to stop at Stockport on his way to the intended 9 August meeting, William Perry of the Stockport Union wrote, 'The idea of your arrival strikes terror to the very foundation of the borough faction in this part of the country'. Hunt did stop at Stockport on 8 August, stayed overnight at Moorhouse's, and proceeded to Manchester on 9 August with Harrison, Moorhouse and a throng of Stopfordians.[69]

The authorities were gaining some assistance at that point from the Royal Proclamation of 30 July against seditious libels. During the early part of August the magistrates of the Stockport division approved of a statement (probably written by Lloyd) which complained of the political writings of Cobbett, Wooler, Sherwin and Wroe–an indication the *Cobbett's Political Register,* the *Black Dwarf, Sherwin's Political Register* and the *Manchester Observer* continued to be the major radical publications in the Stockport district just as they had been for the preceding year and a half. This report also mentioned a few instances of arming and drilling but complained especially about the Union, the Union schools and the female reformers. This magistrates' report formed the basis for a resolution of the adjourned Quarter Sessions on 9 August urging the suppression of radical schools and meetings through the use of existing laws or the passage of new ones. Local magistrates were quick to act on 15 August when Harrison preached a sermon calling for abstinence from excisable articles, a tactic first advocated at the 21 June Manchester meeting. 'The Government have starved the people,' Harrison said, 'and therefore it is fit that the people should starve the Government.' He was arrested almost immediately thereafter.[70]

The events of the infamous 16 August at Manchester have been told countless times over the past century and a half. It may be useful, however, to review the role of Stockport district inhabitants in the proceedings of that day. At least three estimates survive of the numbers of those from Stockport at Peterloo. These range from 1,000 to 5,000 with the middle estimate 1,400 or 1,500 including about 40 women) probably being the most accurate. The latter was made by Francis Philips, a Manchester merchant and manufacturer, who witnessed the Stopfordians' progress along the turnpike road to Manchester.

> On the 16th August I went on the Stockport Road about eleven or a little after, and I met a great number of persons advancing towards Manchester with all the regularity of a regiment, only they had no uniform. They were all marching in file, principally three abreast. They had two banners with them. There were persons by the side, acting as officers and regulating the files. The order was beautiful indeed.

Philips and at least one other witness noted that many Stopfordians brought large sticks with them, just as they had done at the 28 June Stockport meeting. Both banners, or flags, were surmounted by caps of liberty. One of them read 'NO CORN LAWS', and the other read: 'ANNUAL PARLIAMENTS', 'UNIVERSAL SUFF-RAGE', 'VOTE BY BALLOT' and 'SUCCESS TO THE FEMALE REFORMERS OF STOCKPORT'. By the time the Stockport crowd had reached Manchester, the latter standard was borne aloft by 'a profligate amazon, named Mary Waterworth'.[71]

The Stockport district contingent joined tens of thousands of others on St Peter's Fields for those brief minutes before the Manchester and Salford Yeomanry panicked, causing the Hussars and the Stockport Yeomanry to charge and clear the field by hacking people with their swords. A Stopfordian later recalled the sensation created 'when the dark rumours of Peterloo spread rapidly through village and town, and [he remembered], alas, how they proved to be only too true'. The next day there were some 17 wounded victims observed on the road out of Manchester painfully retracing their steps to Stockport and Cheadle. Lists of casualties from the Stockport district reveal a pattern not unexpected (Table 10.2). Those from Stockport and its immediate suburbs (Heaton Norris and Edgeley) comprised a majority of the total. There were no female casualties from other district townships, reflecting the weakness of female radicalism outside Stockport itself. Not sur-prisingly, the most frequently mentioned occupation of the Stock-port district casualties was weaving. Only one of the 54 casualties is known to have died as a direct result of wounds inflicted at Peterloo. This was a 19-year-old lad from Hyde who succumbed to a bullet wound in the head. A Stockport man amazingly survived after having had a piece of his skull cut away. He saved the piece, and Henry Hunt later exhibited it (as Jenkin's ear had been exhibited a century earlier) before the House of Commons to help prove charges of official brutality. Of the eleven major figures arrested after Peterloo, only Moorhouse, the coach proprietor, was from Stockport. Parson Harrison–'the ir-reverend preacher' as *The Times* was beginning to style him–arrived late and missed the affray entirely.[72]

Table 10.2: Stockport District Casualties at Peterloo

Occupation	Stockport and Suburbs: Males	Stockport and Suburbs: Females	Other Stockport District Townships: All Males	Total
Weaver	13	1	1	15
Spinner	2			2
Hatter	2		1	3
Other skilled	8		1	9
Other unskilled	2			2
Unknown	11	7	5	23
Total	38	8	8	54

Sources: *MO,* 22, 29 Jan. 1820: *Report of the Metropolitan and Central Committee appointed for the Relief of the Manchester Sufferers* (London, 1820); *Peterloo Massacre* by 'An Observer' (Manchester, 1819), 199–214.

Lloyd rode with the Stockport Yeomanry at Peterloo and afterwards waxed ecstatic about 'the *glorious* day at Manchester. We have come back with honor . . .' Others supported his evaluation. A soldier stated that 'a troop from *Stockport* cut their way through [the crowd] in form'. John Stavely Barratt, a member of the Stockport Yeomanry, emphasised his own success in seizing flags and banners during the confusion. (He was later rewarded with an appointment to succeed Birch as Stockport's deputy constable.) After the Stockport Yeomanry had been dispersed by a radical crowd in February and 'disgraced' in June, it is little wonder that, given the chance, the troop responded with such brutal zeal at Peterloo. The violence of 16 August in fact put many of the members of the troop in a euphoric state. Within days, they sent an extraordinary offer to the Home Office to serve anywhere for any length of time. The banners seized at Manchester were ordered to be burned in the Stockport Market Place. On 18 August Lloyd played a leading role in a loyalist meeting at which a subscription for Birch was begun and a declaration of loyalty was prepared.[73] All in all, the 'spirit of Peterloo' would not soon be forgotten among Stockport district loyalists.

V

The day after Peterloo, a *Times* reporter observed 'numerous groups of idle men, who were congregated together along [the Manchester-Stockport road]. They appeared ready for any wicked purpose . . .' Peterloo unquestionably engendered deep and justifiable resentment among radicals but it also revived disputes over tactics. The major debate, as after the Blanketeers' march, centred on whether or not violence was to be employed. Historians have tended to speak of two factions in English radicalism at that juncture. The Huntites eschewed violence and pressed for abstinence from excisable articles. Manchester Huntites also proposed a national fast day for 1 January, the day some had proposed for a national delegate meeting. The *Manchester Observer* was advocating abstinence from excisable articles even after New Year's Day, noting that such goods were often adulterated anyway. The Spenceans, by contrast, espoused violence, urged radicals to arm and set various dates (1 and 15 November, 13 December) for a co-ordinated national rising.[74]

It does not appear that the Stockport Union split into two such distinct groups. Harrison, Moorhouse and the Union as a whole were largely Huntite in their sympathies. Harrison urged abstinence from excisable articles as early as 15 August. The idea of a peaceful boycott of tradesmen who acted as Yeomanry at Peterloo supposedly originated among Stockport radicals. Yet Harrison also preached disobedience on 15 August, physical force on 8 November and revolution on 5 December. It is difficult to discredit all the accounts of arming and drilling to the east of Stockport (Torkington, Offerton, Marple), especially after Lloyd found a pike near a radical's house and a model for a pike at an Offerton blacksmith's shop. Believing the rumours that radicals planned to seize the cannon at Lyme Park, the authorities took steps to remove the guns to the safety of Chester Castle. There is also evidence of Spencean connections. A spy reported in September that the Stockport Union had sent delegates out to promote the revolution, that Moorhouse had contacts in London, and that the revolution awaited a signal from a London committee. Thistlewood and Watson were in the area during October. And in November, Stockport radicals advocated the hoarding of silver in preparation for the revolution and warned friendly societies not to keep banknotes.[75]

At the same time, there were some indications of a temporary recrudescence of radical strength in Stockport, perhaps because the Huntite-Spencean debates were not so acrimonious and divisive as they were elsewhere. In October Lloyd wrote that 'matters are carried on with great asperity in this part of the country and the confidence of the disaffected appears to me to be encreasing [*sic*]. We are insulted with threats upon the approaching change as they would have it.' Moorhouse, who was not noted for his oratorical skill, was reported haranguing a Stockport crowd on at least one occasion during the autumn. Harrison continued his lecturing.[76] In Stockport on 5 December his Sunday rhetoric proved to be more inflammatory than ever.

> Kings, Princes, Dukes, Lords, Commons, Parliaments, Arch-bishops, Bishops, Prelates, Rectors, High-Constables, Constables, Sheriffs, Deputy-Constables, and Bailiffs, are all corrupt, and the time is near at hand when they will be upset. The people should rise *en masse* to suppress such a tyrannical government as the one of this country; and it will not be long, but very soon, that it shall be over-turned . . .

This sermon brought about Harrison's arrest one week later and earned him a third indictment for seditious language.[77]

Harrison's unabating demagoguery and the talk of risings after Peterloo occurred amidst new allegations of widening radical influence. In July Lloyd had wondered why some of the highly-paid spinners joined the radical cause. By December an infantry officer wrote (incorrectly) that spinners were the leading revolu-tionaries. He and others also thought that most of the Dissenters supported radical reform. The Stockport Sunday School, although overwhelmingly loyalist, likewise gained a reputation for radicalism because of the views of a handful of its members. A writer in 1820 was still talking about the need for the Stockport Sunday School to vindicate itself.[78] While such changes were over-blown, they did help to energise the forces of order and maintain the exuberant anti-radicalism evinced in their Peterloo victory. Towards the end of August Stockport division Petty Sessions ordered the Watch and Ward into effect. The extensive nightly patrols which resulted were soon reinforced by three companies of regular soldiers.[79]

At the 1819 Summer Assizes, the Grand Jury had made direct reference to public disorders in the Stockport division when it passed resolutions condemning seditious and blasphemous literature, itinerant demagogues and arming and drilling. The resolutions were forwarded to Lord Sidmouth on 3 September. At the same Assizes, Wolseley and Harrison obtained a traverse on the sedition charge growing out of the 28 June meeting. Less than two months later, Parliament passed the Six Acts which were intended to: (1) prevent arming and drilling; (2) allow magistrates to search for arms; (3) prevent delays in justice caused by traversing; (4) prevent meetings of more than 50 persons, with certain exceptions; (5) stiffen penalties for publication of seditious and blasphemous libels; and (6) extend the range of printed matter requiring newspaper stamps. These repressive measures were at least partially influenced by the proceedings at the 1819 Summer Assizes in Cheshire and ultimately by events in the Stockport district.[80]

If the tone of local radicals was becoming more desperate in the latter part of 1819, it was a desperation born of the repression, frustration and, finally, apathy that followed in the wake of Peterloo. It coincided with increasing numbers of published accounts by repatriated emigrants who were critical of the New World and of radicals' romantic emigration schemes. Lloyd provided further reasons for the change in mood at Stockport: 'Harrison has got into some disgrace amongst the radicals by making free with one of his female scholars. Moorhouse has also been publicly hooted for selling his flour dearer than the rest. Some few burnt their white hats, others have enlisted with a recruiting party here.'[81] As an indication of the change, Stockport authorities had little or no fear of incidents on 1 November or 13 December, two of the days scheduled for co-ordinated risings. On the former occasion evening rehearsals of a musical band constituted the only known collective activity by radicals. They were preparing to serenade a 'rising' and a more triumphal march to Manchester than that of August. On the latter occasion Lloyd simply observed: 'The enemy seems to know our strength and to respect it . . .'[82]

As autumn turned into winter, the radicalism of the Peterloo era was simply losing its wide popular appeal in the Stockport district.

A letter of late December in the Home Office papers by the spy 'Alpha' (W.B. Walker) laments that 'unless we can raise some money for both Manchester and Stockport the cause will entirely have to be abandoned in both those places . . .' 'Alpha's' visit to Stockport in early January 1820 tended to confirm his earlier appraisal. He found Harrison amidst 20 'very poor children' but 'in the same cool, deliberate frame that he is so remarkably noted for. And [he] tells me that nothing gives him so much pleasure as the present stillness of the radicals.' This calm was broken momentarily a couple of weeks later when all the windows in Harrison's school and house were broken by vandals. Enrolment in the Union Sunday School was simultaneously declining, reaching 600 by April, the last mention of its existence.[83]

The trials of early 1820 only added to the sense of radical decline. At the January Quarter Sessions six of the leaders of the 31 July 1819 Macclesfield meeting were convicted. Two of them had Stockport links. Joseph Swann, the hatter and vendor of seditious literature, received a sentence of $4\frac{1}{2}$ years on a variety of charges. Joseph Bertinshaw, the Stockport cobbler, received a sentence of two years in prison.[84] This trial foreshadowed much of what was to follow. On 8 April the day-long trial of McInnis and Bruce for shooting Constable Birch ended in convictions and capital sentences for both men. Bruce's sentence was ultimately commuted to transportation for life. McInnis, an avowed atheist, meanwhile decided to convert to Christianity before his appearance on the Chester gallows on 15 April. [85]

Also at the Spring Assizes the trial of Wolseley and Harrison for sedition came up. Wolseley was accused of having said on 28 June (among other things), 'Were all hearts but as firm in the cause as his own, they would soon put an end to the present tyranny and corruption. They should be firm and united, for in a few weeks the struggle would be made and ended.' Harrison was brought to trial for wondering aloud whether the Prince Regent were a pig or a man and for defiling the House of Commons. 'It was absurd to petition them as it would be for a master to petition his groom for his horse,' he had allegedly said. Harrison handled his own defence, speaking 'with the utmost composure, and with a violently method-istical twang' according to one reporter. He remained a flamboyant demagogue to the end. At one point 'the orator stamped emphatic-ally with his foot. He then wiped his forehead, at leisure, with his pocket-handkerchief, and continued.' Such theatrics were to no avail. Indeed, his hours'-long speech to the jury may have hindered his case. The jury deliberated forty-five minutes and delivered a verdict of 'guilty'. King's Bench later sentenced both men to eighteen months' imprisonment.[86] On 18 April Harrison came to trial on the other two indictments, those for seditious sermons on 15 August and 5 December 1819. He was found guilty on both charges, and for each, he received twelve months. His total sentence of 3½ years' imprisonment assured his absence from Stockport radical circles until the autumn of 1823.[87]

The only glimmer of hope for the radicals came at the intervening conspiracy trial of Henry Hunt and nine others for their role at Peterloo (16–27 March). James Moorhouse, the Stockport coach proprietor, was one of the ten defendants and one of the five to be acquitted. The case against him was weak from the outset. It could not be proven that he had seen Hunt or any of the others between 9 and 16 August, the period during which the alleged conspiracy was finally formulated. And though Moorhouse was at Manchester on 16 August, it was never proven beyond a reasonable doubt that he was on the stage and hence an active participant in the day's proceedings. In instructing the jury, the judge himself cautioned that there was much less 'criminal participation' with Moorhouse than with Hunt.[88] Moorhouse's eventual acquittal left him, although a man of limited talents and financially strained by prolonged litigation, as one of the few major radical leaders remaining in Stockport.

The fate of the Stockport 'Permanent Fund' provides further insight into the decline of the Stockport Union. The Fund had been placed under an independent 'Prisoners' Committee' in December 1818 when many Union members objected to its being a formal part of their institution. Disputes over the Fund intensified after Peterloo. In a joint statement of 3 November, the Union and the Prisoners' Committee admitted that 'some animosity has some time prevailed amongst the Reformers in Stockport, relative to the application of their Funds'. The two groups agreed to continue to give 30s. per week to Bagguley, Drummond and Johnston, to expand the Fund to include others under indictment and to place the Fund under the control of the Union. The fact that Harrison soon appeared as a recipient of the Fund suggests that doubts were being expressed as to whether a man involved with collecting the money should be spending large portions of it on himself. This came at a time when charges were circulating that many of the leading radicals were simply living off politics. A writer in the *Manchester Gazette* claimed that

> the Saxtons, the Harrisons, the Wolseleys, the Knights, the Johnstons, the Fittons, and the Ogdens...live by ranting and railing against abuses—remove the abuses and they must perish, for they will not work.[89]

The comment was not entirely fair to Harrison, who did maintain a school. And it is unclear whether he was actually mishandling funds. But as Lloyd had noted in late October, his reputation among Stockport radicals was tarnished. He had already been replaced as secretary to the Union by William Perry, the man to whom all future financial contributions were to be sent. Disputes over the Fund continued during the first half of 1820.[90]

The late spring and early summer of 1820 clearly marked a nadir of radical fortunes at Stockport and elswhere. The *Republican* found 'Lancashire and Cheshire quite still and silent' in April, 'as if there was not a reformer there'. Although there were reports of radical activity in the North around the time of the Cato Street Conspiracy in February and at the time of the various trials in March and April, Stockport figured hardly at all in such accounts. Weapons discovered at Stockport late in April raised fears temporarily—rumours had it that arms caches buried in December after the Six Acts were being dug up in preparation for some sinister plot. Lloyd maintained a cool perspective on the situation, writing in May that 'the radicals are very flat just now. The sentences have astonished them...' With a contingent of the military still on hand and with permanent barracks planned and soon to be built on a hill overlooking Stockport, Lloyd felt rather smug: 'It will not be long before another rising day is fixed—but while they are so well watched they may as well attempt to fly!'[91]

E.P. Thompson has concluded that during the Peterloo era 'the strength of the extreme reformers...lay in the hand-workers' villages of the Midlands and the north'. In this context he makes specific reference to Stockport:

> Although in 1818 Stockport provided an important model of a rather different type of urban reform movement, under the leadership of the Reverend Joseph Harrison, a Methodist minister turned Radical orator and schoolmaster, the 'country' people

were again dominant in 1819.[92]

An urban-to-rural shift from 1818 to 1819 predicated on the increasing adherence of 'country' handloom weavers to the radical cause ignores the important group of urban handloom weavers, including those living directly on the fringes of towns. The vast majority of those baptised by Harrison and of those from the Stockport district wounded at Peterloo were from Stockport and such nearby areas as Edgeley, Lancashire Hill and Stockport Great Moor. Apart from the Stockport Union, the only other political union in the district was at Gee Cross, whose numerous spinning and powerloom factories hardly qualified it as a 'hand-workers' village'. Some handloom weavers from rural areas may have become members of the Stockport and Gee Cross Unions, but they played no prominent role in the former institution, at least. The Stockport Union dominated radicalism in the district, and urban weavers numerically dominated the Stockport Union.

Thompson also tends to ignore the diversity of adherents' goals and the varying strength of their support. How committed were the rank-and-file (would-be emigrants, infidels, opponents to the Corn Laws, and so forth) to the over-arching campaign for parliamentary reform? To a great extent, the Stockport Union had attracted a following far larger than earlier unions by offering a panoply of programmes and thereby diluting the more narrow emphasis of earlier radical groups on political change. So, while there is no answer to the question just posed, it seems plausible to suggest that there existed a basis for potential fissure within the Union even when it appeared outwardly strong during 1819. Without some success, or at least an indication of progress towards one or more of its objectives, fragmentation could occur quite easily in such a heterogenous organisation.

11 THE FRAGMENTATION OF WORKERS' MOVEMENTS

> There is Mr. Carlile...who would make all things straight by
> merely persuading every man to get rid of his conscience, and
> labour, talk, write, and fight, if needful, to advance his own
> interest, and gratify his own passions; a doctrine, in short,
> which says in plain English, 'every man for himself, and the
> devil for us all'. – Thomas Arnold (1832)

Conditions changed dramatically during the 1820s for Stockport
radicals and weavers. The details of these changes are not always
easy to trace in the absence of internal papers of the Stockport
Union and of prominent orators declaring the objects of agitations
before well-publicised open-air meetings. For a decade after the
Six Acts, moreover, the radical press showed decreasing vigour.
Even the *Manchester Observer*, which continued to appear for
two years after Peterloo, became more timid in reporting local
radical schemes and instead devoted long columns to such traditional
newspaper topics as parliamentary proceedings and foreign affairs.
Yet the broad outlines of Stockport district events can be discerned.
They involved the virtual extinction of cotton handloom weaving
and the simultaneous polarisation of radicals into 'Huntites' and
'Carlilites'. These changes were occurring in the early 1820s in
conjunction with a prosperity so pervasive and sustained that its
like had not been experienced locally since the early 1790s. As the
Stockport Advertiser (20 June 1823) rhapsodised:

> Never in our memory was this part of the country in a state
> equally flourishing; our manufacturers are employed, our artisans
> happy and industrious, and loyalty and content have taken place
> to jacobinism and sedition, which distress had mainly contributed
> to foster.

Indeed, with the triumph of the Carlilites by 1822, there were fewer
collective disorders, fewer public agitations, and less worker support
for political reform proposals during the remainder of the decade.

254

I

A generally accepted view is that from the 1820s onwards, and especially after 1826, English handloom weaving was in full decline and handloom weavers were in great distress.[1] This picture must be modified for the Stockport district, where the greatest distress probably occurred under the Regency and where the decrease in numbers of weavers was already apparent during the factory-building boom of the early 1820s. It is not surprising that, as the birthplace of the powerloom, Stockport should have witnessed the decline of handloom weaving earlier than other towns in the cotton districts. Figures on the number of handloom weavers are fragmentary. The 1816 Stockport weavers' petition stated that until 'recently', there had been 15,000 weavers in the town and neighbourhood. This would suggest that from 30 to 40 per cent of the district's population was dependent upon handloom weaving. Lloyd put the figure at one-third of the population in 1816.[2] If this fraction were valid at the time of the first population censuses, the number of people dependent on weaving would have risen from about 12,000 in 1801 to a peak of 15,000 or 16,000 in 1811–14.

Other data seem to apply mostly to Stockport and its immediate suburbs. The weaving census of 1816 recorded over 5,000 weavers in the town and two contiguous townships (Table 9.1). A figure of slightly over 5,000 was still being quoted in 1818 for Stockport and 'vicinity'. In 1822 there were allegedly 2,800 handloom weavers. This figure had dropped to 800 in 1832, and 300 or 400 in 1834. The largest weaving community outside of Stockport in 1826 appeared to be that of 582 weavers to the south at Bullocksmithy.[3] Since these data do not derive from a single series, and it is not known precisely to which areas many of the estimates refer, they should be regarded merely as rough indications of the numerical decline of the handloom weavers. They do suggest certain broad conclusions. From 1818 to 1834, people were quitting the handloom weaving trade by the hundreds each year. According to one observer, many of them actually left town. By the mid-1830s the numbers in handloom weaving had become negligible, amounting to about one per cent of the total district population. Identical percentages were found in Ashton, Stalybridge and Dukinfield in 1834–6.[4]

Adults may have been the first to abandon the trade in many areas. The secretary to the Manchester Chamber of Commerce declared in 1833: 'Hand-loom Weaving has ceased, except in a few of its branches or under peculiar circumstances, to be the work of Adults.' The only exception noted by the secretary was the case in which a whole family, including the father, worked at handloom weaving and thus earned 'a fair means of support'.[5] In other words, one response of handloom weavers to ongoing distress was to increase production by working more looms within the household. Weavers also worked longer hours. Output per weaver in the 1820s is estimated to have increased by 25–30 per cent.[6] Another practice was for the father to continue weaving while putting his children to work in spinning or powerloom weaving factories. The resulting family income might be well above subsistence levels, as is shown by data provided by Joseph Sherwin in 1824:

Sherwin's income from weaving	6s. 6d.
Wife's income from same	3 0
Fifteen-year-old son's income from factory work	7 0
Ten-year-old son's income from same	6 0
Total family income per week	22s. 6d.

Sherwin stated that there were few Stockport children engaged in weaving–'they are sent to the factories in consequence of weaving being so low . . .'[7]

The sufferings, both material and mental, of those caught in the inexorable decline of handloom weaving should never be under-estimated. Yet the few remaining weavers in the Stockport district may not have been so distressed as those in other areas because powerlooms were initially replacing plain weavers, not the more highly paid fine and fancy weavers. The availability of alternate types of weaving also benefited the remaining handloom weavers, especially during the difficult years from 1815 to 1826. With the silk industry thriving at that time, many Stockport district weavers abandoned cotton to work on silk put out from Macclesfield. About one-third of remaining Stockport weavers wove silk in 1832, a fraction which almost certainly increased during the remainder of that decade.[8] Alternation of another kind, that is, between weaving and other occupations also occurred. Weaving could easily be combined with occasional town labour of various sorts, notably building work, and with agricultural employments. A Marple man stated that he worked as a weaver or as an agricultural labourer, both at the rate of 2s. per day.⁹ If alternation of weaving with different occupations was nothing new, it probably became more prevalent during the 1820s and thereafter.

Within such a fluid occupational setting, it is no wonder that thousands could abandon the trade in a generation. The industrialist Jeremiah Bury thought that whereas many had left other occupations to become weavers in earlier years, many in 1808 and subsequent years would have to stop weaving due to depressed wages. Many did. George Smith gave up handloom weaving in 1806 to work in Hope Hill Mills, for example, and Thomas Worsley gave it up in 1810 to work in his father's jenny spinning factory. Many had switched to powerloom weaving by 1819, and many more followed suit thereafter. An exceptional case of abandonment of the trade involved John Jennison who wove until 1829. He then purchased one-half acre of land in Cheadle and, sensing the growing potential of businesses devoted to leisure pursuits, opened his successful 'Monkey House' tea garden featuring caged monkeys, parrots and other animals.¹⁰

It is clear, in short, that the numbers of handloom weavers in the Stockport district declined rapidly in the decade after Peterloo. Those who remained tended to be highly skilled weavers not yet threatened by powerlooms or those whose family incomes were decreasingly dependent on weaving due to the employment of one or more family members in the factories or alternation with other occupations. These facts alone would suggest that the mass movements and public disorders characteristic of the first two decades of the century—events largely dependent on the support of distressed weavers—would be less prominent in the 1820s. Such was precisely the case.

II

At the same time a serious split in the ranks of the radicals was becoming apparent. After the imprisonment of Parson Harrison, James Moorhouse seems to have been the leading figure in the Stockport Union, or rather at the headquarters of the Union in the Windmill Rooms on Sandy Brow. At the branch Union Rooms in London Place, William Perry served as secretary and chief spokesman. The Windmill leaders struggled to maintain public awareness of their cause. They held celebrations of the first anniversary of Peterloo (16 August 1820) and Henry Hunt's birthday (6 November). Both affairs were small and subdued, however, in contrast to the festivities held in other towns of the region.[11] The Windmill leaders also prepared an address of support for Queen Caroline during her protracted 'trial', but her cause inspired only limited local enthusiasm. In November Moorhouse and Jackson (a master hatter) tried unsuccessfully to promote an illumination to celebrate her victory. In a subsequent attempt 21 supporters from the ranks of the lower-middle classes and artisanate published a handbill calling for an illumination on 4 December. Two versions of *Illumination Song, for Stockport* were also printed. Despite the difficulties of November, the tardy celebration proved to be fairly successful. Eight effigies of witnesses against the Queen were prepared, with six of them being hanged and burned during the afternoon behind Moorhouse's residence. The two remaining effigies were paraded through the streets and then also hanged and burned. After the illuminations began at seven o'clock in the evening, the make-believe violence of the reformers was answered by real violence from anti-reformers. Cheetham the surgeon had his windows broken, as did Lawton, the grocer who had earlier provided bail for Sir Charles Wolseley. A pistol shot was fired into Moorhouse's residence. Both John Lloyd and Stockport's mayor stated that there were ultimately few Stockport households with illuminations in their windows.[12]

The desire for a united reform movement remained strong nevertheless. At the end of December Cobbett called for a national reform campaign, and Carlile echoed his call on New Year's Day of 1821. These appeals resulted in a brief flurry of activity during March, climaxing in another delegate meeting at the Stockport Windmill. Those in attendance agreed to a 'Declaration of the Reformers of Yorkshire, Lancashire, Derbyshire, and Cheshire' which called for a national convention to draw up a new British constitution. A furious debate followed in the wake of the meeting, in part because the Stockport Declaration had been formulated by Joseph Brayshaw of Leeds without Hunt's participation or knowledge. Hunt publicly attacked it because of its 'revolutionary tone'; Wooler refused to print it because it was issued anonymously; the *Manchester Observer* condemned it as the product of spies' machinations; and Carlile criticised the idea that a constitution had already been proposed and was circulating in advance of the convening of a national assembly.[13]

After the widespread condemnation of their Declaration, Stockport Huntites became much less prominent. John Lloyd had reported his belief that radicalism was continuing to lose ground to loyalism after the illumination of December. There is no further evidence of any public activity by Moorhouse after 1820. Cheetham the surgeon went bankrupt in June 1821.[14] Bagguley, Drummond and Johnston were released from Chester Castle in April 1821 and thereafter attended a series of dinners in their honour in various towns. None was held in Stockport. Drummond and Johnston settled again in Manchester and had few contacts with Stockport reformers. Bagguley, now 22 years old and bearded, did return temporarily to Stockport. Although he initially behaved 'respectfully' according to Lloyd, he was soon trying to incorporate radical issues into plans for Stockport's celebration of George IV's coronation. He wanted to petition the King to release all political prisoners, and he vowed to lead a procession demanding this object during the coronation festivities. Neither the petition nor the procession materialised. Bagguley was also blocked in his attempt to obtain a licence for a lecture room similar to the one he had used to promote agitations in the summer of 1818. Frustrated at every turn, he finally absconded with about £25 of the Stockport Permanent Fund and a few pounds from the Macclesfield Fund. He was believed to be travelling and lecturing somewhere in Lancashire.[15]

The Stockport Permanent Fund reveals much about the early development of the branch Union Rooms at London Place. The latter worked together for some time with the Windmill headquarters to collect subscriptions for: (1) supporting Harrison, Swann, Bertinshaw, Bagguley, Drummond and Johnston while they were imprisoned in Chester Castle; (2) supporting Mrs Swann, who had moved back to Stockport from Macclesfield in order to obtain poor relief—initially by residing in Daw Bank Workhouse; and (3) helping to support three Macclesfield prisoners in conjunction with the Macclesfield Permanent Fund. The times were not propitious for radical schemes, however. By November 1820 William Perry of the London Place branch had to advertise in the *Black Dwarf* and the *Republican* for outside money to keep the Fund going. He stated that Stockport reformers had paid Bagguley, Drummond and Johnston ten shillings apiece for each of the preceding 15 months. The Union probably sent similar amounts to the other three Stockport prisoners, which would have required a minimum outlay of £3 per month.[16]

During that same period the London Place Union was launching an independent subscription for Richard Carlile. London Place radicals hoped to send the Dorchester prisoner regular contributions of £1, an amount greater than that being sent to any individual Stockport prisoner. Although they had to suspend payments after October 1820 when local financial difficulties intervened, radical finances became stronger (and irresistibly tempting to Bagguley) during the course of 1821. William Perry sent Carlile nearly £2 in April 1821 and nearly £4 in October. It seems likely that during that year, the London Place radicals withdrew their support from the Stockport Permanent Fund and decided to channel all monies to Carlile. Since London Place was rapidly becoming the dominant radical centre in Stockport, this shift would have meant that there would be little or no financial support for Harrison and the other Chester prisoners. A letter written by Perry to Carlile in August 1820 also suggests that new ideological themes were emerging at London Place. Perry referred to the London Place radicals in that early account as 'Friendly Mechanics to Civil and Religious Liberty'. The Friendly Mechanics were primarily opposed to priestcraft and superstition:

> We have a few of the priest-kind in this part, who have joined the ranks of reformers, and who have made great attempts to overthrow your powerful reasoning in support of Universal Freedom; but they having taken up their position in a dark thick fog, such position vanished the moment nature's light made its powerful appearance . . .

Perry later assured Carlile that Stockport's female reformers were still active and expressed his desire that pulpits, 'instead of being filled with the deceitful, fawning, sychophantic, gundy-gutted, and sleek-headed priest, . . . be filled with the philosopher or mathematician, thundering forth immutable and incontrovertible truths'; and that 'the Printing-Press shall really become a part of the household furniture'. The shift away from the political Huntism of the Windmill, apparent in these passages, was also visible in Perry's condemnation of the March 1821 delegate meeting held in the Windmill Rooms. He called it a product of 'the infernal spy system'.[17]

That the subsequent well-being of the Chester prisoners had little relationship to developments in Stockport simply reflects the direction of the growing local schism. London Place radicals, though financially strong, ignored the 'Huntite' prisoners, while the Windmill radicals were becoming too weak (from defections and Bagguley's embezzlement) to help their imprisoned comrades. Harrison's plaintive stories of neglect inspired the Middleton radical Samuel Bamford to write 'Hymn to Hope' in his own Lincoln Castle prison cell and to dedicate it to the Stockport Parson. Others responded with money. Large contributions arrived for Harrison from Nottingham, Leicester and Birmingham, and numerous smaller ones came from such places as Newcastle-upon-Tyne, Great Horton (near Bradford) and Todmorden. This surge in subscriptions, coupled with the fact that after January 1822, Harrison and Swann were the only Stockport district reformers left in Chester Castle, meant that their *per capita* income rose to between £2 and £3 per month. 'It affords us consolation,' they wrote in 1823, 'that when our friends in some parts of the country have become dormant, others are more vigorous...'[18]

The only celebration recorded in the *Black Dwarf* upon Harrison's release later in that year was held not in Stockport but in Great Horton. There, on 31 October, a weaver delivered an ode composed in Harrison's honour, and Harrison renewed his commitment to Huntite reform. He called Hunt 'one of the greatest patriots that ever existed in any age or country'. Such sentiments found little remaining support at Stockport. Harrison tried to revive his Independent congregation, but performed only 14 baptisms from November 1823 to April 1824, after which he stopped. Although he continued his preaching, he remained a figure of little significance in Stockport until the parliamentary reform agitation of the early 1830s.[19]

Adding to the difficulties of the Huntites during this period was, ironically, the formation of the Huntite Grand National Union (GNU) at the end of 1821. On the second anniversary of Peterloo, Hunt had suggested to Manchester radicals that a national fund be established for electing one or more radicals to Parliament. Progress was slow at first, but meetings of support were held at Stockport, Bolton and Royton before the end of September. Sir Charles Wolseley, just out of prison, acted as treasurer and received the first Manchester contribution of £10 at the end of October. Stockport radicals were reported as being 'shy...in intrusting their funds to any but their own Committee, ever since Baguley [*sic*] went off, with monies from Stockport and Macclesfield'.[20]

The tactics espoused by the GNU and by the Stockport Declaration of March 1821 were quite distinct. While the GNU hoped to establish a fund to elect radicals to Parliament, the Declaration advocated the election of a convention of radicals as a sort of Painite alternative to Parliament. The author and chief publicist of the Declaration, Joseph Brayshaw of Leeds, immediately wrote to Carlile complaining that Hunt and Wooler had unjustifiably tried to suppress the convention scheme. Carlile no doubt came to hear other criticisms that were being raised against the GNU and its supporters. Could radicals trust those supervising the collection and disbursement of the election fund, especially at a time when stories were circulating about the financial peccadilloes of Hunt, Cobbett and other radical leaders?[21] Were radical funds to be diverted from the support of needy prisoners to the support of parliamentary candidates? Was Hunt to be the first (or only) radical MP to be elected with the help of the contributions? Were seats to be purchased for Hunt or Cobbett in the same corrupt fashion that radicals had long condemned? In any case, Carlile may have been predisposed to dislike the Huntites because of their religious taint. As early as September 1820 he had criticised the religious tone of the 'National Prayer' which Hunt had composed for the 1820 Peterloo anniversary celebrations. The continuing intransigence of Hunt and Wooler over the Stockport Declaration helped to push Carlile into open opposition. In a pamphlet published at the end of October 1821,[22] he reprinted some of Brayshaw's correspondence and the text of the Stockport Declaration in what amounted to a tacit endorsement of the convention scheme. By December, the second anniversary of his imprisonment, Carlile had shifted his political and religious positions even further. He attacked *Wooler's British Gazette*–and by implication, Hunt–as Whiggish. He likewise ridiculed the GNU and its objectives. Whereas before he could endorse the Huntite emphasis on universal suffrage, he now felt that the Huntite faction could 'do nothing without coming up to all my principles, which consist of the politics of Paine, and the theology of Mirabaud [that is, of the Baron d'Holbach]'.[23] Uncompromising republicanism and atheism were to be the two major principles which Carlile was to advocate for the rest of the decade.

Antagonisms increased during the early months of 1822. Hunt claimed that Carlile was more interested in religion than politics and stated that he did 'not agree with Mr. Carlile, nor ever did agree with him as to the advantage of propagating the theological opinions of Paine and Mirabaud . . .' In the same publication, Hunt eulogised

Harrison, noting that the Stockport preacher had made nothing from politics (since he was not a pamphlet vendor) and was devoted to the cause only due to his 'love of Liberty'. Carlile answered in March by formally breaking with Hunt and attacking Harrison. 'He lived by his politics all the time he was at Stockport,' Carlile claimed, 'by preaching politics, and by teaching politics...' Support or criticism of Harrison thus became a major theme in the national radical schism. Hunt responded to Carlile by stating that he had received a letter which 'says, all that [Carlile] has insinuated against Mr. Harrison, of Stockport, is an infamous falsehood, as Harrison is as good a man as ever lived'.[24]

Wooler, in the *Black Dwarf* of 27 March, vowed not to publish anything on the dispute between Hunt and Carlile since 'the friends of reform are not listed under the banners of *any* individual'. But Carlile had his *Republican* and Hunt his periodic addresses *To the Radical Reformers,* and the debate continued. Carlile repeated his charges against Harrison in April. Hunt countered with a reaffirmation of his support for the parson and a defence of his own position. He charged that Carlile was attacking him merely 'because I do not choose to avow myself a Republican, and an enemy to all religion'. The parting shot came from Carlile in May, when he retold the story of Harrison's having impregnated a female student. With that, the personal schism between Carlile and Hunt was complete, and the stage was set for local schisms between 'republicans' and 'Christian reformers' throughout the country.[25]

The conclusion of the squabble at Stockport was not so dramatic as that at the national level. At the London Place celebration of Paine's birthday on 29 January 1822, the Friendly Mechanics even offered a toast to Hunt, Wolseley and GNU, adding '...and may their pens, and the funds of the Union soon be appropriated to the patriotic purpose of destroying Priestcraft and promulgating the doctrines of unsophisticated Republicanism.' The Stockport Huntites had apparently become so weak and their activities so quixotic as to pose little or no threat to the predominance of the Carlilites. In a letter to Carlile, William Perry seemed almost unconcerned that 'there are a few in this part of the country who are giving vent to their rage and malice against you in consequence of some difference between Mr. Hunt and you...' Just two years later the furniture in the Windmill was being sold off for non-payment of rent.[26] After that time the Huntites played almost no public role in Stockport radicalism for the remainder of the decade and retained no identifiable popular following. There is, moreover, no evidence of any link between Stockport Huntites and the GNU after the gloomy report of Huntite fund-raising efforts in January 1822. The GNU itself was said to have crested in popularity around the same time, but it retained a vestigial institutional form until 1828, when Wolseley turned over the remaining funds in the treasury to Henry Hunt for his personal use.[27]

III

The Friendly Mechanics meanwhile continued to devote their considerable energies to fund-raising campaigns. By the end of 1822 Stockport ranked fifth among provincial towns in terms of the amount of money sent to Carlile.[28] This achievement helped to inspire the Hyde-Denton radicals to go over to Carlile during 1822 without leaving a trace of Huntite support. They sent Carlile £4 at that time and a further £2 in January 1824 (Table 11.1). Samuel Mercer, the leader of the Hyde Carlilites, assured Carlile when he sent the first contribution that 'reason is assuming her proper station in the minds of the people in this part of the country'. Mercer promised to continue purchasing Carlile's works for his family and neighbours. True to his word, he remained an active proselytiser. With the 1824 Hyde subscription he wrote, 'I have this week gained a footing for your *Republican* in a village in a remote part of this country, where none had been sent to, and few read in, before'. As at Stockport, celebrations of Paine's birthday became the major event on the radical calendar.[29] The Hyde Carlilites remained smaller in number, though more generous on average, than Stopfordians because Hyde did not contain many impoverished handloom weavers to recruit to the cause. While Stockport Carlilites numbered a few hundred at their peak, those at Hyde never numbered more than a few dozen.

Carlile fostered his relationship with Stockport district followers not only by publicly thanking them for their contributions in the pages of the *Republican* and other publications but also by making a special effort to publicise the case of the imprisoned Stockport hatter, Joseph Swann. This seemed, in effect, to counter-balance Carlile's denunciations of Parson Harrison during the debates with Hunt. Carlile published the history of the long persecution of Swann and his wife Hannah. When Hunt sent Harrison £10, Carlile sent Swann the same amount. He also reported on other subscriptions for Swann and applauded Swann's successful transition to his old trade after his release in 1824. Carlile's support helped Swann to gain a place in the ranks of the reformers at London Place and (in contrast to Harrison) to play a prominent role in local radical affairs during the ensuing years.[30]

Table 11.1: Individual Subscriptions from Stockport and Hyde to Richard Carlile or the Rev. Robert Taylor, 1821-9

(a) Date	(b) Number of Individual Subscriptions	(c) Total Amount of (b) in £.s.d.	(d) Average = (c) ÷ (b) to nearest d.	(e) Sources
[Stockport:]				
April 1821	51	1. 8. 5	7d.	*To the Reformers,* 24 June 1821
Oct. 1821	71	2.16.10	10	Ibid., 13 Oct. 1821
March 1822	94	3.12. 4	10	*Republican,* 5 April 1822
Sept. 1822	71	2.17.10	10	Ibid., 20 Sept. 1822
Dec. 1822	170	8. 4. 6	12	Ibid., 20 Dec. 1822
March 1828	109	4.19. 6	12	*Lion,* 28 March 1828
March 1829	33	2. 4. 4	14	Ibid., 13 March 1829
[Hyde:]				
March 1822	33	2. 0. 0	15	*Republican,* 12 April 1822
Dec. 1822	32	2. 1. 6	16	Ibid., 31 Jan. 1823
Jan. 1824	18	2. 0. 0½	27	Ibid., 20 Feb. 1824
April 1829	27	2. 0. 0	18	*Lion,* 24 April 1829

Note: In each Stockport subscription campaign, there were additional group contributions, which make the total numbers of individuals subscribing and the total amounts subscribed greater than the above figures indicate. The Hyde figures include subscriptions from Denton and Newton. They compromise the total amounts in each category since there were no additional group contributions.

The social position of Carlile's followers differed somewhat from that of the Huntites. Unfortunately, of the hundreds of Stopfordians who contributed to Carlilite causes from 1821 to 1833, it is possible to determine the occupations of only a small number. Of most importance were Carlilite 'activists', that is, those who either: (1) served as officers in Stockport Carlilite organisations; (2) contributed to at least three subscriptions; (3) remained active in Carlilite affairs for more than two years; or (4) were previously active in such workers' movements as trade unionism, parliamentary reform campaigns or Luddism. The vast majority of activists met more than one of these criteria. The occupations of 40 (out of 111) have been determined (Table 11.2). Slightly more than half were weavers, with hatters and booksellers (or printers) also being notable. By contrast, the occupations of the 21 Huntite leaders who called for an illumination for Queen Caroline in 1820 included no weavers, hatters, booksellers or printers. The majority were shopkeepers or others from the lower-middle classes, and most of the remaining men were skilled artisans. With the exception of Thomas Cheetham the surgeon, none of these Huntites later contributed to Carlile. At the time of the earlier schism between non-violent Huntites and violent Spenceans, a Manchester magistrate made a comment to the effect that the Huntites were reformers of a higher class.[31] In the early 1820s, when the Hunt-Carlile split was primarily over religion, the Stockport Huntite leadership again appears to have had a somewhat higher social status than the leaders of the schismatics. The old Huntite leadership had relied on weavers' support in 1818–20 and simply continued to function in the ensuing years without a substantial popular following of any sort. The Carlilites drew little support from the lower-middle classes and instead derived both their leadership and rank-and-file from weavers and (like the Huntites) from skilled artisans.

As with social standing, so too with the programmes of the Friendly Mechanics: they differed from those of the old Huntite Stockport Union, but not in every respect. It would obscure too many subtleties simply to adopt John Belchem's antithetical model whereby the Huntites are viewed as instrumental, goal-oriented, tolerant and organisation-minded and the Carlilites are regarded as expressive, value-oriented, dogmatic and possessing little concern about organisational structures.[32] Both groups shared a concern about education, for example. Carlile advocated organisations like the mechanics' institutes which had

> one object and only one–that object is strictly good, unalloyed with a particle of evil;–it is intended and calculated to increase the knowledge of the mass of the people, to make every man a scientific schoolmaster in that circle which he can influence . . . It is the very acme of utility in its relation to human happiness.

The Stockport 'Temple of Reason' at London Place succeeded in living up to the Carlilite ideal. It contained the London Place

Table 11.2: Occupations of Stockport Carlilites and Huntites

Occupation	(a) Carlilite Activists	(b) Huntites Calling for an Illumination in 1820
Surgeon	1	1
Coach proprietor	0	1
Grocer, flour dealer, baker	0	4
Draper, hosier	0	3
Druggist	0	2
Shopkeeper	1	0
Salesman	1	0
Printer, bookseller	5	0
Watchmaker	0	1
Reedmaker	0	1
Tinman	0	1
Bricklayer	1	0
Weaver	22	0
Hatter	6	0
Shoe-clog-patten maker	2	3
Tailor	0	1
Pattern drawer	1	0
Ropemaker	0	2
Sweep	0	1
Total	40	21

Sources: (a) Same as for the Stockport subscriptions in Table 11.1; and *Prompter*, 16 July 1831; *Gauntlet*, 14 April 1833; (b) *To the Public* (Manchester, 1820), pr. s.sh.

Reading Society, a group which managed to build up a small library. From time to time, Friendly Mechanics would even contribute pieces to Carlile's publications. In 1824, for example, Thomas Mackintosh sent an ambitious seven-page essay arguing that the intellect was basically physical or material.[33] The Friendly Mechanics placed special emphasis on purity of diet. Carlile himself opposed the use of alcohol, tobacco and snuff. 'As the first of my principles is—*educate, reform yourselves,*' he wrote, 'so I am sensible that health is essential to happiness...' But this trend had also been discernible in Huntism as an extension and elaboration of various schemes to abstain from such excisable items as beer, spirits, tea and coffee.[34] Among Stockport Carlilites of the 1820s, it was to be pushed ever closer to the ideal of vegetarianism.

In politics the Friendly Mechanics were avowedly Painite, or republican. Before 1820, Carlile's republicanism seemed compatible with Hunt's 'democracy' with its emphasis on universal suffrage, annual Parliaments and secret ballots. After 1820, Carlile's republicanism took on an extreme anti-monarchical coloration and consequently became a source of contention. In so far as they interested themselves in politics, the Friendly Mechanics followed the orthodox Carlilite line.

Carlilism differed from Huntism most of all in Carlile's subordination of politics to religion. Religion had played only a minor role in Huntite agitations for political reform. The Huntite leadership was, none the less, openly Christian. With tears streaming down his cheeks, Hunt had denied all charges of religious infidelity in a dramatic opening speech at the Peterloo trial. For the first anniversary of Peterloo, he had composed a 'National Prayer' and thereby caused offence to Carlile. The chaplain attending Hunt on his deathbed in 1835 'went away convinced . . . that Mr. Hunt was a true Christian'.[35] The *Manchester Observer* distanced itself from unbelievers in articles like 'Reformers not Deists' (1820) and 'A Dialogue Between John Fungus, a Magistrate's servant, and Frank Upright, a poor Weaver' (1821). John Lloyd, the Stockport magistrate's clerk, may have provided some of the inspiration for the latter piece. Frank Upright states in one passage of this satire: 'For ma part, a meeon to stick to both Radical and Christian; t' one for politics, an' t' other for religion.' John Bagguley was clearly not an atheist, and James Moorhouse was devoutly religious. Parson Harrison had become a reformer in part 'to prevent the dissemination of infidelity, which he found to his sorrow, had made progress among the reformers'. The executed McInnis was a case in point. An atheist nearly to the end, McInnis (in his own words) 'strove to make as many infidels as he could'. Not surprisingly, Harrison could recall that 'many quarrels had he had with Reformers on account of his defending and propagating the Gospel among them'.[36]

In one sense this movement away from orthodox Christianity comprised a facet of the widespread and complex rejection of Huntite leaders and doctrines. Yet such tendencies did not inevitably lead to blasphemy nor did they always comprise a simple, reflexive reaction against Huntism. The Friendly Mechanics gained some positive inspiration, for example, from the Manchester Swedenborgians or 'Bible Christians'. The latter dabbled in politics, trade unionism and mysticism, and also concerned themselves with disseminating useful knowledge intended to improve the personal habits of their followers. They especially advocated abstinence from alcohol and meat in a combined doctrine of teetotal vegetarianism. The sect's *New System of Vegetable Cookery* was in its second edition by April 1821. Its leading minister, the Rev. James Schofield of Christ Church, Hulme, was preaching at Stockport as early as December 1820.[37] Rowley Barnes, a fervent young member of Schofield's Hulme Chapel congregation, became associated with the Stockport Friendly Mechanics soon thereafter. Born a bastard in 1800, Barnes had become a part-time teacher and lecturer in 1816.[38] In about 1823 he established a Swedenborgian congregation of his own at Brinksway, Stockport, which he called the Society of Universal Benevolence. He also changed his name about that time to Rowland Detrosier. Since he worked as a salesman for a Manchester firm, he was able to spend considerable time in Stockport.

Although his congregation's vegetarianism evoked the popular name 'Beefsteak Chapel' for his house of worship, Detrosier's early sermons did not stray too far from the orthodox Swedenborgian variety of mystical Christianity. Attendance remained small as a result. Then, for some unknown reason, Detrosier came to reject the Son, the Holy Spirit and 'such a place as a hell of brimstone and fire' and converted to deism. He also seems to have devoted more time to 'sermons' on trigonometry, pneumatics, astronomy and social issues. William Blackshaw, a Carlilite bookseller, described Detrosier's oratory in 1826:

> He breathes and preaches the doctrines of the immortal Paine, and his sermons or lectures have such a tendency to moralize the present demoralized state of society, that few can go and hear him, and not admire him. We cannot speak too highly of him for the good that he is doing; for my own part, whenever I hear him, there is a pleasing sensation [which] thrills through my whole frame, which my pen cannot describe—the reason is, because his sentiments are congenial with my own.[39]

These new departures at Brinksway attracted large, curious crowds, including many of Blackshaw's colleagues from the Friendly Mechanics.

The growing popularity of Detrosier, the Beefsteak Chapel and the works of Carlile provoked increasing local opposition. Presbyterian, Congregationalist and Methodist ministers began preaching two or three times a week near Brinksway in an effort to counteract the ideas disseminated inside the Chapel. In 1825 leading Stopfordians established the first Stockport Mechanics' Institute in part to neutralise the impact of the cheap literature in which Carlile specialised. It never attracted much attention, however, and finally closed its doors in May 1827. In the previous year the *Stockport Advertiser* began a sustained attack on the Beefsteak Chapel and the throngs which attended it. 'It affects antiquarian consequence,' one editorial intoned, 'grubs in the rubbish of chronology–burrows among the rocks and fossils of the geologist–stabs the immortality of the soul with the dissecting knife, and degrades the office of the poet . . .'[40] These attacks may have resulted in part from the more public posture taken by local infidels during 1826. Before that time, they had eschewed public meetings, which were, of course, redolent of Huntism. Yet as the distress of the weavers mounted, the Friendly Mechanics (probably mostly weavers themselves) shifted their position and became involved in the weavers' cause.

IV

The Stockport Weavers' Committee, led by Joseph Sherwin and William Longson, had been intermittently active during the Carlilites' rise. In the campaign to repeal the Combination Acts, Longson vociferously supported repeal in the pages of the *Manchester Gazette* and elsewhere beginning in the latter part of 1823. Early in 1824 Joseph Sherwin was chosen to re-enact the role he played in 1811 as spokesman for the Stockport weavers in London. He testified to the Select Committee on Artizans and Machinery that 'we have a small number of a committee now acting; but we have no regular plan to raise our wages'. While the Weavers' Committee still existed, the mass of weavers, according to Sherwin, 'do not meet respecting the price of labour, because their wages are so low, they consider it unnecessary to meet'. The Stockport meeting which had selected Sherwin consisted of just 40 or 50 weavers.[41]

Similar signs of disjunction between the Committee and the operative weavers were to characterise most of the 1820s. With the repeal of the Combination Acts, efforts were made to revive somnolent weavers' groups throughout the Manchester district. In August 1824, 300 weavers' delegates met in Manchester to establish a general union whose function would be to obtain uniformity of wages, prevent wage reductions and, when possible, obtain wage increases. Over the next six or seven months, local committees held meetings in Stockport, Bolton and Manchester to further the cause of the union. But the dwindling numbers of operative weavers remained as apathetic as before, at least in the Stockport district. Organisational efforts were also hindered by internal debates between moderate weavers and those advocating sweeping minimum wage demands enforced by strikes.[42]

It is not without significance in this context that the moderate William Longson had replaced the erstwhile radical Joseph Sherwin as the most prominent spokesman for the Weavers' Committee by the mid-1820s. Well-educated and articulate, Longson nevertheless seemed unable to address himself to the immediate, practical needs of Stockport district weavers. On the contrary, as he began to correspond with Francis Place, he came to endorse many of the London tailor's deductions from the theory of political economy. Place was against apprenticeship restrictions of any kind, and Longson supported this position even though it had negligible relevance to the plight of local weavers. Stockport weavers petitioned Parliament in 1823 for a minimum wage, a perennially popular solution to their distress. Since Place opposed minimum wage legislation, Longson followed suit and suggested as an alternative a rigid and rather idealistic wage-equalisation scheme which never gained much support–certainly not from Place. When Place advocated birth control as the best means of decreasing the population and thereby increasing wages, Longson again offered his enthusiastic public endorsement, oblivious to the indifference of most of his weaving constituency. It can be said on Longson's behalf that he may have thought that the latter stance would help to win the allegiance of the Friendly Mechanics since their national leader, Richard Carlile, had joined Place in advocating contraception for the working classes. Subsequent support for the weavers from the Friendly Mechanics lends plausibility to this assumption.[43]

In general, however, the Stockport Weavers' Committee was becoming increasingly unresponsive and ineffectual under Longson as the economy began to turn downwards in the last half of 1825. Contemporaries blamed the slump on two types of causes: (1) overproduction of cotton goods, which was linked to increased use of powerlooms; and (2) the deficient harvest of 1825, whose effects were exacerbated by the Corn Laws. The slump severely affected the economy of the Stockport district. By January 1826 many factories were working at half time and some were shut down entirely. The *Stockport Advertiser* reported in April that 'hundreds of individuals are wandering about the streets in idleness, who a few months ago were enjoying every comfort that full employment could afford'. Stopfordians generally agreed that of all workers, the handloom weavers were suffering the most. Yet the Stockport Weavers' Committee offered no programme of its own during the earliest months of the slump. It seemed content to follow the lead of Thomas Worsley and the Stockport Committee of Artizans, a body dominated by cotton spinners. One of the last known acts of the Artizans' Committee was to hold a meeting on 16 February to protest the Corn Laws. Longson spoke at the meeting but offered no independent suggestions.[44]

The deteriorating situation of the next few months finally led to collective actions by weavers, with those of the Stockport district merely following examples set elsewhere. Bolton weavers, for instance, agitated for a minimum wage. From 24 to 27 April, weavers in various parts of Lancashire were involved in riots and machine breaking. The Stockport district experienced only threats of violence during the subsequent weeks, although a ritual effigy burning did occur at Bullocksmithy on 8 May. Finally goaded into action by such events, Longson and the Weavers' Committee proposed a distinctive, though moderate, programme. It included opposition to the Corn Laws and a scheme whereby the government would buy up all surplus cloth and hold it in warehouses until a satisfactory selling price could be obtained.[45]

Here was no extremist push for a minimum wage, much less a call to engage in Luddism. The Weavers' Committee did not even actively press for the implementation of its own proposals. Nevertheless, its example of moderation may have helped to diminish violent impulses within the Stockport district, as did the brief amelioration of the economic situation in late May and early June.[46] The extensive charitable efforts which quickly followed the Lancashire riots likewise helped to preserve public order. Early in May, a London Committee for the Relief of the Manufacturing Poor was established along the same lines as the London charitable committees of 1812–13 and 1816–17. By January 1827 it had disbursed over £100,000. The impact of Relief Committee grants on the Stockport district was substantial, particularly during the first months of its operations. From May to September 1826 Stockport, Edgeley, Heaton Norris, Offerton and Bullocksmithy together received an average of about £500 or £600 per month from London. The average monthly totals through February 1827 then dropped to between £200 and £300, although those grants were accompanied by large supplemental shipments of goods.[47]

Only a few days after the London Committee was established, some of Stockport's leading citizens formed a local relief committee which raised subscriptions of its own, disbursed the funds from London and co-ordinated various charitable programmes throughout the district. On 17 May the Stockport Committee began distributing provisions from the Windmill Rooms (long since vacated by the Huntites), a practice it continued twice weekly. Early figures show that between 700 and 1,000 persons typically lined up for free food. Within two weeks of its establishment, the Stockport Committee had raised over £800 locally. During June, inhabitants of Heaton Norris and of Bredbury set up respective relief committees of their own, and the inhabitants of Brinnington soon followed their example. As in 1816 the Stockport Committee soon came to express its preference for outdoor work rather than gratuitous relief. By the end of June some of the poor were set to work moving earth from in front of the National School. Later, they were also engaged in building and repairing roads.[48]

The moderation promoted by the Weavers' Committee and nurtured by charitable largesse was not the only theme apparent in Stockport weavers' circles during 1826. As the slump temporarily worsened towards midsummer, there were reports from Manchester of delegate meetings at which violent schemes were discussed. Whether or not Stockport representatives attended those meetings is unclear, but some local meetings did occur at about the same time. On 19 July Joseph Whitelegg, a weaver linked to the London Place Friendly Mechanics, delivered a fiery address to a crowd of more than 500 people. The Stockport authorities, no doubt energised by recent local government reforms, were quick to react. They arrested Whitelegg and later secured his conviction on five counts of sedition. The magistrates next issued a warning that future meetings 'tending to a breach of the peace' would be suppressed. When a thinly attended public meeting was convened late in the month, special constables had no trouble in dispersing it.[49]

The *Stockport Advertiser* was simultaneously inaugurating its series of attacks on local infidels, probably because they appeared to have taken up the cause of the extremist faction of the weavers. The events of early September lent some credence to such an interpretation. Moderate operatives, including Longson of the Weavers' Committee, held a meeting to express gratitude to the government for allowing special grain imports (in contravention of the Corn Laws) by an Order in Council. William Blackshaw, the infidel bookseller, led the opposition at the meeting by arguing that no gratitude need be displayed for such a tardy and inadequate measure. The majority supported Blackshaw, and the resolution of thanks went down to defeat.[50] Even Rowland Detrosier seemed to be spending less time on deism and geology. In late October he spoke at a Manchester meeting devoted to parliamentary reform and Corn Law repeal. The next month he preached in the Beefsteak Chapel on the desirability of a new constitution. In 1827 he was delivering lectures sympathetic to the weavers' distress.[51]

The Carlilites' brief forays into the public arena must have furnished them with clear evidence of the possible consequences of heightened activism in the 1820s. Whitelegg was imprisoned, and in December 1826, so was Swann. The charge against him was not that of selling radical literature (as in 1819) but of neglecting his wife and children, who had again been forced to apply for poor relief.[52] Detrosier's participation in a reform meeting and his subsequent sermonising may have offended the Swedenborgian hierarchy and thereby helped to set the stage for the troubles which befell him in 1827. The ostensible source of Detrosier's difficulties was, however, Richard Carlile.

During his lengthy provincial tour of 1827, Carlile attended the Swedenborgian services of the Rev. Schofield in Manchester. The London infidel may have found it difficult to conceal his displeasure at the time and soon afterwards wrote that 'the greatest absurdity that I ever heard from a pulpit, I heard that evening from Mr. Scholefield [*sic*]'. Carlile also visited Stockport's Beefsteak Chapel in August and September and delivered 'discourses' after Detrosier had completed Sunday services. He proceeded to debate a local minister from the Swain Street Unitarian Christian Meeting House, a spectacle which attracted an audience of some 2,000 persons. Although hours of argument settled none of the issues, Carlile thought it a moral victory for infidelism that such a debate had even occurred and called it 'the first public discussion that had been held between a preacher of Christianity and its avowed infidel'. At Hyde Carlile met with his long-time supporter, Sam Mercer. Despite harassment by the Hyde constabulary and the interference of 'one of those strange incompatibilities, called a *religious, radical reformer*', Carlile managed to attract a crowd of about 100 persons.[53]

Carlile's presence in the Stockport district during the late summer of 1827 no doubt helped to maintain local interest in his views, as did the subsequent publication of one of his Brinksway 'sermons'. When Carlile's friend, the Rev. Robert Taylor, was imprisoned for blasphemy in 1828, Carlilites at both Stockport and Hyde began extensive new subscription campaigns for his relief (see 1828-9 entries in Table 11.1). Carlile's visit had significant negative effects as well. While he had incurred the displeasure of Manchester Swedenborgians a few years before for propounding his beliefs, Carlile positively enraged them in 1827 by using Detrosier's chapel for atheistical speeches. The Swedenborgian leadership summarily removed Detrosier as a result and then sold the Brinksway Chapel to a dyer for industrial purposes. Thereafter, Detrosier's involvement in Stockport affairs decreased markedly as he tried to make it clear to all who would listen that he still believed in a deity (if, indeed, not the Trinity). Carlile would no more accept such a notion from Detrosier than he would from Schofield or Hunt. He remained uncharacteristically lavish with general praise, calling Detrosier 'a phenomenon as a speech maker' who had 'a fine genius, and almost an [*sic*] universal one – clever at whatever he touches...' But since Carlile insisted on pure atheism, relations between the two men soon became strained.[54]

Stockport Carlilites survived Detrosier's departure just as they had survived the abortive attempts of some of their members to increase support by publicly embracing the handloom weavers' cause in 1826-7. The Friendly Mechanics proceeded to renew their commitment to Carlile's various self-help programmes and remained wary of public activities, especially political agitations. In so doing, they preserved their organisation into the 1830s. They did not, in other words, try again to win mass support from the weavers or any other specific occupational group. The weavers themselves returned to internal squabbling. An extremist group gathered at Compstall Bridge in 1827 with the intention of destroying powerlooms. When confronted not with force but with a cartload of loaves and cheeses provided by a shrewd local manufacturer, the crowd abandoned its attack. William Longson denounced weavers who participated in such activities and also withdrew his support from some of Francis Place's schemes, notably that involving birth control for the masses. Instead, Longson again advocated wage equalisation in 1827 as part of a broad programme encompassing reductions in twist exports, Corn Law levies and general taxation levels.[55] Yet many rank-and-file weavers still hoped to obtain their simple and long-cherished goal of a minimum wage. With such wide disparities in objectives, weavers found it nearly impossible to agree on common agitations. Stockport, consequently, was the only major town in the cotton districts whose weavers failed to petition Parliament for a minimum wage in 1827 and who failed again to petition for a select committee to investigate their distress in 1828.[56]

At least three fissiparous tendencies were thus at work in the 1820s: (1) fragmentation within the trade of handloom weaving, especially in the sense that the Weavers' Committee was losing its hold over dejected operative weavers, and hence, its ability to organise strikes and other collective actions;[57] (2) schisms within the radical movement; and (3) the inability of any radical group to attract the allegiance of substantial numbers of workers in order to sustain mass movements. These were not merely transitory phenomena caused, perhaps, by the defeat at Peterloo. If they had been, the severe economic crisis at mid-decade surely would have elicited the signs of (admittedly incomplete) solidarity found in Luddism, Hampdenism and the Peterloo era. Instead, the brief effort of the Stockport Friendly Mechanics to embrace the weavers' cause comprised nothing more than a belated and unsuccessful attempt to recreate earlier alliances. If there were doubts before, it was clear by the beginning of the later Industrial Revolution in the 1820s that fragmentation among workers was becoming a regular feature of the local scene.

12   CONCLUSION

[Numerous ranks exist]...among the lower orders. The ploughmen hold the mechanics in contempt, as an inferior race of beings, although the latter earn the best wages: the journeymen cabinetmakers cannot degrade themselves by associating with the journeymen tailors: the journeymen shoemakers cannot so far forget their dignity as to make companions of the labourers: the gentleman's lacquey cannot, on any account, lower himself to the level of the carman. – David Robinson in *Blackwood's* (1825)

The Stockport district in the 1820s was far different from what it had been in the 1770s. From its tale of extraordinary growth and development, one can find pieces of evidence to support E.P. Thompson's claim that a working class was made by the early 1830s, Harold Perkin's somewhat more tentative discovery of a working class by 1820, or John Foster's alternate view that only a rudimentary variety of a working class could be found at any point before 1830. Thompson is right, for example, in emphasising that workers' organisations multiplied enormously during the early Industrial Revolution. Whereas the Stockport district contained only a handful of trade and benefit clubs in the 1770s, by the 1820s there were scores of friendly societies and trade unions as well as additional building societies, co-operatives and radical clubs (not to mention religious and educational institutions in which workers played an important, and sometimes predominant, role). The impact of radical ideologies was also important. In the 1770s and 1780s the Stockport district provided a rather stark contrast to the Metropolitan beehive of contending radical views. The few Stopfordians who espoused radical ideologies at that time felt so isolated and helpless that many of them wanted to turn their backs on Britain and migrate to the 'Land of Liberty' across the Atlantic. Then, from the 1790s onwards, advocates of radical political reform gained many adherents in' the Stockport district, and additional calls for an infidel republic or co-operative commonwealth were gaining ground. Moreover, Thompson correctly shifts his focus from the Marxist

277

working-class nucleus (the factory proletariat) to those other groups of workers who were involved more prominently in radical agitations.

At the same time Perkin's caution seems fully justified by Stockport district events and trends. There was a peak of sorts in working-class activity during the Peterloo era, but subsequent occurrences make it difficult to talk about a monolithic working class, certainly not one intent on revolution and intermittently victorious in its struggles. Broadly speaking, this is the theme pursued by Foster for the period down to the 1820s. Leaving aside his talk of guerilla campaigns and revolutionary fervour, his insistence on the incompleteness of working-class development at Oldham could form the basis for a plausible discussion of social change in the Stockport district.

These things being said, it is also true that the weight of evidence for the Stockport district points in a different direction altogether. Taking only the period down to 1820, three generalisations seem inescapable.

First, workers' solidarity was severely limited. Differences in skill, income, sex, age and geographic location within the district were inevitably reflected in different attitudes and living standards. These helped to promote distinctive institutional arrangements and related participation rates for different groups of workers. Trade unions flourished especially in the larger skilled or factory occupations which were dominated by male workers and which were located in Stockport, its suburbs or the Hyde-Denton area. Even these unions had a difficult time achieving comprehensiveness and tended, in general, not to work with one another to achieve objectives which might be in their common interest. Differences can be seen in other areas. Building societies attracted workers who were somewhat better off than the bulk of their fellows, and this was also true of many of the friendly societies. Radicals gained modest support from about 1792 to 1806. In the succeeding decade this support grew principally as a result of the adherence of increasing numbers of handloom weavers. Then, in 1818-20, radicalism reached a peak under the stimuli of regional and national agitations and the dynamic leadership of Parson Harrison. Yet there is no evidence to suggest that anything approaching a majority of the workers of the Stockport district embraced radical views. Many workers simply remained aloof from the radicals, as did nearly all of their combinations (excepting, of course, the weavers' associations).

Second, workers' conflict orientation was also limited. This is not to say that conflicts did not emerge during the early Industrial Revolution or that violence was an unknown phenomenon in the social relationships of the Stockport district. Trade unions, however, generally sought limited objectives and rarely developed critiques of the capitalist system. When confrontations or violence were used, they were not employed to overturn the existing social and economic system but merely to achieve limited sectional goals. Local radicals certainly did develop (or borrow) root-and-branch critiques of the *status quo*. But within radical movements there were some who wanted political reform and others who wanted alterations in attitudes towards religion, some who thought that mass actions were the best means to effect change and others who thought that personal reformation (especially through education) was preferable. One cannot, in other words, automatically assume that adherents to the radical movements of the early Industrial Revolution possessed the kind of conflict mentality which amounted to a 'revolutionary consciousness'. Only a few radicals managed to attain that state of mind.

Third, the solidarity of the middle and upper classes and their hostility towards workers has been vastly over-rated. E.P. Thompson makes many assertions to the contrary. 'In the decades after 1795,' he writes in one place, 'there was a profound alienation between classes in Britain, and working people were thrust into a state of *apartheid* whose effects...can be felt to this day.' And again: 'Magistrates rode through thronged neighbourhoods a few hundred yards from their seats, and found themselves received like hostile aliens.'[1] Yet it was exceedingly difficult for 'bourgeois' solidarity to emerge. The professional classes (medical men, clergymen, attorneys) had numerous gradations within their ranks and were quite distinct from the commercial classes. Before 1820, the latter contained cotton spinners and manufacturers ranged in a steep pyramid of hierarchical distinctions and also included merchants dealing in such things as foodstuffs, coal and metal goods, as well as other entrepreneurs. Religious distinctions cut across such occupational boundaries and by the 1810s, in the wake of the parish church rebuilding project, helped to make it difficult for leading Stockport district citizens to act in concert. But such obstacles were frequently overcome when it came to the maintenance of public order. In crisis situations differences could be forgotten amidst efforts to co-ordinate charitable relief and repression. In quieter times members of the middle and upper classes vied with one another to promote religious observance, educational advances and help for the sick and needy. Clearly, one would err by talking about a monolithic bourgeoisie with a simple set of malign (or, for that matter, beneficent) objectives.

Conclusions in the discipline of history are rarely susceptible to the kind of verification which present-day social scientists routinely insist upon. There is, however, one type of test which is appropriate for the kind of conclusions offered above: are the interpretations advanced for the early Industrial Revolution plausible in light of subsequent developments in the later Industrial Revolution (c. 1820-60)? At various points in the preceding chapters, this kind of test has been employed to a limited extent by carrying the narrative into the 1820s. While the years around 1820 probably did constitute a watershed in social, as well as economic, history,[2] what occurred after that time in the Stockport district is fully consistent with what has been shown to have gone before. Moreover, the 1820s provide a good indication of what was to occur in subsequent decades.

The types of social fissure which were already evident among workers in the 1820s became more pronounced with the passage of time. The number of Irish in the borough of Stockport approximately tripled from 1831 to 1851 and at the latter date comprised about one-quarter of the total population. Ethnic antagonisms increased apace. In the late 1830s and early 1840s, while many English workers in the district were supporting Chartists or Owenites, many Irish workers chose instead to support the anti-Corn Law agitations or temperance movements. Open hostilities erupted in 1852, when savage anti-Irish riots in Stockport gained national attention. At the end of the century certain Stockport public houses still contained wooden partitions to keep English and Irish patrons separated. Stockport thus provides support for Marx's view in 1870 that 'every industrial and commercial center in England now possesses a working-class population divided into two *hostile* camps, English proletarians and Irish proletarians'.[3]

Trade unionism furnishes additional evidence of divisions within the ranks of district workers. Different unions in the cotton factories continued jealously to guard their individuality, as did those which existed among the skilled trades outside the factories. There were instances of co-operation among the different unions, but the general pattern was one of sectional 'labour consciousness' and little more.

Unions tended to stay aloof from radicalism, as has been shown in recent work on the Plug Plot Riots of 1842. While some historians have vainly tried to inflate the episode into a radical general strike, the Reids have conclusively demonstrated that Stockport Chartists and trade unionists found little common ground, either in activity programmes or ideology. Likewise, members of unions exhibited little camaraderie with the unskilled. This was, of course, sanctioned by tradition – a tradition which may well have been strengthened by the widening breach between the average wages of urban skilled and unskilled workers during the later Industrial Revolution.[4]

The framework for radicalism which emerged from the early Industrial Revolution and became established in the 1820s continued in evidence for many years thereafter. It involved two major spheres of ideology and action which, while overlapping, nevertheless retained distinctive characteristics and at times, antagonistic relationships. The one, represented by the Huntites of the 1820s, emphasised political reforms which were to be obtained by means of a network of political clubs, mass meetings and pressure on Parliament – this latter sometimes merging into talk of violence or plans for 'revolution'. The continuity between Huntism, Reform Crisis agitations and Chartism hardly needs to be emphasised. The other radicalism eschewed the political aims, confrontationalist tactics and Christian tinge of the Huntite legacy and concentrated instead on wide-ranging self-help programmes within the context of scientific education and explicit adherence to atheistical/deistical tenets. A veritable culture of infidelity emerged with lines of continuity running from Carlilism to Owenism to secularism.[5] Thus, despite undoubted radical advances and some prominent episodes of violence, it is impossible to follow John Foster and talk about the triumph of revolutionism in the 1830s and 1840s.

Alongside the rich, multiform radical heritage bequeathed by the early Industrial Revolution, paternalism persisted as a popular touchstone for perceiving social responsibilities and guiding behaviour. W. Cooke Taylor was referring to Hyde and similar out-townships when he wrote in 1842 that 'the employer knows the employed and is known by them; an affectionate sense of mutual dependence and mutual interest is created equally advantageous to both parties; the factory displays to a great extent the relations of a family, and the operatives regard themselves as members of one common household'.[6] These impulses were not lacking in Stockport and its suburbs. Neville Kirk has shown that factory owners there provided special social events and day trips for their workers and thereby helped to perpetuate the paternal ideal.[7] The editors of the *Manchester Guardian* commented on aspects of this trend in 1851:

> The last twenty years have witnessed an unprecedented growth of interest and good feeling among our widely-separated social classes, a great improvement in national manners and public morality, the introduction of a more humane and popular spirit into legislation, and, in general terms a patient, but earnest desire of [*sic*] progressive improvement in all ranks of the people.[8]

This rather sanguine view fails to take into account the fact that paternalism could never be a purely voluntary relationship. One should not forget that local government institutions in Stockport, especially those designed to enforce law and order, had been placed on a sounder footing in the 1820s and again in the 1830s under the Municipal Reform Act. As a result, they became increasingly adept at detecting crime, preventing or suppressing public tumults and administering the growing number of activities which fell under their sway, including by the 1850s all of the old manorial functions. Efficient local government helped to provide the essential framework in which paternalism could thrive.[9]

This is not to say that the ideology and behaviour of the middle and upper classes were becoming perfectly homogeneous. While arguing that there did not exist an identifiable 'working class' at Stockport during the years from 1832 to 1870, Paul Thomas Phillips has found that the Whig-Tory dichotomy was assuming immense importance. Local political activities tended to gravitate towards the two poles represented by the major parties. Phillips further demonstrates that the two poles attracted religious activists as well. Dissenter-Anglican conflicts consequently became super-imposed over the Whig-Tory antagonisms. Phillips refers specifically to Stockport when he discusses the resulting politico-religious divisions:

> Sectarianism ensured that the primary clash in industrial society would be between social elites rather than between classes . . . The main channel for this conflict between elite interests was in the area of local politics. Local political stances were, initially at least, defined in relation to one's association with one elite or another.[10]

Independent radical movements consequently declined in significance. Of 56 town councillors in 1836-7, 30 were Whigs with extremely low tax assessments. These were precisely the types of men who, in earlier decades, might have served as leaders of reform movements. Indeed, one finds on this list Thomas Cheetham, the surgeon; G.B. Cheetham, a cotton spinner active during the Reform Crisis; William Clarkson, a weaver prominent in radical affairs since 1810; and at least four other previously-active radicals.

Whether every such man had abandoned radicalism to join the Whigs or whether the Whig label merely served as a convenient electoral badge is unclear. The picture is complicated by the open alliance of radicals (and later, Chartists) with the Whigs from 1836 to 1839. The essential point is that significant numbers of Stockport radicals accepted the leadership of the local Whig elite and worked within the framework of conventional party politics. After the Whig-Chartist alliance dissolved, a Tory-Chartist alliance crystallised around the Conservative Workmen's Ratepayer Association, which was established by a leading Chartist. A latecomer to the growing body of conservative workers' political institutions in the cotton districts, it nevertheless lasted until 1850.[11] Alliances of this sort probably helped to weaken radical impulses at the same time as they helped to strengthen and legitimise various new or reformed municipal institutions. The new liberal order of the later Industrial Revolution thus should not be seen merely as the imposition of social control by the major industrialists; or as a revival of leadership by gentry and professional groups; or as some combination of the two. The participation in many of these changes by some of the leading radicals of the Stockport district must also be recognised.

The Stockport evidence is consistent with a major theme in regional and national social commentaries to the effect that distinctions among workers made it inappropriate to talk, in any meaningful way, about a single, unified working class. One need not leap-frog to late Victorian or Edwardian observers like Robert Roberts and Margaret Penn, nor even to Thomas Wright, W.A. Abrams and the plethora of like-minded commentators of the 1860s and 1870s, to find writers with great sensitivity to the different ranks and categories of workers. Francis Philips, the heir to Bank Hall, Heaton Norris, wrote of 'a class of men' in the cotton districts in 1819 which was 'intermediate between the weavers and the clerks'. This 'class' included spinners and the building trades, had fairly high wages, and did not attend 'meetings of reformers, or wear the badges of rebellion'. In the 1820s William MacKinnon divided the lower classes into two categories on the basis of how many other individuals (like servants or apprentices) they commanded. In the 1830s Jelinger Symons used 'mental and moral criteria' to divide artisans into three groupings. Presumably he would need additional categories in order to encompass other types of workers. John Stuart Mill made a clear distinction between workers who were politically active and those who were involved in industrial agitations: 'Hardly any drunken or profligate working man is a politician. Such men do not read newspapers, or interest themselves in public measures; they take part in strikes, but not in Political Unions.' William Dodd spoke of two classes of workers in the 1840s – the skilled labourers who served apprenticeships (and whom he grouped with the shopkeepers) and the remaining labourers who did not serve apprenticeships. In that same decade William Thornton went further: 'The labouring population has hitherto been spoken of as if it formed only one class, but it is really divided into several, among which the rates of remuneration are far from being uniform...In order to represent with perfect fidelity the state of the labouring population, it would be necessary to describe each class separately.'[12]

Important recent contributions to the historiography of the Industrial Revolution have frequently adopted similar views. Iorwerth Prothero, William Lazonick and Patrick Joyce have, from different geographical and ideological perspectives, stressed the divisions within the ranks of workers and employers which make it well-nigh impossible to talk about class solidarity and class conflict. Using various sociological concepts, Craig Calhoun has offered a sustained and insightful critique of the notion that a radical working class emerged in England during the industrialisation process. Even Harold Perkin has now effectively dissociated himself from the main conclusions of E.P. Thompson and John Foster and has implicitly qualified his earlier views on the birth of an English working class just after Waterloo. Finally, and appropriately for this study, M.E. Rose has likened the working class to the imaginary Cheshire Cat in that it was 'rarely visible as a complete whole'.[13]

Evidence from the Stockport district thus adds further weight to the conclusions of nineteenth-century commentators and recent historians who have found it difficult to accept the view that a class-conscious working class existed during the Industrial Revolution. Yet Stockport alone cannot prove or disprove major hypotheses in the field of labour history. More local and regional studies are needed, studies which do not dwell obsessively on sporadic episodes of conflict and conclude that they reflected the deep-seated commitments of 'most' workers; studies which do not simply add up radical or heterodox ideologies and imagine that the resulting sum could somehow form the basis of a unified class consciousness; and studies which do not ignore the higher ranks of society and their profound influences on workers and workers' movements. If this account of the good-natured, self-effacing inhabitants of 'one of the darkest and smokiest holes in the whole industrial area' can help to promote a re-evaluation of these topics and approaches, then not only will Stopfordians have been rescued from the condescending manipulation of posterity but they will also have provided a valuable impetus for present-day scholarly investigations.

NOTES

Prefatory Remarks

Manuscript correspondence cited in the notes and tables was written at Stockport unless otherwise indicated. Since the volume number and year are provided in all cases of serial publications, indications of 'old series', 'second series', and so forth, have been omitted. For specific volumes of *Parliamentary Debates, Parliamentary History, House of Commons Journal, House of Lords Journal* and *State Trials*, the convention has been followed of indicating in the citation the date(s) covered in the relevant volume rather than the date of publication. Thus, a reference to *House of Commons Journal*, 60 (1805-6), 109, indicates that volume 60 includes entries from the years 1805-6 and not that it was published in those years. The following abbreviations have been used in the notes, the bibliography and the tables in the text:

Add. MSS	Additional Manuscripts (BL)
BL	British Library
BP	British Patent
BRL	Birmingham Reference Library
C	Chancery Papers (PRO)
CHES	County Palatine of Chester Papers (PRO)
CN&Q	*Cheshire Notes and Queries*
CRO	Cheshire Record Office
CS	*Chetham Society*
DDX	Deposited Documents Miscellaneous (CRO)
DNB	*Dictionary of National Biography*
EDV	Articles of Enquiry Preparatory to Visitation (CRO)
Foster, *CSIR*	John Foster, *Class Struggle and the Industrial Revolution: Early Industrial Capitalism in Three English Towns* (London, 1974)
FS	Friendly Society Papers (PRO)
GL	Guildhall Library
HCJ	*House of Commons Journal*
HLJ	*House of Lords Journal*
HO	Home Office Papers (PRO)
JRULM	John Rylands University Library of Manchester
KB	King's Bench Papers (KB)
MCL	Manchester Central Library
MG	*Manchester Guardian*
MGaz	*Manchester Gazette*
MM	*Manchester Mercury*
MO	*Manchester Observer*
PC	Privy Council Papers (PRO)
PD	*Hansard's Parliamentary Debates*

Perkin, *OMES*	Harold Perkin, *The Origins of Modern English Society 1780–1880* (London, 1969)
PH	*Parliamentary History*
PP	Parliamentary Paper
PRO	Public Record Office
pr.s.sh.	printed single sheet
QJB	Quarter Sessions Judicial Books (CRO)
QJF	Quarter Sessions Judicial Files (CRO)
RG	Registrar-General's Papers (PRO)
SA	*Stockport Advertiser*
SC Rept.	*Select Committee Report*
SPL	Stockport Public Library
SSS	Stockport Sunday School
ST	William Cobbett, T.B. Howell and Thomas Jones Howell (eds.), *Complete Collection of State Trials*, 33 vols. (London, 1809-26); and John MacDonell and John E.P. Wallis (eds.), *Reports of State Trials*, 7 vols. (London, 1888-96)
Thompson, *MEWC*	E.P. Thompson, *The Making of the English Working Class* (2nd edn, Harmondsworth, 1968)
THSLC	*Transactions of the Historic Society of Lancashire and Cheshire*
TLCAS	*Transactions of the Lancashire and Cheshire Antiquarian Society*
TS	Treasury Solicitor's Papers (PRO)
WO	War Office Papers (PRO)

Notes to Chapter 1

1. Friedrich Engels, *The Condition of the Working Class in England* (trans. W.O. Henderson and W.H. Chaloner) (Oxford, 1958 [1845]), 52.

2. Ibid., 51, 137.

3. See esp. R.J. Morris, *Class and Class Consciousness in the Industrial Revolution 1780-1850* (London, 1979); R.S. Neale, *Class in English History 1680-1850* (Oxford, 1981); Craig Calhoun, *The Question of Class Struggle: Social Foundations of Popular Radicalism during the Industrial Revolution* (Chicago, 1982).

4. See among other works, Engels, *Condition*; Karl Marx, *Capital: A Critique of Political Economy*, 3 vols. (Moscow, 1965-7 [1867-94]). The references to Marx which follow in the text apply also to Engels.

5. Marx, *Capital*, I, ch. XIV, sect. 1, ch. XV, sect. 1. Cf. Jürgen Kuczynski, a twentieth-century disciple of Marx, who dates the birth of the working class from 1760 and states that the class 'is the product of the machine'. *The Rise of the Working Class* (New York, 1967), 51.

6. Karl Marx, *Economic and Philosophic Manuscripts [1844]* in *Early Texts* (ed. David McLellan)(New York, 1971), 135, 137, and in general, the section on 'Alienated Labour', 133-45. See also *Capital*, I, ch. I, sect. 4; István Mészáros, *Marx's Theory of Alienation* (London, 1970).

7. Karl Marx, *The Communist Manifesto* (New York, 1970 [1848]), 23.

8. Reinhard Bendix and Seymour Martin Lipset, 'Karl Marx's Theory of Social Classes' [1953] in *Class, Status, and Power: Social Stratification in Comparative Perspective* (2nd edn, New York, 1966), 8.

9. Karl Marx, *The Poverty of Philosophy* (New York, 1963 [1847]), 172-3; cf. idem, *Communist Manifesto*, 23-4, 41-2.

10. For a useful summary, see M.H. Cowden, 'Early Marxist Views on British Labor, 1937-1917', *Western Political Quarterly*, 16 (1963), 34-52.

11. In Lenin's *Collected Works*, 45 vols. (Moscow, 1960-70), see for example: *The Three Sources and Three Component Parts of Marxism* [1913], XIX, 23-8; *A Great Beginning* [1919], XXIX, 409-34; *Draft and Explanation of a Programme for the Social-Democratic Party* [1924], II, 93-121.

12. Lenin, *What Is To Be Done? Burning Questions of Our Movement* [1902], *Collected Works*, V, 347-529.

13. This is not to say that other less popular paradigms have not been advanced. See, for example, Georg Lukács, *History and Class Consciousness: Studies in Marxist Dialectics* (trans. Rodney Livingstone)(Cambridge, Mass., 1971 [1923]); István Mészáros, (ed.) *Aspects of History and Class Consciousness* (New York, 1972), esp. the essays by Tom Bottomore and E.J. Hobsbawn.

14. G.D.H. Cole, *A Short History of the British Working-Class Movement 1789-1947* (rev. edn. London, 1948 [1925-7]), 4-5. See also the series of documents which incorporates this periodisation: Max Morris (ed.), *From Cobbett to the Chartists* (London, 1948); James B. Jefferys (ed.), *Labour's Formative Years 1849-1879* (London, 1948); E.J. Hobsbawn (ed.) *Labour's Turning Point 1880-1900* (London, 1948).

15. G.D.H. Cole and Raymond Postgate, *The Common People 1746-1946* (London, 1961 [1938]), 258-72; see also Cole, *Attempts at General Union: A Study in British Trade Union History 1818-1834* (London, 1953).

16. E.J. Hobsbawn, 'The Labour Aristocracy in Nineteenth-century Britain' [1954] in *Labouring Men: Studies in the History of Labour* (New York, 1964), 276. Cf. Richard Johnson, 'Culture and the Historians' in John Clarke, Chas Critcher and Richard Johnson (eds.), *Working-Class Culture: Studies in History and Theory* (London, 1979), 51-60.

17. J.H. Clapham, *An Economic History of Modern Britain: The Early Railway Age 1820-1850* (Cambridge, 1967 [1926]), ch. V; T.S. Ashton, *The Industrial Revolution 1760-1830* (London, 1964 [1948]), 64-5. For a restatement of parts of this argument, see Raphael Samuel, 'Workshop of the World: Steam Power and Hand Technology in mid-Victorian Britain', *History Workshop Journal*, 3 (1977), 6-72.

18. Asa Briggs, 'Social Structure and Politics in Birmingham and Lyons (1825-1848)', *British Journal of Sociology*, 1 (1950), 67-80; idem, 'The Background of Parliamentary Reform in Three English Cities (1830-2)', *Cambridge Historical Journal*, 10 (1950-2), 293-317; idem, *The Making of Modern England 1783-1867: The Age of Improvement* (New York, 1965 [1959]), 63-4; idem, *Victorian Cities* (New York, 1970 [1963]).

19. E.J. Hobsbawn, 'Economic Fluctuations and Some Social Movements since 1800' [1952] in *Labouring Men*, 126-57.

20. Asa Briggs, 'The Local Background of Chartism' in *Chartist Studies* (London, 1959), 6; George Rudé, *The Crowd in History: A Study of Popular Disturbances in France and England 1730-1848* (New York 1964), 218-19.

21. Thompson, *MEWC*, 194, 887.

22. Ibid., 909.

23. Ibid., 9 (emphasis added), 10; cf idem, *The Poverty of Theory & Other Essays* (London, 1978), 238, 298-9.

24. For oscillations between Luddism and politics at Nottingham in 1811-13, see Thompson, *MEWC*, 584-5; and for the apparent end of such oscillations, ibid., 909.

25. R. Currie and R.M. Hartwell, ' The Making of the English Working Class?', *Economic History Review*, 18 (1965), 633-43; Paul T. Phillips, 'Methodism, Political Order, and Revolution', *Studies in Religion*, 5 (1975-6), 186-90.

26. Even this narrower view of oscillations has not remained unchallenged, however; see Roy A. Church and S.D. Chapman, 'Gravener Henson and the Making of the English Working Class' in E.L. Jones and G.E. Mingay (eds.), *Land, Labour and Population in the Industrial Revolution: Essays Presented to J.D. Chambers* (New York, 1968), 131-61. Defences of Thompson can be found in Thompson, 'Postscript', *MEWC*, 924-34; F.K. Donnelly, 'Ideology and Early English Working-class History: Edward Thompson and his Critics', *Social History*, 2 (1976), 219-38.

27. E.P. Thompson, 'Patrician Society, Plebeian Culture', *Journal of Social History*, 7 (1973-4), 396-7; and more generally, idem, 'The Moral Economy of the English Crowd in the Eighteenth Century', *Past and Present*, 50 (1971), 76-136.

28. See, for example, Neil J. Smelser, Review of E.P. Thompson, *MEWC*, in *History and Theory*, 5 (1966), 213-17; James A. Henretta, 'Social History as Lived and Written', *American Historical Review*, 84 (1979), 1317-18; Neale, *Class in English History*, 110-11.

29. E.J. Hobsbawm, *The Age of Revolution* (New York, 1962), 249, 252-3.

30. Idem, *Industry and Empire* (Harmondsworth, 1969), 94.

31. Perkin, *OMES*, 176.

32. Ibid., 193.

33. Ibid., ch. VI.

34. Ibid., 236, 231.

35. Ibid., 178-9.

36. See, for example, 'And That's How Classes Were Born', *Times Literary Supplement* (17 April 1969), 407; E.A. Smith, Review of Harold Perkin, *OMES*, in *English Historical Review*, 85 (1970), 805-8; Morris, *Class*, 13-14, 32.

37. E.P. Thompson, 'Testing Class Struggle', *Times Higher Education Supplement* (8 March 1974), p. I. Thompson's wife Dorothy has likewise criticised certain of the major theses of Foster's work: 'Radical Workers', *Times Literary Supplement* (27 Sept. 1974), 1039.

38. Foster, *CSIR*, 42-3.

39. Ibid., 141, 147.

40. Ibid., 6-7, 146-7 (emphasis in original), 232-3.

41. D.S. Gadian, 'Class Consciousness in Oldham and Other North-West Industrial Towns 1830-1850', *Historical Journal*, 21 (1978), 161-72; but cf. R.A. Sykes, 'Some Aspects of Working-Class Consciousness in Oldham, 1830-1842', ibid., 23 (1980), 167-79.

42. Gareth Stedman Jones, 'Class Struggle and the Industrial Revolution', *New Left Review*, 90 (1975), 35-69.

43. There were exceptions, of course, like the Plug Riots in the early 1840s: A.G. Rose, 'The Plug Riots of 1842 in Lancashire and Cheshire', *TLCAS*, 67 (1957), 75-112.

44. Foster, *CSIR*, 42, 251-2.

45. Derek Fraser, 'Politics and the Victorian City', *Urban History Yearbook* (1979), 36.

46. Asa Briggs, Review of E.P. Thompson, *MEWC*, in *Labor History*, 6 (1965), 84-91; Henry Pelling, *A History of British Trade Unionism* (2nd edn, London, 1972), 4, 295; A.E. Musson, *British Trade Unions, 1800-1875* (London, 1972), 20; idem, 'Class Struggle and the Labour Aristocracy, 1830-60', *Social History*, 3 (1976), 335-56.

47. Asa Briggs, 'The Language of "Class" in Early Nineteenth-Century England' in Asa Briggs and John Saville (eds.), *Essays in Labour History: In Memory of G.D.H. Cole 25 September 1889-14 January 1959* (rev. edn, London, 1967), 43-73.

48. Derek Beales, *From Castlereagh to Gladstone 1815-1885* (New York, 1969), 57-8, 61; cf. Neale, *Class in English History*, 101-2.

49. Cf. Foster, *CSIR*, 3, on the notion that class consciousness can be tested at the local level 'and nowhere else'.

Notes to Chapter 2

1. Samuel Bamford, *Passages in the Life of a Radical*, 2 vols. (3rd edn, London, 1844), I, 54; William MacRitchie, *Diary of a Tour through Great Britain in 1795* (London, 1897), 52.

2. Besides the 'Stockport district', three other expressions require explanation. The 'greater Manchester district' (or simply, the 'Manchester district') will be used to refer to Manchester and the surrounding area to a radius of about ten or twelve miles. It is taken to encompass all of the Stockport district and such prominent satellite towns as Ashton-under-Lyne, Oldham, Bury and Bolton. The 'cotton districts' refer to a somewhat wider area, including also Blackburn, Preston, Wigan and the Peak district of Derbyshire. Finally, references to 'the region' are meant to include the cotton districts and also the remaining parts of Lancashire and Cheshire.

3. Quoted in W.M.P. Taylor, *A History of the Stockport Court Leet* (Stockport, 1971), 33-4; William Harrison, 'Ancient Fords, Ferries, and Bridges in Lancashire', *TLCAS*, 12 (1894), 17; John Whitaker, *The History of Manchester*, 2 vols. (London, 1771-5), I, 145, 174.

4. John Byng, *The Torrington Diaries*, (ed. C. Bruyn Andrews), 4 vols. (London, 1934-8), II, 180.

5. On the 'incompleat' baptismal registers, see CRO, EDV 7/1/104. For a general account of labour migration, sex ratios and related issues, see N.L. Tranter, 'The Labour Supply 1780-1860' in Roderick Floud and Donald McClosky (eds.), *The Economic History of Britain since 1700*: vol. 1, *1700-1860* (Cambridge, 1981), 204-26.

6. *The Nature, Design, and General Rules of the Stranger's Friend Society* ([Stockport?], 1792), pr. s.sh.; HO 42/152, Lloyd to Beckett, 6 July 1816; PP 1834 (44) XXVIII, 16.

7. CRO, QJF 239/1-4, 240/1-4, 241/1, 3-4. QJF 241/2 is missing.

8. PP 1826-7 (550) V, Q 517.

9. [Theophelus Lewis Rupp], *Second Letter to the Inhabitants of Manchester, on the Exportation of Cotton Twist* (Manchester, 1800), 11.

10. E.J.T. Collins, 'Migrant Labour in British Agriculture in the Nineteenth Century', *Economic History Review*, 29 (1976), 45-7; 'Dictionary of Emigrant Scots', *Manchester Genealogist*, 15 (1979), 45.

11. CRO, EDV 7/1-2.

12. HO 42/19, T.B. Bayley and Henry Norris to Lord Grenville, Hope nr. Manchester, 19 July 1791.

13. Henry Heginbotham, *Stockport: Ancient and Modern*, 2 vols. (London, 1882-92), I, 353-4.

14. CRO, EDV 7/3/74, 158; 7/4/76, 101, 221.

15. H.S. Irvine, 'Some Aspects of Passenger Traffic between Britain and Ireland, 1820-50', *Journal of Transport History*, 4 (1959-60), 224-41; CRO, EDV 7/6/306; PP 1833 (394) XVI, 43; PP 1834 (556) X, QQ 6776-8; PP 1835 (341) XIII, QQ 2810-3, 2842-4.

16. CRO, EDV 7/7/164.

17. PP 1836 [40] XXXIV, 86.

18. Ibid., 86-7.

19. Ibid., 85-6; W.H. Shercliff, 'Pickfords and Poynton', *Poynton Local History Society Newsletter*, 2 (1980), 15-16; *CN&Q*, 1 (1886), 19; *SA*, 5 May 1826.

20. *Annual Report of the SSS* (Stockport, 1824), 13; *O'Connel & his Family* (Stockport, [c.1825]). Cf. the following Quaker tract: *A Correct Account of a Blind Irishman Restored to Sight when very Old* (ed. George Jones) (Stockport, [c. 1823]).

21. PP 1824 (51) V, 398; *Black Dwarf*, 30 Sept. 1818; PP 1834 (556) X, Q 6433.

22. Cf. Colin G. Pooley, 'The Residential Segregation of Migrant Communities in mid-Victorian Liverpool', *Transactions of the Institute of British Geographers*, 2 (1977), 364-82; Steve Hochstadt, 'Social History and Politics: A Materialist View', *Social History*, 7 (1982), 78; Michael Hechter, 'Ethnicity and Industrialization: On the Proliferation of the Cultural Division of Labor', *Ethnicity*, 3 (1976), 214-24.

23. William A. Singleton, 'Traditional Domestic Architecture of Lancashire and Cheshire', *TLCAS*, 65 (1955), 43-5.

24. Built in tiers and conceived in agony, according to a local pun. J.H. Ingram, *Companion into Cheshire* (London, 1947), 160. Cf. Daniel Defoe, *A Tour Through the Whole Island of Great Britain*, 4 vols. (7th edn, London, 1769), II, 397.

25. *CN&Q*, 1 (1886), 97; John Britton and Edward Wedlake Brayley, *The Beauties of England and Wales*, 18 vols. (London, 1801-15), II, 279.

26. 13 Geo. III, c. 55; Byng, *Torrington Diaries*, II, 179-80.

27. SPL, HX 130, Deed of 22 Oct. 1788; HX 82, Deed of 1 March 1780; GL, MS 7253/23/127, 468, Policy of Martin Newstead (1792); *MM*, 22 May 1787; cf. P.M. Giles, 'The Enclosure of the Common Lands in Stockport', *TLCAS*, 62 (1950-1), 108-9. (I am grateful to S.D. Chapman for advice on various aspects of the Guildhall Library insurance policy registers.)

28. *MM*, 23 Oct. 1792; *Stranger's Friend Society*, pr. s.sh. On the rapidly increasing building costs during this period, see C.W. Chalklin, *The Provincial Towns of Georgian England: A Study of the Building Process* (Montreal, 1974), 328-9.

29. Walter Gove, Michael Hughes and Omer R. Galle, 'Overcrowding in the Home: An Empirical Investigation of Its Possible Pathological Consequences', *American Sociological Review*, 44 (1979), 59-80.

30. *SA*, 16 Sept. 1825; *MG*, 18 April 1829.

31. PP 1833 (450) XX, D.1., 133-4; on this and related topics, see John Burnett, *A Social History of Housing 1815-1970* (Newton Abbot, 1978), ch. 3.

32. Edwin Chadwick, *Report on the Sanitary Condition of the Labouring Population of Gt. Britain* (ed. M.W. Flinn)(Edinburgh, 1965 [1842]), 91-2; PP 1908 [Cd. 3864] CVII, 430-1.

33. *MGaz*, 29 June 1805, 21 Nov. 1807, 12 March 1808, for references to Stockport cellars capable of holding four handlooms each; PP 1837 (238) XXVIII, 'Stockport' (referring to 1835 data); G.A. Swindells and K. Western (eds.), *Marple in 1851 from Census Returns* (Marple, 1980), 4, 20, for evidence on lodgers and cellar dwellings in Marple in the 1840s and 1850s.

34. PP 1834 (44) XXVIII, 16i; Andrew Ure, *The Philosophy of Manufactures* (London, 1835), 349; PP 1833 (450) XX, D.1., 73, 134.

35. *SA*, 24 June 1831; Chadwick, *Sanitary Condition*, 92, 414; H. Coutie, 'How They Lived On Hillgate', *North Cheshire Family Historian*, 8 (1981), 5-8.

36. This discussion of Stockport district factory housing is mainly based on PP 1834 (167) XX, D.1. See also, Owen Ashmore, *The Industrial Archaeology of Stockport* (Manchester, 1975), 27-8; Ann Ashworth *et al.*, *Historic Industries of Marple and Mellor* (Stockport, 1977), 53, 55; *SA*, 22 April 1825; CRO, EDV 7/3/393; John J. Mason, 'A Manufacturing and Bleaching Enterprise during the Industrial Revolution: The Sykeses of Edgeley', *Business History*, 23 (1981), 83.

37. W. Felkin, 'An Account of the Situation of a Portion of the Labouring Classes in the Township of Hyde, Cheshire', *Journal of the Royal Statistical Society*, 1 (1838-9), 418-19.

38. PP 1834 (167) XX, D.1., 181, 5, 173.

39. P. Gaskell, *Artisans and Machinery* (London, 1836), 294; cf. Patrick Joyce, *Work, Society and Politics: The Culture of the Factory in Later Victorian England* (Brighton, 1980), 121, 168.

40. See especially James Butterworth, *A History and Description of the Towns and Parishes of Stockport, Ashton-under-Lyne, Mottram-Long-Den-Dale and Glossop* (Manchester, 1827), 248, 296, 298; Thomas Middleton, *The History of Hyde and Its Neighbourhood* (Hyde, 1932), 228, 444; *CN&Q*, 1 (1886), 32; Robert Hunter, *A Short History of Bredbury & Romiley with Woodley and Compstall* (Bredbury, 1974), ch. 3; Mason, 'Sykeses', 61.

41. Cf. Robert B. Potter, 'Spatial and Structural Variations in the Quality Characteristics of Intra-urban Retailing Centres', *Transactions of the Institute of British Geographers*, 5 (1980), 207-28.

42. Arthur Young, *A Six Months Tour through the North of England*, 4 vols. (2nd edn, London, 1771), III, 189; HO 55/18/45, 'The Humble Address of the Gentlemen [etc.] . . . of the Town and Neighbourhood of Manchester', Autumn 1775.

43. *MM*, 14 Oct. 1766, 14 Aug. 1770.

44. *HCJ*, 34 (1772-4), 240; B.R. Mitchell and Phyllis Deane, *Abstract of British Historical Statistics* (Cambridge, 1962), 205; *MM*, 6 July 1773.

45. Heginbotham, *Stockport*, II, 343-4; Robert Glen, 'The Milnes of Stockport and the Export of English Technology during the Early Industrial Revolution', *Cheshire History*, 3, (1979), 15-16. See also BP 827 (1765), 968 (1770), 1126 (1776); and in general, Michael M. Edwards, *The Growth of the British Cotton Trade 1780-1815* (Manchester, 1967).

46. Ben Hadfield, 'The Carrs Silk Mills, Stockport', *The Manchester School* 5 (1934), 126-7; SPL, Stockport Poor Ley of 1781; GL, MS 11, 936/241/358, 024, Policy of Wells and Co. (1775); MS 7253/17/112.726, Policy of Wells and Co. (1789); *MM*, 11 Dec. 1781, 15 Oct. 1782.

47. Unless otherwise indicated, the following account is from George Unwin, Arthur Hulme and George Taylor, *Samuel Oldknow and the Arkwrights: The Industrial Revolution at Stockport and Mellor* (Manchester, 1924). Cf. Mason,

'Sykeses', 59-60.

48. JRULM, English MSS 751 (Oldknow Papers), S. and W. Salte to Oldknow, London, 5 Nov. 1787; ibid., Brother von der Becke and Co. to Oldknow, Leipzig, 16 May 1795; Robert Owen, *The Life of Robert Owen by Himself* (New York, 1920), 55.

49. GL, MS 7253/22/124,215, Policy of John Bell (1791); *MM*, 17 Jan. 1797; PP 1808 (179) II, 5. See also the Stockport directories for the 1780s and 1790s.

50. Philip Luckombe, *England's Gazetteer*, 3 vols. (London, 1790), no pagination.

51. BRL, Boulton and Watt Collection, In-Letters, Box 19/5, Ewart to John Southern, 12 Aug. 1791; Box 27, Deeds of 1 March 1791 (Oldknow), 1 Nov. 1791 (Illingworth), 1 March 1792 (Bury), 1 March 1792 (Hunt), 1 Sept. 1792 (Illingworth); Box 31, Deed of 1 Jan. 1793 (Holland and Bridge).

52. *MC*, 3 Dec. 1786; *MM*, 8 Feb. 1791; John Metcalf, *The Life of John Metcalf* (York, 1795), 148. For Stockport's increasing importance as a retailing centre, see Ian Mitchell, 'Pitt's Shop Tax in the History of Retailing', *Local Historian*, 14 (1980-1), 349.

53. Quotation in Samuel Hill, *Bygone Stalybridge* (Stalybridge, 1907), 50; see also Stanley D. Chapman, 'Fixed Capital Formation in the British Cotton Industry, 1770-1815', *Economic History Review*, 23 (1970), 260; L.S. Presnell, *Country Banking in the Industrial Revolution* (Oxford, 1956), 334.

54. William Charles Henry, 'A Biographical Notice of the Late Peter Ewart, Esq.', *Memoirs and Proceedings of the Manchester Literary and Philosophical Society*, 7 (1846), 122-4; BRL, Boulton and Watt Collection, In-Letters, Box 3/0, Oldknow to Boulton and Watt, Mellor, 22 Dec. 1798; *To be Sold by Auction* (Stockport, 1798), pr. s.sh.; Columbia University, Seligman MSS, Box II, Sun Policy No. 698,955 for Oldknow (1799).

55. PP 1833 (690) VI, Q 649.

56. *HCJ*, 58 (1802-3), 890; Alex. B. Richmond, *Narrative of the Condition of the Manufacturing Population* (London, 1824), 8.

57. W.H. Chaloner, 'The Cheshire Activities of Matthew Boulton and James Watt, of Soho, near Birmingham, 1776-1817', *TLCAS*, 60 (1948), 121-36, and the sources cited therein.

58. Ann Radcliffe, *A Journey Made in the Summer of 1794* (London, 1794), 377.

59. See BP 2684 (1803), 2771 (1804), 2876 (1805), 3023 (1807), for Radcliffe; BP 2699 (1803), 2848 (1805), for Horrocks; BP 2869 (1805), 2870 (1805), 2955 (1806), for Marsland; see also 'Specification of the Patent Granted to Peter Marsland . . .', *Repertory of Arts, Manufactures, and Agriculture*, 7 (1805), 327-9; *MM*, 12 Jan. 1802.

60. A.E. Musson and Eric Robinson, *Science and Technology in the Industrial Revolution* (Manchester, 1969), 137, 325n.2; MCL, MS FF 667.3 G1, John Graham 'The Chemistry of Calico Printing from 1790 to 1835 and History of Printworks in the Manchester District from 1760 to 1846' (1846), 356; SPL, Sykes MSS, Miscellaneous Papers (1793-1871).

61. James Wheeler, *Manchester: Its Political, Social and Commercial History, Ancient and Modern* (London, 1836), 244.

62. G.W. Daniels, 'The Cotton Trade at the Close of the Napoleonic War', *Transactions of the Manchester Statistical Society* (sess. 1917-18), 8; Leon Soutierre Marshall, *The Development of Public Opinion in Manchester, 1780-1820* (Syracuse, 1946), 188; JRULM, English MSS 751, Littlewood Andrew to Daniel Oldknow, Rio

de Janiero, 15 Aug. 1809.

63. *MGaz*, 25 April 1812; *HCJ*, 67 (1812), 322; ibid., 68 (1812-13), 151; *HLJ*, 49 (1812-14), 388.

64. Duncan Bythell, *The Handloom Weavers: A Study in the English Cotton Industry during the Industrial Revolution* (Cambridge, 1969), 72-3; see also the enthusiastic reports in *MC*, 26 Feb. 1803; and in Bolton Civic Museum, Crompton MSS, W. MacAlpine to Samuel Crompton, London, 18 Feb. 1805.

65. Richard Guest, *A Compendious History of the Cotton Manufacture* (Manchester, 1823), 46-47; *Gentleman's Magazine*, 94:2 (1824), 636; PP 1808 (179) II, 9.

66. William Radcliffe, *Origin of the New System of Manufacture, Commonly Called 'Power-Loom Weaving'* (Stockport, 1828), 42-4; *MGaz*, 22 Feb. 1812.

67. Ibid., 28 May 1808, 25 July 1812; PRO, B 3/1880, Bankruptcy Papers of John Goodair.

68. *MM*, 16 March 1784, 20 Aug. 1805, 29 Dec. 1807.

69. *MO*, 28 Feb. 1818; HO 52/1, Thomas Sharp to Lord Sidmouth, Manchester, 27 Feb. 1820.

70. BRL, Boulton and Watt Collection, Office Letter Books 40/183-4, William Creighton to Thomas Hope, Soho, 30 Nov. 1816; 41/163, same to John Bentley, Soho, 13 April 1819.

71. PP 1834 (167) XX, D.1., *passim*; PP 1841 (201) VII, 334; *SA*, 16 Aug. 1822, 10 Oct. 1828; G.N. von Tunzelmann, *Steam Power and British Industrialization to 1860* (Oxford, 1978), 32; E.C. Smith, 'Joshua Field's Diary of a Tour in 1821 through the Provinces. Part II', *Newcomen Society Transactions*, 13 (1932-3), 28.

72. Roger Lloyd-Jones and A.A. Le Roux, 'The Size of Firms in the Cotton Industry: Manchester 1815-41', *Economic History Review*, 33 (1980), 72-82; Chapman, 'Fixed Capital Formation', 260-1; T. Midgley, *Statistics Obtained in 1811 by Samuel Crompton* ([Bolton], n.d.), esp. series 151.27.

73. PP 1831-2 (706) XV, 432-3; *SA*, 7 June 1822.

74. Butterworth, *Stockport*, 248-9; PP 1842 (158) XXXV, 116.

75. *Facts and Observations, to Prove the Impolicy and Dangerous Tendency, of the Bill now before Parliament* (Manchester, [1807]), 8; Unwin, *Oldknow*, 51; PP 1833 (450) XX, D.2., 83; *MM*, 17 June 1806; *The Adventures of a Sixpence; Shewing The Method of Setting up Tradesmen without Money* (Manchester, [c. 1800]).

76. *Manchester Journal*, 8 Feb. 1777; *MM*, 23 July 1780.

77. Ibid., 3 Dec. 1793; CRO, QDV 2/398/12, 22, Land Tax Assessments for Stockport (1795, 1806); BRL, Boulton and Watt Collection, In-Letters, Box 6 'A', Randle and John Alcock to Boulton and Watt, 28 Nov. 1792, 2 Jan., 28 Feb. 1793; GL, MS 7253/32A/156,196, Policy of Joseph Dale (1797).

78. PP 1824 (51) V, 610; PP 1833 (519) XXI, D.2., 36.

79. Cf. Hartmut Kaelble, *Historical Research on Social Mobility: Western Europe and the USA in the Nineteenth and Twentieth Centuries* (trans. Ingrid Noakes)(New York, 1981), 41-4.

Notes to Chapter 3

1. Lyme Hall was located in Lyme Handley township and was not therefore in the Stockport district. But the Legh family nevertheless played an important role in

Stockport district affairs (especially with regard to Disley and Norbury townships), and it consequently deserves mention in this context. Cf. Lionel M. Angus-Butterworth, *Old Cheshire Families & Their Seats* (Manchester, 1932), 125.

2. John Watson, *Memoirs of the Ancient Earls of Warren and Surrey, and Their Descendants to the Present Time*, 2 vols. (Warrington, 1782); *Gentleman's Magazine*, 71 (1801), 861-2.

3. PRO, PC 1/40/A. 132, George Warren to the Earl of Chatham, Kingston House, 17 Nov. 1797; HO 42/42, List of Deputy Lieutenants of Cheshire, 1798; A. Hughs and J. Jennings, *List of Sheriffs for England and Wales, from the Earliest Times to A.D. 1831*, List and Index Society, 9 (1898); *MM*, 23 Jan. 1776. H.W. Clemsha, *The New Court Book of the Manor of Bramhall (1632-1657)*, *CS* (1921), 4, gives some seventeenth-century marriage patterns among the Warrens, Leghs, Ardens and Davenports.

4. On magistrates, attorneys, clergymen and medical men, see esp. the Stockport directories from the 1780s to the 1830s.

5. For more detailed accounts, see J. Thorp, 'A History of Local Government in Stockport between 1760 and 1820' (MA thesis, Manchester, 1940); Heginbotham, *Stockport*, I, 159-64, 257-60.

6. MCL, Burton MSS, IX, 13-14.

7. Douglas Hay, 'War, Dearth and Theft in the Eighteenth Century: The Record of the English Courts', *Past and Present*, 95 (1982), 117-60; Thorp, 'Stockport Government', 149n.1. Cf. John Meldrum, *The Care of Providence over Life, and the Sin of Destroying It* (2nd edn, Manchester, 1790).

8. *HCJ*, 35 (1774-6), 153; ibid., 40 (1784-5), 583, 771.

9. [Thomas Seddon], *Characteristic Strictures: or, Remarks on Upwards of One Hundred Portraits, of the Most Eminent Persons in the Counties of Lancaster and Chester* (3rd edn, London, 1779), 38; P.M. Giles, 'The Enclosure of Common Lands in Stockport', *TLCAS*, 62 (1950-1), 80-3, 88.

10. PP 1803-4 (175) XIII, 52-5; SPL, Stockport Poor Ley of 1781; Thorp, 'Stockport Government', 247-8.

11. PP 1816 (511) XVI, *passim*; PP 1826-7 (22) IX, 193-4; PP 1837-8 [103], XXIV, *passim*.

12. *MM*, 6 Sept. 1785.

13. *Manchester Journal*, 25 Sept. 1773; *MC*, 12 Nov. 1785; *MM*, 7 Aug. 1781, 14 July 1789; Middleton, *Hyde*, 259-60.

14. [Evelyn] Newton, *Lyme Letters 1660-1760* (London, 1925), 320; Heginbotham, *Stockport*, II, 380.

15. Sidney and Beatrice Webb, *History of Liquor Licensing* (London, 1903), 137-51; HO 42/7/150, 'Mr Godschall's Plan of Provincial Police' (1785).

16. PC 1/40 A. 132, Warren to the Earl of Chatham, Kingston House, 17 Nov. 1797; Sylvia Harrop, 'Community Involvement in Education in North-east Cheshire in the Late Eighteenth and Early Nineteenth Centuries', *TLCAS*, 80 (1979), 4.

17. Radcliffe, *Origin*, 18.

18. CRO, QJB 26a (1784-91), 467-8; QJF 218/2/108; CHES 24/183/1, Indictment of Terrence Grimes; *MC*, 7 March 1807; SPL, HX 144, Deed of 20 Nov. 1790.

19. WO 17/1037, 'Monthly Returns, Stockport Volunteers', various dates; HO 50/331, Prescot to [Portland], 31 July 1794; WO 1/1094, Watson to [William Windham], 23 May 1795.

20. *Gentleman's Magazine*, 65 (1795), 74-5; WO 1/1094, Watson to [Windham], 5

Aug., 2 Sept. 1795.

21. *Mr. Matthews, (From the Theatre Royal, Hay-Market)* (Stockport, 1804), pr. s.sh.; *By Desire of the Gentlemen of the Stockport Armed Association* (Stockport, 1805), pr. s.sh.; Heginbotham, *Stockport*, II, 421; *Stockport Advertiser Notes and Queries*, 2 (1882-3), 151; CRO, DDX 311/1, Stockport Rifle Corps Minute Book.

22. *HCJ*, 61 (1806), 66, 377, 399, 501, 529.

23. Ibid., 60 (1805), 86, 129, 341, 432; Giles, 'Enclosure', 97-100.

24. PP 1803-4 (175) XIII, 52-5.

25. See sources cited in n. 11 above.

26. *MM*, 13 March 1792; *MGaz*, 16 Nov. 1805, 26 July 1806; David Owen, *English Philanthropy 1660-1960* (Cambridge, Mass., 1964), ch. IV.

27. John Ferriar, 'Account of the Establishment of Fever-Wards in Manchester' in *Medical Histories and Reflections*, 3 vols. (Warrington, 1792-8), III, 92n.; *Manchester Herald*, 21 April 1792.

28. On the immense impact of charitable relief, cf. G.B. Hindle, *Provision for the Relief of the Poor in Manchester 1754-1826*, CS, 22 (1975); Margaret B. Simey, *Charitable Effort in Liverpool in the Nineteenth Century* (Liverpool, 1951), ch. II.

29. PP 1818 (393) V, 153; PP 1819 (59) XVII, 9; CRO, DDX 24/23, Watson to Lloyd, Congleton, 18 June 1808.

30. *The Trial at Large of Thomas Bowen Slaiter* (Stockport, 1815), 121; HO 42/165, Lloyd to Beckett, 17 May 1817; HO 42/179, Lloyd to Hobhouse, Lancaster, 18 Aug. 1818.

31. *Trial of Slaiter, passim; HCJ*, 68 (1812-13), 219-20. On an apparent controversy involving highway leys in 1816, see *To the Rev. Prescot* (Stockport, 1816), pr. s.sh.

32. Giles, 'Enclosure', 101-5.

33. PP 1803-4 (175) XIII, 52-5, 244-7; PP 1818 (82) XIX, 42, 214, 216; PP 1822 (556) V, 16-17, 81; Heginbotham, *Stockport*, I, 77; PP 1833 (450) XX, D.2., 87; CRO QJB 32a (1815-17), 466-7; ibid., 33a (1817-18), 83, 227-8; ibid., 1 (1819-21), 8-10, 60, 107-8.

34. Ibid., 32a (1815-17), 533-4; CRO, EDC 3 (1811-24), entries of 16 Sept. 1811, 13 June 1812; MCL, M22/7/2, Didsbury Vestry Minutes (1812-50), 5-31; F.R. Raines, *The Fellows of the Collegiate Church of Manchester. Part II* (ed. Frank Renaud), CS, 23 (1891), 304.

35. *The Rules of the Pitt Club* (Manchester, 1819), contains a list of original members and subsequent augmentations.

36. George Jackson Hay, *An Epitomised History of the Militia* (London, [1905]), 151-2; HO 51/42/82-3, Lord Hawkesbury to the Earl of Stamford and Warrington, Whitehall, 10 Sept. 1808. On Lloyd's participation, see CRO, DDX 24/22.

37. Frederick Leary, *The Earl of Chester's Regiment of Yeomanry Cavalry: Its Formation and Services 1797 to 1897* (Edinburgh, 1898), 35-8; HO 42/199, H.E. Howard to James Newton, 16 Feb. 1819; Newton to Sir John Fleming Leycester, 16 Feb. 1819; SPL, HX 25, Minute Book of the Stockport Troop Club, 1819-21. On similar divisions within the Lancashire middle classes, see Frank Munger, 'Contentious Gatherings in Lancashire, England, 1750-1830' in Louise A. Tilly and Charles Tilly (eds.), *Class Conflict and Collective Action* (Beverly Hills, 1981), 102.

38. National Library of Scotland, MS 7233/181-2, Hewett Watson to George Combe, Ditton Marsh, 22 Nov. 1834; *A Catalogue of the Valuable Library . . . of the Late Holland Watson* (Liverpool, 1829); cf. CRO, Holland Watson File. (For references to Watson, I am grateful to Frank Egerton, who is preparing a biography of Hewett

Watson.)

39. See, in general, CRO, DDX 24, Lloyd Collection.

40. HO 42/128, John Egerton Killer to Sidmouth, 17 Oct. 1812.

41. William Boulter, *An Evening's Walk in Stockport: A Satirical and Descriptive Poem* (Stockport, 1818), 10; HO 40/1/1/28-9, Broughton to HO, Cheadle, 27 April 1812; HO 42/178, Lloyd to Hobhouse, 18, 19 July 1818.

42. *MO*, 22 July, 5 Aug. 1820; HO 44/2, Lloyd to Sidmouth, 9 Aug. 1820; PP 1834 (44) XXVIII, 278A.

43. See, for example, *SA*, 17, 24, 31 March 1826.

44. SPL, HX 2, Stockport Select Vestry Minutes (1820-3); B/CC/6/1,2, Heaton Norris Vestry Minute Books (1821-4, 1824-30).

45. *CN&Q*, 2 (1887), 49; *Stockport Gas Works* (Stockport, 1821), pr. s.sh.; *HCJ*, 80 (1825), 13, 240, 297; 94, 409, 441; Heginbotham, *Stockport*, II, 417-18; *SA*, 7 July 1826; PRO, PC 1/108, Cholera Returns.

46. *HCJ*, 81 (1826), 45, 218, 261-2, 296, 377; PP 1836 [40] XXXIV, 85-6; *SA*, 15 Sept. 1826; cf. *Stockport: Officers, &c., for the Year 1830* (Stockport, 1830), pr. s.sh.

47. J.S. Morrill, 'Parliamentary Representation' in B.E. Harris (ed.), *A History of the County of Chester*, 2 vols. to date (Oxford, 1979-), II, 126-7; *To Samuel Jowett, Esq.* (Stockport, 1818), pr. s.sh. *MGaz*, 25 July 1812.

48. *MM*, 11 June 1782, 7 April 1789.

49. *MGaz*, 7 Dec. 1805: *An Account of the Celebration of the Jubilee* (Birmingham, [1810?]), 34. Cf. the celebrations at Hyde: Middleton, *Hyde*, 68.

50. *By Desire of the Stewards of the Jubilee Ball. A Benefit for Poor Debtors* (Stockport, 1809), pr. s.sh.; J. Lloyd, *At a Meeting Convened by the Rev. C. Prescot* (Stockport, 1813), pr. s.sh.; *MG*, 21 July 1821; *SA*, 7 July 1826, 9 Sept. 1831; HO 44/10, Thomas Robinson to Warren Bulkeley, 7 Sept. 1821. For an example of the multitude of lesser civic celebrations, see Robert Farren Cheetham, *Odes and Miscellanies* (Stockport, 1796), 107–12, for the local festivities commemorating the Queen's birthday in 1796.

51. W. Clegg, *Jubilean Lines* (Stockport, 1809), pr. s.sh.

52. Cf. Frank Munger, 'Suppression of Popular Gatherings in England, 1800–1830', *American Journal of Legal History*, 25 (1981), 111–40.

Notes to Chapter 4

1. Cf. PP 1834 (167) XIX, D.2., 127, 129.

2. Julia de L. Mann, 'The Textile Industry: Machinery for Cotton, Flax, Wool, 1760–1850' in Charles Singer *et al* (eds.), *A History of Technology*: vol. IV, *The Industrial Revolution* (Oxford, 1958), 277–90; David S. Landes, *The Unbound Prometheus: Technological Change and Industrial Development in Western Europe from 1750 to the Present* (Cambridge, 1969), 82–6; George W. Daniels, *The Early English Cotton Industry with Some Unpublished Letters of Samuel Crompton* (Manchester, 1920), 80.

3. PP 1824 (51) V, 413.

4. A.G. Rose, 'Early Cotton Riots in Lancashire, 1769–1779', *TLCAS*, 73 (1963), 77–88.

5. *The Selected Letters of Josiah Wedgewood* (ed. Ann Finer and George Savage)

(London, 1965), 241–2; WO 1/1003/239–42, John Cross and J. Walshman to Richard Arkwright, Preston, 5 Oct. 1779.

6. WO 1/1003/207–10, Watson to the Commander of HM Troops at Derby, 6 Oct. 1779; /227–30, Lt. Col. W. Radcliffe to Charles Jenkinson [the Secretary of War], Liverpool, 7 Oct. 1779; WO 34/119/81–4, G. Savile to Lord Amherst, Wigan, 10 Oct. 1779.

7. Quoted in 'The Luddites in the Period 1779–1830' in Lionel M. Munby (ed.), *The Luddites and Other Essays* (London, 1971), 35.

8. WO 1/1003/361–4, Maj.-Gen. Faucitt to Jenkinson, Preston, 4 Nov. 1779.

9. 'W.C.' and Ralph Mather, *An Impartial Representation of the Case of the Poor Cotton Spinners in Lancashire* (London, 1780); WO 1/1007/501–4, J. Chippendale to WO, Manchester, 3 June 1780.

10. *MM*, 21 June 1785; PP 1824 (51) V, 410, 413.

11. PP 1833 (690) VI, Q 10,707.

12. Paul Mantoux, *The Industrial Revolution in the Eighteenth Century: An Outline of the Beginnings of the Modern Factory System in England* (rev. edn New York, 1962), 450; *Notice is Hereby Given. To the Mule Spinners of the Town of Manchester, and the Country Adjacent* ([Manchester, 1794]), pr. s.sh.; PP 1824 (51) V, 409–10.

13. PRO, FS 1/24/2; *Articles . . . of the Friendly Associated Mule Cotton Spinners* (Stockport, 1795).

14. On Manchester, see *MM*, 3 March 1795; G.W. Daniels, 'The Cotton Trade during the Revolutionary and Napoleonic Wars', *Transactions of the Manchester Statistical Society* (sess. 1915–16), 59; *Annual Register*, 40 (1798), Chronicle, 21. On the Stockport Friendly Associated Jenny Cotton Spinners, see FS 2/1.

15. Andrew Ure, *The Philosophy of Manufactures* (London, 1835), 364n.; C.H. Lee, *A Cotton Enterprise 1795–1840: A History of M'Connel & Kennedy, Fine Cotton Spinners* (Manchester, 1972), 122; *MC*, 16 July, 15 Oct. 1803; *MO*, 3 Oct. 1818.

16. PP 1824 (51) V, 573–4, 604, 606. Stockport seems to have been District No. 6 of the regional union (ibid., 605) and thus would have contained 22 trade union factories.

17. PP 1812 (210) III, 266, 274; *ST*, 1 (1820–3), 1398n.2.

18. *A Plain Statement of Facts* (Manchester, 1819), pr. s.sh.: PP 1840 (504) X, Q 8475; *HCJ*, 70 (1814–16), 361, 384; PP 1816 (397) III.

19. PP 1824 (51) V, 410–11.

20. Ibid., 411–12; *MO*, 16 May 1818; PP 1825 (417) IV, 33–4, 160–1; PP 1833 (690) VI, Q 10,531.

21. HO 42/174, Lloyd to Hobhouse, 22, 28 Feb. 1818; HO 42/175, same to same, 16 March 1818; *MO*, 2 May 1818.

22. *PD*, 37 (1818), 1259–63; ibid., 39 (1819), 653; *HCJ*, 73 (1818), 213; J.L. Hammond and Barbara Hammond, *The Town Labourer 1760–1832: The New Civilization* (London, 1917), 161–7; *Notice* (Stockport, 1818), pr. s.sh.; Charles Moreton, *To the Public* (Stockport, 1818), pr. s.sh.; *HLJ*, 52 (1818–19), 49.

23. PP 1824 (51) V, 415; *MO*, 18 July 1818; *The Cotton Spinners Address To the Public* (Manchester, 1818), pr. s.sh.

24. Guest, *Compendious History*, 47; PP 1824 (51) V, 302.

25. Ibid., 357, 418; *MGaz*, 14 Feb. 1824.

26. HO 42/178, Prescot, Tatton and Harrison to Sidmouth, 16 July 1818; Lloyd to

Hobhouse, 17, 18, 19 July 1818; *MO*, 25 July, 1, 8, 15 Aug. 1818; *Annual Register*, 60 (1818), Chronicle, 91.

27. HO 42/178, Lloyd to Hobhouse, 23, 25 July 1818; HO 42/179, same to same, 5, 8, 12, 22, 26 Aug. 1818; *MC*, 15 Aug. 1818; CHES 24/188/6, Indictments of Joseph Baker, Joseph Hinchcliffe and Robert Fox.

28. HO 42/179, Lloyd to Hobhouse, 1 Aug. 1818; R.G. Kirby and A.E. Musson, *The Voice of the People: John Doherty, 1798–1854, Trade Unionist, Radical and Factory Reformer* (Manchester, 1975), 19; *Macclesfield Courier*, 3 April 1819; *Chester Guardian*, 22 April 1819; *MO*, 24 April 1819; Hammond, *Town Labourer*, 255–8.

29. PP 1824 (51) V, 415–16; *SA*, 26 July, 9 Aug., 13 Sept. 1822; HO 40/17/734–5, Maj. Eckersley to Sir John Byng, Manchester, 1 Aug. 1822.

30. Kirby and Musson, *Doherty*, 31, 35; BL, Add. MSS 27,801/256–8, 261; N.J. Smelser, *Social Change in the Industrial Revolution: An Application of Theory to the British Cotton Industry* (Chicago, 1959), 233; H.A. Turner, *Trade Union Growth, Structure and Policy: A Comparative Study of the Cotton Unions* (London, 1962), 72.

31. J.T. Ward, *The Factory Movement 1830–55* (London, 1962), 28.

32. *SA*, 21 July, 18 Aug. 1826, 24, 31 Oct. 1828, Jan.–Sept. 1829.

33. PP 1825 (417) IV, 160–3.

34. C. Aspin, *Lancashire, the First Industrial Society* (Helmshore, 1969), 37; PP 1819 (HL 24) CX, 27, 31; PP 1831–2 (706) XV, Q 6639; PP 1833 (450) XX, D.1., 71; D.2., 9–10.

35. Craig Calhoun, 'Transition in Social Foundations for Collective Action: Communities in the Southeast Lancashire Textile Region in the 1820s and 1830s', *Social Science History*, 4 (1980), 443; Sidney and Beatrice Webb, *Industrial Democracy* (London, 1898), 496–7; Louise Tilly and Joan Wallach Scott, *Women, Work, and Family* (New York, 1978), 129–33 and *passim;* R. Burr Litchfield, 'The Family and the Mill: Cotton Mill Work, Family Work Patterns, and Fertility in Mid-Victorian Stockport' in Anthony Wohl (ed.), *The Victorian Family: Structure and Stresses* (London, 1978), 186; *SA*, 20 Aug. 1824, 1 April 1831, 4 May 1832.

36. PP 1833 (450) XX, D.2., 14.

37. R.H. Nichols and F.A. Wray, *The History of the Foundling Hospital* (London, 1935), 191–200; Unwin, *Oldknow,* 170–5; PP 1816 (397) III, 54–5; SPL, SSS MSS. B/T/3/26, Papers of Bury Middleton, Rooth and Mayer, Apprenticeship Indentures.

38. CRO, QJB, 28a (1798–1804), 489–90, 562; ibid., 30a (1808–11), 309–10; *MC*, 10 Dec. 1803. Cf. also SPL, HX 74, Register of Poor Apprentices 1802–15.

39. *Annual Report of the SSS* (Stockport, 1809), 10; ibid, (Stockport, 1814), 5; ibid, (Stockport, 1819), 11.

40. *The Seventh Report of the Stockport Auxiliary Bible Society* (Stockport, 1820), 15; PP 1834 (167) XX, D.1., 69–70, 81, 175; Swindells and Western, *Marple*, 28.

41. PP 1819 (HL24) CX, 442 and Appendix, 3–20; P. Gaskell, *Artisans and Machinery* (London, 1836), 142; cf. Clark Nardinelli, 'Child Labor and the Factory Acts', *Journal of Economic History*, 40 (1980), 746.

42. PP 1816 (397) III, 54; PP 1833 (450) XX, D.1., 72, 133; PP 1834 (167) XX, D.1., *passim*.

43. SPL, S/R43, Glynis Jackson, ' "The House of Mercy" (a History of the Stockport Dispensary and House of Recovery 1792–1833)' (1969); PP 1840 (227) X,

Q 2804; PP 1833 (450) XX, D.1., 133; D.2., 30.

44. Ashmore, *Industrial Archaeology*, 20–1; M.E. Falkus, 'The Early Development of the British Gas Industry, 1790–1815', *Economic History Review*, 35 (1982), 219–20. 232; PP 1834 (167) XX, D.1., *passim.*

45. Wilbur Fisk, *Travels on the Continent of Europe* (New York, 1838), 677; William Boulter, *An Evening's Walk in Stockport: A Satirical and Descriptive Poem* (Stockport, 1818), 12; Chadwick, *Sanitary Condition*, 35; Carlos Flick, 'The Movement for Smoke Abatement in 19th-Century Britain', *Technology and Culture*, 21 (1980), 30.

46. The 1803 Stockport petition against the first Factory Act was probably promoted by the masters' association formed in the preceding year: *HCJ*, 58 (1802–3), 149.

47. William Dodd, *The Factory System Illustrated* (London, 1842), 163; HO 44/14, John Vaughan to Hobhouse, 17 Feb. 1824; PP 1831–2 (706) XV, QQ 6622, 9384, 9388; PP 1833 (450) XX, D.1., 1–3; *SA*, 3 Oct. 1828, 6 April 1832.

48. George Henry Wood, *The History of Wages in the Cotton Trade during the Past Hundred Years* (London, 1910), 69, 127; *MC*, 15 Aug. 1818; *MM*, 18 Jan. 1820; Cole, *Short History*, 131, 135.

49. PP 1857 (211-Sess. 2) XI, QQ 6802–4.

50. *MM*, 8 April 1777, 2 Nov. 1784; see also ibid., 8 Aug. 1786 for further evidence on the calenderers' union.

51. Sidney and Beatrice Webb, *The History of Trade Unionism, 1666–1920* (rev. edn, London, 1920), 25n.1.

52. *MM*, 3, 31 Jan. 1786; *London Gazette*, 24–28 Jan. 1786; *Facts and Observations, to Prove the Impolicy and Dangerous Tendency, of the Bill now before Parliament* (Manchester, [1807]), 13–20.

53. *MM*, 22 Jan. 1788.

54. CRO, QJF 217/4/157, 218/1/108; for an account of the strike of 1789–90, see Geoffrey Turnbull, *A History of the Calico Printing Industry of Great Britain* (ed. John G. Turnbull) (Altrincham, 1951), 185, 188.

55. *MM*, 29 June 1790.

56. Ibid., 20 July 1790; *Considerations Addressed to the Journeymen Calico Printers by One of Their Masters* (Manchester, 1815), 3.

57. PP 1803–4 (150) V, 7; *Observations of the Cotton Weavers' Act* (Manchester, 1804), 14.

58. *MM*, 22 Feb., 22 March 1803; *HCJ*, 58 (1802–3), 180.

59. *MC*, 26 Feb. 1803; *Facts and Observations*, 8; *The Memorial of the Journeymen Calico Printers, and Others Connected with Their Trade* (London, 1804), 6–7.

60. *Ibid., passim*; *HCJ*, 59 (1803–4), 100; PP 1803–4 (150) V, 6–8, 15–16, 18; Turnbull, *History*, 186; Hammond, *Town Labourer*, 293–5.

61. *HCJ*, 60 (1805–6), 109; *HLJ*, 45 (1805–6), 212; *MGaz*, 4 March 1805; *MM*, 4 June 1805.

62. *HCJ*, 61 (1806), 902–3: 'Report from the Committee on the Minutes respecting the Calico Printers Petition.'

63. Ibid., 62 (1807), 272, 297, 343, 359; *PD*, 9 (1807), 532–7; *The Letters of Richard Brinsley Sheridan* (ed. Cecil Price), 3 vols. (Oxford, 1966), III, 10–1, Sheridan to Richard Taylor and Peter Adshead, Richmond, 20 June 1807.

64. *Facts and Observations*, 8–9; *MM*, 30 April 1811; Arthur Redford, *Manchester Merchants and Foreign Trade 1794–1858* (Manchester, 1934), 67.

65. *Considerations*, 6, 14; *MGaz*, 2 March 1805; *The Times*, 3 July 1807.

66. *HCJ*, 68 (1812–13), 248; *Rules for the Conducting of the Union Society of Printers, Cutters, and Drawers in Lancashire, Cheshire, Derbyshire, &c.* (Manchester, 1813); *At an Adjourned Meeting of the Master Calico Printers* (Manchester, 1814), pr. s.sh. HO 42/138, C. Swainson & Co. to [Sidmouth], Bannister Hall near Preston, 31 March 1814.

67. *Considerations*, 16; *MM*, 27 Dec. 1814.

68. *To the Various Bodies of Mechanics* by the Journeymen Calico Printers (Preston, 1815), pr. s.sh; HO 42/144, Lloyd to Beckett, 20 June [1816]; William Kiddier, *The Old Trade Unions, from Unprinted Records of the Brushmakers* (London, 1930), 26. The interest-free loans from the brushmakers were not fully repaid until 1823.

69. *HCJ*, 70 (1814–16), 474.

70. *MM*, 30 Jan. 1816; HO 48/17, 'Memorial of the Undersigned Merchants, Manufacturers and Inhabitants of . . . Manchester and Salford'. The incident in Webb, *Trade Unionism*, 79, appears to be a garbled account of the 1815–16 episode.

71. Turnbull, *History*, 191–2; HO 42/158, William Booth, John Sawyer and Owen Clark to Sidmouth, London, 21 Jan. 1817; cf. *Observations on the Use of Machinery in the Manufactories of Great Britain* (London, 1817).

72. Disley calico printers sent contributions to Bolton cotton spinners in 1823. *We are requested to inform you* (Bolton, 1823), pr. s.sh.

73. K.L. Wallwork, 'The Calico Printing Industry of Lancastria in the 1840s', *Transactions of the Institute of British Geographers*, 45 (1968), 148–9; Swindells and Western, *Marple*, 28. Printed goods charged with duties rose from an annual average of 59 million yards in 1811–15 to 101 million yards in 1821–9, although these figures include silks, linens and stuffs as well as calicoes. Mitchell and Deane, *Abstract*, 184.

74. *Facts and observations*, 7; *SA*, 27 Jan. 1832.

75. PP 1824 (51) V, 307; Baines, *Cotton Manufacture*, 450n.; cf. Gaskell, *Artisans*, 259.

76. *SA*, 14 Aug. 1829.

77. Quoted in Aspin, *Lancashire*, 107.

78. Webb, *Trade Unionism*, 86–7; Cole, *Short History*, 59–60.

79. James R. Cuca, 'Industrial Change and the Progress of Labor in the English Cotton Industry', *International Review of Social History*, 22 (1977), 241–55.

80. Edward Baines, Jr, *History of the Cotton Manufacture in Great Britain* (London, 1835), 446.

Notes to Chapter 5

1. G. von Schulze-Gaevernitz, *The Cotton Trade in England and on the Continent* (trans. Oscar S. Hall) (London, 1895), 30; Engels, *Condition*, 51–2.

2. *SA*, 16 Sept. 1831; Aiken, *Manchester*, 178; PP 1824 (51) V, 545.

3. *HCJ*, 29 (1761–4), 905; for statistics on the increasing exports of felt hats, see Elizabeth Boody Schumpeter, *English Overseas Trade Statistics 1697–1808* (Oxford, 1960), 39–47.

4. George Unwin, 'A Seventeenth Century Trade Union', *Economic Journal*, 10 (1900), 394–403; *MM*, 20 March 1753.

5. Henry Mayhew, *The Unknown Mayhew: Selections from the Morning Chronicle,*

1849–1850 (ed. E.P. Thompson and Eileen Yeo) (London, 1971), 450.

6. *Annual Register*, 11 (1768), Chronicle, 107; *ibid.*, 13 (1770), Chronicle, 74; Webb, *Trade Unionism*, 28–9; *HCJ*, 36 (1776–8), 192–3.

7. *MM*, 6 June, 5 Dec. 1775. Note that hat makers and finishers, who might have only a handful of journeymen and apprentices working under them, were called 'masters' in these notices. The same appellation was also given to proprietors of large firms which put out materials and took charge of the marketing of finished hats.

8. *Manchester Journal*, 8 Feb. 1777.

9. *HCJ*, (1776–8), 192–3, 240, 257, 280–1, 287–8, 329, 454, 539.

10. Ibid., 36 (1776–8), 289, 518, 535–6.

11. *MM*, 5 April 1785.

12. PRO, C 107/104, Letter Book, Thomas Davies to [Thomas Hope, London], 17 Sept., 12 Nov. 1785. (I am grateful to Ian Mitchell for drawing my attention to this cache of documents.)

13. *MC*, 12 Nov. 1785; *MM*, 29 Nov. 1785, 3 Jan. 1786; HO 42/7, Thomas B. Bayley to Lord Sydney, Hope, 15 Dec. 1785; C 107/104, Letter Book, Davies to Hope [London], 11 Feb. 1786.

14. P.M. Giles, 'The Felt-Hatting Industry, c. 1500–1850, with Particular Reference to Lancashire and Cheshire', *TLCAS*, 69 (1959), 121; *MM*, 19 July 1791; [James Dawson Burn], *A Glimpse at the Social Condition of the Working Classes during the Early Part of the Present Century* (London), [1868]), 38; D.M. Smith, 'The Hatting Industry in Denton, Lancashire', *Journal of Industrial Archaeology*, 3 (1966), 1. Denton hatters were, however, participating in a friendly society as early as 1794: FS 2/4–5. On a minor Stockport hatters' dispute in 1799 over the employment of 'foul' men, see C.R. Dobson, *Masters and Journeymen: A Prehistory of Industrial Relations 1717–1800* (London, 1980), 170.

15. PP 1808 (119) X, 4, 8–9; CRO, QJB 29a (1804–8), 180; *MGaz*, 19 Nov. 1808.

16. *At a General Congress of the Journeymen Hat-makers and Finishers, of Stockport* (Stockport, 1808), pr. s.sh. Some inventions were being developed locally. BP 1871, for instance, was granted in 1792 to James Daniel, a Stockport hat manufacturer, for an 'improved machine for felting and making hats'. For other early trends in the mechanisation of hatting, see Ashmore, *Industrial Archaeology*, 37.

17. HO 42/99, Daniel Cooper's Memorial to the Earl of Liverpool, 31 Jan. 1809; *MGaz*, 19 Nov. 1808, 4 March 1809; *Tradesman*, 1 Feb. 1809.

18. *MGaz*, 22 July 1809; W.O. Henderson (ed.), *Industrial Britain under the Regency: The Diaries of Escher, Bodmer, May and de Gallios 1814–18* (London, 1968), 146.

19. HO 42/144, Lloyd to Beckett, 20 June [1816]; HO 42/165, same to same, 17 May 1817; *MM*, 8 Oct. 1816.

20. *MO*, 20 June 1818. For mention of the depressed state of the hatters, see ibid., 22 Aug. 1818.

21. HO 42/178, 'X.Y.' to Byng, Oldham, 16 July 1818; Byng to Hobhouse, Pontefract, 18 July 1818; *MO*, 30 Oct. 1819, 20 April 1820. By 1824 it was said to be typical of hatters of different towns to support one another during strikes. PP 1824 (51) V, 92.

22. Cf. the disputes in London at that time: BL, Add. MSS 27,799/85–6; PP 1824 (51) V, 64, 73–6; *To the Journeymen Hat Finishers, and Stiffeners, in Manchester, Oldham, Denton, and Ashton* (n.p., 1820), pr. s.sh.

23. HO 44/7, Lloyd to Hobhouse, Chester, 12 April 1821; CHES 24/189/3.

24. *MGaz*, 13, 27 March 1824. Masters had met openly at the end of 1822 to fix prices. *At a Meeting of the Master Hat-Manufacturers* (Manchester, 1822), pr. s.sh.

25. *HCJ*, 79 (1824), 161; *MGaz*, 1 May 1824; *SA*, 2 Feb., 3, 17 Aug., 14 Sept. 1827.

26. *A List of Journeymen Hatters and Apprentices Belonging to the Union of the United Kingdom* (London, 1831), 5–12; PP 1843 [431] XIV, b 41–2.

27. *A Letter to a Member of Parliament, on the importance of Liberty* (London, 1745); *A Particular Account of the Processions of the Different Trades in Manchester* (Manchester, 1761), pr. s.sh.; F.W. Galton (ed.), *Select Documents Illustrating the History of Trade Unionism I. The Tailoring Trade* (London, 1923); HO 42/179, bundle of papers on shoemakers.

28. PP 1834 (556) X, QQ 7259–60.

29. FS 2/1; PP 1824 (51) V, 609–10; PP 1825 (522) IV, 8; *MG*, 21 July 1821; *SA*, 9 Sept. 1831.

30. Webb, *Trade Unionism*, 37, 79–80; *HCJ*, 56 (1801), 269–70; *MM*, 20 April 1802. Cf. Neale, *Class and Ideology*, 49.

31. HO 42/161, Deposition of W. Lloyd Caldecot, 17 March 1817; cf. HO 42/79, Deposition of Thomas Hudson, 9 Aug. 1804; *HCJ*, 62 (1812), 186; PP 1824 (51) V, 97, 133–5, 146–7.

32. HO 50/98, Nathaniel Wright to Charles Yorke, Poynton, 24 Jan. 1804; Sidney Pollard, 'A New Estimate of British Coal Production, 1750–1850', *Economic History Review*, 33 (1980), 229–30; Hammond, *Town Labourer*, 132–3.

33. Jelinger C. Symons, *Arts and Artisans at Home and Abroad* (Edinburgh, 1839), 5; *MO*, 4 July 1818; *To the Public* (Manchester, 1818), pr. s.sh; HO 42/179, William Chippendale to Hobhouse, Oldham, 27 Aug. 1818; HO 42/181, Lloyd to R.H. Clive, 10 Oct. 1818.

34. FS 2/1; Keith Burgess, *The Origins of British Industrial Relations: The Nineteenth Century Experience* (London, 1975), 177–8.

35. Thompson, *MEWC*, 546–7.

36. [George White and Gravener Henson], *A Few Remarks on the State of the Laws, at Present in Existence, for Regulating Masters and Work-People* (London, 1823), 84; M. Dorothy George, 'The Combination Laws Reconsidered', *Economic History*, 1 (1926–9), 214–28; idem, 'The Combination Laws', *Economic History Review*, 6 (1935–6), 172–8; Malcolm I. Thomis, *Politics and Society in Nottingham 1785–1835* (Oxford, 1969), 65.

37. HO 42/179, Lloyd to Hobhouse, 25 Aug. 1818; HO 42/181, Norris to Sidmouth, Manchester, 4, 11 Oct. 1818.

38. PP 1824 (51) V, 413; [J.R. McCulloch], 'Restraints on Emigration', *Edinburgh Review*, 39 (1823–4), 329.

39. I.J. Prothero, *Artisans and Politics in Early Nineteenth-Century London: John Gast and his Times* (Baton Rouge, 1979), ch. 9, esp. pp. 175, 178–9; *HCJ*, 79 (1824), 161, 211, 217, 265.

40. Ibid., 80 (1825), 351, 426–7, 605.

41. *SA*, 27 Jan. 1825; BL, Add. MSS 27,803/268, 273–4, Blackett to Francis Place, 5 March, 18 April 1825;/280, Worsley to Place, 23 May 1825: /316–17, Longson to Place, 16 Oct. 1825.

42. *ST*, 1 (1820–3), 1395-8.

43. CHES 24/180/5. Indictments of Edward Brooks and John Richardson; *MC*, 5 March, 30 July, 1 Oct. 1803; *SA*, 4 Feb. 1831, 6 April 1832; S.I. Mitchell, 'Retailing

in Eighteenth- and Early Nineteenth-Century Cheshire'. *THSLC*. 130 (1981). 37-60.

44. Cf. Eric Hopkins. 'Working Hours and Conditions during the Industrial Revolution: A Re-Appraisal'. *Economic History Review*. 35 (1982). 52-66.

45. Elizabeth W. Gilboy. *Wages in Eighteenth Century England* (Cambridge. Mass.. 1934). 195: Chalklin. *Provincial Towns*. 221: HO 42/95. Fletcher to Hawkesbury. [Bolton. received 24] Feb. 1808: Leon Soutierre Marshall. *The Development of Public Opinion in Manchester. 1780-1820* (Syracuse. 1946). 27: PP 1840 (43-1) XXIII. 508: Donald R. Adams. Jr. 'Some Evidence on English and American Wage Rates. 1790-1830'. *Journal of Economic History*. 30 (1970). 513.

46. PP 1833 (612) V. 280: William Radcliffe. *Letters on the Evils of the Exportation of Cotton Yarns* (Stockport. 1811). 18.

47. Thompson. *MEWC*. 456-62.

48. 33 Geo. III. c. 54.

49. FS 2/1: cf *Rules and Articles to be Observed and Kept by the True Blue Friendly Society . . . Instituted the 24th day of August. 1764* (Chester. 1809).

50. FS 1/252B/351: 1/28/186. For another early Stockport society, see *Articles and Orders. Made. Agreed Upon. and Appointed to be Observed by the Members Belonging to the Old Association Club. Heretofore Called The Weavers Club* (Manchester. 1771).

51. Cf. P.H.J.H. Gosden. *Self-Help: Voluntary Associations in 19th-century Britain* (New York. 1974). 13-14. Calculations are based on two sources: FS 2/1 and CRO. A List of Friendly Society Rules Filed with the Clerk of the Peace for the County of Chester Previous to 1794 to 1829'.

52. FS 1/292/1051-2: 1/283/879.

53. Ibid.. 1/25/23.

54. PP 1831-2 (90) XXVI. 5. 15-16.

55. See the contrasting hypothesis in P.H.J.H. Gosden. *The Friendly Societies in England 1815-1875* (Manchester. 1961). 237-43.

56. *Strictures on Benefit or Friendly Societies* (Stockport. [1799?]). 17: *Observations on the Cotton Weavers' Act* (Manchester. 1804). 15.

57. Quoted in C. Stella Davies. *A History of Macclesfield* (Manchester. 1961). 180.

58. CRO. QJB 29a (1804-8). 256.

59. HO 42/132. W.R. Hay to Sidmouth. Manchester. 4 Feb. 1813.

60. *Friendly Societies* (Stockport. 1818). pr. s.sh.: HO 42/179. Lloyd to Hobhouse. Lancaster. 19 Aug. 1818.

61. See. for example. FS 1/25/17: *Rules and Orders of the Stockport Sunday School Benevolent Male Society* (Stockport. 1810).

62. FS1/30/262; *CN&Q*. 2 (1887). 209: *SA*. 7 July 1826.

63. HO 42/149. James Warr to Fletcher. Bolton. 1 March 1816.

64. MCL. Burton MSS. V. 507-8: PP 1803-4 (175) XIII. 54-5: PP 1818 (82) XIX. 42-3: J. Marshall. *An Analysis and Compendium of all the Returns made to Parliament* (London. 1835). 21-3.

65. FS 1/26/24: on the Gardeners' Order. see J. Frome Wilkinson. *Mutual Thrift* (London. 1891). 13.

66. The following account of Stockport Masons is based on John Armstrong. *A History of Freemasonry in Cheshire* (London. 1901). 275-344: James Bertram Oldham. *A Short History and Centenary Souvenir of the Lodge of Peace* (Stockport. 1906).

67. *SA*. 9 Sept. 1831: PP 1842 (158) XXXV. 31-2.

68. John Tidd Pratt. *The History of Savings Banks in England. Wales. Ireland. and Scotland* (London. 1842). xx: *Philanthropist.* 4 (1818). 17-18: *MC.* 10 Jan.. 16 May 1818.

69. *SA.* 20 Sept. 1822. 6 Aug. 1824: Heginbotham. *Stockport.* II. 425: John Tidd Pratt. *The History of Savings Banks* (London. 1830). 23: *A Century of Thrift: An Historical Sketch of the Stockport Savings Bank 1824-1924* (Stockport. 1925). 3-14.

70. 59 Geo. III. c. 128. On attempts to enforce this Act in Cheshire. see *Ordered by the Court* (Chester. 1820). pr. s.sh.: CRO. QJB 1 (1819-21). 273-4.

71. *Stockport Co-operative Society Ltd. Centenary 1860-1960* (Stockport. 1960). 1-2: W. Longson. *An Appeal to Masters. Workmen & the Public. Shewing the Cause of the Distress of the Labouring Classes* (Manchester. 1827). 26: PP 1833 (690) VI. QQ 10.572-3. Cf. Jennifer Tann. 'Co-operative Corn Milling: Self-help During the Grain Crises of the Napoleonic Wars'. *Agricultural History Review.* 28 (1980). 45-57.

72. GL. MSS 7253/15/109.096. Policy of James Antrobus Newton and others (1788): *To Be Sold* (Stockport. 1804). pr. s.sh.: SPL. Hurst MSS. I. 73. 171: MX 49. Schedule of Edgeley Title Deeds.

73. *SA.* 11 July 1823. 16 June. 29 Sept. 1826; *Annual Report of the SSS* (Stockport, 1823). 10: Gosden. *Self-Help.* 143.

74. Marx. *Communist Manifesto.* 23-4. 41: idem. *Poverty of Philosophy.* 172-5.

75. Webb. *Trade Unionism.* 83-4.

76. Richard Price. 'The Labour Process and Labour History'. *Social History.* 8 (1983), 61-2.

Notes to Chapter 6

1. See. for example. Christopher Hill. *The World Turned Upside Down: Radical Ideas during the English Revolution* (New York. 1972): Caroline Robbins. *The Eighteenth-Century Commonwealthman* (Cambridge. Mass.. 1959).

2. John Brewer. *Party Ideology and Popular Politics at the Accession of George III* (Cambridge. 1976). 19-25: see also Colin Bonwick. *English Radicals and the American Revolution* (Chapel Hill. 1977).

3. Brewer. *Party Ideology.* 175: Robert Glen. 'Industrial Wayfarers: Benjamin Franklin and a Case of Machine Smuggling in the 1780s'. *Business History.* 23 (1981). 309-26.

4. Egon Bittner. 'Radicalism'. *International Encyclopedia of the Social Sciences.* 17 vols. (New York. 1968). XIII. 294-300: idem. 'Radicalism and the Organization of Radical Movements'. *American Sociological Review.* 28 (1963). 928-40.

5. Cf. Thompson. *MEWC.* 200-1. 507-8: Elie Halévy. *The Growth of Philosophic Radicalism* (trans. Mary Morris)(Boston. 1955). 261.

6. *Cheshire Sheaf.* 3 (1901). 115-16: *MM.* 20 Sept. 1757. For parallels at Oldham. see Foster. *CSIR.* 31-2.

7. See R.M. Wiles. *Freshest Advices: Early Provincial Newspapers in England* (Columbus. Ohio. 1965). 295: *Manchester Politics* (London. 1748): and the numerous and not unfavourable accounts of Wilkes' activities in the *Lancashire Magazine.* 1 (1763-4).

8. *MM.* 21 Sept. 1790: William E.A. Axon. *The Annals of Manchester* (Manchester. 1886). 117-18: F.E. Sanderson. 'The Structure of Politics in Liverpool 1780-1807'.

THSLC, 127 (1978), 68; *Chester Poll Book* (Chester, 1784); [Ralph Eddowes], *Sketch of the Political History of Chester* (Chester, 1790); Joseph Hemingway, *History of the City of Chester*, 2 vols. (Chester, 1831), II, 382, 401-5.

9. *MM*, 5 April 1791; Donald Grove Barnes, *A History of the English Corn Laws from 1660-1846* (London, 1930), 59-62, 71; James Wheeler, *Manchester: Its Political, Social and Commercial History, Ancient and Modern* (London, 1836), 90.

10. *Brother Fustian's Advice to the Inhabitants of Manchester and Salford* ([Manchester], 1792), pr. s.sh.; Thomas Walker, *A Review of Some of the Political Events which Have Occurred in Manchester, during the Last Five Years* (London, 1794), 11-16; Pauline Handforth, 'Manchester Radical Politics, 1789-1794', *TLCAS*, 67 (1956), 87-106.

11. Philip Anthony Brown, *The French Revolution in English History* (London, 1918), 53-8, 61-2; J. Taylor, 'The Sheffield Constitutional Society (1791-1795)', *Transactions of the Hunter Archaeological Society*, 5 (1937-43), 133-46; Henry Collins, 'The London Corresponding Society' in John Saville (ed.), *Democracy and the Labour Movement: Essays in Honour of Dona Torr* (London, 1954), 109-11; *Manchester Herald*, 4 Aug. 1792.

12. The *Chester Chronicle* included a series of extracts from *Rights of Man* commencing in its issue of 22 April 1791.

13. See *Manchester Herald*, 14 April 1792 and subsequent issues for advertisements stating that the *Patriot* was sold by John Reddish of Stockport. He had earlier sold the radical *Sheffield Register* (as noted in ibid., 9 June 1787).

14. N. Hibbert and John Andrew, *In the Cause of Liberty* (Stockport, 1792), pr. s.sh.; *Manchester Herald*, 1 Sept. 1792.

15. BL. Add. MSS 27,812/21. The three LCS addresses had appeared in April, May and August 1792, respectively. They are reprinted in *ST*, 24 (1794), 377-87.

16. Add. MSS 27,812/22, 24; *ST*, 24 (1794), 388-9; *HCJ*, 48 (1794), 669.

17. PRO, TS 11/952/3496, Andrew to the editors of the *Patriot*, 4 Oct. 1792; *ST*, 24 (1794), 825-31; ibid., 25 (1794-5), 186-8; *Patriot*, 13 Nov. 1792.

18. *Manchester Herald*, 10 Nov. 1792; Brown, *French Revolution*, 64; *MC*, 15 Dec. 1792. At Didsbury, for example, an effigy of Paine was burned in January 1793, no doubt to frighten would-be Jacobins in that area. Ivor R. Million, *A History of Didsbury* (Didsbury, 1969), 69.

19. HO 42/21/478-85, 'List of Addresses to His Majesty'; Clive Emsley, 'The Home Office and its Sources of Information and Investigation 1791-1801', *English Historical Review*, 94 (1979), 538.

20. Somewhat later, another active loyalist referred to Stockport Jacobins as being of 'the poorer sort' and said that their numbers were small despite the fact that some country people had joined the society. He also said that Dissenters had been active in circulating *The Rights of Man* among the 'lower class of people'. TS 24/2/20, Robert Newton to Chamberlayne and White, 18 Dec. 1792.

21. TS 11/952/3496, Andrew to the editors of the *Patriot*, 4 Oct. 1792.

22. *A Rod for the Burkites*, by 'Tyrtaeus' (2nd edn. Manchester, [1792]), 10, 15. Tyrtaeus was a lame Greek poet of the seventh century BC who inspired Spartans to heroic deeds with his war poems.

23. *The readers of the letters of H.W.*, by 'Mancuniensis' (Manchester, 1792), pr. s.sh.

24. *Proceedings of the Association for Preserving Liberty against Republicans and Levellers* (London, [1792]); TS 24/2/3, Chamberlayne and White to Holland

Watson, Lincoln's Inn, 7 Dec. 1792; same to Robert Newton.

25. *Manchester Herald*, 5, 12 Jan. 1793; *At a Meeting held... the tenth day of December, 1792* (|Stockport|, 1792), pr. s.sh.; QJF 221/1/56, Indictment of Thomas Bailey; TS 24/2/20, Newton to Chamberlayne and White, 18 Dec. 1792; Archibald Prentice, *Historical Sketches and Personal Recollections of Manchester* (London, 1851), 422.

26. QJF 221/1/54-5, Indictments of James Hartley and Henry Wharmby; Add. MSS 16,923, Watson to Reeves, 29 Dec. 1792; ibid., 16,924, Watson to John Moore, 14 Jan. 1793; *Publications of the Society for Preserving Liberty and Property against Republicans and Levellers*, 2 series (London, |1792-3|).

27. TS 24/2/23, Watson to Chamberlayne and White, 29 Dec. 1792; /20, Newton to same, 18 Dec. 1792; Add. MSS 27,812/61; ibid., 16,924, Watson to Moore, 14 Jan. 1793.

28. Ibid.; TS 24/2/23, Watson to Chamberlayne and White, 29 Dec. 1792. It is not known if Watson decided to brave the criticism and circulate *Britannia's Address*.

29. Henry W. Meikle, *Scotland and the French Revolution* (Glasgow, 1912), 139-42; *The Political Martyrs... Persecuted in the Year 1793-4 for Advocating the Cause of Reform in Parliament* (London, 1837).

30. Editions of four, six and eight pages ultimately appeared. The tract has been reprinted by the Stockport Municipal Museum (Stockport, 1975).

31. HO 42/30/94-5, 'A Lover of Liberty and Order' to Pitt, 14 May 1794; *ST*, 24 (1794), 745-8.

32. HO 43/5/232, Henry Dundas to Prescot, Whitehall, 18 June 1794; HO 42/32, Watson to HO, 3 July 1794.

33. TS 11/1026/4298, Watson to |Dundas|, 10 July 1794; Watson to Chamberlayne and White, 22 July 1794; CHES 24/178/2, Depositions of Joseph Hibbert, 20 July, 6-7 Sept. 1794; Indictments of Gordon, Atkinson and Baxter; *London Chronicle*, 15 Oct. 1794.

34. George Lloyd *et al.*, *An Appeal to the Inhabitants of Manchester and Its Neighbourhood* (Manchester, 1795), pr. s.sh.; *HLJ*, 40 (1794-6), 578-9.

35. *MGaz*, 2, 16 Jan. 1796; *MC*, 9 Jan. 1796; HO 65/1, J. King to Prescot, Whitehall, 24 Dec. 1795; HO 49/3/46, King to Joseph White, Whitehall, 24 Dec. 1795; Marshall, *Public Opinion*, 127.

36. *MGaz*, 13 Feb. 1796; Charles Cestre, *John Thelwall: A Pioneer of Democracy and Social Reform in England during the French Revolution* (London, 1906), 128. Cestre states (p. 159) that Thelwall stayed with 'artisans, shopkeepers, dissenting ministers, |and| schoolmasters' on his provincial tour.

37. HO 42/45, Examination of James Dixon, 5 May 1798; PC 1/41 A, 136, Information of Robert Gray, 23 March 1798; for anti-war pieces, see, for example, *MGaz*, 18 March 1796, 18 Feb. 1797.

38. CHES 24/179/6, Examinations of John Cockin, 8 April 1798; and Thomas Hadfield, 12 April 1798.

39. *PH*, 34 (1798-1800), 603; Add. MSS 27,808/91-5; HO 42/45, Deposition of Robert Gray, 12 April 1798.

40. HO 42/40, paper beginning 'Gentlemen of the Union Society of Manchester...' cf. PC 1/41 A, 139, Examination of Robert Gray, 15 April 1798. The Gee Cross Union Society was probably given a copy of *The Declaration, Resolutions, and Constitution of the Society of United Englishmen* (n.p., |1797?|).

41. J. Auchincloss, *The Sophistry of the First Part of Mr. Paine's Age of Reason*

(Stockport, 1796); idem, *Paine's Confession of the Divinity of the Holy Scriptures: or the Sophistry of the Second Part of the Age of Reason* (2nd edn, Stockport 1796); see also the combined edition (Edinburgh, 1796). For the industrialist, see Abraham Binns, *Remarks on a Publication Entitled 'A Serious Admonition to the Disciples of Thomas Paine, and All Other Infidels'* (Stockport, 1796); review of Abraham Binns, *Remarks on a Publication*, in *Critical Review*, 20 (1797), 109.

42. PC 1/38 A. 123, |William Barlow| to Ford, |Liverpool, c. July 1797|; PC 1/40 A. 132, Thomas Bancroft to ?, Bolton, 24 Nov. 1797; PC 1/41 A. 136, 'List of Books'; PC 1/44 A. 161, |Barlow| to Mr. Harrop |Liverpool?, 1799?|; *Republican*, 18 March 1825; J.M. Wheeler, *A Biographical Dictionary of Freethinkers of All Ages and Nations* (London, 1889), 100. James Davies is also sometimes referred to as 'John' Davies.

43. HO 42/46, Bundle L.n.4, John Waring to HO, Stonyhurst, 15 Feb. 1798; Bundle L.n.7, 'Extract of Information Respecting the United Irishmen'; PC 1/40 A. 133, Thomas Bancroft to |Portland|, Bolton, 7 Jan. 1798.

44. CHES 24/179/6, Examination of Joseph Jackson, 3 May 1798; CHES 35/25, sess. 27 Aug. 1798; Clive Emsley, 'An Aspect of Pitt's "Terror": Prosecutions for Sedition during the 1790s', *Social History*, 6 (1981), 178.

45. J.R. Dinwiddy, 'The "Black Lamp" in Yorkshire 1801-2', *Past and Present*, 64 (1974), 113-23; J.L. Baxter and F.K. Donnelly, 'The Revolutionary "Underground" in the West Riding: Myth or Reality', ibid., 124-32; Dinwiddy, 'Rejoinder', ibid., 133-5; Marianne Elliott, 'The "Despard Conspiracy" Reconsidered', ibid., 75 (1977), 46-61; Albert Goodwin, *The Friends of Liberty: The English Democratic Movement in the Age of the French Revolution* (Cambridge, Mass., 1979), 461-4.

46. A.W. Smith, 'Irish Rebels and English Radicals 1798-1820', *Past and Present*, 7 (1955), 79-82.

47. PC 1/44 A. 158, R. F|oxley| to Lord Viscount Belgrave, Manchester, |1 Aug.? 1799|.

48. PC 1/44 A. 161, R. F|oxley| to Portland, Manchester, 8 Aug. 1799; W. Barlow to Richard Ford, Sheffield, 14 Aug. 1799; PC 1/45 A. 164 pt. I, newspaper clipping dated 9 Dec. 1799; Bayley to John King, Hope, 21, 30 Nov. 1799; *At a Meeting of Labourers, Mechanics and Artificers of Manchester* (Manchester, 1799), pr. s.sh.; *On Combinations* (Manchester, 1799), pr. s.sh.

49. *At a Meeting of the Acting Magistrates* (Manchester, 1799), pr. s.sh.; Radcliffe, *Origin*, 72-3, 107.

50. *The Magistrates Inform the Farmer* (Stockport, 1799), pr. s.sh.; Samuel Bamford, *Early Days* (London, 1849), 174-5; *MM*, 14 Jan. 1800; SPL, 'Lloyd Scrapbook', 52, pr. s.sh. dated 29 Jan. 1800; WO 40/17, Holland Watson to William Windham, 2 Feb. 1800; *The Times*, 10 Feb. 1800.

51. HO 42/51/346-7, Prescot to |Portland|, 25 Sept. 1800 (emphasis added). Cf. Barnes, *Corn Laws*, 79; Alan Booth, 'Food Riots in the North-West of England 1790-1801', *Past and Present*, 77 (1977), 84-107.

52. HO 42/55/89-90, Bancroft to King, Bolton, 15, 21 Dec. 1800.

53. *Annual Register*, 42 (1800), Chronicle, 141-4; CHES 24/180/5, Indictment of Joshua Castle; HO 42/53/297, Watson to Bayley, 15 Nov. 1800; /318, 320, Bayley to Portland, Manchester, 15, 16 Nov. 1800.

54. HO 42/56, 'A Return Made by the Clerk of the Peace for the County of Chester', 27 April 1801; S.I. Mitchell, 'Food Shortages and Public Order in Cheshire, 1757-1812', *TLCAS*, 81 (1982), 54-6, 60-1 and, esp., the conclusions at 66.

55. HO 42/61/432-3, T. Coke to Portland, Manchester, 4 April 1801; HO 42/62, William Robert Hay to Portland, Dukinfield, 4 May 1801; *The Times*, 12 May 1801.

56. HO 42/62, Fletcher to Pelham, Bolton, 28 July, 31 Aug. 1801; HO 42/65, same to same, Bolton, 7 Jan. 1802.

57. The following account is based on HO 42/65 Fletcher to Pelham, Bolton, 3 April, 7 July 1802. Mellish was a sometime Wigan tailor and infantry sergeant, whose examination of 27 Nov. 1803 (in PC 1/3583) has also been used.

58. *MGaz*, 7 Aug. 1802; William Clegg, *Freedom Defended or the Practice of Despots Exposed* (Manchester, |1802?|).

59. HO 42/64, Richard Walker to Earl Fitzwilliam, Ridings, 28 June 1802.

60. HO 42/65, Fletcher to Pelham, Bolton, 3 April 1802. Fletcher also stated that Manchester delegates went up to London on 23 March.

61. HO 42/65, Fletcher to King, Bolton, 31 July 1802; Elliott, 'Despard Conspiracy', 56-8. It is unclear whether this is the same McCabe who temporarily resided in a Stockport lodging house with the spy Mellish and who was an active local proselytiser for a short time.

62. PC 1/3583, Deposition of John Mellish, 27 Nov. 1803; HO 42/70, Fletcher to King, Bolton, 8 April 1803.

63. HO 42/68, Peploe Ward to HO, Chester, 28 Aug. 1803; HO 42/81, Fletcher to Hawkesbury, Bolton, 10 Aug. 1805.

64. CHES 24/182/1, Indictment of Hugh Davies; CHES 24/182/2-3, Recognisances of Edward Dixon and John Howard; W. Clegg, *Peace, and No War: or, Hints on the Necessity of a Change of His Majesty's Present Ministers* (Manchester, 1805). See also the *Anti-Gallican*, 1 (1804), which includes reprints of many loyalist tracts from the North-west of England.

65. HO 42/83, Fletcher to King, Bolton, 24 Dec. 1805.

66. It may have been the case that Bullocksmithy Jacobinism was thereafter amalgamated with the radical movement at nearby Stockport. The events of 1797-8 already revealed links between the two.

67. *Lion*, 25 April 1828, 31 July 1829; cf. *MGaz*, 4 May 1805, for a description of an aged 'eccentric genius' at Gee Cross; and W. Cooke Taylor, *Notes of a Tour in the Manufacturing Districts of Lancashire* (2nd edn, London, 1842), 142-60.

68. HO 42/153, Lloyd to Beckett, 7 Oct. 1816; HO 42/158, Lloyd to Beckett and Addington, 13 Jan. 1817; *SA*, 16 Feb. 1826.

69. Goodwin, *Friends*, 489-90.

Notes to Chapter 7

1. Bythell, *Handloom Weavers*, 43-4; S.J. Chapman, *The Lancashire Cotton Industry: A Study in Economic Development* (Manchester, 1904), 25; *HCJ*, 55 (1799-1800), 494; Unwin, *Oldknow*, 46-7; Radcliffe, *Origin*, 41-2.

2. 'Loomshops' adjoining or near weavers' cottages, and cellars containing four or fewer looms were, however, common. *MGaz*, 12 March 1808; Ashmore, *Industrial Archaeology*, 7.

3. PP 1842 (158) XXXV, 124; Andrew Corrie, *An Illustrated History of Methodism in Bramhall* (Manchester, 1971), 5; PP 1826-7 (550) V, Q 2262. On weavers leaving to fight in the war, see HO 42/47, John Singleton to HO, Wigan, 27 May 1799.

4. This analysis is based on the Stockport piece rate series found in PP 1808 (177) II, 28; PP 1812 (210) III, 274; PP 1824 (51) V, 419; *MGaz*, 27 Dec. 1823; BL, Add. MSS 27,804/185.

5. Unwin, *Oldknow*, 113.

6. Ibid., 112-13; *HCJ*, 55 (1799-1800), 493-4. Radcliffe's label 'golden age' can be found in his *Origin*, 63.

7. PP 1834 (44) XXVIII, 279A; Bythell, *Handloom Weavers*, 276.

8. Ibid., 12-13; PP 1808 (177) II, 4-7; PP 1812 (210) III, 274. For later variations, see PP 1834 (556) X, QQ 7174, 7176-7.

9. *The Times*, 2 June 1808; Guest, *Compendious History*, 38.

10. David Levine, *Family Formation in an Age of Nascent Capitalism* (New York, 1977), 33-4.

11. See *MM*, 17 June 1806, for an advertisement of a Gee Cross weaver who was seeking a position as a putter-out.

12. Unwin, *Oldknow*, 112; Radcliffe, *Origin*, 16, 40; *Plain Facts* ([Stockport?], 1810), pr. s.sh.; PP 1808 (177) II, 3.

13. These small masters were in an analogous position to the big masters in that they purchased cotton wool, put it out, and then sold the finished cloth. Another type of small master was in a *subordinate* position, taking out raw materials from a capitalist and receiving wages in compensation. He nevertheless might have had a small group working under him in his house or in the neighbourhood. In Oldknow's business empire, however, it was rare for an individual weaver to have more than four looms under his control. Unwin, *Oldknow*, 112-13.

14. PP 1808 (177) II, 5; William Radcliffe, *Letters on the Evils of the Exportation of Cotton Yarns* (Stockport, 1811), 18; Bythell, *Handloom Weavers*, 15.

15. Guest, *Compendious History*, 46-7.

16. Turner, *Trade Union Growth*, 59-61; Thomas Percival, *A Letter to a Friend* (Halifax, [1758]); *Articles and Orders, Made, Agreed Upon, and Appointed to be Observed by the Members Belonging to the Old Association Club, Heretofore Called The Weavers Club* (Manchester, 1771); FS 1/252B/351.

17. *MM*, 11, 18 Sept. 1781, 31 Dec. 1782.

18. HO 42/150, Lloyd to Beckett, 21 May 1816; Foster, *CSIR*, 36.

19. All accounts agree that the volume of twist exports first became a serious problem in the mid-1790s; see, for example, Radcliffe, *Origin*, 24-5; PP 1833 (690) VI, Q 652. Note also the formation of the Stockport Friendly Associated Cotton and Linen Weavers' Society at the end of 1797, which is mentioned in FS 2/1.

20. Radcliffe, *Origin*, 67; cf. Bamford, *Early Days*, 117, 119.

21. PP 1808 (177) II, 22,26; *MM*, 2 April 1799. The latter notice may have been made by the same Stockport masters' association which was formed in 1781 to prevent embezzlements during another slump; see *MM*, 7 Aug. 1781.

22. *An Address to the Inhabitants of Bolton* (Bolton, 1799), pr. s.sh.; *The Association of Weavers, &c. &c. To the Public* (Bolton, 1799), pr. s.sh.

23. See Radcliffe, *Origin*, 76-7, on what was apparently a weavers' delegate meeting on 29 June; see also PC 1/44/A. 158, Rev. Thomas Bancroft to Portland, Bolton, 30 July 1799; PC 1/44/A. 161, same to same, Bolton, 22 Aug. 1799.

24. *To the Cotton Weavers of the Several Counties of Chester, York, Lancaster, and Derby* (Manchester, 1799), pr. s.sh.; *To the Nobility, Gentry, and People of Great Britain* ([Bolton?], 1799), pr. s.sh.; *MGaz*, 21 Dec. 1799.

25. *HCJ*, 55 (1799-1800), 261-2, 493-4, 784.

26. Ibid., 57 (1801-2), 136-7; *MM*, 23 Feb., 2 March 1802.

27. *MC*, 19 Feb. 1803; *HCJ*, 58 (1802-3), 168, 275-6, 511-12, 630. The central masters' committee at Manchester ultimately spent £2,000 to oppose the Act. *MM*, 5 June 1804.

28. PP 1802-3 (114) VIII, 20-2, 63-6. That the Stockport masters' complaints were generally voiced is borne out by the anonymous *Observations on the Cotton Weavers' Act* (Manchester, 1804), 6-8.

29. *HCJ*, 59 (1803-4), 79, 431; PP 1803-4 (41) V; J.L. Hammond and Barbara Hammond, *The Skilled Labourer 1760-1832* (London, 1919), 68; but cf. PP 1834 (556) X, QQ 7195, 7197.

30. *HCJ*, 58 (1802-3), 890; Chapman, *Lancashire Cotton,* 65n.1.

31. In opposition to twist export see especially [William Radcliffe?], *Thoughts on the State of the Manufacturers, and the Exportation of Twist* (Stockport, 1800); for the opposing side, see *On the Exportation of Twist. Twenty-Two Queries to the Manufacturers* (Manchester, [1800?]), pr. s.sh.

32. *At a Special Meeting Held . . . the 22nd of April, 1800* (Manchester, 1800), pr. s.sh.; *At a Numerous and Respectable Meeting* (Manchester, 1800), pr. s.sh.; Samuel Marsland, *At a Numerous and Respectable General Meeting* (Manchester, 1800), pr. s.sh.; Radcliffe, *Origin,* 11-12.

33. John Foster, 'The Making of the First Six Factory Acts', *Bulletin of the Society for the Study of Labour History,* 18 (1969) 4-5.

34. J[ohn] S[ilvester], *A View of the Cotton Manufactories of France* (Manchester, 1803); see also [Theophelus Lewis Rupp], *A Third Letter to the Inhabitants of Manchester, on the Exportation of Cotton Twist* (Manchester, 1803). For anti-export arguments at this time, see George Walker, *Observations Founded on Facts, upon the Propriety or Impropriety of Exporting Cotton Twist* (London, 1803).

35. Radcliffe, *Origin,* 30-5; PP 1808 (179) II, 7.

36. Radcliffe, *Origin,* 35; idem, *Letters,* 5-13.

37. This Act pegged bounties on grain exports and duties on imports to a new schedule of domestic price levels. It has been called 'a piece of class legislation [which] was harmless in the end only because even more unusual circumstances rendered inoperative the price levels fixed'. Barnes, *Corn Laws,* 89.

38. HO 42/80, Fletcher to King, Bolton, 16 Feb. 1805; HO 42/82, same to same, Bolton, 16 Jan., 7 March 1805; *HCJ*, 60 (1805), 83; *MGaz*, 25 Aug. 1804, 2, 9 March 1805.

39. In Radcliffe, *Letters,* 15-30; see also *HCJ*, 62 (1807), 169; *MC*, 14 March 1807.

40. *MGaz*, 22 Aug. 1807; Henry Hunt, *Memoirs of Henry Hunt, Esq.,* 3 vols. (London, 1821), II, 275-80. Hunt (ibid., 301) referred to Manchester district inhabitants as 'misguided men [who] had not then been taught to look for redress by obtaining a reform in the representation'.

41. *MGaz*, 28 Nov., 5, 12, 26 Dec. 1807, 16 Jan. 1808; HO 42/91, Fletcher to Hawkesbury, Bolton, 27 Dec. 1807. In a paper written with John Griffith, the Rev. John Gatliffe of Didsbury argued that distress was caused not by the Continental wars but by '*War with Heaven and its God,* by men opposing Divine Counsels and rejecting Divine Government in the heart and life'. *An Address to the Inhabitants of Manchester and Salford* (Manchester, 1808).

42. *MGaz*, 26 Dec. 1807, 5, 12 March 1808; *A Short Sketch, or Memoir of the Late Joseph Hanson, Esq.* (Salford, 1811), 13-15.

43. *HCJ*, 63 (1808), 123; HO 42/95, Fletcher to Hawkesbury, [Bolton, received 24]

Feb. 1808. For Sir Robert Peel's claim that over 95 per cent of the signatures on the Manchester peace petition were phoney, see *PD*, 11 (1808), 35.

44. PP 1808 (179) II, 7; PP 1834 (556) X, QQ 7300-2.

45. Ibid., QQ 5400, 5676; *HCJ*, 63 (1808), 81, 183; 150-1, 157, 170, 180, 261.

46. PP 1808 (177) II, 3-7.

47. *PD*, 9 (1808), 425-8; HO 42/95, Farington to |Hawkesbury?|, Manchester, 26 May 1808. Average prices for oats in Cheshire were 22 per cent higher on 21 May than they had been just two weeks before. *London Gazette*, 10-14 May, 24-28 May 1808.

48. For this and the broad outlines of the account that follows, see CHES 24/183/4, 'Journal of Proceedings at Stockport', 23 May to 4 July 1808.

49. *The Times*, 27, 28 May 1808; *ST*, 31 (1809-13), 1-99; L.W. Praizer, *Remarks on Slander and Envy* (Manchester, |1809|), 55.

50. See the note on persons apprehended in CHES 24/183/4.

51. HO 42/95, Prescot and John Philips to Hawkesbury, 28 May 1808. Cf. TS 11/836/2821/6-12, Crown Brief in *R. v. Leah and others*.

52. *The Times*, 3 June 1808; HO 42/95, Farington to Hawkesbury, Manchester, 31 May 1808; Ralph Wright to Perceval, Manchester, 31 May 1808.

53. Ibid., Farington to Hawkesbury, Manchester, 9 June 1808; *To the Public in General, and to the Cotton Manufacturers and Weavers* (Manchester, 1808), pr. s.sh. A handbill printed on 1 June gives a minimum wage schedule: *Prices of Weaving* (Bolton, 1808), pr. s.sh.

54. HO 42/95, Farington to Hawkesbury, Manchester, 16 June 1808.

55. It was apparently on this occasion that another Volunteer, Thomas Bunting, threw down his arms while on duty: see the note on persons apprehended in CHES 24/183/4.

56. TS 11/836/2821/13-20, Crown Briefs in *R. v. Handford* and *R. v. Wharmby*; CHES 24/183/4, 'List of Persons Apprehended on the 14th June 1808 at Cross Acres Green'.

57. Ibid., Deposition of Thomas Steel and others; ibid., 'List of Persons Apprehended on the 15th June Coming from Thatcher's Wood'.

58. Peter Brown and T. Cartwright, *Protection for the Industrious Weavers* (Stockport, 1808), pr. s.sh.; Bythell, *Handloom Weavers*, 101.

59. The Manchester crowd explicitly rejected the use of violence at its 24 May meeting. The actions of Stockport crowds suggest a similar determination. HO 42/95, Farington to Hawkesbury, Manchester, 24 May 1808.

60. TS 11/836/2821/1-5.

61. HO 42/95, Farington to Hawkesbury, Manchester, 4, 9, 14 June 1808; CHES 24/183/4, Deposition of Thomas Gatley.

62. Wood was arrested on 15 June. For the Artificers' Society, see FS 1/25/20, 1/29/251.

63. QJB 30a (1808-11), 16-17.

64. HO 42/188, E. Shawney and Richard Molloy, Account of 28 June 1819 Stockport Meeting; PRO, RG 4/7; HO 42/153, Lloyd to Beckett, 7 Oct. 1816; HO 42/158, Lloyd to the Under-Secretary of State, Macclesfield, 2 Jan. 1817; Bamford, *Passages*, I, 215; *To the Reformers* |Carlile|, 24 June, 13 Oct. 1821; *Republican*, 5 April, 20 Sept., 20 Dec. 1822.

65. *MO*, 29 Aug. 1818; HO 42/195, Deposition of ?, 18 Sept. 1819; HO 42/199, Information of Samuel Fleming, 27 Nov. 1819; *Lion*, 28 March 1828; PP 1824 (51)

V, 417.

66. *HCJ*, 64 (1809), 95, 196; Norman Murray, *The Scottish Hand Loom Weavers 1790-1850: A Social History* (Edinburgh, 1978), 186-7.

67. *The Times*, 25 June 1808.

Notes to Chapter 8

1. Thompson, *MEWC*, 646.

2. Malcolm I. Thomis, *The Luddites – Machine Breaking in Regency England* (London, 1970), 27. Cf. John Stevenson, *Popular Disturbances in England 1700-1870* (London, 1979), 158-9; *MGaz*, 1 Aug. 1812; Robert Eveleigh Taylor, *Letter on the Subject of the Lancashire Riots in the Year 1812* (Bolton, 1813), 7.

3. Harold Priestley, *Voice of Protest: A History of Civil Unrest in Great Britain* (London, 1968), 196; John Dinwiddy, 'Luddism and Politics in the Northern Counties', *Social History*, 4 (1979), 41.

4. Hammond, *Skilled Labourer*, 277-86; Malcolm I. Thomis, *The Town Labourer and the Industrial Revolution* (London, 1974), 129-30.

5. Prentice, *Manchester*, 37-40; Radcliffe, *Origin*, 18.

6. Quoted in Howard Hodson, 'Martin Swindells I: His Diary' in *Cotton Town: Bollington and the Swindells Family in the 19th Century* (Wilmslow, 1973), 17.

7. Thomis, *Town Labourer*, 78; idem, *Luddites*, 17-21, 57-8, 78, 95; idem and Peter Holt, *Threats of Revolution in Britain 1789-1848* (London, 1977), 33-5.

8. PP 1812 (210) III, 266-70, 273-6.

9. HO 40/1/1/3, Lloyd to Richard Ryder, 3 March 1812, enclosing deposition.

10. HO 42/120, Lloyd to Ryder, 26 Feb. 1812.

11. Cole, *Short History*, 63; E.J. Hobsbawm, 'The Machine Breakers' [1952] in *Labouring Men: Studies in the History of Labour* (New York, 1964), 5-22.

12. Frank Ongley Darvall, *Popular Disturbances and Public Order in Regency England* (Oxford, 1934), 197; Thomis, *Luddites*, 78, 95.

13. *Annual Register*, 54 (1812), 132; HO 40/1/1/236-9, Maitland to Ryder, Manchester, 4 May 1812; Dinwiddy, 'Luddism', 63; Foster, *CSIR*, 40, 139, 143; Thompson, *MEWC*, 624, 646-56; idem, 'The Moral Economy of the English Crowd in the Eighteenth Century', *Past and Present*, 50 (1971), 107-8, 128-9.

14. *HCJ*, 68 (1812-13), 521. For Cheshire grain prices in 1811-12, see CRO, QJF 238/2-4, 240/1-4, 241/1.

15. PRO, CHES 24/184/4-5. One of Swindell's employees damaged some machinery belonging to the firm in June, but whether this was due to malicious intentions or negligence is unclear from the evidence. CRO, QJB 30a (1808-11), 311-12.

16. Bythell, *Handloom Weavers*, 101-2; François Crouzet, *L'Economie britannique et le blocus continental (1806-1813)*, 2 vols. (Paris, 1958), II, 630-1; *To the Manufacturers of Blackburn* (Blackburn, 1810), pr. s.sh.

17. [George Beaumont], *The Beggar's Complaint* (2nd edn, Sheffield, 1812), 46-7, 106-7; HO 42/115, 'The Humble Petition of the Cotton Weavers of the Town of Stockport and Neighbourhood'; PRO, BT 5/20/411-12.

18. Cf. ibid., 5/20/294-6; *HCJ*, 66 (1810-11), 383, 394, 425, 452; PP 1810-11 (232) II, 3.

19. HO 42/114, Fletcher to Beckett, Bolton, 25 Feb. 1811; Dinwiddy, 'Luddism', 37.

20. Radcliffe, *Letters*, *passim*; idem, *Origin*, 4-5; *HCJ*, 64 (1809), 95.

21. *MGaz*, 13 May, 10 June 1809; *Hampden Club* (London, 1814); Hunt, *Memoirs*, II, 435-79; F.D. Cartwright, *The Life and Correspondence of Major Cartwright*, 2 vols. (London, 1826), II, 10, 374; Naomi C. Miller, 'Major John Cartwright and the Founding of the Hampden Club', *Historical Journal*, 17 (1974), 615-17.

22. HO 42/117, Fletcher to Beckett, [Bolton], 12 Oct. 1811, and reports of 'B' enclosed.

23. Richard Taylor, *To the Manufacturers, Mechanics, Artizans, and Others (Inhabitants of Manchester and Its Vicinity)* (Manchester, 1811), pr. s.sh. It is believed that the radical John Knight was the real author of this broadside; see Marshall, *Public Opinion*, 133.

24. HO 42/117, Fletcher to Beckett, Bolton, 21 Nov. 1811, enclosing reports of 'B'; Dinwiddy, 'Luddism', 40, 49, 51.

25. HO 42/118, Warren Bulkeley to Ryder, 26 Dec. 1811; same to same, Poynton, 1 Jan. 1812. Cf. *The Journal and Correspondence of William, Lord Auckland*, (ed. George Hogge), 4 vols. (London, 1860-2), IV, 377-8, Warren Bulkeley to Auckland, Poynton, 18 Dec. 1811: 'Trade in this country is low, but rather livelier than it has been . . .'

26. HO 42/119, Fletcher to Beckett, Bolton, 21 Jan. 1812, enclosing reports of 'B'; HO 42/120, same to same, Bolton, 25 Feb. 1812, enclosing reports of 'B'.

27. Dinwiddy, 'Luddism', 49; *London Gazette*, 20–24 March 1792. For a common version of the Luddite oath and background on the Luddite system, see PP 1812 (335) II.

28. HO 42/120, Fletcher to Ryder, Bolton, 6 Feb. 1812; Fletcher to Beckett, Bolton, 25 Feb. 1812, enclosure; HO 40/1/1/170–3, John Lloyd, 'Memorandums of Conversations with Yarwood on the 19th June 1812'; /47–53, 'Copy of H. Yarwood's Statement 27 June 1812'.

29. *HCJ*, 67 (1812), 207–8, 220–1; HO 42/131, 'Account of Factories, Mills, etc. Attacked or Destroyed'.

30. HO 42/120, Lloyd to Warren Bulkeley, Manchester, 11 Feb. 1812.

31. Ibid., J. Mayer to ?, Manchester, 11 Feb. 1812. Mayer was involved with the thriving Stockport Sunday School, the largest institution of its kind in England at that time.

32. HO 42/128, Declarations of Oliver Nicholson and James Lyon, 7 Oct. 1812; HO 42/121, James Warr to Fletcher, Bolton, 21 March 1812; HO 42/127, Lloyd to Beckett, Huddersfield, 10 Sept. 1812. See also n. 9 above.

33. HO 42/120, Fletcher to Beckett, Bolton, 25 Feb. 1812, enclosing reports of 'B'; Lloyd to Ryder, 26 Feb. 1812; HO 42/128, Richard Clayton to Sidmouth, Adlington nr. Wigan, 12 Oct. 1812, enclosure.

34. PP 1824 (51) V, 417–18; *MGaz*, 28 March 1812.

35. HO 40/1/1/5–6, Lloyd to Ryder, 21 March 1812; /7–8, Radcliffe's Memorial to Ryder, same date; *Cobbett's Political Register*, 25 April 1812; *A Most Daring Attack* (Stockport, 1812), pr. s.sh. For a useful contemporary survey of Stockport district Luddism, see Francis Raynes, *An Appeal to the Public* (London, 1817).

36. KB 8/90/58–9, Examination of John Parnell, 17 April 1812; /68, Deposition of John Lloyd, 20 April 1812.

37. Bamford, *Early Days*, 295–7; *Now or Never* (Manchester, 1812), pr. s.sh.; *Gentleman's Magazine*, 82:1 (1812), 381; Hammond, *Skilled Labourer*, 286.

38. HO 40/1/1/10–11, Lloyd to Ryder, Chester, 13 April 1812. For a discussion of

General Ludd's wives in the context of traditional protest-transvestism, see Natalie Zemon Davis, 'Women on Top' in *Society and Culture in Early Modern France: Eight Essays* (Stanford, 1975), 148.

39. It may have been on this occasion that Radcliffe's wife 'was so alarmed and injured by the rioters that she died a few weeks later'. See entry on Radcliffe in the *DNB*.

40. *Cobbett's Political Register*, 25 April 1812; TS 11/370/1160, Cheshire Special Commission, Spring 1812.

41. Cf. the hyperbole already entering the tale by 1814: Henderson, *Industrial Britain*, 50.

42. I am indebted to John B. McKee, a descendant of Goodair's, for details on Goodair's career.

43. HO 42/1/1/22–3, 'General Justice' to ?, 16 April 1812.

44. HO 40/1/1/159–60, Deposition of Thomas Whitehead, 18 June 1812; /163–4, Deposition of Joseph Taylor, 18 June 1812; *Much Injured! Long Oppressed Countrymen!!!* (Manchester, 1812), pr. s.sh. See also Yarwood's statements cited in n. 28 above.

45. *HCJ*, 67 (1812), 348–9, 374–5; Cartwright, *Life*, II, 30–2.

46. TS 11/1059/4766, Crown Brief in *R. v. Washington and others* (1812); *Trial at Full Length of the 38 Men. From Manchester* (Manchester, 1812).

47. HO 40/1/1/10–11, Lloyd to Ryder, Chester, 13 April 1812; *Chester Chronicle*, 24 April 1812.

48. TS 11/370/1160, Crown Brief in *R. v. Renshaw;* KB 8/90/100, Deposition of Thomas Croft, 2 May 1812.

49. TS 11/370/1160, Crown Brief in *R. v. London and others*; KB 8/90/52–3; HO 40/1/1/14–18, Lloyd to Ryder, 18 April 1812.

50. HO 40/1/1/24–7, Prescot to Ryder, 21, 27 April 1812.

51. TS 11/370/1160, Crown Brief in *R. v. Temple.*

52. HO 42/123, Whitaker to the Governor of Chester Castle, Chester Castle, n.d. [c. 29 May 1812]; HO 42/121, Information of Thomas Whitaker, 4 July 1812.

53. HO 40/1/1/16–17, Lloyd to Ryder, 18 April 1812; Thompson, *MEWC*, 618–19.

54. TS 11/370/1160, Crown Briefs in *R. v. Haywood* and *R. v. Redfern and Hurst*; Davies, *Macclesfield*, 180; Bamford, *Early Days*, 360; *MGaz*, 18, 25 April 1812.

55. Quoted (from the MS diary of the Rev. James Brooks) in Thomas Middleton, *The History of Hyde and Its Neighbourhood* (Hyde, 1932), 72.

56. John Aiken, *Annals of the Reign of King George the Third*, 2 vols. (2nd edn, London, 1820), II, 380; cf. Mitchell, 'Food Shortages'. 64–6.

57. *From Bishop Blaze to the Misguided Men who Destroy Machinery* (Manchester, 1812), 3.

58. HO 102/22/282–4, Francis Ronaldson to Francis Freeling, Glasgow, 1 June 1812; HO 40/1/1/33–4, Lloyd to Ryder, 2 May 1812.

59. *London Gazette*, 28–31 March 1812; HO 42/122, 'Special General Session of the Peace, 23 April 1812'; SPL, HX 440, Cheadle Bulkeley Constables' Accounts, 24 April 1812, and additional related entries through Aug. of that year; *MGaz*, 16, 23 May 1812; CRO, MG 24/2, Ryder to the Earl of Stamford and Warrington, Whitehall, 28 April 1812.

60. [W. Duckworth], *Fellow Weavers!* (Manchester, 1812), pr. s.sh.; [idem], *Second Letter, Fellow Weavers!* (Manchester, 1812), pr. s.sh.; *To All Brave and Loyal Englishmen* (Manchester, 1812), pr. s.sh.; Middleton, *Hyde*, 69.

61. On Luddite colliers, see Darvall, *Popular Disturbances*, 173.

62. KB 8/90, Cheshire Special Commission, 1812.

63. *Philanthropist*, 2 (1812), 229–38; ibid., 3 (1813), 143–4, 374–8; *Macclesfield Courier*, 13 June 1812.

64. HO 40/2/1/12–13, Lt. Col. Nelthorpe to Maj.-Gen. Acland, 2 June 1812; /24–5, same to same, 19 June 1812; HO 40/1/1/147–8, 'Extract of a Letter from R.W. -Stockport' and 'Extract from the Second Letter from R.W. 17 June 1812' ; *Chester Chronicle*, 26 June 1812; *Cobbett's Political Register*, 4 July 1812.

65. PP 1812 (210) III, 267; SPL, SSS MSS, B/G/4/1, Scholars' Register, 1 (1789–1824); HO 40/2/1/37–8, Nelthorpe to Acland, 24 June 1812.

66. HO 100/168/74–5, Michael Farrell to Charles Saxton, Dublin, 16 Aug. 1812; /120–1, 'E.H.' to Edward Knight, 23 Aug. 1812.

67. HO 42/129, Deposition of James Knott, 8 Sept. 1812.

68. HO 40/1/1/264–5, Maitland to Sidmouth, Manchester, 16 June 1812; HO 42/124, same to same, Manchester, 19 June 1812; HO 40/1/1/141–2, Broughton and Tatton to Sidmouth, Cheadle Bulkeley and Manchester, 17 June 1812; HO 40/2/1/20–1, 'Accounts received by the Magistrates of unlawful seizure of fire arms', 17 June 1812; *MGaz*, 27 June 1812; Middleton, *Hyde*, 70.

69. HO 40/1/1/56–7, Lloyd to HO, 17 June 1812; HO 40/2/1/24–5, 37–8, 39–40, Nelthorpe to Acland, 19, 24, 25 June 1812; HO 40/2/7/1077–81, Acland to Maitland, Manchester, 25, 30 June 1812; Raynes, *Appeal*, 29–31.

70. HO 42/125, Hay to Beckett, Manchester, 26 July 1812; Lloyd to Beckett, 30 July 1812; HO 40/2/1/75–6, Raines to Maitland, Roe Cross nr. Mottram, 25 July 1812; HO 42/125, Lloyd to Beckett, 30 July 1812.

71. HO 49/6/281–2, Beckett to H.C. Litchfield, Whitehall, 29 Aug. 1812; HO 43/21/217–19, J.H. Addington to G.H. Clarke and others, Whitehall, 24 Sept. 1812.

72. HO 42/126, Prescot to [Sidmouth], 23 Aug. 1812; *Courier*, 26 Aug. 1812.

73. HO 40/2/1/110–11, 134–5, Prescot to Acland, 25 Aug., 12 Sept 1812; HO 42/126, Robert Pratt to [Sidmouth], 29 Aug. 1812; HO 42/127, Prescot to Beckett, 20 Sept. 1812; Raynes, *Appeal*, 60–82; *MGaz*, 12 Sept. 1812.

74. HO 42/127, Farington to Sidmouth, Didsbury, 13 Sept. 1812; HO 42/128, same to same, Didsbury, 2 Oct. 1812.

75. R.A. Farington *et al.. Illegal Oaths* (Manchester, 1812), pr. s.sh.

76. *MGaz*, 31 Oct. 1812; HO 42/128, Lloyd to J.H. Addington, Congleton, 9 Oct. 1812; HO 42/129, Prescot to Beckett, 8 Nov. 1812; HO 42/132, Earl of Stamford and Warrington to Sidmouth, Enville, 1 Feb. 1813; *HCJ*, 68 (1812–13), 521.

77. Ibid., 172, 185, 229, 282, 308, 416; Hammond, *Skilled Labourer*, 86–8.

78. Cartwright, *Life*, II, 34–42, 47–50; *MGaz*, 5 Sept. 1812.

79. Thompson, *MEWC*, 668; HO 42/153, Lloyd to Beckett, 18 Sept. 1816; Dinwiddy, 'Luddism', 60.

80. *MGaz*, 11 Jan., 25 Jan. 1812.

81. HO 40/1/1/28–9, H.D. Broughton to HO, Cheadle, 27 April 1812; *MGaz*, 19 Sept. 1812. It is not clear whether this was the same John Thorp whose Manchester warehouse was robbed of various pieces of cloth on the night of 13–14 Oct.; cf. ibid., 17 Oct. 1812. See also ibid., 28 Nov. 1812, for a report that croft breaking in the vicinity of Manchester 'has of late, we are sorry to observe, extended to an unprecedented degree'.

82. PP 1812 (210) III, 269.

83. Perkin, *OMES*, 181; Dinwiddy, 'Luddism', 63. Cf. Francis Hearn, *Domination*,

Legitimation, and Resistance: The Incorporation of the Nineteenth-Century English Working Class (Westport, Conn., 1978), 115.

Notes to Chapter 9

1. Cartwright, *Life*, II, 38–42; J.R. Dinwiddy, 'Sir Francis Burdett and Burdettite Radicalism', *History*, 65 (1980), 23; T[homas] P[arsons], *Christianity, a System of Peace* (2nd edn, Stockport, 1813); *War Inconsistent with the Doctrine and Example of Jesus Christ* (Stockport, 1814); HO 42/136, Fletcher to Beckett, Bolton, 16 Dec. 1813; HO 42/138, Joseph Nadin to HO, Manchester, 26 March 1814.

2. PP 1821 (668) IX, 454; cf. John D. Post, *The Last Great Subsistence Crisis in the Western World* (Baltimore, 1977).

3. Quoted in Graham Wallas, *The Life of Francis Place 1771–1854* (London, 1898), 141; Heginbotham, *Stockport*, I, 76.

4. HO 42/150, Lloyd to Beckett, 13, 20, 21 May 1816.

5. Ibid., Prescot to Sidmouth, 21 May 1816; Joseph Sherwin to Wilbraham Egerton, 21 May 1816; Lloyd to Beckett, 26 May 1816; *HCJ*, 71 (1816–17), 393–4.

6. HO 42/150, Prescot to Sidmouth, 21 May 1816; Lloyd to Beckett, 20 May 1816.

7. Ibid., Lloyd to Beckett, 26, 27 May 1816; HO 42/151, same to same, 25 June 1816; Fletcher to Beckett, Bolton, 27 May 1816; Hammond, *Skilled Labourer*, 99; *The Humble Memorial of the . . . Manufacturers of Cotton Goods, and Workmen* (Stockport, 1816), pr. s.sh.

8. Radcliffe *Origin*, 199; *Manchester Magazine*. 2 (1816), 329; HO 42/152, Sherwin to Warren Bulkeley, 29 July 1816; Warren Bulkeley to Sidmouth, Stanhope St. [London], 12 August 1816.

9. HO 42/150, Lloyd to Beckett, 20 May 1816; HO 42/152, same to same, 23 July 1816

10. HO 42/151, Lloyd to Beckett, 25 June 1816.

11. HO 42/152, Lloyd to Beckett, 6, 11 July 1816; *The Times*, 31 July 1816; John Lloyd, *The Committee for Employing the Poor* (Stockport, 1816), pr. s.sh.

12. HO 42/152, E.R. Travers to Sidmouth, Preston, 13, 19 Aug. 1816; Lloyd to Beckett, 17 Aug. 1816.

13. Ibid., Lloyd to Beckett, 26, 27, 29, 31 Aug. 1816; HO 42/153, same to same, 1, 2 Sept. 1816.

14. Ibid.; HO 42/153, Lloyd to Beckett, 18 Sept., 8 Oct. 1816; a remark of Bamford's (himself a weaver) suggests that weavers also predominated in the Middleton Club. Bamford, *Passages*, I, 44.

15. *The Times*, 22 Aug. 1816; HO 42/152, Fletcher to Beckett, Bolton, 28 Aug. 1816; HO 42/153, William Fitton to John Kay, Royton, 3 Sept. 1816; Lloyd to Beckett, 26, 30 Sept. 1816; MCL, MS F363 D1, Documents concerning the Formation of Hampden Clubs 1816–17; Hunt, *Memoirs*, III, 410; Thompson, *MEWC*, 678–9; H.W.C. Davis, 'Lancashire Reformers, 1816–17', *Bulletin of the John Rylands Library*, 10 (1926), 51–2.

16. HO 42/153, Lloyd to Beckett, 18 Sept. 1816; Prescot and Marsland to Sidmouth, 18 Sept. 1816; Prescot to Beckett, 23 Sept. 1816; Fletcher to Beckett, Bolton, 26 Sept. 1816, enclosing report of 'B'.

17. Ibid., Lloyd to Sidmouth, 30 Sept., 6 Oct. 1816; *Parliamentary Reform* (Stockport, 1816 [30 Sept.]), pr. s.sh.; John Lloyd, *Reforming Parliament* (Stockport,

1816), pr. s.sh.; *Public Meeting* (Stockport, 1816), pr. s.sh.

18. HO 42/153, Lloyd to Beckett, 7, 8 Oct. 1816; *The Petitions of the People to the Prince Regent* (Bath, 1816), pr. s.sh.

19. Leary, *Yeomanry*, 48; HO 42/155, Byng to the Under-Secretary of State, Pontefract, 24 Nov. 1816; Fletcher to Addington, Bolton, 5, 30 Nov. 1816; HO 42/156, William Chippendale to Joseph Warren, Oldham, 2 Dec. 1816; Lloyd to Beckett, 3 Dec. 1816.

20. SPL, SSS MSS, B/S/5/3, E. Howard to SSS Committee, 7 Dec. 1816; HO 42/156, Lloyd to Beckett and Addington, 12 Dec. 1816; HO 42/157, Lloyd to Addington, 19, 21, 24 Dec. 1816.

21. *To the Public* (Manchester, 1816), pr. s.sh.; *To the People of England* (Manchester, 1816); Bamford, *Passages*, I, 9–10.

22. *Public Meeting* (Manchester, 1816), pr. s.sh.; *Manchester Meeting* (Manchester, 1816), pr. s.sh.; HO 42/157, Lloyd to Addington, 24 Dec. 1816; HO 42/162, Lloyd to Beckett and Addington, [31 Dec. 1816]; HO 42/158, Lloyd to the Under-Secretary of State, Macclesfield, 2 Jan. 1817; Lloyd to the Under-Secretaries of State, 4 Jan. 1817.

23. *Public Meeting* (Manchester, 1817 [10 Jan.]), pr. s.sh.; [John Lloyd], *Public Meeting* (Stockport, 1817), pr. s.sh.; HO 42/158, Lloyd to Beckett and Addington, 13 Jan. 1817; Ralph Wright to Sidmouth, Flixton, 11 Jan. 1817; Joseph Green and others to Sidmouth, Manchester, 18 Jan. 1817.

24. Cf. also the subsequent anti-reform pamphlet campaign of the Manchester Pitt Club directed primarily towards an audience of weavers: MCL, MS FF 367 M56, Manchester Pitt Club, Minutes of the Select Committee on Political Tracts, entries of 17–31 Jan. 1817; [Francis Philips], *A Dialogue between Thomas, the Weaver, and his Old Master* (Manchester, 1817); [C.D. Wray], *The Street Politicians: or, a Debate About the Times* (Manchester, 1817).

25. HO 42/3/13–14, Lloyd to the Under-Secretary, 7 Jan 1817; HO 42/158, same to same, 21 Jan. 1817; HO 42/159, same to same, 2, 8 Feb. 1817; *At a Special General Meeting of the Members of the Orange Institution* (Manchester, 1817), pr. s.sh.; John Philips, *To John Philips, Esq.* (Stockport, 1817), pr. s.sh.; Charles Prescot, *Stockport* (Stockport, 1817), pr. s.sh.

26. HO 40/3/117–18, 'Middleton Meeting of Delegates', 13 Jan. 1817; HO 42/158, Lloyd to the Under-Secretaries, 21 Jan. 1817; HO 42/159, same to same, 10 Feb. 1817; *Manchester Political Register*, 1 Feb. 1817.

27. PP 1817 (34) IV; HO 42/158, Ethelston to Sidmouth, Longsight, 29 Jan. 1817; TS 11/1029/4414, Information of 'A.B.', 31 Jan. 1817; HO 42/164, 'A.B.' to [Fletcher?], Bolton, 2 March 1817; *Public Meeting* (Manchester, 1817 [28 Feb.]), pr. s.sh.; Bamford, *Passages*, I, 32; HO 42/161, Lloyd to the Under-Secretaries, 3, 5 March 1817; *HCJ*, 72 (1817), 128.

28. HO 42/162, W.D. Evans to Sidmouth, Manchester, 18 March 1817.

29. *Macclesfield Courier*, 15 March 1817; *Hone's Reformists' Register*, 12 April 1817; HO 42/164, Hay to Sidmouth, Manchester, 10 March 1817; HO 42/161, Lloyd to Beckett, 10, 13, 15 March 1817; TS 11/1029/4414, 'The Meeting at St Peter's Church, March 10th 1817'.

30. HO 42/164, bundle of papers relating to the Blanketeers; PP 1818 (HL 23) XCIV; *Annual Report of the SSS* (Stockport, 1817).

31. Bamford, *Passages*, I, 37–9, 76–9; HO 42/162, Joseph Green and others to Sidmouth, Manchester, 18 March 1817; TS 11/1029/4414, J. Warr to ?, Bolton, 24

March 1817; HO 42/164, William Chippendale to Joseph Green, Oldham, 25 March 1817.

32. HO 42/163, Lloyd to W.R. Hay or W.D. Evans, 9 April 1817; John Stephens to Sidmouth, Chester, 14 April 1817; Bamford, *An Account of the Arrest and Imprisonment of Samuel Bamford, Middleton, on Suspicion of High Treason* (Manchester, 1817); HO 42/164, Examination of Richard Flitcroft, 22 April 1817; Proceedings before Lord Sidmouth, 29 April 1817; HO 42/165, John Reys (for Richard Flitcroft) to HO, Chelmsford Gaol, 7 May 1817; HO 41/3/469, Addington to the Keeper of Chelmsford Gaol, 12 Nov. 1817. Flitcroft discussed his arrest and imprisonment in a letter to the *Black Dwarf*, 13 May 1818.

33. TS 11/1029/4414, Narrative of Richard Flitcroft, 23 May 1817. Many prominent radicals (including Bamford) in fact disapproved of the Blanketeers' march. Hammond, *Skilled Labourer*, 343; Bamford, *Passages*, I, 30-1. Bamford adds (I, 44) that the Middleton Club also went out of existence at about the time of the march.

34. HO 42/165, Lloyd to Becket, 17 May 1817.

35. For the London and Stockport petitions, see *HCJ*, 72 (1817), 244-5, 325. See also J.B. Sharp, *Letters on the Exportation of Cotton Yarns* (London, 1817); Radcliffe, *Origin*, 169.

36. *MC*, 23 Sept. 1817; Marshall, *Public Opinion*, 142.

37. *Proceedings of the Hampden Club* (London, 1816); H.W.C. Davis, *The Age of Grey and Peel: Being the Ford Lectures for 1926* (Oxford, 1929), 174.

38. Thomas Evans, *Christian Policy the Salvation of the Empire* (2nd edn, London, 1816); Rudkin, *Spence*, 142-7.

39. Ibid., 187-8. In order to justify and defend his actions, Henry Hunt minimised the role of the Spenceans at the two Spa Fields meetings. *Memoirs*, III, 328-34, 366-8.

40. Meikle, *Scotland*, 294; Iorwerth Prothero, 'William Benbow and the Concept of the "General Strike"', *Past and Present*, 63 (1974), 150-1; *PD*, 37 (1818), 223.

41. J.C. Belchem, 'Henry Hunt and the Evolution of the Mass Platform', *English Historical Review*, 93 (1978), 746-8; idem, 'Republicanism, Popular Constitutionalism and the Radical Platform in Early Nineteenth-century England', *Social History*, 6 (1981), 5-6.

42. HO 42/156, Prescot to Robert Langley Appleyard, 12 Dec. 1816; Donald Read, 'Lancashire Hampden Clubs: A Spy's Narrative', *Manchester Review*, 8 (1957-60), 84; Bamford, *Passages*, I, 8; *The Voice of God!!! In Support of the Grand Object of Parliamentary Reform* (Manchester, 1817).

43. HO 42/151, Lloyd to Beckett, 25 June 1816; HO 43/25/432, J.H. Addington to [Joseph Lane], Whitehall, 3 Feb. 1817; W.W. Pole, *Notice. New Silver Coinage* (Westminster, 1817), pr. s.sh.; HO 42/180, Prescot to [Sidmouth], 24 Sept. 1818.

44. HO 42/165, Lloyd to Beckett, 14 June 1817; PP 1817 (387), IV; PP 1817 (399) IV. The former parliamentary report concludes that 'the most active and determined insurgents' were not those suffering from great privations.

45. Leary, *Yeomanry*, 55; HO 42/165, Lloyd to Addington, 31 May 1817.

46. HO 42/153, Lloyd to Beckett, 8 Oct. 1816; HO 42/158, same to same, 13 Jan. 1817; *Hone's Reformists' Register*, 27 Sept. 1817.

47. Critic's remarks quoted in George Pellew, *The Life and Correspondence of the Right Honble Henry Addington, First Viscount Sidmouth*, 3 vols. (London, 1847), III, 176n.; see also Bamford, *Passages*, I, 7; *To the Journeymen Mechanics & Labouring Poor* (Stockport, [1816?]), pr. s.sh.

48. *HCJ*, 72 (1817), 839; HO 42/162, Lloyd to Beckett, 31 March 1817; HO 42/165, same to same, 17 May 1817; HO 42/169, Lloyd to the Under-Secretaries, [rec. 18 Aug. 1817]; HO 40/7/5/2160-2, same to same, 18 Jan. 1818; HO 42/175, Lloyd to Hobhouse, 7 March 1818; *Lion*, 10 April 1829.

49. On Lancashire reading societies which purchased reform tracts late in 1817, see *Black Dwarf*, 8 Oct. 1817; cf. A. Aspinall, 'The Circulation of Newspapers in the Early Nineteenth Century', *Review of English Studies*, 22 (1946), 30-2.

Notes to Chapter 10

1. *MO*, 2 May 1818. For early evidence of its availability at Stockport public houses, see ibid., 18 April 1818.

2. Ibid., 24, 31 Jan., 7 Feb. 1818, *The Times*, 3 Feb. 1818.

3. Olive D. Rudkin, *Thomas Spence and His Connections* (London, 1927), 189; *The Times*, 13 Feb., 5 March 1818; HO 42/173, Reports of N. Conant, London, 24-27 Jan. 1818; HO 42/174, Lloyd to Hobhouse, 7 Feb. 1818; *PD*, 37 (1818), 191-7, 438-44, 820-62; Prothero, *Artisans*, 100.

4. HO 42/174, Lloyd to Hobhouse, 12 Feb. 1818; *MO*, 14, 21 March 1818.

5. Ibid., 4 April 1818; HO 42/176, Prescot to Sidmouth, 2 April 1818; Lloyd to Hobhouse, 13 April 1818; *Black Dwarf*, 13 May 1818.

6. HO 42/177, Lloyd to Hobhouse, 19 May 1818.

7. HO 42/178, [Lloyd] to Byng, 14 Sept. 1818; *MO*, 17 Sept. 1818.

8. Ibid., 25 July 1818; cf. HO 42/178, Lloyd to Hobhouse, 19 July 1818.

9. *MO*, 25 July, 8, 15, 22, 29 Aug. 1818; [John Bagguley], *Oh! Horrible! Horrible! most Horrible!* (Manchester, 1818), pr. s.sh.; HO 42/179, Lloyd to Hobhouse, 10 Aug. 1818. The title of Bagguley's broadside was taken from *Hamlet*, I:5.

10. HO 42/179, Lloyd to Hobhouse, 11, 24, 25 Aug. 1818; David Ramsay to Sidmouth, 20 Aug. 1818; HO 42/180, [Lloyd] to Byng, 14 Sept. 1818; *MO*, 29 Aug. 1818.

11. HO 42/180, John Livesey, 'The Outlines of the Different Speeches made by the Reformers on Sandy Brow in Stockport', 1 Sept. 1818; Lloyd to Hobhouse, Chester, 3 Sept. 1818; *MO*, 17 Sept. 1818.

12. HO 42/178, Ramsay to Sidmouth, 18 July 1818; cf. PP 1824 (51) V, 356-7, 394-5.

13. *MO*, 25 July 1818; HO 42/178, Lloyd to Hobhouse, 23 July 1818; Fletcher to Hobhouse, Bolton, 26 July 1818; John Hibbert and Robert Ellison, *An Address to the Cotton Manufacturers of Lancashire, Yorkshire, Cheshire, Derbyshire, &c* (Bury, 1818), pr. s.sh.

14. Hammond, *Skilled Labourer*, 112 and nn.1-2; HO 42/179, Lloyd to Hobhouse, 5 Aug. 1818; *MC*, 8 Aug. 1818.

15. *To the Weavers of the Town of Stockport* (Manchester, 1818), pr. s.sh.; HO 42/179, Ramsay to Sidmouth, 20 Aug. 1818; James Brooks and Richard Kay, *At a Meeting of Deputies, for the Cotton Weavers* (Bury, 1818), pr. s.sh.

16. HO 42/179, Lloyd to Hobhouse, 24, 26 Aug. 1818; Hammond, *Town Labourer*, 261; *MO*, 29 Aug. 1818.

17. HO 42/179, Norris to Clive, Manchester, 31 Aug. 1818; HO 42/180, Lloyd to Hobhouse, Chester, 3 Sept. 1818; Norris to Clive, Manchester, 3 Sept. 1818; Prescot to Sidmouth, 3 Sept. 1818; *MC*, 5 Sept. 1818; Winifred M. Bowman, *England in*

Ashton-under-Lyne (Altrincham, 1960), 421.

18. HO 42/180, Chippendale to Sidmouth, Oldham, 6 Sept. 1818.

19. Ibid., Lloyd to Hobhouse, 10, 12 Sept. 1818; Lloyd to the Under-Secretary of State, 19 Sept. 1818; Lloyd to the Under-Secretaries, 26 Sept. 1818; PP 1824 (51) V, 417; HO 42/181, Lloyd to Clive, Knutsford, 22, 28 Oct. 1818.

20. HO 42/180, Ethelston to Sidmouth, Longsight, 29 Sept. 1818.

21. Ibid., Prescot to Sidmouth, 23 Sept. 1818; [Joseph Harrison], *Report of the Proceedings of a Numerous and Respectable Meeting* (Stockport, 1818); *Sherwin's Political Register*, 31 Oct. 1818; *Black Dwarf*, 4 Nov. 1818; *Manchester Spectator*, 7 Nov. 1818.

22. *A Full, Accurate, and Impartial Report of the Trial, of John Bagguley ... John Johnston ... and Samuel Drummond* (Manchester, 1819), 55, 63-4; HO 42/194, 'B' to Fletcher, n.p., 29 Aug. 1819; HO 42/203, same to same, n.p., 6 Jan. 1820.

23. *Declaration of the Object and Principles of the Union formed at Stockport, In October, 1818 for the Promotion of Human Happiness* (Stockport, 1819); *Black Dwarf*, 28 April 1819; *Sherwin's Political Register*, 5 June 1819; *Blanketteer*, 27 Nov. 1819.

24. In the United States Cobbett eventually received word of the 28 Sept. meeting which had voted him thanks. In response he devoted the whole 20 Feb. 1819 issue of his *Political Register* to the meeting and associated topics. The *Gorgon* (6 March 1819) then picked up Cobbett's account of the meeting. On Hunt and Wolseley, see *DNB*; HO 42/182, Lloyd to Clive, 3, 7 Dec. 1818; HO 42/183, Lloyd to Hobhouse, 20, 26, 28 Jan. 1819.

25. HO 42/181, Lloyd to Clive, 7, 12 Oct. 1818; HO 41/4/207-8, Clive to Lloyd, Whitehall, 14 Oct. 1818; T.M. Parsinnen, 'Association, Convention and Anti-parliament in British Radical Politics, 1771-1848', *English Historical Review*, 88 (1973), 516.

26. *MO*, 6 Feb. 1819. Membership cards, which appeared as early as November 1818, called the Union simply the 'Stockport Union Society for Constitutional Reform'.

27. *Black Dwarf*, 13 Jan. 1819.

28. Another source of Harrison's moderation in promoting human happiness may have been the ideas of Jeremy Bentham. See J.R. Dinwiddy, 'Bentham's Transition to Political Radicalism, 1809-1810', *Journal of the History of Ideas*, 36 (1975), 699-700; Richard Hendrix, 'Popular Humor and "The Black Dwarf"', *Journal of British Studies*, 16 (1976-7), 111; *PD*, 38 (1818), 1118-85. In *The Works of Jeremy Bentham* (ed. John Bowring), 11 vols. (Edinburgh, 1843), see: *Plan of Parliamentary Reform ...* [1817], III, 433-557; *The King against Sir Charles Wolseley, Baronet, and Joseph Harrison, Schoolmaster ...* [1820], V, 253-61.

29. HO 42/181, Lloyd to Clive, 5 Oct. 1818; TS 11/48/195/212, Crown Brief in *R. v. Harrison* (1820).

30. *MO*, 10 July 1819; PRO, RG 4/7.

31. Notably Robert F. Wearmouth, *Methodism and the Working-Class Movements of England 1800-1850* (London, 1947), 66-72.

32. Historical Manuscripts Commission, *Report on the Manuscripts of S.B. Fortescue, Esq., Preserved at Dropmore*, 10 vols. (London, 1892-1927), X, 450-1; cf. HO 42/175, Fletcher to Sidmouth, Bolton, 29 March 1818.

33. *Black Dwarf*, 2 June 1819; Samuel Bamford, *Passages in the Life of a Radical*, 2 vols. (3rd edn, London, 1844), I, 8; MCL, MS F363 D1, Documents concerning the

Formation of Hampden Clubs 1816-17, p. 29.

34. *MC*, 27 Nov. 1819; HO 42/181, Lloyd to Clive, 12 Oct. 1818; *MO*, 10 July 1819; Thomas Walter Laqueur, *Religion and Respectability: Sunday Schools and Working Class Culture 1780-1850* (New Haven, 1976), 198-9.

35. PP 1819 (224) IX. 83, 1461; HO 44/18, Report of the Magistrates in the Stockport Division, August 1819; J. Knight, *A Full and Particular Report of the Proceedings of the Public Meeting Held in Manchester On Monday the 18th of January, 1819* (London, 1819), 3.

36. *Black Dwarf*, 6 April, 2 June 1819; *MC*, 27 Nov. 1819.

37. *Plots at Midnight: Being the Confessions of a Radical* (Stockport, n.d. [c. 1820]), pr. s.sh.

38. *Trial of Bagguley*, 63-4; *MO*, 12 June 1819.

39. Bamford, *Passages*, I, 165; Bagguley and Drummond spoke at the Lydgate meeting. *MO*, 25 April, 4 July 1818; *Black Dwarf*, 9 Sept. 1818.

40. PRO, RG 4/7; HO 44/18, Report of the Magistrates in the Stockport Division, August 1819 (emphasis in original).

41. *MO*, 20 Feb., 3 July 1819; HO 42/188, Lloyd to Hobhouse, 26 June 1819, enclosing Bagguley's letter to the female reformers of Stockport.

42. *MO*, 17, 31 July 1819.

43. *The following Address* (Stockport, 1819), pr. s.sh.; cf. *The Times*, 21 July 1819; John Aiken, *Annals of the Reign of King George the Third*, 2 vols. (2nd edn, London, 1820), II, 519.

44. *MO*, 13 Feb. 1819; *MGaz*, 31 July 1819.

45. Hammond, *Skilled Labourer*, 118-22; *MM*, 18 May 1819.

46. HO 42/188, Lloyd to Hobhouse, 15 June 1819; Prescot to Warren Bulkeley, 23 June 1819; *MO*, 3 July 1819; Joseph Sherwin, *A Committee of the Cotton Weavers of Stockport* (n.p., 1819), pr. s.sh.

47. 'Marshall, Benjamin (1782-Dec. 2, 1858)', *Dictionary of American Biography*; *MO*, 4 April, 6 June, 15 Aug., 17 Oct., 26 Dec. 1818; *Black Dwarf*, 1 April, 5 Aug. 1818; *Gorgon*, 7, 14 Nov. 1818.

48. HO 42/182, Lloyd to Hobhouse, 7 Dec. 1818.

49. *MO*, 26 June 1819.

50. *South America* (Manchester, 1819), pr. s.sh.; HO 42/190, John Ogle Ogle to Sidmouth, Liverpool, 20 July 1819; Lloyd to Hobhouse, 28 July 1819.

51. *Annual Register*, 62 (1820), Chronicle, 910-11: Harrison to Bagguley, 30 June 1819; PP 1835 (492) XIII, 6.

52. Donald Read, *Peterloo* (Manchester, 1958), 50; Thompson, *MEWC*, 709, 739n.1.

53. *Black Dwarf*, 13 Jan. 1819.

54. *MO*, 2, 9 Jan. 1819; Knight, *Full and Particular Report, passim*.

55. On the meeting and its background, see *MO*, 30 Jan., 6, 20 Feb. 1819.

56. Samuel Bamford, *Homely Rhymes, Poems, and Reminiscences* (London, 1864), 177-9; *MO*, 27 Feb. 1819. For two additional poems, see ibid., 20 March, 10 April 1819.

57. HO 42/184, Prescot to Sidmouth, 18 Feb. 1819; Lloyd to Hobhouse, 24, 27 Feb. 1819; HO 42/185, same to same, 4, 10 March 1819; *MO*, 8, 15 May 1819.

58. Ibid., 14 Nov. 1818, 8 May 1819; *Black Dwarf*, 13 Jan., 12 May, 2 June 1819; PRO, CHES 24/188/7; HO 42/186, Lloyd to Hobhouse, Chester, 15, 17, 19 April 1819; *Trial of Bagguley, passim*.

59. HO 42/182, Lloyd to Hobhouse and Clive, 21 Dec. 1818; Joseph Harrison *et*

al., Windmill, Stockport (Oldham, 1818), pr. s.sh., *MO*, 15, 22 May 1819.

60. HO 42/187, Lloyd to Hobhouse, 10 May 1819; 'A.S.B.D.' to Norris, Ashton, 25 May 1819; *The Times*, 22 July 1819. The Stockport petition, signed by Harrison, can be found in HO 42/183.

61. *MO*, 12, 19 June, 10 July 1819.

62. HO 42/188, Lloyd to Hobhouse, 28 June 1819; *MO*, 3 July 1819; Charles Fanning, *To the Inhabitants of Stockport and its Neighbourhood* (Manchester, 1819), pr. s.sh.; Anne Bayliss, 'Radical Meeting at Stockport', *Cheshire History*, 7 (1981), 79-81.

63. *ST*, 1 (1820-3), 1373: Joseph Johnson to Hunt, [Manchester], 3 July 1819.

64. HO 42/189, Lloyd to Hobhouse, 3, 5, 8, 14 July 1819 (the latter written from Knutsford); [John Lloyd], *Hundred of Macclesfield (Stockport Division)* (Stockport, 1819), pr. s.sh.; SPL, HX 70/6, 'Laws and Regulations of a Society Called the Stockport Troop Club Established 12th July 1819'; *MO*, 24 July 1819.

65. HO 42/189, Lloyd to Hobhouse, 12, 19 July 1819; same to same, Knutsford, 15 July 1819; *MO*, 24 July 1819; *PD*, 41 (1819-20), 94; *Black Dwarf*, 21, 28 July 1819; *The Times*, 22 July 1819.

66. HO 42/190, Lloyd to Hobhouse, 24 July 1819 (two letters); *A Report of the Meeting Held in Smithfield* (London, 1819). After Birch's death some years later, an autopsy was performed to smother lingering rumours that he had not been shot at all. The breastbone encasing the bullet was removed and placed on public display. The Stockport Municipal Museum was still displaying it from time to time in the 1970s.

67. CHES 38/42/1, Statement of Bruce, [c. 27 July 1819]; *The Times*, 11 April 1820; *Felony. £400 Reward* (Stockport, 1819), pr. s.sh.; HO 42/192, Information of William Pearson, 16 August 1819; HO 42/194, Lloyd to Hobhouse, Chester, 4 Sept. 1819.

68. HO 42/191, Lloyd to Hobhouse, 7 Aug. 1819; *Black Dwarf*, 28 July 1819; *MO*, 10, 31 July, 14 Aug. 1819.

69. *MO*, 31 July, 7 Aug. 1819; *ST*, 1 (1820-3), 1377; see also ibid., 171-496, for excellent, neglected contemporary accounts of Peterloo and its background.

70. HO 42/191, 'At an Adjournment of the General Quarter Sessions for the County of Chester', 9 Aug. 1819.

71. *ST*, 1 (1820-3), 201-2, 226-9, 243, 252, 264.

72. *The Times*, 20 Aug. 1819; *CN&Q*, 3 (1898), 190; *PD*, 11 (1832), 255. Donald Read (*Peterloo*, 24) notes that about three-quarters of those killed or wounded at Peterloo were weavers.

73. HO 42/192, Lloyd to Hobhouse, 18 Aug. 1819; TS 11/1056/4673, Maj. Dyneley to ?, Manchester, 16 Aug. 1819; ibid., Information of John Staveley Barratt, 20 Jan. 1820, *MC*, 21 Aug. 1819.

74. *The Times*, 19 Aug. 1819; *We, the Union of Manchester* (Manchester, 1819), pr. s.sh.; *MO*, 29 Jan. 1820; Read, *Peterloo*, 149-59.

75. HO 42/194, 'B' to Fletcher, n.p., 23 Aug. 1819; Ethelston to Sidmouth, Longsight, 13 Sept. 1819; HO 42/195, Information of Samuel Fleming, 23 Sept. 1819; HO 42/197, Norris to Sidmouth, Manchester, 26 Oct. 1819; HO 42/198, Lloyd to Hobhouse, 2 Nov. 1819.

76. HO 42/197, Lloyd to Hobhouse or Clive, 16 Oct. 1819; same to the Under-Secretaries, 11 Nov. 1819; HO 42/194, Prescot to Sidmouth, 11 Sept. 1819; [John Edward Taylor], *Notes and Observations, Critical and Explanatory, on the Papers*

Relative to the Internal State of the Country (London, 1820), 128.

77. *Annual Register*, 62 (1820), Chronicle, 954-5.

78. HO 42/189, Lloyd to Hobhouse, 18 July 1819; HO 42/200, Lt. Col. George Burrell to Palmerston, 4 Dec. 1819; SPL, SSS MSS, B/S/5/3, William Griffiths to Joseph Mayer, Portwood, 22 Dec. 1819; Rev. N.K. Pugsley to the Chairman of the SSS Committee, [March 1820]; R. Philip to Joseph Mayer, Liverpool, 28 March 1820.

79. Leary, *Yeomanry*, 81-9; S.P. Humphreys, *At a Numerous and Highly-respectable Meeting* (Stockport, 1819), pr. s.sh.; HO 42/193, 'At a Special General Sessions of the Peace', 24 Aug. 1819; *List of the Stockport Nightly Patrol* (Stockport, 1819), pr. s.sh.; PP 1819-20 (1) IV, 31.

80. HO 42/194, Lloyd to Hobhouse, Chester, 6 Sept. 1819. The Six Acts are conveniently reprinted in *PD*, 41 (1819-20), 1645-90.

81. *The Times*, 8, 20 Oct. 1819; *Things as They Are; or, America in 1819* (Manchester, 1819); *A Clear and Concise Statement of New York and the Surrounding Country* (Belper, Derbyshire, 1819); HO 42/197, Lloyd to Hobhouse or Clive, 30 Oct. 1819.

82. HO 42/198, Lloyd to Hobhouse, 2 Nov. 1819; HO 42/201, same to same, 13 Dec. 1819.

83. HO 42/200, Norris to Sidmouth, Manchester, 1, 12 Dec. 1819; HO 42/201, 'Alpha' to J. Langshaw, Bolton, 26 Dec. 1819; HO 42/203, same to same, 12 Jan. 1820; *MO*, 12 Feb. 1820; *The Times*, 21 April 1820; Taylor, *Notes*, 133-5.

84. *Chester Chronicle*, 21 Jan. 1820; *MO*, 26 Feb. 1820.

85. Ibid., 14 April 1820; HO 40/12/177-8, 230-3, 322-5, 386-9, Lloyd to Hobhouse, Chester, 8, 9, 13, 15 April 1820; *The Times*, 11, 17 April 1820.

86. *ST*, 1 (1820-3), 1347 and n. (c); *Annual Register*, 62 (1820), Chronicle, 908-20; TS 11/1071/5034, Chester Spring Assizes 1820; *The Times*, 12 April 1820.

87. *ST*, 1 (1820-3), 1348; *Annual Register*, 62 (1820), Chronicle, 952; *The Times*, 20, 21 April 1820.

88. *ST*, 1 (1820-3), 277-80, 391, 482; *Republican*, 10 Sept. 1819.

89. *MO*, 6 Nov. 1819; *MGaz*, 7 Aug. 1819.

90. *MO*, 26 Feb., 11 March, 8 April, 13 May, 22 July 1820.

91. *Republican*, 21 April 1820; *MO*, 13 May 1820; HO 40/13/153-6, Burrell to Palmerston, 5 May 1820; HO 40/13/393-4, Lloyd to Hobhouse, Strand, 23 May 1820.

92. Thompson, *MEWC*, 709-10. It should be noted again that Harrison was Presbyterian, not Methodist, and did not 'turn' schoolmaster when he became a radical. He had been a schoolmaster long before.

Notes to Chapter 11

1. Bythell, *Handloom Weavers*, 53, 75; but cf. idem, *The Sweated Trades: Outwork in Nineteenth-century Britain* (New York, 1978), 46.

2. *HCJ*, 71 (1816-17), 393-4; HO 42/152, Lloyd to Beckett, 23 July 1816. Cf. Foster, *CSIR*, 293-4n.7; Hammond, *Town Labourer*, 110.

3. For the weaving census of 1816, see Table 9.1; for later estimates, see HO 42/179, David Ramsay to Sidmouth, 20 Aug. 1818; Charles Babbage, *On the Economy of Machinery and Manufactures* (London, 1832), 335; PP 1834 (556) X, QQ 6741,

7234; *SA*, 13 April 1826.

4. PP 1834 (556) X, Q 6744; PP 1835 (341) XIII, QQ 1743-4, 2241; Bythell, *Handloom Weavers*, 52, 56; [William Rathbone Greg], *An Enquiry into the State of the Manufacturing Population* (London, 1831), 3.

5. Quoted in Arthur Redford, *Manchester Merchants and Foreign Trade 1794-1858* (Manchester, 1934), 240.

6. Bythell, *Handloom Weavers*, 117.

7. PP 1824 (51) V, 419.

8. PP 1835 (341) XIII, xii; PP 1831-2 (678) XIX, Q 11,712; W. Cooke Taylor, *Notes of a Tour in the Manufacturing Districts of Lancashire* (2nd edn, London, 1842), 194-210.

9. PP 1810-11 (232) II, 2-3; HO 40/1/1/39-40, Depositions of Joseph Jackson, 10, 12, 13 May 1812; W.R. Goudie, *Grove Methodist Sunday School, Marple, Cheshire. 1795 to 1945* (Oldham, 1945), 7.

10. PP 1808 (177) II, 6; PP 1833 (450) XX, D.1., 1, 71; PP 1819 (HL 24) CX, 369; 'The Early History of Belle Vue, Manchester' in J.D. Beckett (ed.), *The Manchester Genealogist: Selected Reprints 1964-1974*, 3 vols. (Manchester, 1977), I, 26-8.

11. *MO*, 19 Aug., 25 Nov. 1820.

12. Ibid., 16 Sept., 16 Dec. 1820; HO 40/15/211-14, Lloyd to Hobhouse, 13 Nov. 1820; /419-22, same to same, Congleton, 25 Nov. 1820; /483-6, Thomas Robinson to Sidmouth, [5] Dec. 1820; /551-4, Lloyd to Hobhouse, 9 Dec. 1820, enclosure. Thomas W. Laqueur sees this as a more significant and resonant episode in other parts of Britain: 'The Queen Caroline Affair: Politics as Art in the Reign of George IV', *Journal of Modern History*, 54 (1982), 417-66.

13. *Black Dwarf*, 27 Dec. 1820, 4, 18 April 1821; *To the Reformers* [Carlile], 1 Jan., 23 April 1821; *To the Radical Reformers* [Hunt], 11 April 1821; *MO*, 21 April 1821; Belchem, 'Republicanism', 24.

14. HO 40/15/547-50, Lloyd to Hobhouse, 9 Dec. 1820; John D. Crosfield, 'Richard Smith and his Journal 1817-1824', *Journal of the Friends Historical Society*, 14 (1917), 59-60; *MG*, 9 June 1821.

15. HO 40/16/635-8, Lloyd to Hobhouse, 8 May 1821; HO 44/8, same to same, 28 June, 28 July 1821; /10, Thomas Robinson to Viscount Warren Bulkeley, 7 Sept. 1821.

16. *Republican*, 22 Dec. 1820; *Black Dwarf*, 13 Dec. 1820, 8 Oct. 1823.

17. *Republican*, 8 Sept., 13 Oct. 1820; *To the Reformers*, 24 June, 13 Oct. 1821. Stockport's female Carlilites were not nearly so active as those in some other towns, however; cf. Iain McCalman, 'Females, Feminism and Free Love in an Early Nineteenth Century Radical Movement', *Labour History*, 38 (1980), 1-25.

18. Samuel Bamford, *Hours in the Bowers, Poems, &c.* (Manchester, 1834), 50-1; *To the Radical Reformers*, 12 Jan. 1822; *Black Dwarf*, 23 July 1823.

19. Ibid., 20 Nov. 1823; PRO, RG 4/7; *SA*, 15, 22 Dec. 1826.

20. *To the Radical Reformers*, 24 Sept. 1821; *Black Dwarf*, 21 Nov. 1821, 30 Jan 1822; HO 40/17/37-40, Eckersley to Byng, Manchester, 24 Jan. 1822.

21. Joseph Johnson, *A Letter to Henry Hunt, Esq.* (2nd edn, Manchester, 1822); *Cobbett's Ten Cardinal Virtues* (3rd edn, Manchester, 1832), 23-4, referring to events of 1820.

22. Richard Carlile, *An Effort to Set at Rest some Little Disputes and Misunderstandings between the Reformers of Leeds* (London, 1821); *Republican*, 8 Sept. 1820.

23. *To the Reformers*, 20 Dec. 1821; cf. [Richard Carlile], *The Character of a Priest* (London, 1821).

24. *To the Radical Reformers*, 11 Feb., 11 March 1822; *Republican*, 1 March 1822.

25. Ibid., 12 April, 31 May 1822; *To the Radical Reformers*, 24 April 1822. A concomitant development was Carlile's split with Cobbett – but this had no discernible repercussions in the Stockport district. *Cobbett's Political Register*, 22 Sept. 1821, 2 Feb., 13 April 1822; *Republican*, 15 Feb., 1 March 1822.

26. Ibid., 22 Feb., 5 April 1822; *SA*, 28 May 1824; HO 40/17/122-5, Lloyd to Hobhouse, Congleton, 23 Feb. 1822.

27. University of Chicago MS 563/64, 68, Wolseley to Hunt, Brussels, 30 Oct. 1826, 17 Feb. 1828; Read, *Peterloo*, 162.

28. *Republican*, 27 Dec. 1822.

29. Ibid., 8 March, 28 June 1822, 21 March 1823, 19 Jan. 1824.

30. See ibid., 22 May to 8 July 1825.

31. HO 42/200, Norris to Sidmouth, Manchester, 12 Dec. 1819.

32. Belchem, 'Republicanism', 29. Belchem (in 'Henry Hunt', 769) also goes astray when he declares: 'Carlile's call for a redirection of radical endeavor won little favour in the north . . .'

33. *Republican*, 23 Jan. 1824, 26 Aug. 1825; Richard Carlile, *An Address to Men of Science* (2nd edn, London, 1822).

34. *Moralist*, 1 (1823), 17-29, 33-4, 84; *Republican*, 28 May 1824; and for earlier Huntite views, *Black Dwarf*, 8 March 1820.

35. *ST*, 1 (1820-3), 312; *To the Radical Reformers*, 28 Aug. 1820; *Poor Man's Guardian*, 28 Feb. 1835; *Black Dwarf*, 24 Nov. 1819.

36. *MO*, 17 July 1819, 1 Jan. 1820; *The Times*, 15, 20 April 1820; *ST*, 1 (1820-3), 202; Bamford, *Passages*, II, 21-2.

37. *MO*, 16 Dec. 1820, 7 April 1821; HO 40/15/739-42, Lloyd to Hobhouse, 28 Dec. 1820.

38. George Jacob Holyoake, *The History of Co-operation*, 2 vols. (rev. edn, London, 1908), I, 227; *DNB*; Gwyn A. Williams, *Rowland Detrosier: A Working-Class Infidel 1800-34, Borthwick Papers*, 28 (1965).

39. *Republican*, 14 July 1826.

40. *SA*, April 1825 to May 1827; Heginbotham, *Stockport*, II, 38, 398.

41. *MGaz*, Dec. 1823 to Feb. 1824; W. Longson, *The Impolicy, Injustice, Oppression and Commercial Evils Resulting from the Combination Law* (Manchester, 1823), pr. s.sh.; PP 1824 (51) V, 416-17. Longson resided briefly at Manchester during this period but still kept in close contact with the Stockport Weavers' Committee.

42. *MGaz*, 18 Sept. 1824; BL, Add. MSS 27,801/259; 27,803/255; *MC*, 15 Jan. 1825; HO 40/18, Eckersley to Byng, Manchester, 27 Jan. 1825; HO 44/15, J. Brown to Robert Peel, Bolton, 25 March 1825.

43. Wallas, *Francis Place*, 181; *PD*, 9 (1823), 598-9; W. Longson, *To the Working Classes* (Manchester, 1825), pr. s.sh.; idem, *On Population and Their Wages* (Manchester, 1824), pr. s.sh.; George W. Hilton, 'The Controversy Concerning Relief for the Hand-loom Weavers', *Explorations in Entrepreneurial History*, 1 (1963-4), 169; William L. Langer, 'The Origins of the Birth Control Movement in England in the Early Nineteenth Century', *Journal of Interdisciplinary History*, 5 (1974-5), 673-7.

44. Radcliffe, *Origin*, 88n.-89n.; PP 1826-7 (550) V, QQ 2828-9; *SA*, Jan. to May

1826 (quotation in 21 April issue); *HCJ*, 81 (1826), 115.

45. PP 1834 (556) X, Q 6849; Edward Baines, Jr, *Address to the Unemployed Workmen of Yorkshire and Lancashire, on the Present Distress and on Machinery* (2nd edn, London, 1826); *SA*, 5, 12 May 1826; Bythell, *Handloom Weavers*, 246.

46. HO 44/16/64, 68, J. Fred Foster to Peel, Manchester, 18 May, 1 July 1826.

47. Bythell, *Handloom Weavers*, 243; *SA*, May 1826 to Jan. 1827; PP 1826-7 (550) V, Q 2350.

48. *SA*, 19 Jan. 1827.

49. Ibid., 21 July, 4 Aug. 1826; HO 44/16/72, Norris to Peel, Manchester, 14 July 1826; CHES 24/192/1, Indictment of Joseph Whitelegg; *Notice is hereby given* (Stockport, 1826), pr. s.sh.

50. *SA*, 18 Aug., 8, 15 Sept., 13 Oct. 1826.

51. Ibid., 24 Nov. 1826; *Republican*, 3 Nov. 1826; *Bolton Chronicle*, 1 Sept. 1827.

52. *SA*, 15 Dec. 1826.

53. Ibid., 17, 31 Aug. 1827; *Lion*, 18 Jan., 25 April, May to June 1828.

54. *Richard Carlile's First Sermon upon the Mount* (London, 1827); Robert Hindmarsh, *Christianity against Deism, Materialism, and Atheism. Occasioned by a Letter Addressed to the Author by R. Carlile* (Manchester, 1824); *SA*, 21 Sept. 1827; Rowland Detrosier, *A Form of Public Worship* (London, 1827); *Lion*, Jan. to March 1828, 23 Jan. 1829; Huntington Library, Richard Carlile Papers 96, Detrosier to Carlile, n.p., n.d. [c. 1830].

55. R.E. Thelwall, *The Andrews and Compstall Their Village* (Marple, 1972), 2; Longson, *Appeal, passim*; Prothero, *Artisans*, 205-7.

56. See, for example, *HCJ*, 82 (1826-7), 341, 368, 399; ibid., 83 (1828), 264, 289, 390.

57. Cf. PP 1834 (556) X, Q 7462; *PD*, 24 (1834), 367.

Notes to Chapter 12

1. Thompson, *MEWC*, 195, 531.

2. C. Knick Harley, 'British Industrialization Before 1841: Evidence of Slower Growth During the Industrial Revolution', *Journal of Economic History*, 42 (1982), 276.

3. *New Moral World*, 10 (1841-2), 15; PP 1842 (158) XXXV, 100; *The Times*, 3 July 1852; H. Coutie, 'How They Lived on Hillgate', *North Cheshire Family Historian*, 8 (1981), 37; Karl Marx and Friedrich Engels, *Letters to Americans 1848-1895: A Selection* (trans. Leonard E. Mins) (New York, 1953), 78; Neville Kirk, 'Ethnicity, Class and Popular Toryism, 1850-1870' in Kenneth Lunn (ed.), *Hosts, Immigrants and Minorities: Historical Responses to Newcomers in British Society 1870-1914* (New York, 1980), 64-106.

4. T.D.W. Reid and Naomi Reid, 'The 1842 "Plug Plot" in Stockport', *International Review of Social History*, 24 (1979), 55-79; Carole Ann Naomi Reid, 'The Chartist Movement in Stockport' (MA thesis, Hull, 1974), ch. 3; Joseph L. White, 'The Tenacity of Sectional Differences' in *The Limits of Trade Union Militancy: The Lancashire Textile Workers. 1910-1914* (Westport, Conn., 1978); Jeffrey G. Williamson, 'The Structure of Pay in Britain, 1710-1911', *Research in Economic History*, 7 (1982), 1-54.

5. These themes are developed in Robert Glen, 'The Working Classes of Stockport

during the Industrial Revolution' (PhD dissertation, Berkeley, 1978), chs. 11-12. On latter-day Christian reformers at Stockport and elsewhere, see Eileen Yeo, 'Christianity in Chartist Struggle 1838-1842', *Past and Present*, 91 (1981), 109-39.

6. Taylor, *Tour*, 165.

7. Neville Kirk, 'Class and Fragmentation: Some Aspects of Working-Class Life in South-east Lancashire and North-east Cheshire, 1850-1870' (PhD dissertation, Pittsburgh, 1974), 126. For a nearby comparison, see H.J. Perkin, 'The Development of Modern Glossop', in A.H. Birch (comp.), *Small-Town Politics: A Study of Political Life in Glossop* (Oxford, 1959), 8-33.

8. *MG*, 27 Dec. 1851.

9. Cf. H.I. Dutton and J.E. King, 'The Limits of Paternalism: The Cotton Tyrants of North Lancashire, 1836-54', *Social History*, 7 (1982), 59-74.

10. Paul Thomas Phillips, 'The Sectarian Spirit: A Study of Sectarianism, Society and Politics in the North and West of England, 1832-1870' (PhD dissertation, Toronto, 1971), 217-18. John Seed discusses the provincial bourgeoisie as 'a complex and deeply fissured formation' in 'Unitarianism, Political Economy and the Antinomies of Liberal Culture in Manchester, 1830-50', *Social History*, 7 (1982), 1–25.

11. Phillips, 'Sectarian Spirit', 195-6, 202-3, 208.

12. Francis Philips, *An Exposure of the Calumnies Circulated by the Enemies of Social Order* (London, 1819), xv–xvi n.,7n.a.; William Alexander MacKinnon, *On the Rise, Progress, and Present State of Public Opinion in Great Britain, and Other Parts of the World* (London, 1828), 3-4; Symons, *Arts and Artisans*, 157; [John Stuart Mill], 'Reorganization of the Reform Party', *Westminster Review*, 32 (1839), 203-4; [William Dodd], *The Laboring Classes of England, Especially Those Engaged in Agriculture and Manufactures* (Boston, Mass., 1847), 9-10; William Thomas Thornton, *Over-Population and Its Remedy* (London, 1846), 10.

13. Prothero, *Artisans and Politics, passim*; William Lazonick, 'Industrial Relations and Technical Change: The Case of the Self-Acting Mule', *Cambridge Journal of Economics*, 3 (1979), 231-62; idem, 'Conflict and Control in the Industrial Revolution: Social Relations in the British Cotton Factory' in Robert Weible, Oliver Ford and Paul Marion (eds.), *Essays from the Lowell Conference on Industrial History 1980 and 1981* (Lowell, 1981), 14-32; Patrick Joyce, *Work, Society and Politics: The Culture of the Factory in Later Victorian England* (Brighton, 1980); Calhoun, *Question of Class Struggle, passim*; Harold Perkin, '"The Condescension of Posterity": Middle-Class Intellectuals and the History of the Working Class' [1979] in *The Structured Crowd: Essays in English Social History* (Brighton, 1981), 168-85; M.E. Rose, 'Social Change and the Industrial Revolution' in Roderick Floud and Donald McCloskey (eds.), *The Economic History of Britain since 1700:* vol. 1, *1700-1860* (Cambridge, 1981), 253-75. See also Robert Glen, Review of Craig Calhoun, *The Question of Class Struggle* in *American Historical Review*, 87 (1982), 1386-7.

SELECT BIBLIOGRAPHY OF PRIMARY SOURCES

I. Manuscripts

Birmingham – Birmingham Reference Library

Boulton and Watt Collection

Bolton – Bolton Civic Museum

Crompton MSS

Chester – Cheshire Record Office

DDX 24: Lloyd Collection
DDX 311: Stockport Rifle Corps, 1803-4
EDC 3: Consistory Court Citation Books
EDV 7: Articles of Enquiry Preparatory to Visitation
MG 24: Lieutenancy and Militia: Letters from the War Office 1811-12
QDV 2: Land Tax Assessments
QJB: Quarter Sessions Judicial Books
QJF: Quarter Sessions Judicial Files
Holland Watson File
'A List of Friendly Society Rules filed with the Clerk of the Peace for
    the County of Chester previous to 1794 to 1829'

Chicago – University of Chicago Library

MS 563: Henry Hunt Papers

Edinburgh – National Library of Scotland

MS 7233: Papers of George Combe

London – British Library

Add. MSS 16,923-4: Association for Preserving Liberty and Property, Corres-
    pondence
Add. MSS 27,799-813: Place Papers

London – Guildhall Library

MS 7253: Royal Exchange Assurance Company, Fire Policy Registers
MS 11, 936: Sun Insurance Office Policy Registers

London – Public Record Office

Bankruptcy Papers
    B 3: Commissions: Files
Board of Trade Papers
    BT 5: Minutes
Chancery Papers
    C 107/104: Chancery Masters' Exhibit

County Palatine of Chester Papers
 CHES 24: Gaol Files
 CHES 35: Rule Books and Minute Books
 CHES 38: Miscellanea
Friendly Society Papers
 FS 1: Deeds of Registration
 FS 2: Indexes to Rules and Amendments
Home Office Papers
 HO 40: Disturbances, Correspondence and Papers
 HO 41: Disturbances, Entry Books
 HO 42: Domestic and General Correspondence, George III
 HO 43: Domestic and General Entry Books
 HO 44: Domestic and General Correspondence, George IV and later
 HO 48: Law Officers' Reports and Correspondence
 HO 49: Law Officers' Letter Books
 HO 50: Military Correspondence
 HO 51: Military Entry Books
 HO 55: Addresses (Miscellaneous)
 HO 65: Police Entry Books
 HO 102: Scotland, Correspondence
King's Bench Papers
 KB 8/90: Baga de Secretis, '1812. Cheshire. Special Commissions and Proceedings under them for Trial of the Rioters for Destroying Machines &c. in the Woollen and Cotton Manufactory'
Papers of the Ministry of Agriculture, Fisheries and Food
 MAF 10: Corn Returns
Privy Council Papers
 PC 1: Non-Colonial Papers
Registrar-General's Papers
 RG 4/7: Non-Parochial Registers, Windmill Room, Edward Street, Stockport, Baptismal Register
Treasury Solicitor's Papers
 TS 11/952/3496: Papers relating to the London Corresponding Society and the Society for Constitutional Information
 TS 11/1026/4298: Crown Brief in *R. v. William Holdby Atkinson*, 1794
 TS 11/836/2821: Cheshire Assizes, Autumn, 1808
 TS 11/370/1160: Cheshire Special Commission, 1812
 TS 11/1029/4414: Seditious Meeting at Manchester, 10 March 1817
 TS 11/1071/5034: Cheshire Assizes, Spring, 1820
 TS 11/48/195: Crown Brief in *R. v. Harrison*, 1820
 TS 11/1056/4673: Crown Brief in *R. v. Hunt and others*, 1820
 TS 24: Sedition Cases, Miscellaneous Papers
War Office Papers
 WO 1: In-Letters
 WO 17: Monthly Returns
 WO 34: Amherst Papers
 WO 40: Correspondence, Selected Unnumbered Papers

Manchester – Chetham's Library

'An Enumeration of the Houses and Inhabitants in the Town and Parish of Manchester', 3 vols. (1773-4)

Manchester – John Rylands University Library of Manchester

English MSS 751: Samuel Oldknow Papers

Manchester – Manchester Central Library

MS F363 D1: Documents concerning the Formation of Hampden Clubs, 1816-17
MS FF367 M56: Manchester Pitt Club Papers
MS FF667.3 G1: John Graham, 'The Chemistry of Calico Printing from 1790 to 1835 and History of Printworks in the Manchester District from 1760 to 1846' (1846)
MS M22/7/2: Didsbury Vestry Minutes (1812-50)
Burton MSS

New York – Columbia University Library

Seligam MSS

Oxford – Bodleian Library

MS Topography Cheshire b.1., Watson MSS

San Marino, California – Huntington Library

Richard Carlile Papers

Stockport – Stockport Public Library

B/CC/6/1, 2: Heaton Norris Vestry Minute Books (1821-4, 1824-30)
B/G, S, T: Stockport Sunday School MSS
HX series, various numbers: Miscellaneous deeds for the eighteenth and nineteenth centuries
HX 2: Stockport Select Vestry Minutes (1820-3)
HX 25: Minute Book of the Stockport Troop Club, 1819-21
HX 70: Stockport Troop Club Papers and Miscellaneous Military Papers, eighteenth-twentieth centuries
HX 74: Register of Poor Apprentices, 1802-15
HX 440: Accounts of the Constables of Cheadle Bulkeley, 1776-1830
Hurst MSS
'John Lloyd Scrapbook'
Stockport Poor Ley of 1781
Sykes MSS

II. Printed Sources

Books, Pamphlets and Articles

An Account of the Celebration of the Jubilee. Birmingham, [1810?]
Address to the United Britons. n.p., [1798?]

The Adventures of a Sixpence; Shewing The Method of Setting up Tradesmen without Money. Manchester, [c. 1800]

Aiken, J. *A Description of the Country from thirty to forty Miles round Manchester*. London, 1795

Aiken, John. *Annals of the Reign of King George the Third*. 2 vols., 2nd edn, London, 1820

Annual Reports of the Stockport Auxiliary Bible Society. 8 vols., Stockport, 1815-22

Annual Reports of the Stockport Sunday School. 36 vols., Stockport, 1795-1830

Articles and Orders, Made, Agreed Upon, and Appointed to be Observed by the Members Belonging to the Old Association Club, Heretofore Called The Weavers Club. Manchester, 1771

Articles . . . of the Friendly Associated Mule Cotton Spinners. Stockport, 1795

Aspinall, A. *The Early English Trade Unions: Documents from the Home Office Papers in the Public Record Office*. London, 1949

Auchincloss, J. *The Sophistry of the First Part of Mr. Paine's Age of Reason*. Stockport, 1796

    Paine's Confession of the Divinity of the Holy Scriptures: or the Sophistry of the Second Part of the Age of Reason. 2nd edn, Stockport, 1796

    The Sophistry of Both the First and Second Part of Mr. Paine's Age of Reason. Edinburgh, 1796

Babbage, Charles. *On the Economy of Machinery and Manufactures*. London, 1832

Baines, Edward, Jr. *Address to the Unemployed Workmen of Yorkshire and Lancashire, on the Present Distress and on Machinery*. 2nd edn, London, 1826

    History of the Cotton Manufacture in Great Britain. London, 1835

Bamford, Samuel. *An Account of the Arrest and Imprisonment of Samuel Bamford, of Middleton, on Suspicion of High Treason*. Manchester, 1817

    Hours in the Bowers. Poems, &c. Manchester, 1834

    Passages in the Life of a Radical. 2 vols., 3rd edn, London, 1844

    Early Days. London, 1849

    Homely Rhymes, Poems, and Reminiscences. London, 1864

[Beaumont, George?] *The Beggar's Complaint*, by 'One Who Pities the Oppressed'. 2nd edn, Sheffield, 1812

Bentham, Jeremy. *The Works of Jeremy Bentham* (ed. John Bowring). 11 vols., Edinburgh, 1843

Binns, Abraham. *Remarks on a Publication Entitled, 'A Serious Admonition to the Disciples of Thomas Paine, and All Other Infidels'*. Stockport, 1796

Boulter, William. *An Evening's Walk in Stockport: A Satirical and Descriptive Poem*. Stockport, 1818

Britton, John and Edward Wedlake Brayley. *The Beauties of England and Wales*. 18 vols., London, 1801-15

[Burn, James Dawson]. *A Glimpse at the Social Condition of the Working Classes during the Early Part of the Present Century*. London, [1868]

Butterworth, James. *A History and Description of the Towns and Parishes of Stockport, Ashton-under-Lyne, Mottram-Long-Den-Dale, and Glossop*. Manchester, 1827

Byng, John. *The Torrington Diaries* (ed. C. Bruyn Andrews). 4 vols., London, 1834-8

C., W. and Ralph Mather. *An Impartial Representation of the Case of the Poor*

Cotton Spinners in Lancashire. London, 1780

[Carlile, Richard]. *The Character of a Priest.* London, 1821

  An Effort to Set at Rest some Little Disputes and Misunderstandings between the Reformers of Leeds. London, 1821

   An Address to Men of Science. 2nd edn, London, 1822 [1821]

   Richard Carlile's First Sermon upon the Mount. London, 1827

Cartwright, F.D. *The Life and Correspondence of Major Cartwright.* 2 vols., London, 1826

A Catalogue of the Valuable Library . . . of the Late Holland Watson, Esq. Liverpool, 1829

Chadwick, Edwin. *Report on the Sanitary Condition of the Labouring Population of Gt. Britain* (ed. M.W. Flinn). Edinburgh, 1965 [1842]

Chambers, R[obert] (ed.) *The Book of Days.* 2 vols., Edinburgh, 1863-4

Cheetham, Robert Farren. *Odes and Miscellanies.* Stockport, 1796

Chester Poll Book, Chester, 1784

A Clear and Concise Statement of New York and the Surrounding Country. Belper, Derbyshire, 1819

Clegg, William. *Freedom Defended or the Practice of Despots Exposed.* Manchester, [1802?]

   Peace, and No War; or, Hints on the Necessity of a Change of His Majesty's Present Ministers. Manchester, 1805

Clemesha, H.W. (ed.) *The New Court Book of the Manor of Bramhall (1632-1657),* CS, 80 (1921)

Cobbett, William. *Paper Against Gold.* London, 1817

   T.B. Howell and Thomas Jones Howell (eds.) *Complete Collection of State Trials.* 33 vols., London 1809-26

Cobbett's Ten Cardinal Virtues [anon.]. 3rd edn, Manchester, 1832

Considerations Addressed to the Journeymen Calico Printers by One of Their Masters. Manchester, 1815

A Correct Account of a Blind Irishman Restored to Sight When Very Old (ed. George Jones). Stockport, [c. 1823]

Corry, John. *The History of Macclesfield.* London, 1817

Davies, James. *A Short Sketch of the Scripturian's Creed.* Manchester, 1839

Dawson, W. *Stockport Flim Flams.* Manchester, 1807

Declaration of the Object and Principles of the Union Formed at Stockport, in October, 1818 for the Promotion of Human Happiness. Stockport, 1818

The Declaration, Resolutions, and Constitution of the Society of United Englishmen. n.p., [1797?]

Defoe, Daniel. *A Tour Through the Whole Island of Great Britain.* 4 vols., 7th edn, London, 1769

Detrosier, Rowland. *A Form of Public Worship.* London, 1827

Dodd, William. *The Laboring Classes of England, Especially Those Engaged in Agriculture and Manufactures.* Boston, Mass., 1847

Eden, William. *The Journal and Correspondence of William, Lord Auckland* (ed. George Hogge). 4 vols., London, 1860-2

[Eddowes, Ralph]. *Sketch of the Political History of the City of Chester.* Chester, 1790

Engels, Friedrich. *The Condition of the Working Class in England* (trans. W.O. Henderson and W.H. Chaloner). Oxford, 1958 [1845]

Evans, Thomas. *Christian Policy the Salvation of the Empire.* 2nd edn, London, 1816

Facts and Observations, to Prove the Impolicy and Dangerous Tendency, of the Bill now before Parliament. Manchester, [1807]

Fawkes, Walter. *The Englishman's Manual: or, a Dialogue between a Tory and a Reformer.* London, 1817

Felkin, W. 'An Account of the Situation of a Portion of the Labouring Classes in the Township of Hyde, Cheshire' *Journal of the Royal Statistical Society*, 1 (1838-9), 416-20

Ferriar, John. *Medical Histories and Reflections.* 3 vols., Warrington, 1792-8

From Bishop Blaze to the Misguided Men Who Destroy Machinery. Manchester, 1812

A Full, Accurate, and Impartial Report of the Trial of John Bagguley . . . John Johnston . . . and Samuel Drummond. Manchester, 1819

Galton, F.W. (ed.) *Select Documents Illustrating the History of Trade Unionism I. The Tailoring Trade.* London, 1923

Gaskell, P. *Artisans and Machinery.* London, 1836

[Greg, William Rathbone]. *An Enquiry into the State of the Manufacturing Population.* London, 1831

Griffith, John and John Gatliffe. *An Address to the Inhabitants of Manchester and Salford.* Manchester, 1808

Guest, Richard. *A Compendious History of the Cotton-Manufacture.* Manchester, 1823

Hampden Club. London, 1814

Hanshall, J.H. *The History of the County Palatine of Chester.* n.p., [1817]

[Harrison, Joseph]. *Report of the Proceedings of a Numerous and Respectable Meeting.* Stockport, 1818

Hemingway, Joseph. *History of the City of Chester.* 2 vols., Chester, 1831

Henderson, W.O. (ed.) *Industrial Britain Under the Regency: The Diaries of Escher, Bodmer, May and de Gallois 1814-18.* London, 1968

Henry, William Charles. 'A Biographical Notice of the Late Peter Ewart, Esq.' *Memoirs and Proceedings of the Manchester Literary and Philosophical Society*, 7 (1846), 113-36

Hindmarsh, Robert. *Christianity Against Deism, Materialism, and Atheism. Occasioned by a Letter Addressed to the Author by R. Carlile.* Manchester, 1824

Historical Manuscripts Commission. *Report on the Manuscripts of S.B. Fortescue, Esq., Preserved at Dropmore.* 10 vols., London, 1892-1927

[Hone, William]. *A Political Catechism.* 4th edn, Manchester, 1816

A Political Litany. Manchester, [1817]

Hunt, Henry. *Memoirs of Henry Hunt, Esq.* 3 vols., London, 1820-2

Johnson, Joseph. *A Letter to Henry Hunt, Esq.* 2nd edn, Manchester, 1822

Knight, John. *The Emigrant's Best Instructor, or, the Most Recent and Important Information Respecting the United States of America.* 1st-2nd edn, London, 1818

Important Extracts from Original and Recent Letters: Written by Englishmen in the United States of America to their Friends in England. 1st-2nd series, Manchester, 1818

A Full and Particular Report of the Proceedings of the Public Meeting Held in Manchester on Monday the 18th of January, 1819. London, 1819

A Letter to a Member of Parliament, on the Importance of Liberty. London, 1745

A List of the Journeymen Hatters and Apprentices Belonging to the Union of the United Kingdom. London, 1831

Longson, W. *An Appeal to the Masters, Workmen & the Public, Shewing the Cause of the Distress of the Labouring Classes.* Manchester, 1827

Luckombe, Philip. *England's Gazetteer.* 3 vols., London, 1790

[McCulloch, J.R.]. 'Restraints on Emigration.' *Edinburgh Review,* 39 (1823-4), 315-45

MacDonell, John and John E.P. Wallis (eds.) *Reports of State Trials.* 7 vols., London, 1888-96

MacKinnon, William Alexander. *On the Rise, Progress, and Present State of Public Opinion in Great Britain, and Other Parts of the World.* London, 1828

MacRitchie, William. *Diary of a Tour Through Great Britain in 1795.* London, 1897

Manchester Politics. A Dialogue between Mr. True-blew and Mr. Whiglove. London, 1748

Marshall, J. *An Analysis and Compendium of all the Returns made to Parliament (Since the Commencement of the Nineteenth Century).* London, 1835

Marx, Karl. *Economic and Philosophic Manuscripts* [1844] in *Early Texts* (ed. David McLellan) (New York, 1971), 130-83

    The Poverty of Philosophy. New York, 1963 [1847]

    The Communist Manifesto. New York, 1970 [1848]

    Capital: A Critique of Political Economy. 3 vols., Moscow, 1965-7 [1867-94]

    and Friedrich Engels. *Letters to Americans 1848-1895: A Selection* (trans. Leonard E. Mins). New York, 1953

The Memorial of the Journeymen Calico Printers, and Others Connected with Their Trade. London, 1804

Metcalf, John. *The Life of John Metcalf.* York, 1795

[Mill, John Stuart]. 'Reorganization of the Reform Party.' *Westminster Review,* 32 (1839), 252-69

Morris, Max (ed.) *From Cobbett to the Chartists 1815-1848.* London, 1948

Newton, [Evelyn]. *Lyme Letters 1660-1760.* London, 1925

Observations on the Cotton Weavers' Act. Manchester, 1804

Observations on the Use of Machinery in the Manufactories of Great Britain by 'A Mechanic'. London, 1817

O'Connel & his Family. Stockport, [c. 1825]

Owen, Robert. *The Life of Robert Owen by Himself.* New York, 1920

Paine, Tom. *The Rights of Man.* 2 pts, London, 1791-2

    The Age of Reason. 2 pts, London, 1794-5

P[arsons], T[homas]. *Christianity, a System of Peace.* 2nd edn, Stockport, 1813

Pellew, George. *The Life and Correspondence of the Right Honble Henry Addington, First Viscount Sidmouth.* 3 vols., London, 1847

Percival, Thomas. *A Letter to a Friend.* Halifax, [1758]

The Petitioning Weavers Defended by 'Operator'. Manchester, [1817]

[Philips, Francis]. *A Dialogue between Thomas, the Weaver, and his Old Master.* Manchester, 1817

    An Exposure of the Calumnies Circulated by the Enemies of Social Order. London, 1819

The Political Martyrs . . . Persecuted in the Year 1793-4 for Advocating the Cause of Reform in Parliament. London, 1837

Praizer, L.W. *Remarks on Slander and Envy.* Manchester, [1809]

Pratt, John Tidd. *The History of Savings Banks*. London, 1830
    The History of Savings Banks in England, Wales, Ireland, and Scotland. London, 1842

Prentice, Archibald. *Historical Sketches and Personal Recollections of Manchester.* London, 1851

Proceedings of the Association for Preserving Liberty and Property Against Republicans and Levellers. London, [1792]

Proceedings of the Hampden Club. London, 1816

Publications of the Society for Preserving Liberty and Property Against Republicans and Levellers. 2 series; London, [1792-3]

Radcliffe, Ann. *A Journey Made in the Summer of 1794.* London, 1794

[Radcliffe, William?]. *Thoughts on the State of the Manufactures, and the Exportation of Twist.* Stockport, [1800]

Radcliffe, William. *Letters on the Evils of the Exportation of Cotton Yarns.* Stockport, 1811

    Origin of the New System of Manufacture, Commonly Called 'Power-Loom Weaving'. Stockport, 1828

Raynes, Francis. *An Appeal to the Public.* London, 1817

A Report of the Meeting held in Smithfield. London, 1819

Review of Abraham Binns, *Remarks on a Publication...* In *Critical Review*, 20 (1797), 109

Richmond, Alex. B. *Narrative of the Condition of the Manufacturing Population.* London, 1824

Rights of Swine: An Address to the Poor by 'A Friend to the Poor'. [Stockport?], 1794

A Rod for the Burkites. 2nd edn, Manchester, [1792]

Rules and Articles to be Observed and Kept by the True Blue Friendly Society... Instituted the 24th day of August, 1764. Chester, 1809

Rules for the Conducting of the Union Society of Printers, Cutters and Drawers in Lancashire, Cheshire, Derbyshire, &c. Manchester, 1813

The Rules of the Pitt Club. Manchester, 1819

[Rupp, Theophelus Lewis]. *Second Letter to the Inhabitants of Manchester, on the Exportation of Cotton Twist.* Manchester, 1800

    A Third Letter to the Inhabitants of Manchester, on the Exportation of Cotton Twist. Manchester, 1803

[Seddon, Thomas]. *Characteristic Strictures: or, Remarks on Upwards of One Hundred Portraits, of the Most Eminent Persons in the Counties of Lancaster and Chester.* 3rd edn, London, 1779

Sharp, J.B. *Letters on the Exportation of Cotton Yarns.* London, 1817

A Short Sketch, or Memoir of the Late Joseph Hanson, Esq. Salford, 1811

S[ilvester], J[ohn]. *A View of the Cotton Manufactories of France.* Manchester, 1803

Smith, E.C. 'Joshua Field's Diary of a Tour in 1821 Through the Provinces. Part II'. *Newcomen Society Transactions*, 13 (1932-3), 15-50

'Specification of the Patent Granted to Peter Marsland...' *Repertory of Arts, Manufactures, and Agriculture*, 7 (1805), 327-9

Strictures on Benefit or Friendly Societies. Stockport, [1799?]

Symons, Jelinger C. *Arts and Artisans at Home and Abroad.* Edinburgh, 1839

[Taylor, John Edward]. *Notes and Observations, Critical and Explanatory, on the*

Papers Relative to the Internal State of the Country, Recently Presented to Parliament. London, 1820

Taylor, Robert Eveleigh. *Letter on the Subject of the Lancashire Riots in the Year 1812.* Bolton, 1813

Taylor, W. Cooke. *Notes of a Tour in the Manufacturing Districts of Lancashire.* 2nd edn, London, 1842

The Theory of Money by 'John Hampden, Jr'. Manchester, 1817

Things as They Are; or, America in 1819. Manchester, 1819

Thornton, William Thomas. *Over-Population and Its Remedy.* London, 1846

To the People of England. Manchester, 1816

Trial at Full Length of the 38 Men, From Manchester. Manchester, 1812

The Trial at Large of Thomas Bowen Slaiter. Stockport, 1815

Ure, Andrew. *The Philosophy of Manufactures.* London, 1835

    The Cotton Manufacture of Great Britain Systematically Investigated. 2 vols., London, 1836

The Voice of God!!! In Support of the Grand Object of Parliamentary Reform. Manchester, 1817

Walker, George. *Observations Founded on Facts, Upon the Propriety or Impropriety of Exporting Cotton Twist.* London, 1803

Walker, Thomas. *A Review of Some of the Political Events which Have Occurred in Manchester, during the Last Five Years.* London, 1794

War Inconsistent with the Doctrine and Example of Jesus Christ. Stockport, 1814

Watson, John. *Memoirs of the Ancient Earls of Warren and Surrey, and Their Descendants to the Present Time.* 2 vols., Warrington, 1782

Wedgwood, Josiah. *The Selected Letters of Josiah Wedgwood* (ed. Ann Finer and George Savage). London, 1965

Wheeler, James. *Manchester: Its Political, Social and Commercial History, Ancient and Modern.* London, 1836

Whitaker, John. *The History of Manchester.* 2 vols., London, 1771-5

[White, George and Gravener, Henson]. *A few Remarks on the State of the Laws, at Present in Existence, for Regulating Masters and Work-People.* London, 1823

[Wray, C.D.]. *The Street Politicians: or, a Debate About the Times.* Manchester, 1817

Young, Arthur. *A Six Months Tour through the North of England.* 4 vols., 2nd edn, London, 1771

Periodicals

Annual Register

Anti-Gallican

Black Dwarf

Blanketteer

Bolton Chronicle

Carlile's Political Register

Chester Chronicle

Chester Guardian

Cobbett's Political Register

Co-operative Magazine

Courier

Gauntlet

Gentleman's Magazine

Gorgon

Hone's Reformists' Register

Lancashire Magazine

Lion

London Chronicle

London Gazette

Macclesfield Courier

Manchester Chronicle

Manchester Gazette

Manchester Guardian

Manchester Herald

Manchester Journal; Or, Prescott's
　Lancashire Advertiser
Manchester Magazine
Manchester Mercury
Manchester Observer
Manchester Political Register
Manchester Spectator
The Moralist
New Moral World
Patriot
Philanthropist
Poor Man's Guardian

The Prompter
Republican
Sheffield Register
Sherwin's Political Register
Stockport Advertiser
The Times
To the Radical Reformers, Male and
　Female, of England, Ireland, and
　Scotland
To the Reformers of Great Britain
Tradesman

Parliamentary Proceedings and Papers

Hansard's Parliamentary Debates
Journal of the House of Commons
Journal of the House of Lords
Parliamentary History
Parliamentary Papers:

　PP 1802-3 (114) VII, *SC Minutes on Disputes between Masters and Workmen*

　PP 1803-4 (41) V, *SC Rept. on Differences between Masters and Workmen in the Cotton Manufacture*

　PP 1803-4 (150) V, *SC Rept. on the Journeymen Callico Printers' Petition*

　PP 1803-4 (175) XIII, *Abstract of the Answers and Returns...Relative to the Expence and Maintenance of the Poor*

　PP 1808 (177) II, *SC Rept. on Cotton Weavers' Petitions*

　PP 1808 (179) II, *SC Rept. on Dr. Cartwright's Petition*

　PP 1808 (119) X, *Minutes of Evidence Upon Several Petitions Respecting the Orders in Council*

　PP 1810-11 (232) II, *SC Rept. on the Weavers' Petitions*

　PP 1812 (335) II, *Rept. from the Committee of Secrecy*

　PP 1812 (210) III, *Minutes of Evidence Taken Before the Committee of the Whole House Relating to the Orders in Council*

　PP 1816 (397) III, *SC Rept. on Children Employed in the Manufactories*

　PP 1816 (511) XVI, *Abstract of Returns of Charitable Donations*

　PP 1817 (34) IV, *1st Rept. from the Committee of Secrecy*

　PP 1817 (387) IV, *2nd Rept. from the Committee of Secrecy*

　PP 1817 (399) IV, *Rept. of the Secret Committee of the House of Lords*

　PP 1818 (393) V, *SC Rept. on the Laws Relating to the Salt Duties*

　PP 1818 (82) XIX, *Abridgement of Abstract of Answers and Returns Relative to the Expense and Maintenance of the Poor*

　PP 1818 (HL 23) XCIV, *Return of Persons...Arrested or Committed for Having been Unlawfully Assembled.*

　PP 1819 (224) IX, *Digest of Parochial Returns on the Education of the Poor*

　PP 1819 (59) XVII, *Statement of the Number of Persons Committed to the Different Gaols in England and Wales, 1805-1818*

　PP 1819 (HL 24), CX, *Minutes of Evidence Taken Before the Lords Committees on Children in the Cotton Manufactories*

PP 1819-20 (1) IV, *Papers Relative to the Internal State of the Country*

PP 1821 (668) IX, *SC Rept. on the Depressed State of Agriculture*

PP 1822 (556) V, *SC Rept. on Poor Rate Returns*

PP 1824 (51) V, *SC Rept. on Artizans and Machinery*

PP 1825 (437, 417) IV, *SC Rept. on Combination Laws*

PP 1825 (522) IV, *SC Rept. on Laws Respecting Friendly Societies*

PP 1826-7 (550) V, *3rd SC Rept. on Emigration*

PP 1826-7 (22) IX, *16th Rept. of the Charity Commissioners*

PP 1830 (590) X, *SC Rept. on Manufacturers' Employment*

PP 1831 (348) XVIII, *Comparative Account of the Population of Great Britain, in the Years 1801, 1811, 1821 and 1831*

PP 1831-2 (706) XV, *SC Rept. on Children's Labour*

PP 1831-2 (678) XIX, *SC Rept. on the Silk Trade*

PP 1831-2 (90) XXVI, *Return of the Number of Friendly Societies filed . . . Since 1st January 1793*

PP 1833 (612) V, *SC Rept. on Agriculture*

PP 1833 (690) VI, *SC Rept. on Manufactures, Commerce, and Shipping*

PP 1833 (394) XVI, *SC Rept. on Irish Vagrants*

PP 1833 (450) XX, *1st Rept. of the Factories Inquiry Commission*

PP 1833 (149) XXXVI-XXXVII, *Enumeration Abstract, 1831*

PP 1834 (556) X, *SC Rept. on Hand-loom Weavers' Petitions*

PP 1834 (167) XIX, *Factories Inquiry Commission, Suppl. Rept., Pt. I*

PP 1834 (167) XX, *Factories Inquiry Commission. Suppl. Rept., Pt. II*

PP 1834 (44) XXVIII, *Rept. on the Poor Laws in England and Wales*

PP 1835 (341) XIII, *SC Rept. on Hand-Loom Weavers' Petitions*

PP 1835 (605) XVII, *SC Rept. on Orange Institutions*

PP 1836 [40] XXXIV, *Rept. on the Irish Poor in Great Britain*

PP 1836 (24) XLV, *Return of the Number of Power Looms Used in Factories*

PP 1837 (238) XXVIII, *Rept. of the Commission on Municipal Corporations Boundaries*

PP 1837-8 [103] XXIV, *31st Rept. of the Charity Commissioners*

PP 1840 (227) X, *SC Rept. on the Regulation of Mills and Factories*

PP 1840 (43-I) XXIII, *Rept. on Hand-Loom Weavers, Pt. II*

PP 1841 (201) VII, *1st SC Rept. on the Exportation of Machinery*

PP 1842 (158) XXXV, *Rept. on the State of the Population of Stockport*

PP 1908 [Cd. 3864] CVII, *Cost of Living of the Working Classes*

INDEX

abstinence proposals 244, 247, 267-9, 280

Acts of Parliament: Arbitration Acts (1800, 1804) 148-50, 152; Combination Laws 92, 105-6, 132, 138, repeal of 71, 75-6, 102, 114, 270; Corn Laws 119, 152, 195; Factory Acts (incl. bills) 70, 72, 76, · 78-9, 81-2, 151; Hatters' Act (1777) 97; Six Acts (1819) 249, 254; Statute of Artificers (1563) 188; Stockport Church Rebuilding Act (1810) 56, 165; Stockport Court of Requests Act (1806) 52; Stockport Enclosure Act (1805) 52; Stockport Gas Act (1825) 61; Stockport Water Act (1825) 61; Two Acts (1795) 127-8; see also habeas corpus, suspension of

Addington, Henry see Sidmouth, Lord

air pollution 30, 81

Andrew family 29, 189

Andrew, John 120-3, 137

anonymous letters 84, 100, 146, 173-4, 178

anti-Corn Law agitations 137, 152, 271-2, 274, 280; in 1810s 204, 206, 213, 225, 236, 239, 253

anti-war agitations: pre-1802 126, 128, 131; post-1802 153-4, 162, 170-3 passim, 179, 189, 194

apprentices, apprenticeship 107, 146, 206, 271, 284; in calico printing 84-9, 189-90, 192; in hatting 97-100, 102

Arden family 35, 44, 48, 62

Ardwick Conspiracy 207-8

Arkwright, Richard 31-2, 67, 144

artisans 32-3, 57, 94-5, 107-8, 121-2, 246, 277; see also building trades; calico printers; hatters; leather trades; metal trades; shoemakers; tailors; wood-working trades

Ashton family 28-30, 81-2, 90, 108, 182; industrial activities of 35, 38, 41

Ashton-under-Lyne 20, 99, 101-2, 183, 255; Luddism 176, 180; radicalism 13, 134, 154, 220, 239-40; strikes 104, 146, 160, 222-3

Assizes 156, 168; combinations tried at 74-5, 101, 105-6, 156, 161; radicals tried at 136, 237-8, 249-51

Bagguley, John 206, 212, 217-20, 236, 259-61, 268; imprisonment of 221, 223-7, 232, 238-9, 251

Bamford, Samuel 15, 45, 162; in Blanketeer period 203, 208-9, 213, 215; in Peterloo era 229, 231, 237, 261

bankruptcies 36-8, 54, 133

banks 34, 113-14

Beefsteak Chapel (Brinksway, Stockport) 269-70, 274-5

Belchem, John 212, 266

Bentley, John 30, 38, 143, 150-2, 155-6, 177

Bentley, Thomas 168

Bertinshaw, Joseph 202, 218, 243, 250, 259

Birch, William 237, 242-3, 246

Birmingham 6-7, 208, 214, 225, 242, 261

birth control 271, 275

Bittner, Egon 118

Blackburn 67, 168, 229, 232, 240

blacklegs see strike breakers

blacklisting 69, 73-4, 81

Blackshaw, William 215, 269, 274

Blanketeers 205-12, 225, 247

bleachers 66, 82, 190

bleachworks see printworks, bleachworks, dyeworks

Bolsover, George L. 227, 237

Bolton 20, 108, 196, 209; handloom weavers 147-8, 152, 188, 270-2; Luddism 67, 174, 176, 178; radicalism 13, 129-30, 134, 154, 173, 261; strikes 69, 104, 112, 194, 222

booksellers 120, 126, 133, 215, 224; in 1820s 266-7, 269, 274

340